IoT and Cloud Computing Advancements in Vehicular Ad-Hoc Networks

Ram Shringar Rao
Ambedkar Institute of Advanced Communication Technologies and Research, India

Vishal Jain
Bharati Vidyapeeth's Institute of Computer Applications and Management, New Delhi, India

Omprakash Kaiwartya
School of Science and Technology, Nottingham Trent University, UK

Nanhay Singh
Ambedkar Institute of Advanced Communication Technologies and Research, India

A volume in the Advances in Computational Intelligence and Robotics (ACIR) Book Series

Published in the United States of America by
    IGI Global
    Engineering Science Reference (an imprint of IGI Global)
    701 E. Chocolate Avenue
    Hershey PA, USA 17033
    Tel: 717-533-8845
    Fax: 717-533-8661
    E-mail: cust@igi-global.com
    Web site: http://www.igi-global.com

Library of Congress Cataloging-in-Publication Data

Names: Rao, Ram Shringar, 1973- editor. | Jain, Vishal, 1983- editor. |
   Kaiwartya, Omprakash, 1981- editor. | Singh, Nanhay, 1973- editor.
Title: IoT and cloud computing advancements in vehicular ad-hoc networks /
   Ram Shringar Rao, Vishal Jain, Omprakash Kaiwartya, and Nanhay Singh,
   editors.
Description: Hershey, PA : Engineering Science Reference, an imprint of IGI
   Global, 2020. | Includes bibliographical references and index. |
   Summary: "This book explores new VANET architectures, challenges,
   technology gaps, business opportunities, future applications, and
   worldwide applicability"-- Provided by publisher.
Identifiers: LCCN 2019042205 (print) | LCCN 2019042206 (ebook) | ISBN
   9781799825708 (hardcover) | ISBN 9781799825715 (paperback) | ISBN
   9781799825722 (ebook)
Subjects: LCSH: Vehicular ad hoc networks (Computer networks) | Internet of
   things. | Cloud computing.
Classification: LCC TE228.37 .I68 2020 (print) | LCC TE228.37 (ebook) |
   DDC 338.3/12--dc23
LC record available at https://lccn.loc.gov/2019042205
LC ebook record available at https://lccn.loc.gov/2019042206

This book is published in the IGI Global book series Advances in Computational Intelligence and Robotics (ACIR) (ISSN: 2327-0411; eISSN: 2327-042X)

British Cataloguing in Publication Data
A Cataloguing in Publication record for this book is available from the British Library.

For electronic access to this publication, please contact: eresources@igi-global.com.

Advances in Computational Intelligence and Robotics (ACIR) Book Series

Ivan Giannoccaro
University of Salento, Italy

ISSN:2327-0411
EISSN:2327-042X

MISSION

While intelligence is traditionally a term applied to humans and human cognition, technology has progressed in such a way to allow for the development of intelligent systems able to simulate many human traits. With this new era of simulated and artificial intelligence, much research is needed in order to continue to advance the field and also to evaluate the ethical and societal concerns of the existence of artificial life and machine learning.

The **Advances in Computational Intelligence and Robotics (ACIR) Book Series** encourages scholarly discourse on all topics pertaining to evolutionary computing, artificial life, computational intelligence, machine learning, and robotics. ACIR presents the latest research being conducted on diverse topics in intelligence technologies with the goal of advancing knowledge and applications in this rapidly evolving field.

COVERAGE

- Intelligent control
- Artificial Intelligence
- Adaptive and Complex Systems
- Agent technologies
- Robotics
- Computational Logic
- Fuzzy Systems
- Pattern Recognition
- Artificial Life
- Natural Language Processing

IGI Global is currently accepting manuscripts for publication within this series. To submit a proposal for a volume in this series, please contact our Acquisition Editors at Acquisitions@igi-global.com or visit: http://www.igi-global.com/publish/.

Titles in this Series

For a list of additional titles in this series, please visit:
https://www.igi-global.com/book-series/advances-computational-intelligence-robotics/73674

Smart Systems Design, Applications, and Challenges
João M.F. Rodrigues (Universidade do Algarve, Portugal & LARSyS, Institute for Systems and Robotics, Lisbon, Portugal) Pedro J.S. Cardoso (Universidade do Algarve, Portugal & LARSyS, Institute for Systems and Robotics, Lisbon, Portugal) Jânio Monteiro (Universidade do Algarve, Portugal & INESC-ID, Lisbon, Portugal) and Célia M.Q. Ramos (Universidade do Algarve, Portugal & CIEO, ortugal)
Engineering Science Reference • © 2020 • 459pp • H/C (ISBN: 9781799821120) • US $245.00

Deep Learning Applications and Intelligent Decision Making in Engineering
Karthikrajan Senthilnathan (VIT University, India) Balamurugan Shanmugam (Quants IS & CS, India) Dinesh Goyal (Poornima Institute of Engineering and Technology, India) Iyswarya Annapoorani (VIT University, India) and Ravi Samikannu (Botswana International University of Science and Technology, Botswana)
Engineering Science Reference • © 2020 • 335pp • H/C (ISBN: 9781799821083) • US $245.00

Implementing Computational Intelligence Techniques for Security Systems Design
Yousif Abdullatif Albastaki (Ahlia University, Bahrain) and Wasan Awad (Ahlia University, Bahrain)
Information Science Reference • © 2020 • 332pp • H/C (ISBN: 9781799824183) • US $195.00

Managerial Challenges and Social Impacts of Virtual and Augmented Reality
Sandra Maria Correia Loureiro (Business Research Unit (BRU-IUL), Instituto Universitário de Lisboa (ISCTE-IUL), Lisboa, Portugal)
Engineering Science Reference • © 2020 • 318pp • H/C (ISBN: 9781799828747) • US $195.00

Innovations, Algorithms, and Applications in Cognitive Informatics and Natural Intelligence
Kwok Tai Chui (The Open University of Hong Kong, Hong Kong) Miltiadis D. Lytras (The American College of Greece, Greece) Ryan Wen Liu (Wuhan University of Technology, China) and Mingbo Zhao (Donghua University, China)
Engineering Science Reference • © 2020 • 403pp • H/C (ISBN: 9781799830382) • US $235.00

Avatar-Based Control, Estimation, Communications, and Development of Neuron Multi-Functional Technology Platforms
Vardan Mkrttchian (HHH University, Australia) Ekaterina Aleshina (Penza State University, Russia) and Leyla Gamidullaeva (Penza State University, Russia)
Engineering Science Reference • © 2020 • 355pp • H/C (ISBN: 9781799815815) • US $245.00

701 East Chocolate Avenue, Hershey, PA 17033, USA
Tel: 717-533-8845 x100 • Fax: 717-533-8661
E-Mail: cust@igi-global.com • www.igi-global.com

Table of Contents

Detailed Table of Contents

    Kamlesh Kumar Rana, Galgotia College of Engineering and Technology, India
    Vishnu Sharma, Galgotia Collge of Engineering and Technology, India
    Vishal Jain, Bharati Vidyapeeth's Institute of Computer Applications and Management, New
        Delhi, India
    Sanjoy Das, Indira Gandhi National Tribal University, Manipur, India
    Gagan Tiwari, Galgotias College of Engineering and Technology, India
    Vikram Bali, JSS Academy of Technical Education Noida, India

Vehicular ad-hoc network (VANET) is an autonomous system of mobile vehicles in which vehicles are a source of information. In VANET, direct communication between vehicles provides high-level safety and hassle-free drive. Large moving vehicles such as trucks or buses may affect direct communication of vehicles as a nonline of sight (NLOS) may occur. NLOS restricts direct communication of vehicles. Even the corresponding vehicle is within the communication range of the communicating vehicle. To overcome the NLOS problem and verify the location of the vehicles, this chapter has presented a routing mechanism, namely Directional Location Verification and Routing (DLVR) in Vehicular Ad-hoc Network. DLVR model prevents the false location information of the nodes by reduced packet drop and increased packet delivery ratio. Before transmitting data packets DLVR verifies data packets through reliability check. Through simulation work, it has shown the proposed DLVR model reduced packet drop and increased packet delivery ratio which increases the network performance.

    Mekelleche Fatiha, Department of Computer Science, University of Oran1 Ahmed BenBella,
        Algeria
    Haffaf Hafid, Department of Computer Science, University of Oran1 Ahmed BenBella,
        Algeria

Vehicular Ad-Hoc Networks (VANETs), a new mobile ad-hoc network technology (MANET), are currently receiving increased attention from manufacturers and researchers. They consist of several mobile vehicles (intelligent vehicles) that can communicate with each other (inter-vehicle communication) or with fixed road equipment (vehicle-infrastructure communication) adopting new wireless communication technologies. The objective of these networks is to improve road safety by warning motorists of any event on the road (accidents, hazards, possible deviations, etc.), and make the time spent on the road more pleasant and less boring (applications deployed to ensure the comfort of the passengers). Practically, VANETs are designed to support the development of Intelligent Transportation Systems (ITS). The latter are seen as one of the technical solutions to transport challenges. This chapter, given the importance of road safety in the majority of developed countries, presents a comprehensive study on the VANET networks, highlighting their main features.

Walaa Abd el aal Afifi, Faculty of Graduate Studies for Statistical Research, Cairo University, Egypt

Hesham Ahmed Hefny, Faculty of Graduate Studies for Statistical Research, Cairo University, Egypt

Nagy Ramadan Darwish, Faculty of Graduate Studies for Statistical Research, Cairo University, Egypt

Imane Fahmy, Cairo University, Egypt

Position is a vital element for ITS applications. Its accuracy helps to deliver services quickly to drivers to increase their satisfaction. GPS is a well-known position system but it suffers from multipath effect and non-line of sight in tunnel environments. Relative Position or sometimes called cooperative localization is an alternative position estimation. It utilizes different forms of v2x communication to exchange position, distance, direction, and velocity parameters. It will benefit in collecting a large amount of data to increase the accuracy of position estimation. However, the dependency of radio range communication methods has drawbacks such as poor-received signal, multipath, lose packets, delay, and overhead communication that will have inverse impact on position accuracy. In addition, safety applications require fewer seconds to make quick response. This chapter provides the latest related papers, the state art of radio range, the well-known localization algorithms, and current challenges and future direction.

Parul Agarwal, Jamia Hamdard, India

Syed Imtiyaz Hassan, Maulana Azad National Urdu University, India

Jawed Ahmed, Jamia Hamdard, India

Today, the technology is moving at a fast pace and has also changed the pace at which the commuter is moving. No longer is the commuter ready to waste time and resources while travelling. This has led to a revolution in the transport sector. ICT, smart devices, and different enabling technologies make intelligent transport systems (ITS) a reality. If well implemented, they can save time and money, help to reduce the environmental threats, and also create business opportunities for many. Today's era is an era of revolution, technological advances, Internet, digitalization, mobile communications, big data, and an era of harnessing the potentials of Cloud Computing. Realizing the benefits of each of these and their utilization and need, a global potential for a powerful and less costly ITS has to be created. This chapter shall give a complete insight into the ITS: its history, components, benefits, issues, and challenges. It would also discuss the future that is in store for ITS but with a realization that the environment is not at stake.

Mamoon Rashid, School of Computer Science and Engineering, Lovely Professional University, Jalandhar, India

Aabid Rashid, School of Electronics and Communication Engineering, Shri Mata Vaishno Devi University, Katra, India

Sachin Kumar Gupta, School of Electronics and Communication Engineering, Shri Mata Vaishno Devi University, Katra, India

This chapter is related to quality of service in the network. The congestion is the factor which affects quality of service in the network. The AODV is the routing protocol used to establish path from source to destination. To maintain quality of the service, novel approach is proposed. The technique of back propagation is proposed in this work for the congestion avoidance in the network. The back propagation algorithm calculates changes of congestion on each node in network. The node with the least chances of congestion is selected for path establish from source to destination. The proposed approach is implemented in network simulator version 2 and results are analyzed in terms of throughput, packet-loss, delay, and load. It is analyzed that network throughput is increased, packet-loss, delay, and load is reduced in the proposed methodology as compared to state-of-art.

Chapter 6

Parul Choudhary, Teerthanker Mahaveer University, India & Bharati Vidyapeeth's Institute of Computer Applications and Management, New Delhi, India

Rakesh kumar Dwivedi, Teerthanker Mahaveer University, Moradabad, India

Umang Singh, Institute of Technology and Science, Ghaziabad, India

The exponential increase of traffic on roads has led to numerous disastrous consequences. These issues demand an adaptive solution that ensures road safety and decreases the traffic congestion on roads. New paradigms such as Cloud computing and internet of things are aiding in achievement of the inter-communication among the vehicles on road. VANETs are designed to provide effective and efficient communication systems to develop innovative solutions but are restricted due to mobility constraints. This chapter proposes an IP-based novel framework composed of open threads integrated with VANETs exchanging information to create a mesh network among vehicles. This novel Open Threads-based infrastructure can help in achieving a more economical, efficient, safer, and sustainable world of transportation which is safer and greener. This chapter also discusses and compares various thread-enabled microcontrollers by different vendors that can be utilized to create a mesh network.

Chapter 7

Harjit Singh, Guru Kashi University, India

Vijay Laxmi, Guru Kashi University, India

Arun Malik, Lovely Professional University, India

Isha Batra, Lovely Professional University, India

Vehicular Ad hoc Networks (VANets) are designed to provide reliable wireless communications between high-speed mobile nodes. To improve the performance of VANets' applications, and make a safe and comfort environment for VANets' users, Quality of Service (QoS) should be supported in these networks. The delay and packet losses are two main indicators of QoS that dramatically increase due to the congestion occurrence in the networks. Indeed, due to congestion occurrence, the channels are saturated and the packet collisions increase in the channels. Therefore, the congestion should be controlled to decrease the packet losses and delay, and to increase the performance of VANets. Congestion control in VANets is a challenging task due to the specific characteristics of VANets such as high mobility of the nodes with high speed, and high rate of topology changes, and so on.

Preety Khatri, Institute of Management Studies, Noida, India
Priti Rani Rajvanshi, Institute of Management Studies, Noida, India

This chapter includes a relative study of mobile ad-hoc networks (MANET), vehicular ad hoc networks (VANET), and Flying ad-hoc networks (FANET). The approaches and protocol applicable to MANET are equally applicable to VANET or FANET. Authors discuss several emerging application and the future trends of MANET, VANET, and FANET. The common attacks on ad hoc networks are also introduced. The chapter enhances the overall concepts relative to MANET, VANET, and FANET. Authors compare mobile ad-hoc networks (MANET), vehicular ad hoc networks (VANET), and flying ad-hoc networks (FANET) in all aspects with the help of several examples. The chapter includes a relative and detailed study of mobile ad-hoc networks (MANET), vehicular ad hoc networks (VANET), and Flying ad-hoc networks (FANET).

Nirbhay Kumar Chaubey, Ganpat University, India
Dhananjay Yadav, Gujarat Technological University, India

Vehicular ad hoc networks (VANETs) are a class of ad hoc networks in which vehicle communicate with each other to show the traffic situation and any mishappening on the road. VANET is vulnerable to a number of attacks due to its infrastructure-less nature. One of these attacks is the Sybil attack. Security of data dissemination in VANET is very crucial, otherwise any mishappening can occur on road. Sybil attack is very difficult to be defended and detected, especially when it is launched by some conspired attackers using their legitimate identities, and this has become a growing research interest in VANETs in past few years. This chapter studies various dimension of VANETs including its structure, communication architecture, security issues, and critical review of technique to detect Sybil attacks.

Ananthi Govindasamy, Department of Electronics and Communication Engineering,
Thiagarajar College of Engineering, India
S. J. Thiruvengadam, Thiagarajar College of Engineering, India

Vehicular Ad-hoc Networks (VANET) is a mobile ad-hoc network in which vehicles move rapidly through the road and topology changes very frequently. VANET helps to provide safe, secure, and more comfort travel to travelers. Vehicles intelligence is an important component in high mobility networks, equipped with multiple advanced onboard sensors and contain large volumes of data. Datascience is an effective approach to artificial intelligence and provides a rich set of tools to exploit such data for the benefit of the networks. In this chapter, the distinctive characteristics of high mobility vehicular ad-hoc networks are identified and the use of datascience is addressing the resulting challenges. High mobility vehicular ad-hoc networks exhibit distinctive characteristics, which have posed significant challenges to wireless network design. Vehicle traffic data, and road traffic future condition data are analyzed and incorporated to enhance the VANET performance. VANETs technologies are useful to efficiently model and reliably transmit big data.

Chapter 11

Deena Nath Gupta, Jamia Millia Islamia, India

Rajendra Kumar, Jamia Millia Islamia, India

Ashwani Kumar, United College of Engineering and Research, India

A secure environment is needed to communicate without any information leakage. From large devices having UPS to small devices having a battery, the parameter about security changes over time. Researchers need to work in three basics of security: (1) Mutual authentication between devices, (2) Strong encryption methodology for transmission, and (3) Secure storage environment with anytime availability. The IoT-enabled devices demand a lightweight secure environment. In this chapter, authors are concerning on all three points, i.e. Mutual authentication between devices, Strong encryption methodology for transmission, and Secure storage environment with anytime availability. Authors study some of the methods related to lightweight mutual authentication, lightweight cryptography, and local storage techniques; will talk about different issues in the field of secure communication, secure transmission, and secure storage; and will try to find out some research gap with a possible countermeasure.

Chapter 12

Aruna Pathak, Government Engineering College, Bharartpur, India

Ram Shringar Raw, Ambedkar Institute of Advanced Communication Technologies and Research, India

Pratibha Kamal, Guru Gobind Singh Indraprastha University, Delhi, India

Sensor nodes are supposed to function independently for a long timespan through a restricted source of energy in Wireless sensor networks (WSNs). For prolonging the network lifespan, sensor nodes need to be energy-efficient. To split the sensing region of WSNs into clusters is a noble methodology is to lengthen network lifespan. Clustering methods rotate the extra burden of head of cluster nodes among other nodes of the network through head rotation and re-clustering techniques. Overhead cost is greater in case of Re-clustering as compared to rotation method due to its global approach. Head rotation takes place when residual energy of cluster head falls below a fixed energy threshold. However, this fixed threshold does not consider the existing load of cluster head which become foremost cause for enhancing their early death. This chapter proposes an Energy-Efficient Rotation Technique of Cluster Head (EERTCH) for WSNs, which takes existing load of cluster head in consideration for their rotation.

Chapter 13

Sudesh Kumar, Indira Gandhi National Tribal University, Amarkantak, India

Abhishek Bansal, Indira Gandhi National Tribal University, Amarkantak, India

Recently, with the rapid technological advancement in communication technologies, it has been possible to establish wireless communication between small, portable, and flexible devices like Unmanned Aerial Vehicles (UAVs). These vehicles can fly autonomously or be operated without carrying any human being. The workings with UAVs environment often refer to flying ad-hoc network (FANETs), currently a very important and challenging area of research. The usage of FANETs promises new applications in military and civilian areas. The data routing between UAVs also plays an important role for these real-time applications and services. However, the routing in FANETs scenario faces serious issues due to fast mobility and rapid network topology change of UAVs. Therefore, this chapter proposes a comparative study on topology-based routing protocols like AODV, DSDV, and DSR. Furthermore, investigate the performance of these different protocols for a FANETs environment based on different parameters by using the NS-2 simulator.

Chapter 14

VANET, a type of MANET, connects vehicles to provide safety and non-safety features to the drivers and passengers by exchanging valuable data. As vehicles on road are increasing to handle such data cloud computing, functionality is merged with vehicles known as Vehicular Cloud Computing(VCC) to serve VANET with computation, storage, and networking functionalities. But Cloud, a centralized server, does not fit well for vehicles needing high-speed processing, low latency, and more security. To overcome these limitations of Cloud, Fog computing was evolved, extending the functionality of cloud computing model to the edge of the network. This works well for real time applications that need fast response, saves network bandwidth, and is a reliable, secure solution. An application of Fog is with vehicles known as Vehicular Fog Computing (VFC). This chapter discusses cloud computing technique and its benefits and drawbacks, detailed comparison between VCC and VFC, applications of Fog Computing, its security, and forensic challenges.

Preface

It gives us immense pleasure to put forth the book title "IoT and Cloud Computing Advancements in Vehicular Ad-Hoc Networks". The optimization of traffic management operations has become a considerable challenge in today's global scope due to the significant increase in the number of vehicles, traffic congestions, and automobile accidents. Fortunately, there has been substantial progress in the application of intelligent computing devices to transportation processes. Vehicular ad-hoc networks (VANETs) are a specific practice that merges the connectivity of wireless technologies with smart vehicles. Despite its relevance, empirical research is lacking on the developments being made in VANETs and how certain intelligent technologies are being applied within transportation systems. IoT and Cloud Computing Advancements in Vehicular Ad-Hoc Networks provides emerging research exploring the theoretical and practical aspects of intelligent transportation systems and analyzing the modern techniques that are being applied to smart vehicles through cloud technology. Featuring coverage on a broad range of topics such as health monitoring, node localization, and fault tolerance, this book is ideally designed for network designers, developers, analyst, IT specialists, computing professionals, researchers, academics, and post-graduate students seeking current research on emerging computing concepts and developments in vehicular ad-hoc networks. The many academic areas covered in this publication include, Cross-Layer Design, Data Dissemination, Energy Consumption, Fault Tolerance, Health Monitoring, Intelligent Transportation Systems, Machine Learning, Middleware, Network Scalability, Node Localization, Protocol Design and Smart City Environment. We believe the book is ready to serve as a reference for larger audience such as system architects, practitioners, developers, and researchers.

Chapter 1

This chapter has presented a routing mechanism namely Directional Location Verification and Routing (DLVR) in Vehicular Ad-hoc Network. DLVR model prevents the false location information of the nodes by reduced packet drop and increased packet delivery ratio. Before transmitting data packets DLVR verifies data packets through reliability check. Through simulation work, it has shown the proposed DLVR model reduced packet drop and increased packet delivery ratio which increases the network performance.

Chapter 2

This chapter gives the importance of road safety in the majority of developed countries and presents a comprehensive study on the VANET networks.

Chapter 3

This chapter discusses relative position estimation in vehicle ad hoc network.

Chapter 4

This chapter shall give a complete insight into the ITS: its history, components, benefits, issues and challenges. It would also discuss the future that is in store for ITS but with a realization that the environment is not at stake.

Chapter 5

This chapter proposes a novel congestion control model for maintaining Quality of Service in MANET. The proposed approach is implemented in network simulator version 2 and results are analyzed in terms of throughput, packet-loss, delay and load. It is analyzed that network throughput is increased, packet-loss, delay and load is reduced in the proposed methodology as compared to state-of-art.

Chapter 6

This chapter proposes an IP-based novel framework composed of open threads integrated with VANETs exchanging information to create a mesh network among vehicles. This novel Open Threads based infrastructure can help in achieving a more economical, efficient, safer and sustainable world of transportation which is safer and greener. This paper also discusses and compares various thread enabled microcontrollers by different vendors that can be utilized to create a mesh network.

Chapter 7

This chapter presents a review on Role and Importance of Congestion Control for Traffic Optimization in Vehicular Ad-Hoc Networks.

Chapter 8

This chapter discusses about a relative study of mobile ad-hoc networks (MANET), vehicular ad hoc networks (VANET) and Flying ad-hoc networks (FANET). Also covers about the approaches and protocol applicable to MANET are equally applicable to VANET or FANET.

Chapter 9

This chapter studies various dimension of VANETs including its structure, communication architecture, security issues and critical review of technique to detect Sybil attacks.

Chapter 10

In this chapter, the distinctive characteristics of high mobility vehicular ad-hoc networks are identified and the use of data science in addressing the resulting challenges. High mobility vehicular ad-hoc networks exhibit distinctive characteristics, which have posed significant challenges to wireless network design. VANETs technologies are useful to efficiently model and reliably transmit big data.

Chapter 11

This chapter presents a study of methods related to lightweight mutual authentication, lightweight cryptography, and local storage techniques; will talk about different issues in the field of secure communication, secure transmission, and secure storage; and will try to find out some research gap with a possible countermeasure.

Chapter 12

This chapter presents an energy-efficient rotation technique of cluster-head method for wireless sensor networks.

Chapter 13

This chapter investigates the performance of different protocols for a FANETs environment based on different parameters by using the NS-2 simulator.

Chapter 14

This works well for real time applications that needs fast response, saves network bandwidth and is a reliable, secure solution. An application of Fog is with vehicles which is known as Vehicular Fog Computing (VFC) and discussed the cloud computing technique and its benefits and drawbacks, detailed comparison between VCC and VFC, applications of Fog Computing, it's security and forensic challenges.

We further also express our sincere thanks to Dr. Jan Travers, IGI-Global for giving us an opportunity to convene the book in his esteemed publishing house and Ms. Courtney Tychinski, IGI-Global for her kind cooperation in completion of this book. We thank our esteemed authors for having shown confidence in the book and considering it as a platform to showcase and share their original research work. We would also wish to thank the authors whose papers were not published in this book, probably because of their minor shortcomings.

Ram Shringar Rao
Ambedkar Institute of Advanced Communication Technologies and Research, India

Vishal Jain
Bharati Vidyapeeth's Institute of Computer Applications and Management, New Delhi, India

Omprakash Kaiwartya
School of Science and Technology, Nottingham Trent University, UK

Nanhay Singh
Ambedkar Institute of Advanced Communication Technologies and Research, India

Chapter 1
Directional Location Verification and Routing in Vehicular Ad-Hoc Network

Kamlesh Kumar Rana

Galgotia College of Engineering and Technology, India

Vishnu Sharma

Galgotia Collge of Engineering and Technology, India

Vishal Jain

🆔 https://orcid.org/0000-0003-1126-7424

Bharati Vidyapeeth's Institute of Computer Applications and Management, New Delhi, India

Sanjoy Das

Indira Gandhi National Tribal University, Manipur, India

Gagan Tiwari

Galgotias College of Engineering and Technology, India

Vikram Bali

JSS Academy of Technical Education Noida, India

ABSTRACT

Vehicular ad-hoc network (VANET) is an autonomous system of mobile vehicles in which vehicles are a source of information. In VANET, direct communication between vehicles provides high-level safety and hassle-free drive. Large moving vehicles such as trucks or buses may affect direct communication of vehicles as a nonline of sight (NLOS) may occur. NLOS restricts direct communication of vehicles. Even the corresponding vehicle is within the communication range of the communicating vehicle. To overcome the NLOS problem and verify the location of the vehicles, this chapter has presented a routing mechanism, namely Directional Location Verification and Routing (DLVR) in Vehicular Ad-hoc Network. DLVR model prevents the false location information of the nodes by reduced packet drop and increased packet delivery ratio. Before transmitting data packets DLVR verifies data packets through reliability check. Through simulation work, it has shown the proposed DLVR model reduced packet drop and increased packet delivery ratio which increases the network performance.

DOI: 10.4018/978-1-7998-2570-8.ch001

INTRODUCTION

The vehicular ad-hoc network (VANET) is a decentralized wireless ad hoc network that assists in inter-vehicular communication among the mobile vehicles on the road and communication between mobile vehicles and roadside unit (RSU). In daily life, VANET offers several advantages; it sends traffic-related update messages i.e. crossroads, accident warning, and congestion on the road of preferred route opted by drivers (Rana et al., 2019). Therefore, it can be said by contributing distributed wireless ad hoc network VANET enhances traffic conditions and safe driving on the road.

VANET uses in developing Intelligent Transportation System (ITS) which enhances the performance of the transportation system. Through ITS vehicles enthusiastically communicate with other vehicles in the network to identify traffic circumstances on the road i.e. fatal, and traffic jams. VANET works as a safeguard for vehicle drivers and passengers because during critical situations the vehicle driver could be able to make proper judgment based on received traffic-related messages (Shakya et al., 2019).

In the multi-hop vehicular ad hoc network to accomplishing interaction between source to destination node a number of intermediate next hops are needed. VANET is a decentralized wireless ad hoc network so that it does not exist on predefined infrastructure in the network (Rana et al., 2017). Therefore, mobile nodes in VANET construct routing infrastructure to deliver data packets at the destination node without prior global knowledge of the network. Since, in VANET global knowledge of the network is not needed that's why VANET lacks reliable next hops, may acknowledge spoofing and various attacks (Shendurkar &, Chopde, 2014).

In VANET when a vehicle wants to send data packets to another vehicle and receiving vehicle is directly not reachable then data delivery is accomplished by multi-hop forwarding. In VANET vehicles construct decentralized routing infrastructure without global knowledge of the network (Rana, Triparhi, Raw, 2016). VANET is a decentralized wireless ad hoc network so that each vehicle must know own current physical location and their neighbor vehicles physical location along with the surrounding environment information. In VANET, such kind of information vehicles shares through beacon, direct communication, and group communication (Rossi, Leung, Gkelias, 2015). The large size moving vehicles such as trucks or buses can interfere between vehicles communication and block driver visuals that may lead to a non-line of sight that causes driver may make a poor judgment during lanes change or crossroad on the highway (Rana, Tripathi, Raw, 2019).

To increase driving awareness for drivers, VANET is expected to deliver traffic related and surrounding environment message to assist vehicle drivers. The vehicles in VANET are capable to determine their current geographical location through global positioning system (GPS) and other location positioning devices (Dahmane & Lorenz, 2016). But some physical obstacles like moving large vehicles as shown in Figure 1 interfere between two communicating vehicles which could block driver visuals that cause reliability and data packet delivery rate decreases. Therefore, direct communication between vehicles increases reliability and data delivery rate. For direct communication between vehicles each vehicle must enable to determine their current geographical location and need to have surrounding traffic environment message (Yang, Rongxi, Lin, Wang, 2014; Shelly & Babu, 2015). This surrounding traffic environment message should be exchanged among neighbor vehicles through beacon of direct message.

Figure 1. Non-line of sight

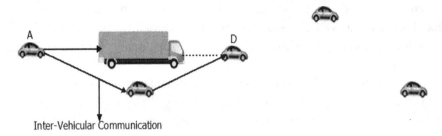

Inter-Vehicular Communication

As shown in Figure 1, vehicle C detects a message sent from the vehicle A for the vehicle D which is ahead of the large size vehicle B. The vehicle D does not receive the message directly from the vehicle A because large size vehicle B is an obstacle between vehicle A and D. Due to large size vehicle B between vehicle A and D, vehicle A is not aware with exact location information of the vehicle D that causes a non-line of sight occurs and message cannot be delivered to vehicle D within a proper time.

The vehicle location verification awareness can improve the vehicular communication affected by obstacles to delivering message within a specified time interval. In the multi hops vehicular ad- hoc network; the mechanism to maintain neighbor vehicles information is very important for routing in an efficient manner. Developing of a trustworthy, safe and sound localization technique capable to overcome the effects of the obstacles on vehicular communication is important as well (Bachir, Ali, Ahmed, Mohamed, 2014).

LITERATURE SURVEY

In location-based routing (LBR) mechanism prior familiarity of the overall network topology does not require because LBR uses latest physical position coordinate values of the nodes in network to sending packets towards intended destination (Sivakumar, 2015). LBR broadcast data packets in to adequate neighbor nodes which help to setup a route from sending to intended receiving node. Therefore, LBR gives the minimum routing overhead for the route establishment and maintenance. To forward data packets, LBR uses greedy forwarding approach that is guarantees of the loop-free operation (Kumar, & Kumar, 2015; Stojmenovic, Ruhil, Lobiyal, 2006).

Dynamic nature causes of the vehicles in the VANET, delivery of messages at anticipated location is a very typical job. Therefore, an adaptable and competent location-based steering mechanism needs for healthier operation of the network (Chi & Oh, (2014). Menouar et al. (2007) designed a vehicle movement prediction-based location-based routing in that vehicles mobility pattern based on the vehicle life span at the meticulous place decided for routing. For routing the mobility model utilized the latest location, life span, movement track and speed of the vehicles.

Using concept of the request and expected zone the authors Ko and Vaidya (1998) presented a location-based routing model for VANET namely location added routing (LAR) protocol. Once the request zone is formed, the nodes falling out of request zone are removed. Thus, the nodes exist inside the request zone accept and process the route request message. LAR controls flooding of the route request message that turns in minimum routing overhead.

Karp & Kung (2000) proposed geographical secure path routing protocol in which data authentication process scheme has introduced for secure data transmission in the network. The drawback of this proposed protocol is that authors are not addressed location verification process of vehicles globally for a large area. This drawback exploits node distance bounding, apparent validity, and distance estimation to validate location claimed by vehicles.

Using autonomous location verification scheme authors Kaleem, Hussain, Raza, Chaudhry, Raza (2014) increased security issues in geographical ad hoc routing. The vehicles broadcast their latest location as a beacon packets at regular intervals the neighbouring vehicles updates the routing table if there is any change in their location information. According the predefined rule the sending node finds the next hop based on the information of the routing table.

In LBR all the vehicles transmit the data packet that's why congestion of the network increases, therefore, for the healthier operation of the network the data packets could be transmitted to an adequate quantity of neighbors. To balance network functionality authors Raw, Lobiyal, Das, Kumar, (2015) proposed a probability-based routing mechanism that uses latest physical position coordinates values of the vehicles. The vehicles build merely solitary copy of message and send it to choosy neighbors that balance the network operation and future contact of vehicles depends upon the earlier location of the nodes.

LBR uses rectangular request zone (RZ) and expected zone (EZ), as dimension of RZ grows the route setup overhead grows also. For minimum routing overheads the size of request zone should be smaller. Authors Rana, Tripathi, and Raw (2017) improved functioning of DLR that is an example of the LBR. To improve the functioning of DLAR the authors partitioned request zone in smaller subrequest zone that reduced control flooding to setup the best route from sending to receiving node.

Song et al. (2014) proposed a cooperative infrastructure-less secure location verification (SLV) scheme has proposed by authors Joo-Han Song et al. which potentially recognizes spoofing attacks. SLV used radio frequency based measured distance between two node to identify malicious vehicles in the network. SLV verified claimed location of a node through a series of acceptability checks i.e. received location, speed, and movement direction on node. Lastly, claimant location controlled by the ellipse with foci at both ends such as verifier and supportive neighbor vehicle.

Unlike topology-based routing protocols the location-based routing protocols present various challenging issues and special characteristics. (Shelly & Babu, (2017). Location-based routing protocols do not need network topology information globally uses only geographical location information of vehicles for routing. Due to geographical location information of vehicles, location-based routing protocols give low routing overhead and maintenance cost. From the last few years researchers have proposed various location-based routing protocols (Rana, Tripathi, Raw, 2016).

Using global positioning system *LAR* finds the latest physical position coordinate values of vehicles to setup the path from sending to intended receiving end. Authors Ko and Vaidya (2000) modified the *LAR* using concept of the fractional flooding that minimizes routing control overhead. Due to the restricted and dense explore area, the route setup message forwarded to inadequate neighbours; therefore, route discovery overhead decreased.

Rana et al. (2016) observed one hop delay in greedy forwarding based location-based directional location routing (*DLR*) protocol where sender node uses current location updates of the node to decide the movement track. Selection mechanism of the next-hop node consists of two steps. At first, *DIR* estimates the sharp divergence of neighbors. Secondly, it selects the neighbor as the next hop that has lower sharp divergence from the baseline drawn from source to destination. This approach is followed until data packets reached at intended destination. Such kind data forwarding mechanism reaches at intended destination covering less spatial distance (Raw et al. 2012).

DIRECTIONAL LOCATION VERIFICATION AND ROUTING (DLVR)

A location verification mechanism has proposed for a secure location-based routing when *NLOS* occurs in *VANET*. In the proposed *DLVR* model, nodes explicitly broadcast current location information encoded through location hashes to its neighboring nodes after a specific time interval known as beacon messages. For secure communication between nodes, *DLVR* uses private and public key of the nodes. For further transmission of data packets *DLVR* selects the next hop, only when location is verified and neighbor node insures reliability. Three key values i.e. timestamp, transmission range, and velocity of the node are used to check reliability of the nodes.

Distance Authentication

For direct communication of the vehicles they should be within communication range of each other. As shown in Figure 2, suppose (S_x, S_y) and (I_x, I_y) represent current coordinate values of the source node S and I^{th} neighbor node of the node S. Let $d(S, I)$ is distance between the node S and I, these node scan communicate with each other only when satisfies the following condition.

$$d(S,I) \leq R \tag{1}$$

where $d(S, I)$ is.

$$d(S,I) = \sqrt{(S_X - I_X)^2 + (S_Y - I_Y)^2} \tag{2}$$

Figure 2. Distance calculation between sender and border nodes

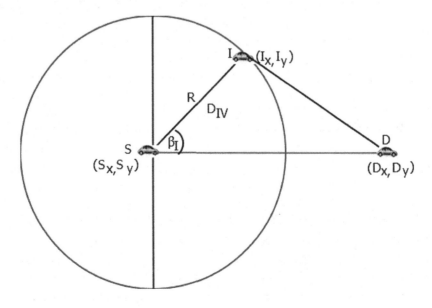

As shown in Figure2, current location (I_X, I_Y) of Ith node is on the circle; therefore, the current location of both sender and receiver nodes will satisfy the equation of the circle as:

$$R^2 = (S_X - I_X)^2 + (S_Y - I_Y)^2 \tag{3}$$

The line *SI* passing through a point (S_X, S_Y) which makes an angle β1 can be given as:

$$S_Y - I_Y = \tan(â_1)(S_X - I_X) \tag{4}$$

$$S_Y - I_Y = \frac{\sin(â_1)}{\cos(â_1)}(S_X - I_X) \tag{5}$$

Putting the value of (S_Y, I_Y) in Eq. (3).

$$R^2\cos^2(â_1) = (S_X - I_X)^2 \cos^2(â_1) + (S_X - I_X)^2 \sin^2(â_1) \tag{6}$$

$$R^2\cos^2(â_1) = (S_X - I_X)^2 (\cos^2(â_1) + \sin^2(â_1)) \tag{7}$$

$$(S_X - I_X)^2 = R^2\cos^2(â_1) \tag{8}$$

$$S_X - I_X = \pm R\cos(â_1) \tag{9}$$

$$I_X = S_X + R\cos(â_1) \tag{10}$$

Similarly,

$$I_Y = S_Y + R\cos(â_1) \tag{11}$$

Thus, distance *d(S, I)* between the nodes *S* and *I* is:

$$d(S,I) = \sqrt{(S_X - S_X - R\cos(\beta_1))^2 + (S_Y - S_Y - R\cos(\beta_1))^2} \tag{12}$$

$$d(S,I) = \sqrt{2}.R\cos(\beta_1) \tag{13}$$

Eq. (13) shows that distance*d(S, I)* between sender node *S* and neighbor *I* is less than the communication range *R*.

Location Verification

As shown in Figure 3, the vehicle S would like to send data packets to the vehicle *C* but there is large size vehicle *D* between the vehicle *S* and *C* is an obstacle that's why a non-line of sight creates between the vehicle *S* and *C*. Therefore, before delivering data packets to the vehicle *C* the vehicle *S* needs location verification of the vehicle *C*. It can be observed in Figure 3, the vehicle *B* is communicating directly with the vehicle *S* and *C* and each node knows their current location information. The vehicle *S* sends current location (C_X, C_Y) of the vehicle *C* to the vehicle *B* and request to verify it. The vehicle *B* verified current location of the vehicle *C* by determining distance D_{BC} of the vehicle C using coordinate values. If the coordinate value (C_X, C_Y) of the vehicle C stored in the vehicle *B* matched with the coordinate value (C_X, C_Y) send by the vehicle *S*, the vehicle *B* sends an acknowledgement to the vehicle *S*.

Figure 3. Location verification of the node C

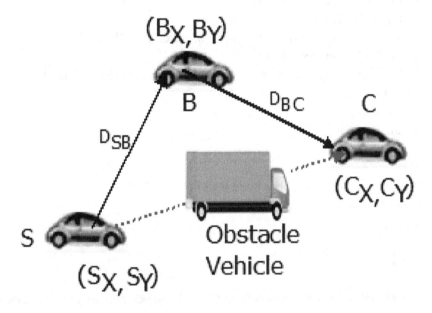

Algorithm to verify location of the vehicle *C* consists of two parts given below.

Algorithm 1: Location verification

    Notations Used:

        LREQ: Location verification request message

        C_{ID}: ID of vehicle C

        C_{Loc}: Coordinates of vehicle C

        C_V: Velocity of vehicle C

        C_θ: Movement direction of the vehicle C

        S_{ID}: ID of the vehicle S

        S_{Loc}: Coordinates of vehicle S

        S_V: Velocity of the vehicle S

Part A: Node S sends location verification (LREQ) message

Step 1: If (NLOS) then

Step 2: Node S sends LREQ message to node B, LREQ contains information i.e. message id LREQID, Id of vehicle S and C i.e. S_{ID} and C_{ID}, current location of vehicle S and C i.e. S_{Loc} and C_{Loc}, velocity of vehicle S and C i.e. S_V and (C_V), movement direction C_θ of vehicle C.

Step 3: end if.

Step 4: Node S continues communication with the node C.

Step 5: end else

Part B: Node B received message LREQ

Step 1: If (Node B received (LREQ)) Then

Step 2: Node B verifies the sender node

Step 3: If (Location of S and C is in neighbor list of node B) then

Step 4: Compute distance D_{SB} of sender node S.

Step 5: Compute distance D_{BC} of node C.

Step 6: Compute Ð SBC

Step 7: Match Ð SBC with movement direction stored in LREQ.

Step 8: If (Node C is verified) then

Step 9: Node C sends reply LREP message that contains information i.e. C_{ID}, C_{Loc}, C_V, C_θ.

Step 10: End If

Step 11: Else

Node is not verified

Step 12: End Else

Step 13: Else

Node S and C are not in neighbor node list of B.

Step 14: End Else

Step 15: End If

Reliability Check

As a node receives data packets from a previous node, the node checks reliability of data packets as follows:

1. As a node receives data packets from a previous node checks timestamp of data packets to ensure data packet is not stale. If it is a stale message the vehicle discards the message, otherwise; checks speed of the vehicle.
2. To verify the vehicle speed stored in received message, the receiving vehicle compare it with defined maximum speed V_{MAX}. The vehicle speed stored in the message should be less than or equal to the Vmax.
3. The node movement direction specifies that the node is how much away from the base line. The node movement direction stored in the message is compared with defined maximum node movement direction θ_{MAX}. For reliable message it should be smaller or equal to defined θ_{MAX}.

Reliability Check Algorithm

Notations Used:

S: Source node
D: Destination node
      Step 1:   Movement direction
D$_{PACKETS}$: Data packets
T$_W$: time window
V$_{MAX}$: Maximum speed
θ$_{MAX}$: Maximum movement direction
R$_{MAX}$: Maximum transmission range
      Step 1:   Let the node N_i sends data packets to the node N_{i+1} towards the destination node D, where i=1, 2, 3, 4... N.
      Step 2:   The node N_{i+1} checks timestamp of data packets.
      Step 3:   If (Timestamp (D$_{PACKETS}$) £ T$_W$) then
      Step 4:   If (Speed (D$_{PACKETS}$) £ V$_{MAX}$) then
      Step 5:   If (MD (D$_{PACKETS}$) £ θ$_{MAX}$) then
      Step 6:   Packet is digitally signed by the node N_{i+1}.
      Step 7:   Else
      Step 8:   D$_{PACKETS}$ is discarded.
      Step 9:   End IF
      Step 10:   Else
      Step 11:   D$_{PACKETS}$ is discarded.
      Step 12:   End If
      Step 13:   Else
      Step 14:   D$_{PACKETS}$ is discarded.
      Step 15:   End If

Next Hop (NH) Selection

As shown in Figure 4, the nodes N_1, N_2, and N_3 are neighbor of sending node S where to obtain their distance from nodes D, the DLVR projects them on the baseline SD which joints the node S and D. The node N_3 has least distance from node D so that it selects as next hop. The distance of the neighbor vehicles NH_i of the sending node can be obtained as:

$$Dist_{N_{Hi}} = \sqrt{\left(X_D - X_{NH_i}\right)^2 + \left(X_D - X_{NH_i}\right)^2} \tag{14}$$

The neighbor who is nearby intended destination selects as the next hop.

$$NH = min\left(Dist^D_{N_1}, Dist^D_{N_2}, Dist^D_{N_3}\right) \tag{15}$$

$$NH = min\left(Dist^{D}_{NH_i}\right) \tag{16}$$

$$Nearest_{Vehicle} = NH \tag{17}$$

Figure 4. Nexthop selection

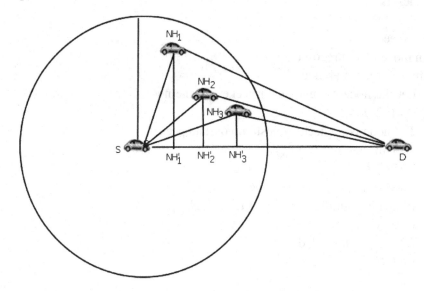

Data Forwarding Delay (D$_{FD}$)

Data forwarding delay is a time requires to delivering messages from sending to intended receiving node. Basically data forwarding delay depends upon the data packet size, communication range of nodes and number of the links with sending node. Suppose P_{Size} and N represents message packet size and counting of neighbors of sending node respectively. Therefore, data transmission time can be obtained as:

$$D_{TX} = \frac{(Packet\ Size).(Number\ of\ Links)}{Communication\ Range}$$

$$D_{TX} = \frac{S_{SIZE}.N}{R} \tag{18}$$

Throughput (*TH*)

Throughput is number of data packets successfully sent from one location to at destination in the network. Let NHC represents average number of next forwarders which are needed to delivering the messages at intended receiving end. Therefore, $1 + N_{HC}$ transmissions are needed to delivering the messages at intended receiving end. Suppose T_P and P_{col} represents throughput of one next forwarder communication and collision probability respectively then throughput of the network can be given as:

$$Th = \frac{(1-P_{col})T_P}{1+N_{HC}}$$
(19)

As shown in Figure 5, the vehicle S would like to deliver data packets to destination vehicle D which is not in direct communication with vehicle S. Therefore, to sending data packets at intended destination vehicle D intermediate vehicles are needed. As shown in Figure 4, vehicle $H1$ is in direct communication of the vehicle S so that vehicle S sends data messages to vehicle $H1$. In the same manner vehicle $H1$ forwards data packets to the vehicle $H2$ which is in reach of $H1$. The destination vehicle D is reachable from vehicle $H2$ so that vehicle $H2$ delivers data packets at destination vehicle D.

Figure 5. Next hops between sender and destination node

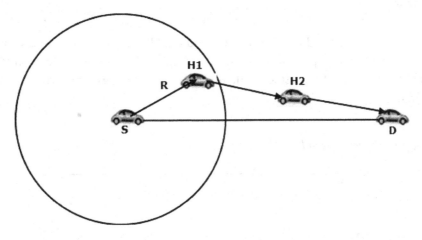

SIMULATION AND RESULT ANALYSIS

The simulation work of the proposed DLVR model is done using NS-2.35 (network simulator 2, version 3.5) for the network area of 2500meter X 2500meter where 10 to 100 mobile vehicles move for 30 seconds simulation time. DLVR used the circle round the nodes to represent the transmission range of the vehicles for free space propagation model. In the simulation work used parameters are given in simulation parameters Table1.

Functionality of the proposed *DLVR* model has examined under consideration of key routing metrics i.e. routing overhead, packet delivery ratio, data forwarding delay, and throughput and compared with *LAR* and *D-LAR* protocols.

Table 1. Simulation parameters

Parameters	Values
Network Area	2500meter X 2500meter
Number of Nodes	10 -100
Communication Range	250meter
Packet Size	512 Bytes
Data Sending Rate	20-70 Pkts/second
Pause	4 second
Traffic Type	CBR
CBR Interval	0.5 second
MAC Protocol	IEEE802.11
Simulation Time	3500 second

Routing Overhead

In Figure 6 shows routing overhead for *DLVR*, *LAR*, and *DLAR* concerning the nodes counts, the routing overhead grows in all routing protocols as quantity of the vehicles grows. The control messages are directly related to the number of the vehicles, therefore, the control messages grows as the quantity of the vehicles grows.

Figure 6. Routing overhead vs. number of nodes

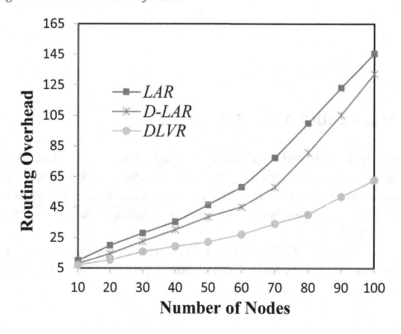

Figure 7 shows the routing overhead with varying sending data rate in term of amount of packets, the routing overhead hikes as data sending rate hikes. The routing overhead in *DLVR* model is incurred and it is least as compared to the *LAR* and *DLAR* protocols.

Figure 7. Routing overhead vs. data sending rate

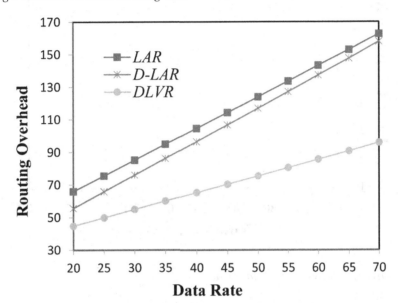

Packet Delivery Ratio

Figure 8 depicts packet delivery ratio under augmenting quantity of nodes, it hikes as the quantity of the nodes hikes. Because as the quantity of the vehicles hikes they augment possibility of optimal next hop to forward messages towards the intended destination side.

Figure 9 illustrates packet delivery ratio against variable packet sending rate, the packet delivery ratio decreases as the packet sending rate increases. Higher packet sending causes probability of network congestion and packets collision increases so that packet delivery ratio goes down. The packet delivery ratio in the proposed DLVR model is higher as compared to the *LAR* and *D-LAR* protocols.

Figure 10 shows packet delivery ratio with varying data size 512Mb to 1012Mb. It can be concluded from the Figure 10 that the packet delivery ratio decreases as data size increase. The reason behind this is that as the data size increases it takes more time to reach at the destination node.

Data Forwarding Delay

Figure 11 exhibits performance of *DLVR*, *LAR*, and *D-LAR* in term of data forwarding delay concerning variable nodes, it goes down as the quantity of the nodes goes up. The higher quantity of nodes maximizes possibility of best next hop towards destination. The best next hop forwards data packets efficiently towards destination takes least time to carry the messages at intended destination.

Figure 8. Packet delivery ratio vs. number of nodes

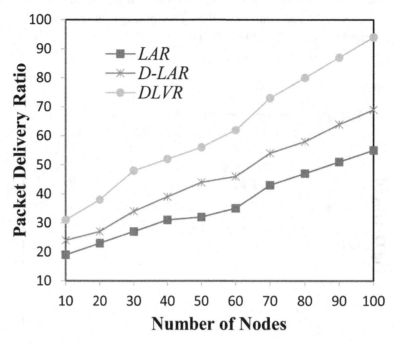

Figure 9. Packet delivery ratio vs. data sending rate

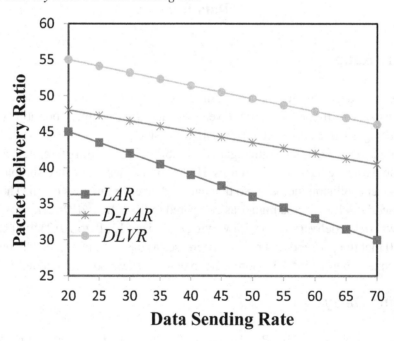

Figure 10. Packet delivery ratio vs. data size in Mb

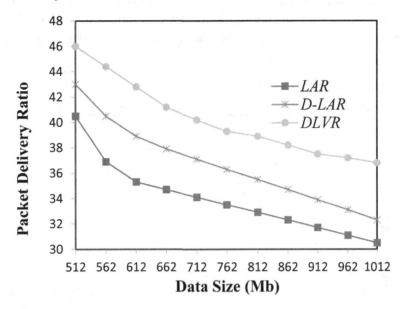

Figure 11. Data forwarding delay vs. number of nodes

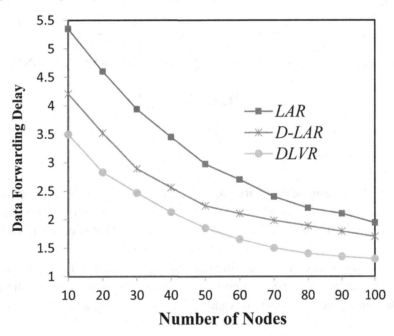

Figure 12 depicts data forwarding delay with the varying data size; it increases as data size increases because the larger data size needs more time to delivering at intended destination. The data forwarding delay in the proposed *DLVR* model comparatively low against *LAR* and *D-LAR* protocols.

Figure 12. Data forwarding delay vs. data size (Mb)

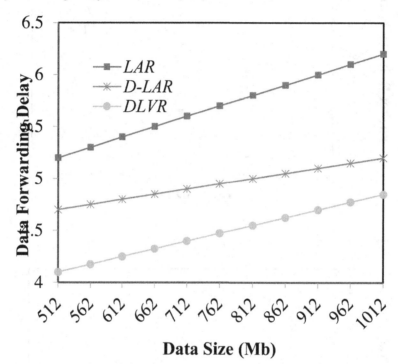

Data Size (Mb)

Throughput

Figure 13 depicts the throughput against variable node; the throughput in all the routing protocols goes up as quantity of nodes goes up. The more nodes maximize possibility of optimal next hop that forwards messages efficiently. The throughput in proposed model *DLVR* is comparatively higher so that it performs better.

Figure 14 shows throughput with the varying data size transmission; it goes down as message size grows because larger message size need more time to delivering at intended destination. Therefore, throughput in all the routing protocols decreases and is comparatively higher in the proposed model *DLVR*.

CONCLUSION

It is notable that due to the certain characteristics of the VANET like nodes mobility and fixed short range communication the links breaking prone frequently. We have fruitfully designed and implemented DLVR to hike performance of a *VANET* based wireless ad hoc networks in term of data forwarding delay and throughput. As data size increases throughput in the *LAR* and *D-LAR* decreases very fast but in

Figure 13 Throughput vs. number of nodes

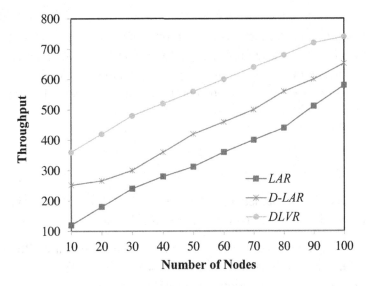

Figure 14. Throughput vs. data size in Mb

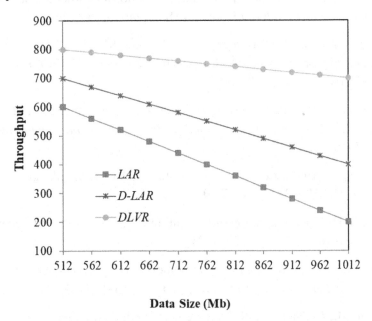

DLVR it decreases very slow. We have improved data forwarding delay towards the intended destination. As the quantity of nodes hikes the message forwarding delay shrinks gradually that is much lower in the *DLVR* protocol. Though the proposed algorithm outperform compare to *LAR* and *D-LAR* for all the parameters. However, following observations are worthy to mention; packet delivery ratio much higher in the proposed model *DLVR*. Throughput drastically increases as the number of the nodes increases in the network.

FUTURE SCOPE

In this chapter a novel routing model directional location verification and routing in Vehicular Ad-hoc Network has proposed and successfully implemented for various scenarios. In this model current location of vehicles are verified before transmission of data packets. In future work we can introduce secure routing algorithms in this proposed model to prevent from various attacks. This proposed model can be to monitor traffic to avoid congestion on the road.

REFERENCES

Bachir, B., Ali, O., Ahmed, H., Mohamed, E., (2014). Proactive schema-based link lifetime estimation and connectivity ratio. Hindawi Publishing Corporation the Scientific World Journal, 2014(4), 1-6.

Chi, T. N., & Oh, H. (2014). A link quality prediction metric for location-based Routing protocols under shadowing and fading effects in vehicular ad-hoc networks. In *Proceedings International Symposium on Emerging Inter-Networks, Communication, and Mobility, 34*, 565-570.

Dahmane, S., & Lorenz, P. (2016). Weighted probabilistic next-hop forwarder decision-making in VANET environments. In *Proceedings IEEE International Conference on Global Communication Conference*, 1-6.

Kaleem, M., Hussain, S. A., Raza, I., Chaudhry, S. R., & Raza, M. H. (2014). A direction and relative speed (DARS) based routing protocol for VANETs in a highway scenario. *Taylor Francis Journal of the Chinese Institute of Engineers, 38*(3), 399-405.

Karp, B., & Kung, H. T. (2000). GPSR: greedy perimeter stateless routing for wireless networks. *Mobi-Com 00 proceedings of the 6th annual international conference on mobile computing and networking*, 243-254. 10.1145/345910.345953

Ko, Y. B., & Vaidya, N. H. (1998). Location-aided routing (LAR) in mobile ad-hoc networks. In *Proceedings of ACM/IEEE MOBICOM'98*, 66 –75. IEEE.

Ko, Y. B., & Vaidya, N. H. (2000). Location-aided routing (LAR) in mobile ad-hoc networks. *International Journal of Wireless Networks, 6*(4), 307–321.

Kumar, V., & Kumar, S. (2015). Position based beaconless routing in wireless sensor networks. *International Journal Wireless Personal Communication, 86*(2), 1061-1085.

Menouar, H., Lenardi, M., & Filali, F. (2007).Movement Prediction-Based Routing (MOPR) Concept for Position-Based Routing in Vehicular Networks. In *Proceedings IEEE International conference on vehicular technology conference*, 556-561. IEEE.

Rana, K., K., Triparhi, S., & Rao, R. S. (2016). VANET: Expected delay analysis for location aided routing protocol. *International Journal of Information Technology, 8*(2), 1029-1037.

Rana, K., K., Triparhi, S, Rao, R., S., (2016). Analysis of expected hop counts and distance in VANETs. *International Journal of Electronics, Electrical, and Computational System, 5*(4), 66-71.

Rana, K., K., Triparhi, S., Rao, R., S., (2017). Analysis of expected progress distance in vehicular ad-hoc network using greedy forwarding. In *Proceedings IEEE International Conference on Computing for Sustainable Global Development,* 5171-5175.

Rana, K. K., Triparhi, S., & Rao, R. S. (2019). Opportunistic Directional Location Aided Routing Protocol for Vehicular Ad-hoc Network. *International Journal of Wireless Personal Communication, 108*(392), 119–137.

Rana, K. K., Tripathi, S., & Raw, R. S. (2016). Feasibility Analysis of Directional-Location Aided Routing Protocol for Vehicular Ad-hoc Networks. [IJCSIS]. *International Journal of Computer Science and Information Security, 16*(4), 214–225.

Rana, K. K., Tripathi, S., & Raw, R. S. (2016). VANET: Expected Delay Analysis for Location Aided Routing (LAR) Protocol. *International Journal of Information Technology, 8*(2), 1029–1037.

Rana, K. K., Tripathi, S., & Raw, R. S. (2017).Analytical analysis of improved directional-location aided routing protocol for VANETs. *International Journal of Wireless Personal Communication, 98*(2), 2403-2426.

Raw, R. S., Das, S., Singh, N., & Kumar, S. (2012). Feasibility evaluation of VANET using directional-location aided routing ((D-LAR) protocol. *International Journal of Computational Science, 9*(5), 404–410.

Raw, R. S., Lobiyal, D. K., Das, S., & Kumar, S. (2015).Analytical evaluation of improved directional-location aided routing protocol for VANETs. *International Journal of Wireless Personal Communication, 82*(3), 1877 - 1891.

Rossi, G. V., Leung, K. K., & Gkelias, A. (2015). Density-based optimal transmission for throughput enhancement in vehicular ad-hoc networks communications. In *Proceedings IEEE International Conference on Communications,* 6571-6576. IEEE.

Shakya, R. K., Rana, K. K., Gaurav, A., Mamoria, P., & Srivastava, P. K. (2019). Stability Analysis of Epidemic Modeling Based on Spatial Correlation for Wireless Sensor Networks. *International Journal of Wireless Personal Communication.* doi:10.100711277-019-06473-0

Shelly, S., & Babu, A. V. (2015). Link reliability based greedy perimeter stateless routing for vehicular ad-hoc networks. International Journal of Vehicular Technology. *Hindawi Publishing Corporation, 2015*(1), 1–16.

Shelly, S., & Babu, A. V. (2017). Link residual lifetime-based next hop selection scheme for vehicular ad-hoc networks. *EURASIP Journal on Wireless Communications and Networking, 2*(6), 1–13. doi:10.118613638-017-0810-x

Shendurkar, A., M., & Chopde, N., R. (2014). A review of position-based routing protocol in mobile ad-hoc networks. *International Journal of Advanced Research in Computer Engineering and Technology, 3*(6), 2047-2053.

Sivakumar, T., & Manoharan, R. (2015). OPRM: An efficient hybrid routing protocol for sparse VANETs. *International Journal of Computer Applications in Technology, 51*(2), 97–104. doi:10.1504/IJCAT.2015.068920

Song, J. H., Wong, V. W., & Leung, V. C. (2014). Secure Location Verification for Vehicular Ad-Hoc Networks, in *Journal of Theoretical and Applied Information Technology, 63*(3), 636-644.

Stojmenovic, I., Ruhil, A. P., & Lobiyal, D. K. (2006). Voronoi diagram and convex hull based geocasting and routing in wireless networks. *Wireless Communications and Mobile Computing, 6*(2), 247-258.

Yang, S., Rongxi, H., Lin, S., Lin, B., & Wang, Y. (2014). An improved geographical routing protocol and its OPNET-based simulation in VANETs. In *Proceedings IEEE International Conference on Bio Medical Engineering and Informatics,* 913-917.

Chapter 2
Towards the Development of Vehicular Ad-Hoc Networks (VANETs):
Challenges and Applications

Mekelleche Fatiha

Department of Computer Science, University of Oran1 Ahmed BenBella, Algeria

Haffaf Hafid

Department of Computer Science, University of Oran1 Ahmed BenBella, Algeria

ABSTRACT

Vehicular Ad-Hoc Networks (VANETs), a new mobile ad-hoc network technology (MANET), are currently receiving increased attention from manufacturers and researchers. They consist of several mobile vehicles (intelligent vehicles) that can communicate with each other (inter-vehicle communication) or with fixed road equipment (vehicle-infrastructure communication) adopting new wireless communication technologies. The objective of these networks is to improve road safety by warning motorists of any event on the road (accidents, hazards, possible deviations, etc.), and make the time spent on the road more pleasant and less boring (applications deployed to ensure the comfort of the passengers). Practically, VANETs are designed to support the development of Intelligent Transportation Systems (ITS). The latter are seen as one of the technical solutions to transport challenges. This chapter, given the importance of road safety in the majority of developed countries, presents a comprehensive study on the VANET networks, highlighting their main features.

INTRODUCTION

The technological advances that the world has experienced today in terms of embedded systems and wireless communication techniques have led man to deal with more and more complex problems. Among these problems, there are the transport problems. In fact, the popularization of vehicles for example has

DOI: 10.4018/978-1-7998-2570-8.ch002

led to problems of safety and efficiency. For that, in a road environment, a transport system is essential to manage road traffic, on the one hand, and develop new applications to improve the comfort of travelers and drivers on the other hand.

Nowadays, several means of transport have appeared, the vehicle is the most common means of transport. This vehicle is increasingly equipped with electronic and computer equipment that has led to the emergence of the term "smart vehicle" or "connected vehicle". More precisely, a smart vehicle is a vehicle equipped with computers, cameras, network interfaces as well as sensors capable of collecting information and processing it. A set of smart vehicles builds what we call "intelligent transport systems" (ITS) (Figueiredo et al., 2001) (Perallos, Hernandez-Jayo, Zuazola, & Onieva, 2015), which aims to strengthen road safety significantly through safe roads (traffic information, accidents, hazards, possible deviations, etc.) and improve efficiency and user-friendliness in road transport. The architecture on which the Intelligent Transportation Systems (ITS) is based is known as Vehicular Ad-Hoc Network (VANET).

A VANET network (Al-Sultan, Al-Doori, Al-Bayatti, & Zedan, 2014) (Yousefi, Mousavi, & Fathy, 2006) is an emerging technology adopting new communication technologies and wireless devices. Figure 1 shows that the VANETs represent a subclass of MANETs (Mobile Ad-Hoc Networks) (Hoebeke, Moerman, Dhoedt, & Demeester, 2004). A VANET consists of hardware components that include vehicles which are capable to communicate among each other or with fixed equipment from the road based on radio and software components. In other words, a VANET is an ad hoc network characterized by a highly dynamic topology due to the high mobility of vehicles as well as the heterogeneity of their speed and the diversity of their trajectories as a function of road infrastructures. In addition, it is very dense in certain environments such as urban areas. Recently, this type of network has aroused a real interest by research organizations, industrial units and also by cooperation projects because the improvement of road safety has become a government priority in the majority of developed countries.

Figure 1. Hierarchy of wireless networks where the inclusion of VANET in MANET is illustrated

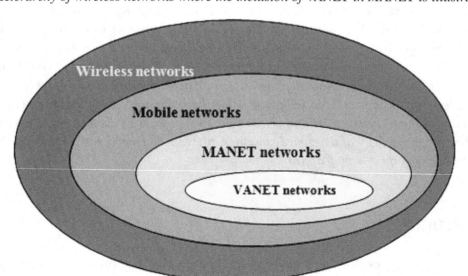

In this first chapter, we will trace the functioning of VANETs through a synthetic description, as we describe their architectures, their characteristics and their various fields of application. We also try to highlight their different issues and challenges where we identify the data dissemination and vehicle location.

AD-HOC VEHICLE NETWORKS (VANETS)

Definition

A Vehicle Ad-Hoc Network (VANET) (Al-Sultan, Al-Doori, Al-Bayatti, & Zedan, 2014) is an emerging paradigm in wireless networks providing efficient, fast and cost-effective communications in the automotive industry and new applications that enhance the security and the comfort in road transport (like reducing the number of undesirable events, ease of circulation in difficult situations, etc.). The VANET network is considered as a special type of MANET networks, in which mobile nodes are intelligent vehicles (safe, economical and comfortable vehicles) that encompasses a set of technologies such as environmental perception devices (radar, cameras), a tracking system (GPS) (Hofmann-Wellenhof, Lichtenegger, & Collins, 2012), calculators and sensors. More precisely, as illustrated in Figure 2, a VANET is distributed system putting into communication a large number of vehicles. In a typical application scenario, these vehicle nodes use wireless communication to route data with multi-hop routing. The size of a VANET network is highly variable because of the diversity of road environment topologies and traffic conditions. For instance, in the case of traffic congestion (overcrowding) the size of the network increases considerably.

Figure 2. Example of a VANET

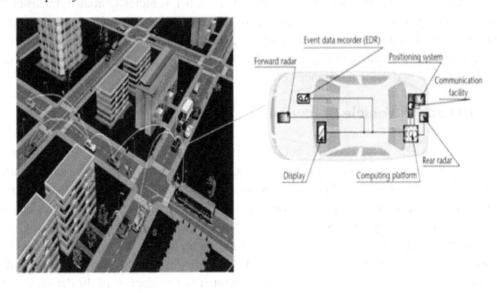

Currently, Intelligent Transportation Systems (ITS) are considered as one of the technical and economic solutions to the transport challenge. They offer several advantages in terms of safety and comfortability. They encompass all modes of transport and take into account all components of the transportation system: the vehicle, the infrastructure, and the driver. Vehicular networks (VANETs) represent a projection of these transport systems where vehicles communicate with each other via inter-vehicle communication (IVC). They can also communicate with the equipment of the road via the Road-to-Vehicle Communication (RVC). These two modes of communication are discussed later.

VANET Characteristics

Each type of computer network is characterized by very particular properties. So, it is important to point out that VANETs have some characteristics that distinguish them from other types of ordinary wireless networks. For example, compared to a typical ad hoc network, VANETs are characterized by a high mobility of nodes making the topology of the network highly dynamic. These specific features can open horizons for new challenges that defy all the applications already realized in the context of ad hoc networks on the one hand, and offering new possibilities related to vehicular networks on the other hand. For this purpose, when designing protocols dedicated to this type of network, these specificities must be taken into account. In this section, we will unveil some characteristics (Kumar, Mishra, & Chand, 2013) (Lee, Lee, & Gerla, 2010) and constraints related to vehicle networks. As, three classes are planned:

Features Related to The Technological Advancement of Vehicles

Among the most important constraints when dealing with ad hoc networks are the energy constraint. However, in VANETs, this constraint is ignored because the power system of the platforms embedded in the vehicles allows to these networks to have largely sufficient energy. In addition, vehicles are able to exchange and store different types of information from other vehicles or road infrastructure. This information can be updated continuously to enable the driver to make appropriate decisions in the face of a situation. VANETs have also a large capacity for processing and calculation (several communication interfaces: Wireless, Bluetooth, etc.). These advantages make it possible to propose more and more advanced applications of driving assistance.

Features Related to Vehicle Behaviour

Among the major concerns in the VANETs networks, the high mobility of the vehicles, the heterogeneity of their speed according to the behavior of the drivers and the diversity of their trajectories according to the road environments. This mobility causes rapid changes in network topology that are difficult to manage. Indeed, in a very short time, the vehicle can quickly join or leave the network. This leads to sporadic network connectivity and frequently partitioned network topology in the form of groups. The arrival / departure rate depends on their speed, the environment, and the drivers' needs to be connected to the network. Typically, the mobility of vehicles depends on deployment mode, so their trajectories can be predicted using information about road infrastructure and the reaction of the driver. In highways, for example, vehicles often move at high speeds, while in urban areas they are slow. Furthermore, the mobility is limited by road directions as well as by traffic regulations. As a result, mobility models can now include some level of predictability of movement.

Otherwise, VANET networks have been designed primarily for applications that offer secure collaborative driving (alert message broadcasting: emergency braking, collision, slowdown, etc.) and a safer environment. These applications require that the vehicles communicate with each other by the successive diffusion of the messages (all the nodes share the same channel). Vehicles are concerned with the dissemination of information according to their geographical positions and their degree of involvement in the event triggered. However, the links between the vehicle nodes can be broken frequently because of the high speed and the high number of obstacles. for this, VANETs are characterized by very limited coverage.

Features Related to The Road Environment

In the design of VANET protocols, it is imperative to take into account the great environmental diversity. Unlike other wireless networks that have a very specific environment depending on how they work. The deployment environments of vehicular networks are of various characteristics related to their location (urban, rural, mountainous, etc.) and their means (national road, highway, urban roads, subterranean environment, tunnel, etc.).

In addition, in a context of vehicle deployment, the density of vehicles in a VANET is highly variable, and depends on several factors. For instance, the density of vehicles in an urban environment is much higher than in a rural area or on highways; it is also dense on intersections, and when certain types of events are present on the road such as accidents and works (Fiore, Harri, Filali, & Bonnet, 2007).

Communication Architecture in VANET

Advances in wireless technologies have opened the door to new trends in deploying VANET on the highway, in urban and other environments. This deployment is done by operators of networks and/or services according to the following configurations (or combination of these configurations) (Cunha et al., 2016):

Vehicle-to-Vehicle Communication (V2V)

The vehicle-to-vehicle (V2V) communication mode, also known as IVC (Inter-Vehicle Communication), is a decentralized mode, and represents a special case of MANETs networks. This communication system is a recent area of research that caught the attention of the scientific community, car manufacturers and telecom operators. Indeed, IVC systems can be used to implement several types of ITS applications. More precisely, this IVC model relies on a distributed and autonomous system that is formed by the vehicles themselves. No infrastructure is used, no facilities are needed on the roads and all vehicles can communicate directly with each other anywhere, whether on highways, mountain roads or urban roads, giving less expensive and more flexible communication. In the case where two communicating vehicles are separated from several jumps from one another, the other vehicles of the network serve as relays and these communications are done by means of a multi-hop protocol which is responsible for transmitting the messages from end to end (Al-Sultan, Al-Doori, Al-Bayatti, & Zedan, 2014) (Rawat, Bista, Yan, & Olariu, 2014).

The mode of communication IVC favors the speed of the diffusion of the messages, for that it is much used in the applications of the road safety where often messages of alerts are communicated. We can quote the applications of emergency braking, automatic deceleration and cooperative driving. Nevertheless, this mode requires a sufficient number of vehicles for the communications to be done efficiently and without interruption.

Vehicle to Infrastructure Communication (V2I)

In this communication mode, we don't rely on simple inter-vehicle communication systems, but we use base stations or infrastructure points RSUs (Road Side Units). RSUs are often referred to as access points or gateways to principal servers. The vehicles rely on these RSUs which are placed along the roads to send, receive and relay information from the network. As a result, two communication models are emerged: infrastructure-to-vehicle (I2V) and vehicle-to-infrastructure (V2I). V2I communications allow vehicles to send messages to infrastructures and I2V communications allow sending in the other direction (Dey, Rayamajhi, Chowdhury, Bhavsar, & Martin, 2016) (Cunha et al., 2016). These communications are based on cellular networks such as GSM, UMTS, WIMAX, etc. More precisely, this architecture is based on the client / server model where the vehicles are the clients and the stations installed along the road are the servers. These servers are connected to each other via an interface. They can offer users several services regarding traffic, internet access, vehicle-to-home data exchange and even car-to-garage communication for remote diagnostics.

The mode of communication V2I enriches vehicle knowledge with centralized information in RSUs such as internet access or accident alert. However, its major drawback is that the installation of stations along the roads is an expensive task and takes a long time, not to mention the costs related to the maintenance of stations. For that the majority of the works do not rest this mode of communication but on the two others.

Hybrid Communication (V2V + V2I)

The vehicles can use the two modes mentioned previously (V2V or V2I) or combine them (V2V + V2I) if they can't communicate directly with the infrastructures of the road. This combination makes it possible to achieve a hybrid communication very interesting and very useful in many applications such as road traffic management (congestion, slowdowns, average traffic speed, etc.). Indeed, this mode makes it possible to cover a maximum of infrastructures thanks to the communication V2V where the vehicles serve as relay to extend the informations. This saves infrastructure costs and avoids the proliferation of base stations at every corner of the road. Moreover, compared to V2V networks, this mode can address the problem of long-distance connectivity. Such as infrastructures, not having mobility constraints, in turn serve as fixed relays to extend the distance in inter-vehicle communication.

Previously, the existing communication modes in VANETs are introduced theoretically but in Figure 3 they are illustrated schematically.

Figure 3. Communication architectures in VANETs

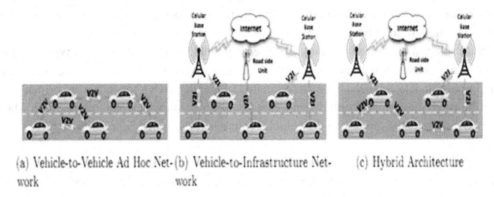

(a) Vehicle-to-Vehicle Ad Hoc Network (b) Vehicle-to-Infrastructure Network (c) Hybrid Architecture

It is clear that the architecture of a VANET is composed of communicating entities (RSU, vehicles and road infrastructures). These entities create and exchange messages that allow the dissemination of useful information to the various VANET applications. This is the case for example of a vehicle that creates a message about a detected accident or a RSU that creates a message about weather conditions. In addition, some messages are generated and are not transferred to other communicating entities. This is the case of control messages created by vehicles containing information (position, speed, trajectory), they allow vehicles to be known by the network. As a result, a new "intra-vehicle" or "in-vehicle" communication mode has emerged which makes possible to develop communications inside the vehicles (Pinart et al., 2008). The intra-vehicle communication system refers to a local area network within each vehicle. It is logically composed of two units: an On-Board Unit (OBU) and one or more Application Units (AU). Each intelligent vehicle must be equipped with these two devices (Abdelhamid, Hassanein, & Takahara, 2015). The first device, the OBU, is a communication platform that allows vehicles to communicate with each other and with other network entities. The second device, the AU, allows one or more VANET applications to be executed when using the communication capabilities of the OBU. Then, the AU is in permanent connection with the OBU.

Services and Applications of VANETS

Thanks to recent technological advances, a multitude of new features are associated to the vehicles. In VANETs, the data is shared, in a collaborative way between the vehicles. These networks have been very successful and have invaded many application fields (Kumar, Mishra, & Chand, 2013) where they can offer better contributions. These applications can be oriented towards road safety applications, applications for driver assistance systems and road traffic management and comfort applications that mainly require an internet connection. We will detail these domains below and then give examples of applications (Hartenstein & Laberteaux, 2010) (Hartenstein & Laberteaux, 2008).

Applications for Road Safety

This category is undoubtedly the most important category because road safety has become a priority in most developed countries, today. This priority is motivated by the increasing number of accidents on the roads. In order to enhance the prevention of travel and to cope with dangerous situations, VANETs offer the possibility of preventing collisions and road works, of detecting obstacles (fixed or mobile) and of distributing weather information by sending warning messages. These latter must be reduced in size to be transmitted as quickly as possible to give to driver enough time to react.

In the road safety applications (Cheng, Shan, & Zhuang, 2011), there are two types of messages: periodic messages and event messages. Periodic messages also called driver assistance messages, such as, contain important data and need to be disseminated frequently. Event messages are priority messages containing the type of event, sent only when a dangerous situation is detected on the road. These messages must be disseminated quickly to the vehicles to prevent them from danger.

- Alert in case of accidents: the purpose of this service is to avoid the risk of road accidents (road collisions) by providing drivers with relevant information about the road situation in real-time. To do this, event data is collected via on-board sensors in vehicles to be processed and disseminated as alert messages containing information on the position and direction of the event. The role of these messages is to warn other communicating entities heading to the scene of the accident (the necessity to intensify vigilance). Figure 4 is an example of this alert.

Figure 4. Vigilance in the case of accident

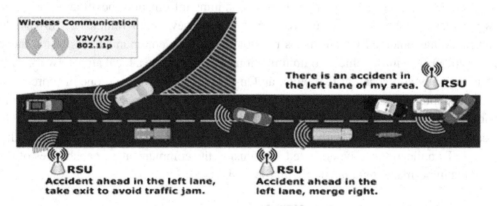

- Alert in case of abnormal slowdown (like works, congestion, weather): this service aims to warn motorists about the particular traffic situations that have occurred. Vehicles detect information on traffic difficulties (For instance: road work, heavy braking, low visibility due to heavy fog, traffic jams, traffic jams, rockslides, slippery substances on the roadway or ice storms, rain, etc.) and then disseminate them collaboratively, using V2V communications. to warn drivers. In the case of works on the road, a vehicle participating to the works may also be the source of the warning message (as depicted in Figure 5). As for the warning message informing of an accident, the warning message informing of a slowdown must be transmitted to the other vehicles in an efficient and fast way.

Figure 5. Alert in the case of road works

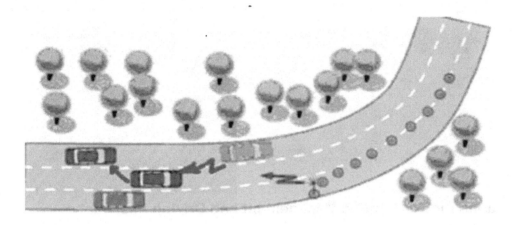

- Alert of an emergency vehicle: this service ensures a free path for emergency vehicles. First, the sensors retrieve information about the existence of an emergency vehicle on a road lane. This information is then analyzed and processed then through V2V communications between vehicles circulating on the same path as the emergency vehicle, an alert message (as shown in Figure 6) containing the information about (speed and direction) is disseminated.

Figure 6. Warning in the event of an emergency vehicle on a lane

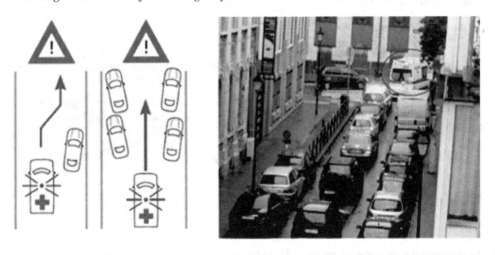

- Collaborative conduct: this service aims to significantly enhance the safety of road transport and improve vehicular traffic. In addition, when it comes to motor vehicles, collaborative driving is responsible for reducing the risk of accidents. As we can notice in Figure 7, this concept is based on multi-hop V2V communications to share information between vehicles equipped with sensors. The vehicles collaborate in dynamically trained groups. These vehicle groups include a collective driving strategy that doesn't require driver intervention (Gunther, Trauer, & Wolf, 2015).

Figure 7. Collaborative driving

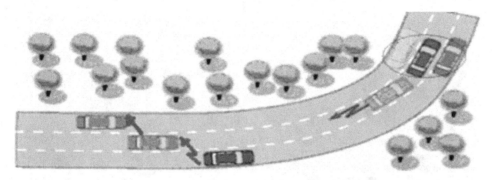

Applications for Road Traffic Management and Driving Assistance

Traffic management applications aim to improve road traffic and avoid traffic congestion (Jayapal & Roy, 2016). Indeed, to optimize road traffic, this service consists of balancing traffic on roads and intersections through the selection of routes and appropriate paths, taking into account traffic jams or obstacles on the road. This makes it possible to distribute the road traffic, to avoid congestion and the risk of accidents, to reduce the duration of journeys and to save on fuel consumption. An example of traffic management application is represented in Figure 8.

Figure 8. Road traffic administration

Road traffic management

In addition, the current systems present in vehicles aim to mitigate driver failures, but the recent developments add the integration of new goals to driving. This drive improvement trend has brought a new generation of systems with significant challenges. Driver assistance systems (Cunha et al., 2016) are one of the technologies to solve the problems of this new era of embedded systems. They are designed mainly to lighten and facilitate the task of the driver. They can be greatly improved through the collection and sharing of collected data on road traffic status by vehicles, which becomes a technical support for drivers in critical situations. Specifically, they help to prevent the occurrence of a dangerous situation that could lead to an accident, release the driver of a number of tasks that could mitigate his alertness and assist the driver in his perception of the environment (overtaking, freezing, pedestrian, etc.). These systems include: an electronic braking system, a cruise control system, a radar at the front of the vehicle to measure the distance with the nearest vehicle and therefore to warn the driver if there is a risk, a Driver Visibility Improvement System Using Cameras Capable of Viewing in the Night or in Fog, etc.

Comfort and Entertainment Applications

The messages exchanged within information and entertainment applications (also called infotainment applications) are intended to increase the comfort of drivers and passengers and make travel more comfortable and enjoyable (Sarakis, Orphanoudakis, Leligou, Voliotis, & Voulkidis, 2016). These applications are considered to provide certain services. One of these services, Internet access. This access can be made at strategic points, such as RSU infrastructures or gas stations. In addition to the Internet connection, other services are used to perform instant messaging, inter-vehicle chat and download files, music or videos. The passengers in vehicles can also play in networks, or even browse the internet. This concept of Internet availability in the vehicles is evidently illustrated in Figure 9.

Figure 9. Internet access in vehicles

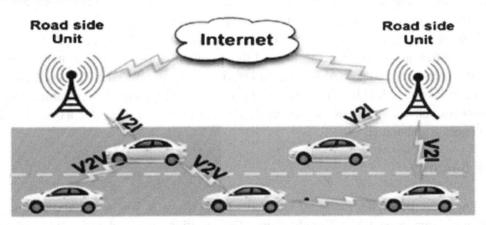

On the other hand, these applications announce to vehicles general utility information such as weather information, information on the location of (a gas station, a restaurant or a hotel) and advertising information on the edges roads. These applications can also be informative like in the case of parking management in car parks (Lu, Lin, Zhu, & Shen, 2009). In fact, this service makes it possible to inform the driver of the available places via the data provided by a RSU. This concept of managing the free spaces in a car park is well illustrated in Figure 10.

Figure 10. Parking assistance with VANETs

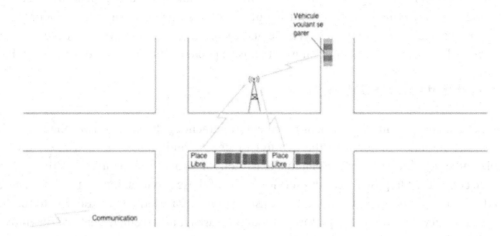

ISSUES AND CHALLENGES OF VANETS

As mentioned above, VANETs represent one of the most important components of Intelligent Transport Systems (ITS). These aim to integrate the new technologies of information and communication in the field of transport in order to improve the safety and comfort of users. These networks do not have the same characteristics as traditional networks, and their particularities make them more complex. For that, several technical challenges (Al-Sultan, Al-Doori, Al-Bayatti, & Zedan, 2014) (Zeadally, Hunt, Chen, Irwin, & Hassan, 2012) have been generated such as, routing, data dissemination, access to the channel, network connectivity, network security, location of vehicles, Hereinafter a brief description of these challenges is elaborated.

Network Security

Security (Engoulou, Bellaïche, Pierre, & Quintero, 2014) (Raya & Hubaux, 2005) is a major challenge with a big impact on VANET applications. The sensitivity of the data conveyed in a VANET demonstrates a strong need for security in order to guarantee the operational safety of the network, in particular and of Intelligent Transport System (ITS), in general. So, the importance of security in this context is crucial given the serious consequences on all vehicles that result from an attack or intrusion, For instance, as depicted in Figure 11, an attacker can create alert messages that have falsified content or prevent the delivery of a legitimate message to cause an accident. For that, several research has been projected to develop a security mechanisms that make the data dissemination in VANETs: fast, reliable and particularly fulfilling the security needs.

To detail the security issue in VANETs, it is important to discuss some of the concepts (security needs) that must be taken into account when designing security protocols for these networks. When a requirement is not respected, this presents a security gap. These requirements are presented as follows:

- **Confidentiality:** The confidentiality of the messages in the VANETs makes possible to secure the exchanged data (this protection is ensured by the addition of specific fields within the message) and to ensure the anonymity of the sources. The encryption of messages during the communica-

Figure 11. Broadcast of a falsified message by an opponent

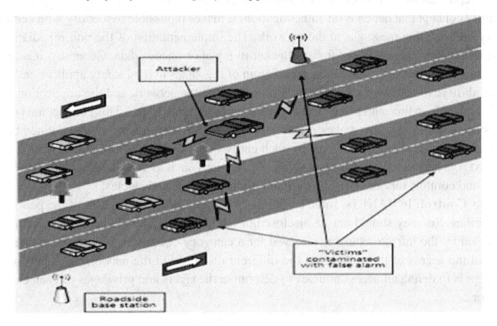

tion allows to set up the confidentiality service. Generally, asymmetric and symmetric cryptography algorithms (Raya & Hubaux, 2005) are used to encrypt and decrypt data using public / private keys. However, this encryption process depends on the application and the communication scenario; for example, alert messages informing of a dangerous situation can be read by any member of the network. So, this type of message doesn't need to be encrypted. On the other hand, for a comfort application, in the case of inter-vehicle chat, it is important that the messages are encrypted so as not to disclose sensitive information.

- **Authentication:** In VANETs, it is very important to know several information about the sending node (vehicle) such as its identifier, its address, and its geographical position. It is therefore important to authenticate the sender of the message and the message circulating on the network. From this, we can deduce two types of authentication: entity authentication and message authentication. Entity authentication is used to identify the network node while message authentication is used to reveal the source of the message. In other words, authentication is a security service that allows different nodes to trust the messages broadcast in the network and thus strengthen the relationship between them. In a road scenario, authentication aims to greatly enhance road safety by preventing attacks by specifying a unique identifier for each vehicle.

- **Data Integrity:** One of the important requirements for ensuring a secure road environment is the integrity of the messages exchanged. Indeed, this service consists in protecting the vehicles against destruction and preventing the alteration of messages. Generally, the integrity is ensured if the packet sent by the source has not undergone any modification or alteration throughout its routing in the network. If a circulated message is corrupted or modified, it is considered that there is a security breach (integrity violation). The electronic signature (Guo, Baugh, & Wang, 2007) allows to set up the integrity service in certain security protocols. The mechanisms that are also used to manage the data integrity are the hash functions and the Message Authentication Code (MAC) (Raw, Kumar, & Singh, 2013).

- **Non-Repudiation (Non-Rejection):** The non-repudiation service in VANETs is an important security concept that depends on authentication. It makes it possible to identify with certainty any entity broadcasting messages in the network. The implementation of the non-repudiation policy thus eliminates any possibility for an attacker to inject erroneous data. Generally, it is the digital signature that is used to ensure non-repudiation of messages in road safety applications.

- **Availability:** In vehicular networks, it is essential that the network and the applications must remain available in time and place even in the presence of breakdowns. This concept not only makes the system secure but also makes it fault-tolerant. Availability service is also defined by permanent access to services or resources by each entity in the network. More precisely, in a vehicular context, the services provided by VANET applications such as road safety, road traffic management and comfort services must be available for any legitimate vehicles.

- **Access Control:** In VANETs, some communications are sensitive like that of the police or other authorities. So, they should not be disclosed in the network. Thus the access to certain services provided by the infrastructures is reserved for a category of entities. It is therefore necessary to control the access of the vehicles to the different resources in the network. The purpose of this concept is to define all access policies to determine the rights and privileges of each entity in the network.

Data Routing

Routing challenge in VANETs (Singh & Agrawal, 2014) represents a real issue and recent research axis. It is considered a method of routing data to the right destination (unicast routing) through a connection network. It consists in exploiting a strategy that guarantees, at all times, an efficient and optimal route establishment between any pair of vehicles. The purpose of routing service is therefore to ensure the exchange of messages between vehicles in a continuous manner. Nevertheless, in order for vehicles to communicate with each other, we need to put in place appropriate routing protocols.

The problem of routing in VANETs resides essentially in the high mobility of the nodes, which leads to a very dynamic topology, unstable network connectivity and security constraints. Indeed, for instance, in the VANETs, the speed can be much higher than the MANETs especially in certain communication environments like highways. In this case, the network must be robust and have a very short wait time (to deliver the messages quickly from a source vehicle to the destination vehicle.). In order to answer these problems, researchers have developed a number of routing protocols. Generally, as shown in Figure 13, these protocols can be classified into three categories: (i) Routing protocols based on network topology that are divided into protocols: proactive, reactive and hybrid. (ii) Routing protocols based on node localization. (iii) Hierarchical routing protocols based on the concept of clusters for better dissemination of information. In what follows, we will detail each class.

- Routing protocols based on topology: this family of protocols uses the information on the links that exist between the nodes for the transmission of packets in the network. Depending on how routes are created and maintained between nodes during data routing, these protocols can be classified into three classes: proactive, reactive, and hybrid protocols (Li & Wang, 2007).
  - **Proactive Protocols (Table-Driven):** In this category of protocols, each node retains all possible routes for each destination in the network (any route in the network will be available immediately). In a more specific way, each node keeps an image (in the form of routing

tables) of the topology of the entire network. This image is updated periodically and with each topological modification by means of control messages. The two main methods using this principle are: Link State method (Singh & Agrawal, 2014) and the Vector Distance method (Fazio, De Rango, Sottile, Manzoni, & Calafate, 2011). In the literature, there are several protocols that are proactive (Hamid & El Mokhtar, 2015), we can quote: DSDV (Destination-Sequenced Distance-Vector) and OLSR (Optimized Link State Routing).

○ **Reactive Protocols (On-Demand Driven):** In reactive routing protocols (Chowdhury, Lee, Choi, Kee, & Pyun, 2011), the routes between nodes are established only on demand and only routes in use are retained (unlike proactive protocols, all routes are backed up even if they are not used). In this case, an additional period of time is required at the beginning of each communication session for searching the path. In this category of protocols, two steps are planned: (i) Road discovery stage. (ii) Road maintenance stage. The major disadvantage of on-demand routing resides in the slowness of the data routing operation to the destination because of the search for paths, which can degrade the performance of the applications. Moreover, it is impossible to know beforehand the quality of the path (in terms of bandwidth, delays, etc.). Looking at the review of the literature, finding several protocols basing on this principle among them we have (Paul, Ibrahim, Bikas, & Naser, 2012): AODV (Ad hoc On-demand Distance Vector), DSR (Dynamic Source Routing) and SSR (Signal Stability-based Routing).

○ **Hybrid Protocols:** Hybrid protocols (Al-Rabayah & Malaney, 2012) combine the two previous approaches; proactive and reactive. Specifically, they use the principle of proactive protocols to discover nearby neighbors, then, for the rest of the network, this category acts as the reactive protocols. The best-known routing protocol in this class is: ZRP (Zone Routing Protocol). Its principle is simple, as it divides the network in different zones. For each node, it defines a routing area expressed in maximum number of hops n. the routing area of a node includes all nodes that are at a maximum distance of n hops. Within this zone, ZRP uses a proactive protocol and outside this zone, it uses a reactive protocol. For more details about the operation of this protocol, refer to (Beijar, 2002).

• **Routing Protocols Based on Geographic Position (Geographical Routing):** VANET Geographical routing (Liu, et al., 2016) represents a data routing mechanism adapted to vehicular network. This is a routing that takes into account the physical location (the geographical coordinates) of the nodes to find a path to the destination (the positions of the nodes are included in the routing tables). To achieve this goal, it is essential that all the nodes of the network have a means of localization (GPS). In addition, a source node must know imperatively the position of the destination node. Several protocols have been developed, in the literature, to ensure geographic routing namely: DREAM (Distance Routing Effect Algorithm for Mobility), GPSR (Greedy Perimeter Stateless Routing), A-STAR (Anchor-based Street and Traffic Aware Routing) and VADD (Vehicle-Assisted Data Delivery).

• **Hierarchical Routing Protocols (Hierarchical Routing):** The hierarchical routing (Li & Wang, 2007) (Luo, Zhang, & Hu, 2010) is considered as a well-adapted and compatible data routing mechanism for the particularities of VANETs. Indeed, the strong dynamicity due to the rapid mobility of vehicles and the discontinuous connectivity of the entire network, lead to the fragmentation of the network (formation of groups). As shown in Figure 12, the hierarchy of VANET (process of Clustering) consists in hierarchically organizing the network into groups of nodes (clusters). Inside each constituted cluster, there are three types of nodes ("Cluster-Head (CH)", "Gateway nodes" and " member nodes"): the CH manages all communications within of the cluster and has additional functions (routing, access to the medium, etc.). A gateway is a non-cluster-head node that has inter-cluster links and can therefore access neighboring clusters and route data between them, whereas an ordinary node is a non-cluster-head node that doesn't have links with other clusters. In addition, the hierarchy of vehicular networks becomes profitable and brings undeniable advantages, which are: (i) Introduce stable structures (clusters) in an unstable environment (VANETs). (ii) Reduce the size of the routing table that is based on the clustering structure used. (iii) The scaling of protocols, in fact, the division of space makes the network easier to manage and reduces the number of messages exchanged between all nodes.

Figure 12. Hierarchical architecture of a VANET.

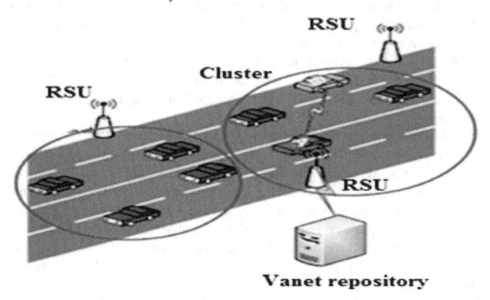

Clustering in VANETs is naturally distributed and requires a large number of messages for building and maintaining clusters using clustering algorithms (Vodopivec, Bešter, & Kos, 2012). In the literature, different clustering approaches devoted to VANETs have been depicted. They are based on certain metrics relating to vehicles such as: clustering according to the path where the vehicle is located, clustering according to the distance between the vehicles, clustering according to the moving direction (movement-based), clustering according to the position, clustering according to speed, etc. Among the routing protocols proposed for clustering a vehicle network: CONVOY (Vèque, Kaisser, Johnen, & Busson, 2013) in a motorway context.

Figure 13. Routing protocols in VANETs.

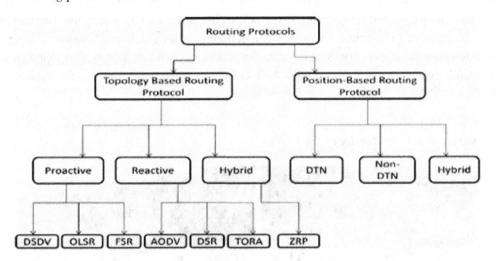

Location (Geo-Localization)

At present, particular interest has been given to research work focused on vehicular networks. This interest is due to the crucial role that these types of networks can play in Intelligent Transport Systems (ITS). Node localization is a very important point that should not be overlooked in any type of computer network. VANETs are no exception. Localization (Benslimane, 2005) is used in many applications and road transport services such as geographic routing. The purpose of localization in VANETs is to assign an exact or estimated position (geographic coordinates) to each of the vehicles. However, in these networks, in order to guarantee a precise and efficient location, it is essential to adapt to the changes occurring in the network and to take into account its constraints, such as: the speed of the vehicles and the rapid change of the topology, the variable density of the network, discontinuous connectivity as well as the extent of geographic areas to be covered. In order to limit the impact of these constraints, several localization solutions (Boukerche, Oliveira, Nakamura, & Loureiro, 2008) proposed in the literature. Each of these solutions proposes various hypotheses on the capacities of the vehicles. The first and most used is the use of GPS (Hofmann-Wellenhof, Lichtenegger, & Collins, 2012), i.e. equip each vehicle with a GPS module. This technique is not applicable to the entire network because it is too expensive from a financial point of view. To reduce this cost, other localization techniques have been proposed, see (Kuutti et al., 2018).

Variable Density and Discontinuous Network Connectivity

In VANETs, the density of vehicles is very variable. It may vary depending on the road environment (highway, rural environment or city) and travel time (peak hours, late at night or early morning). Indeed, the density can be very high in the case of traffic jams during peak hours in large cities (i.e. congested urban network), as it can be low in a rural environment or early in the morning in cities (in this case the vehicles are scattered). This has an impact on delivery rate and time of release of packets. In the first situation, as revealed in Figure 14. (a), the number of nodes in the transmission range of a vehicle increases considerably which poses several problems for wireless communications such as, competition for access to the communication channel causing interference, collisions and consequently a lot of packet loss and low message delivery rate. Nevertheless, in Figure 14. (b), when the disconnections are frequent in the network (low connectivity between vehicles), a long delivery times may have resulted and a low rate of message delivery. Several research works have recently been developed to solve the problems related to density variations of the VANETs by proposing new strategies for the data dissemination (Darwish & Bakar, 2015).

Figure 14. Variations in the density of the VANET

Sharing Channel Resources

In vehicular networks, communications are based on wireless links (radio waves) and the vehicles communicate with each other using the same channel. As a result, several problems may occur during data dissemination: congestions of the communication channel, collisions especially in high density environments, radio interference, electromagnetic irregularities, and distributed resource allocation (the bandwidth), etc. In order to overcome these problems and to manage resources equitably (access to the channel and bandwidth sharing), it is necessary to design specific mechanisms for traffic management such as: MAC protocols (Menouar, Filali, & Lenardi, 2006), packet scheduling protocols.

Passage in The Scale (Scalability)

In VANETs, especially in urban areas (city centers or motorways) where intersections and multi-lane roads are common, the number of vehicles increases significantly, as well as the amount of information exchanged within the network. For this, any solution proposed in the context of vehicular networks, must consider from its conception, the problem of scalability. For instance, compared to the channel access protocols, the scalability is materialized by taking into account any possible collisions on the communication medium and interferences between the vehicles during the data transmission.

Self-Organization

In most VANETs applications, particularly those aimed at improving road safety, the communications used are of the V2V type. A VANET is formed when vehicles are present in their deployment area and disappears when vehicles leave the area. This requires that all the vehicles in the network organize themselves (the nodes adapt to the topological change of the network) without any intervention of an external entity or a centralized control. In addition, self-organization (oussama Cherif, Senouci, & Ducourthial, 2009) must also be based on local interactions to ensure the maintenance of the entire network.

Standards Dedicated to VANETS

Vehicular environments are characterized by the diversity of car manufacturers. The latter are generally in competition with each other to gain market share. Nevertheless, for the development and progression of VANET technology, they must work together with the major standardization organizations (IEEE, ISO, IETF, ETSI, ASTM, SAE) (Fischer, 2015) to ensure interoperability between equipment from different car manufacturers. For this reason, the use of standards in VANETs becomes an important aspect. Indeed, the use of standards greatly simplifies the development of equipment, reduce costs and allows users to compare the equipments and the competing products. Many standards that relate to wireless access in VANETs have been created to establish the exchange of information between vehicles. These standards (Karagiannis et al., 2011) extend protocols that apply to transmission equipment going through the security specifications, packet routing and interoperability protocols.

- **DSRC (Dedicated Short Range Communication)**

A set of frequencies dedicated to vehicular communications in ITS has been allocated in different regions of the world. A short-range communication channel DSRC (short-range communication) (Bai, Stancil, & Krishnan, 2010) has been specifically designed for vehicular communications (V2V and V2I). This new standard has evolved from IEEE 802.11a to IEEE802.11p or WAVE (Wireless Access in Vehicular Environments) to meet the particularities of VANETs. It is divided into 7 channels of 10 MHZ for each. All of these channels are functionally divided into 1 control channel (CCH) and 6 service channels (SCH). The control channel is reserved for the transmission of the most important messages (messages related to road safety applications). The other 6 channels are dedicated to the dissemination of management messages and messages related to other road services. The DSRC is characterized by a range that can reach 1 km, it can withstand speeds of up to 300 km/h. This technology of communication is adapted to mobility with a very short connection setup time. Therefore, it is considered, today, as the most appropriate standard for VANETs (It ensures smooth operation for road safety applications).

IEEE 802.11p \ WAVE (Wireless Access in Vehicular Environment)

The IEEE 802.11 standard has been defined primarily by the IEEE organization for wireless access. It is imposed for the first experiments and the simulations of the VANETs, many studies use the versions 802.11b or 802.11g, which are very widespread and built at low cost. In recent years, the IEEE working group has resumed this work to define a new standard dedicated to communications (V2V and V2I) and based on the family of IEEE 1609 protocols to operate in the communication channel of DSRC [48]. This standard known as IEEE 802.11p or WAVE (Wireless Access in Vehicular Environments) (Eichler, 2007). The latter uses the multichannel concept to ensure communications for road safety applications and the various road transport services.

The IEEE 802.11p (WAVE) standard introduces new specificities to the physical layer, as well as to the MAC layer. Indeed, at the physical layer level, IEEE 802.11p offers a rate of between 6 and 27 Mb/s over a distance of 1000 meters and with type modulation OFDM (Orthogonal Frequency Division Multiplexing). On the other hand, at the level of the MAC layer, the IEEE 802.11p is based on the CSMA/CA approach (Carrier Sense Multiple Access with Collision Avoidance) as in the IEEE 802.11a protocol.

ISO: CALM (Continuous Air Interface Long and Medium Range)

At the universal level, ISO TC204/WG16 has established a set of rules proportional to the radio interface in short or long range (distance) known as CALM (Continuous Air interface, Long and Medium Range) (Böhm, Lidström, Jonsson, & Larsson, 2010). The CALM standard aims to develop a software platform embedded in vehicles (make transparent the use of standards) that claims the interface between several communication technologies (WiFi, GSM, DSRC, 2G, 3G, etc.) (Anwer & Guy, 2014). It also consists of switching between these technologies depending on the availability of networks and the message to be transmitted.

Research Projects and Consortia in VANETS

After having presented in the previous section the main standards designed for VANETs, in this section, we will try to highlight the various research projects developed in the vehicular context. In recent years, several consortia and research projects (Zeadally, Hunt, Chen, Irwin, & Hassan, 2012) (Hartenstein & Laberteaux, 2008) (Kuklinski, Matei, & Wolny, 2010) have been launched as in Europe (the CVIS project and the C2C-CC consortium), in Japan (the JARI project and the ASV project) and in the United States (as project VII). The first works appeared in the 1980 in Japan by the association AETATD (Association of Electronic Technology for Automobile Traffic and Driving). The main objective is the standardization and the implementation of the new inter-vehicular communication protocols to improve road safety and effectively manage road traffic. Since 2002, with the emergence of new wireless communication technologies, several researchers have been oriented towards different issues related to vehicular environments, and they have participated in the increase of a number of publications in this field. In this dynamic, several workshops and conferences have been created. In what follows, we will present and describe the most representative projects.

FleetNet

The European project FleetNet (Internet on the Road) is a German project initiated by a consortium of six industrial and three universities. It was launched in September 2000. Its goal is to develop a platform to enable vehicular communication using UMTS technology (UTRA-TDD) and standardize proposed solutions and internet access to provide better security and greater comfort. The FleetNet architecture focuses on a routing mechanism based on network topology and vehicle position.

NoW (Network on Wheels)

The project NOW (Network on Wheels) is the successor of the German project FleetNet. It was launched in 2004 by the Federal Government of Research and Education in Germany (car manufacturers, telecom operators and universities). It cooperates strongly with the Car2Car (Baldessari et al., 2007) consortium to improve data security and implement communication protocols based on IEEE 802.11 wireless technologies.

CVIS (European Commission's Cooperative Vehicle-Infrastructure System)

The European Cooperative Vehicle Infrastructure Systems (CVIS) project is seen as a technical solution that allows all vehicles and infrastructures to communicate with each other in a continuous and transparent manner using different communications media. It was launched in 2006 until 2009. As part of this project, open standards are being developed as CALM (Böhm, Lidström, Jonsson, & Larsson, 2010) to create a single communication architecture providing total interoperability.

Consortium Car-to-Car (C2C-CC)

Recently, European car manufacturers have undertaken a Car2Car Communication Consortium (C2C-CC) (Baldessari et al., 2007). This consortium, accessible by suppliers, research organizations and other partners in order to have a rapid deployment of VANETs. Its aim is to improve road safety and effectively manage road traffic. To achieve these objectives, this consortium plans several missions which are:

- Create an open European standard for V2V communications based on wireless LAN components.
- Encourage the allocation of an exclusive free frequency band for Car2Car applications in Europe.
- Develop prototypes and demonstrators of V2V systems for road applications.
- Develop deployment strategies and business models for market acuity.

   This consortium was able to have great success thanks to the interoperability it has generated between cars from different car manufacturers and the equipment manufacturers of RSU (Road Side Unit).

PReVENT

The PReVENT project (PReVENTive and Active Safety Applications) is proposed by the European Union (EU) in 2004. It aims to contribute to road safety by developing preventive safety applications and technologies, especially at intersections. In other words, it consists in avoiding accidents by alerting drivers to dangerous situations. Thereby, it is used to help lower component costs to bring quickly designed solutions to market.

GéoNet

The GeoNet (geo-networking) project was developed by seven European partners. Its objective is to design and develop a communication architecture, this architecture is based on multi-jump geographic routing (V2V) in the routing of messages to all destinations over a given geographical area.

VII (Vehicle-Infrastructure Integration)

The American project VII (Vehicle Infrastructure Integration) was undertaken in 2004 by car manufacturers (BMW, Honda, Hyundai, Toyota, Ford, etc.) and the USDoT (US Department of Transportation). Improving the safety, efficiency and maintenance of roads is the priority of this consortium. It is based on DSRC technology and the GPS location system to provide a range of security services and applications that enable V2V and V2I communications. These applications are varied such as: active security systems (alerts), accident and incident reactive systems, hazard warning systems, data collection (using sensors), etc.

JARI (Japan Automobile Research Institute)

The Japanese project JARI (Japan Automobile Research Institute) is an organization launched by more than 200 automotive industries. This project is used to investigate road safety, conduct research and work on vehicle environments and Intelligent Transportation Systems (ITS).

Table 1. Advantages and limitations of VANETs.

	VANETs
Benefits	• VANETs are not limited by constraints related to memory space, computing capacity and energy amount. • VANETs are decentralized and open systems. Nodes (vehicles) move through streets, roads, highways in different mobility patterns (speed, orientation...) resulting in changes in network topology (unstable topology) Thus, the links between the nodes are intermittent and of very short duration (a node can reach and leave the network in a very short time). • VANETs are scalable, i.e., they can grow rapidly, especially in urban areas where intersections and multi-lane roads are common. • The VANETs are (heterogeneous) of different brands and the network components that constitute them use different communication techniques (WIFI, DSRC, CALM, etc.), but they can all lead to a good exchange of information thanks to the standards and protocols established by cooperation between standardization bodies, car manufacturers and network designers. • Data dissemination in Ad-hoc networks is done, most often, in a collaborative way. In VANETs, the vehicles agree to cooperate, to relay and transmit messages from their neighbors (as relay nodes).
Limits	• Vehicular networks suffer from the large amount of data to be sent and the extent of geographical areas (dispersion and high mobility of vehicles as well as the variable density of the network) to be covered. • The environment of a vehicular network can be urban, rural or motorway. The constraints imposed by this type of environment such as traffic lights and speed limits strongly affect mobility and vehicle density (low / high density). • VANETs do not have a coordinator for the allocation of resources from the communication channel to the vehicles. Then, it becomes the responsibility of each vehicle to use and manage, in a fair way, these resources. This makes it possible to increase the waiting times before the access to the channel and thus the latency of the messages. However, security applications require packets to be delivered on time. Indeed, in these applications, the packets carry security information that can have an impact on human lives. So an information (for example: grubbing braking) that arrives late will be useless. • In VANETs, vehicles communicate with each other using the same radio channel. Simultaneous use of channel resources can lead to several problems such as: channel congestion problem, message collision problem that can occur especially in high density environments, radio interference problem (which makes signal sent incomprehensible by the receiver and increases the rate of transmission errors), problems of multipath waves, etc. • In VANETs, nodes move in changing environments (tunnels, city center, rural environment, highway ...) infecting the connectivity (sporadic connections) of the network and the signal strength.

SAFESPOT (Cooperative System for Road Safety)

The SAFESPOT project (Cooperative System for Road Safety) was started in 2006. It is similar to the CVIS project for V2V communications (using the IEEE802.11p standard). It aims to set up a platform for sharing information (cooperative system) concerning safety events (accidents, work, etc.) on the road.

ADVANTAGES AND CONSTRAINTS OF VANETS

After presenting the concepts and fundamental challenges of the VANETs framework, in the previous sections, in this section, we try to reveal some of the advantages/downsides of these networks that have been quoted and summarized in Table 1.

CONCLUSION

This chapter depicts an overview of VANETs. The latter are very dynamic, very heterogeneous and generate considerable interest in providing better road safety and reducing problems related to ecology context and traffic congestion field.

In this chapter, we saw that the VANET are beginning to be appreciated and recognized by vehicle users and are increasingly being used in different countries. They help users in their driving, minimize the risk of accidents, as well offer more comfort and access to leisure activities. Thus, the purpose of this chapter is to provide readers with a more in-depth understanding of vehicle networks and research trends in this area.

We also saw that the partnership projects between car manufacturers and those of telecommunication devices are constantly increasing. And that for modernize cars by equipping them with the necessary peripherals (devices) to integrate VANET, this may be possible, in the future close, to create a global vehicular network.

REFERENCES

Abdelhamid, S., Hassanein, H. S., & Takahara, G. (2015). Vehicle as a resource (VaaR). *IEEE Network*, *29*(1), 12–17. doi:10.1109/MNET.2015.7018198

Al-Rabayah, M., & Malaney, R. (2012). A new scalable hybrid routing protocol for VANETs. *IEEE Transactions on Vehicular Technology*, *61*(6), 2625–2635. doi:10.1109/TVT.2012.2198837

Al-Sultan, S., Al-Doori, M. M., Al-Bayatti, A. H., & Zedan, H. (2014). A comprehensive survey on vehicular ad hoc network. *Journal of Network and Computer Applications*, *37*, 380–392. doi:10.1016/j.jnca.2013.02.036

Anwer, M. S., & Guy, C. (2014). A survey of VANET technologies. *Journal of Emerging Trends in Computing and Information Sciences*, *5*(9), 661–671.

Bai, F., Stancil, D. D., & Krishnan, H. (2010, September). Toward understanding characteristics of dedicated short range communications (DSRC) from a perspective of vehicular network engineers. In *Proceedings of the 16th Annual International Conference on Mobile Computing and Networking* (pp. 329-340). ACM. 10.1145/1859995.1860033

Baldessari, R., Bödekker, B., Deegener, M., Festag, A., Franz, W., Kellum, C. C., ... & Peichl, T. (2007). Car-2-car communication consortium-manifesto.

Beijar, N. (2002). Zone routing protocol (ZRP). Networking Laboratory, Helsinki University of Technology, Finland, 9, 1-12.

Benslimane, A. (2005, August). Localization in vehicular ad hoc networks. In Proceedings 2005 Systems Communications (ICW'05, ICHSN'05, ICMCS'05, SENET'05) (pp. 19-25). IEEE. doi:10.1109/ICW.2005.54

Böhm, A., Lidström, K., Jonsson, M., & Larsson, T. (2010, October). Evaluating CALM M5-based vehicle-to-vehicle communication in various road settings through field trials. In *IEEE Local Computer Network Conference* (pp. 613-620). IEEE. 10.1109/LCN.2010.5735781

Boukerche, A., Oliveira, H. A., Nakamura, E. F., & Loureiro, A. A. (2008). Vehicular ad hoc networks: A new challenge for localization-based systems. *Computer Communications*, *31*(12), 2838–2849. doi:10.1016/j.comcom.2007.12.004

Cheng, H. T., Shan, H., & Zhuang, W. (2011). Infotainment and road safety service support in vehicular networking: From a communication perspective. *Mechanical Systems and Signal Processing*, *25*(6), 2020–2038. doi:10.1016/j.ymssp.2010.11.009

Chowdhury, S. I., Lee, W. I., Choi, Y. S., Kee, G. Y., & Pyun, J. Y. (2011, October). Performance evaluation of reactive routing protocols in VANET. In *The 17th Asia Pacific Conference on Communications* (pp. 559-564). IEEE. 10.1109/APCC.2011.6152871

Cunha, F., Villas, L., Boukerche, A., Maia, G., Viana, A., Mini, R. A., & Loureiro, A. A. (2016). Data communication in VANETs: Protocols, applications and challenges. *Ad Hoc Networks*, *44*, 90–103. doi:10.1016/j.adhoc.2016.02.017

Darwish, T., & Bakar, K. A. (2015). Traffic density estimation in vehicular ad hoc networks: A review. *Ad Hoc Networks*, *24*, 337–351. doi:10.1016/j.adhoc.2014.09.007

Dey, K. C., Rayamajhi, A., Chowdhury, M., Bhavsar, P., & Martin, J. (2016). Vehicle-to-vehicle (V2V) and vehicle-to-infrastructure (V2I) communication in a heterogeneous wireless network–Performance evaluation. *Transportation Research Part C, Emerging Technologies*, *68*, 168–184. doi:10.1016/j.trc.2016.03.008

Eichler, S. (2007, September). Performance evaluation of the IEEE 802.11 p WAVE communication standard. In *Proceedings 2007 IEEE 66th Vehicular Technology Conference* (pp. 2199-2203). IEEE.

Engoulou, R. G., Bellaïche, M., Pierre, S., & Quintero, A. (2014). VANET security surveys. *Computer Communications*, *44*, 1–13. doi:10.1016/j.comcom.2014.02.020

Fazio, P., De Rango, F., Sottile, C., Manzoni, P., & Calafate, C. (2011, March). *A distance vector routing protocol for VANET environment with Dynamic Frequency assignment. In Proceedings 2011 IEEE Wireless Communications and Networking Conference* (pp. 1016–1020). IEEE. doi:10.1109/WCNC.2011.5779274

Figueiredo, L., Jesus, I., Machado, J. T., Ferreira, J. R., & De Carvalho, J. M. (2001, August). Towards the development of intelligent transportation systems. In Proceedings 2001 IEEE Intelligent Transportation Systems (Cat. No. 01TH8585) ITSC 2001. (pp. 1206-1211). IEEE. doi:10.1109/ITSC.2001.948835

Fiore, M., Harri, J., Filali, F., & Bonnet, C. (2007, March). Vehicular mobility simulation for VANETs. In *Proceedings 40th Annual Simulation Symposium (ANSS'07)* (pp. 301-309). IEEE. 10.1109/ANSS.2007.44

Fischer, H. J. (2015). Standardization and harmonization activities towards a global C-ITS. In *Vehicular ad hoc Networks* (pp. 23–36). Cham, Switzerland: Springer. doi:10.1007/978-3-319-15497-8_2

Gunther, H. J., Trauer, O., & Wolf, L. (2015, December). The potential of collective perception in vehicular ad-hoc networks. In *Proceedings 2015 14th International Conference on ITS Telecommunications (ITST)* (pp. 1-5). IEEE. 10.1109/ITST.2015.7377190

Guo, J., Baugh, J. P., & Wang, S. (2007, May). *A group signature based secure and privacy-preserving vehicular communication framework. In Proceedings 2007 Mobile Networking for Vehicular Environments* (pp. 103–108). IEEE. doi:10.1109/MOVE.2007.4300813

Hamid, B., & El Mokhtar, E. N. (2015, December). Performance analysis of the Vehicular Ad hoc Networks (VANET) routing protocols AODV, DSDV, and OLSR. In *Proceedings 2015 5th International Conference on Information & Communication Technology and Accessibility (ICTA)* (pp. 1-6). IEEE.

Hartenstein, H., & Laberteaux, K. (2010). *VANET: vehicular applications and inter-networking technologies* (Vol. 1). Chichester, UK: Wiley. doi:10.1002/9780470740637

Hartenstein, H., & Laberteaux, L. P. (2008). A tutorial survey on vehicular ad hoc networks. *IEEE Communications Magazine, 46*(6), 164–171. doi:10.1109/MCOM.2008.4539481

Hoebeke, J., Moerman, I., Dhoedt, B., & Demeester, P. (2004). An overview of mobile ad hoc networks: Applications and challenges. *Journal-Communications Network, 3*(3), 60–66.

Hofmann-Wellenhof, B., Lichtenegger, H., & Collins, J. (2012). *Global positioning system: theory and practice*. Springer Science & Business Media.

Jayapal, C., & Roy, S. S. (2016, March). Road traffic congestion management using VANET. In *Proceedings 2016 International Conference on Advances in Human Machine Interaction (HMI)* (pp. 1-7). IEEE.

Karagiannis, G., Altintas, O., Ekici, E., Heijenk, G., Jarupan, B., Lin, K., & Weil, T. (2011). Vehicular networking: A survey and tutorial on requirements, architectures, challenges, standards and solutions. *IEEE Communications Surveys and Tutorials, 13*(4), 584–616. doi:10.1109/SURV.2011.061411.00019

Kuklinski, S., Matei, A., & Wolny, G. (2010, June). NGVN: A framework for Next Generation Vehicular Networks. In *Proceedings 2010 8th International Conference on Communications* (pp. 297-300). IEEE. 10.1109/ICCOMM.2010.5509082

Kumar, V., Mishra, S., & Chand, N. (2013). Applications of VANETs: Present & future. *Communications and Network, 5*(1), 12–15. doi:10.4236/cn.2013.51B004

Kuutti, S., Fallah, S., Katsaros, K., Dianati, M., Mccullough, F., & Mouzakitis, A. (2018). A survey of the state-of-the-art localization techniques and their potentials for autonomous vehicle applications. *IEEE Internet of Things Journal, 5*(2), 829–846. doi:10.1109/JIOT.2018.2812300

Lee, K. C., Lee, U., & Gerla, M. (2010). Survey of routing protocols in vehicular ad hoc networks. In Proceedings *Advances in vehicular ad-hoc networks: Developments and challenges* (pp. 149–170). IGI Global. doi:10.4018/978-1-61520-913-2.ch008

Li, F., & Wang, Y. (2007). Routing in vehicular ad hoc networks: A survey. *IEEE Vehicular Technology Magazine, 2*(2), 12–22. doi:10.1109/MVT.2007.912927

Liu, J., Wan, J., Wang, Q., Deng, P., Zhou, K., & Qiao, Y. (2016). A survey on position-based routing for vehicular ad hoc networks. *Telecommunication Systems, 62*(1), 15–30. doi:10.100711235-015-9979-7

Lu, R., Lin, X., Zhu, H., & Shen, X. (2009, April). SPARK: A new VANET-based smart parking scheme for large parking lots. In Proceedings IEEE INFOCOM 2009 (pp. 1413-1421). IEEE. doi:10.1109/INFCOM.2009.5062057

Luo, Y., Zhang, W., & Hu, Y. (2010, April). A new cluster-based routing protocol for VANET. In *Proceedings 2010 Second International Conference on Networks Security, Wireless Communications, and Trusted Computing* (Vol. 1, pp. 176-180). IEEE. 10.1109/NSWCTC.2010.48

Menouar, H., Filali, F., & Lenardi, M. (2006). A survey and qualitative analysis of MAC protocols for vehicular ad hoc networks. *IEEE Wireless Communications, 13*(5), 30–35. doi:10.1109/WC-M.2006.250355

oussama Cherif, M., Senouci, S. M., & Ducourthial, B. (2009, June). A new framework of self-organization of vehicular networks. In *Proceedings 2009 Global Information Infrastructure Symposium* (pp. 1-6). IEEE.

Paul, B., Ibrahim, M., Bikas, M., & Naser, A. (2012). Experimental analysis of aodv & dsr over tcp & cbr connections with varying speed and node density in vanet. *arXiv preprint arXiv:1204.1206.*

Perallos, A., Hernandez-Jayo, U., Zuazola, I. J. G., & Onieva, E. (Eds.). (2015). *Intelligent Transport Systems: Technologies and Applications.* John Wiley & Sons. doi:10.1002/9781118894774

Pinart, C., Sanz, P., Lequerica, I., García, D., Barona, I., & Sánchez-Aparisi, D. (2008, March). DRIVE: a reconfigurable testbed for advanced vehicular services and communications. In *Proceedings of the 4th International Conference on Testbeds and research infrastructures for the development of networks & communities* (p. 16). ICST (Institute for Computer Sciences, Social-Informatics and Telecommunications Engineering). 10.4108/weedev.2008.3141

Raw, R. S., Kumar, M., & Singh, N. (2013). Security challenges, issues and their solutions for VANET. *International journal of network security & its applications, 5*(5), 95.

Rawat, D. B., Bista, B. B., Yan, G., & Olariu, S. (2014, July). Vehicle-to-vehicle connectivity and communication framework for vehicular ad-hoc networks. In *2014 Eighth International Conference on Complex, Intelligent, and Software Intensive Systems* (pp. 44-49). IEEE. 10.1109/CISIS.2014.7

Raya, M., & Hubaux, J. P. (2005, November). The security of vehicular ad hoc networks. In *Proceedings of the 3rd ACM workshop on Security of ad hoc and sensor networks* (pp. 11-21). ACM. 10.1145/1102219.1102223

Sarakis, L., Orphanoudakis, T., Leligou, H. C., Voliotis, S., & Voulkidis, A. (2016). Providing entertainment applications in VANET environments. *IEEE Wireless Communications*, *23*(1), 30–37. doi:10.1109/MWC.2016.7422403

Singh, S., & Agrawal, S. (2014, March). VANET routing protocols: Issues and challenges. In Proceedings 2014 Recent Advances in Engineering and Computational Sciences (RAECS) (pp. 1-5). IEEE.

Vèque, V., Kaisser, F., Johnen, C., & Busson, A. (2013). CONVOY: A New Cluster-Based Routing Protocol for Vehicular Networks. *Vehicular Networks: Models and Algorithms*, 91-129.

Vodopivec, S., Bešter, J., & Kos, A. (2012, July). A survey on clustering algorithms for vehicular ad-hoc networks. In *Proceedings 2012 35th International Conference on Telecommunications and Signal Processing (TSP)* (pp. 52-56). IEEE. 10.1109/TSP.2012.6256251

Yousefi, S., Mousavi, M. S., & Fathy, M. (2006, June). Vehicular ad hoc networks (VANETs): challenges and perspectives. In *Proceedings 2006 6th International Conference on ITS Telecommunications* (pp. 761-766). IEEE.

Zeadally, S., Hunt, R., Chen, Y. S., Irwin, A., & Hassan, A. (2012). Vehicular ad hoc networks (VANETS): Status, results, and challenges. *Telecommunication Systems*, *50*(4), 217–241. doi:10.100711235-010-9400-5

Chapter 3
Relative Position Estimation in Vehicle Ad–Hoc Network

Walaa Abd el aal Afifi
Faculty of Graduate Studies for Statistical Research, Cairo University, Egypt

Hesham Ahmed Hefny
Faculty of Graduate Studies for Statistical Research, Cairo University, Egypt

Nagy Ramadan Darwish
Faculty of Graduate Studies for Statistical Research, Cairo University, Egypt

Imane Fahmy
Cairo University, Egypt

ABSTRACT

Position is a vital element for ITS applications. Its accuracy helps to deliver services quickly to drivers to increase their satisfaction. GPS is a well-known position system but it suffers from multipath effect and non-line of sight in tunnel environments. Relative Position or sometimes called cooperative localization is an alternative position estimation. It utilizes different forms of v2x communication to exchange position, distance, direction, and velocity parameters. It will benefit in collecting a large amount of data to increase the accuracy of position estimation. However, the dependency of radio range communication methods has drawbacks such as poor-received signal, multipath, lose packets, delay, and overhead communication that will have inverse impact on position accuracy. In addition, safety applications require fewer seconds to make quick response. This chapter provides the latest related papers, the state art of radio range, the well-known localization algorithms, and current challenges and future direction.

DOI: 10.4018/978-1-7998-2570-8.ch003

INTRODUCTION:

By increasing the development in car manufacturing and increasing the number of vehicles. There is a necessary need to feel drivers more comfortable and provide more services during driving tour. Intelligent transportation systems (ITS) depend more on vehicle position to provide more services like warning system and driver assistance. As a result, localization accuracy is the main challenge especially in urban and tunnel environment (Mrunmayi S Sahasrabudhe et al, 2014). Global position system (GPS) is a well-known absolute position system. Its accuracy is limited to 10m: 30m (K. Golestan et al, 2015). It requires line of sight condition and suffers from multipath. Differential GPS (DGPS) is an extension of GPS (Rainer Mautz, 2012). It consists a set of stationary nodes or roadside units (RSU)and vehicle nodes. Roadside units are placed at known position in advance. In addition, they calculate the correction rates (i.e. localization error) and send them to nearby mobile vehicles. Unknown vehicle uses these corrections to fix its position calculation. DGPS achieves accuracy level about ten of centimeters. The drawbacks of DGPS are (A. Benslimane, 2005):

1.   Both mobile and stationary nodes must be within coverage area of each other. Otherwise, vehicles cannot use correction rate.
2.   Large number of roadside units represents high cost deployment.
3.   The local error of pseudo range measurement still exists.

Recently, cooperative localization is an alternative solution to estimate relative position. It depends on v2v or v2I or both communications. Cooperative localization combines more than one source of position information such as GPS, navigation system, nearby vehicle position or road side unit and mobility metrics (i.e. direction, speed). After that, it utilizes one of optimization algorithms to minimize position errors like Kalman filter, extended Kalman filter, particle filter, double difference method, least square methods...etc. Authors proposed VANET location improve algorithm (VLOCI) (Farhan Ahamed et al,2012). Nearby vehicles exchanged the position and estimated the distance between them. Authors used weight function of distance measurements. This weight function might be the inverse distance or inverse exponential function of distance. It evaluated the nearest neighbor node by more weight. The estimated x coordinate was the average weight distance and plus or minus the x-coordinate of neighbor nodes. The plus or minus sign returned to front or back neighbor vehicle. The authors assumed linear network topology, single lane and one direction. The distance wasn't the only parameter to guarantee accurate position estimation. The drawbacks of wireless communication impact on distance estimation and can cause overhead communication. The VLOCI achieved more accuracy in dense environment. (Drawil et al, 2010) authors proposed Inter-vehicle communication-assisted Localization (IVCAL) algorithm. IVCAL used three different algorithms. First, Kalman filter minimizes error for GPS position, Inertial Navigation System (INS) and nearby vehicles. Secondly, IVCAL used neural network to classify nearby vehicles into two classes: multipath affected or not. Finally, Nelder and Mead algorithm minimizes error in position estimated. Data collecting from nearby vehicles entered the same environment like GPS from signal fading effect and uncertainty mobility metric. IVCAL consumed more computation resources. IVCAL depends only on position information. (Nabil Drawil & Otman,2010) Basir authors proposed a Constrained Weighting Scheme of Inter-Vehicle Communication Assisted Localization (CWS-IVCAL). Distance between inter-vehicles are calculated and participate in position estimation. Trilateration method is used to estimate location if there are 3 anchor nodes, otherwise, it will utilize all available neighbor nodes as anchor nodes. A constrained weighting schema is used as uncertainty measure. Weight indicates the confidence degree of estimated parameter for neighbor nodes. The final location is the average weighted position estimated. CWS-IVCAL outperforms IVCAL where average of localization error in urban city for CWS-IVCAL is 2.308 m and for IVCAL is 4.38 m. CWS-IVCAL confirms small region around target vehicle that has a positive effect on localization error rather than all neighbors. CWS-IVCAL ignores other parameters like link quality in constraint weight schema. As mention above, the dynamic behavior causes a large amount of noise data and multipath effect. Localization accuracy is measured as absolute difference between real position and estimated position. Almost research papers use various optimization algorithms as attempting for reducing position errors. They may also use digital map information aligns the estimated position to the boundary of road. However, the position accuracy is more related with the accuracy of digital map. They ignore uncertainty wireless communication. They restricted to road width, number of lane, traffic light displacement and road length. All previous parameters conclude for GPS position, direction, velocity, distance. Other parameters such as bandwidth consumption, link quality may have role to enhance position accuracy. These parameters help to reduce overhead communication and to increase packet delivery ratio. Research papers work extensively on reducing error in collecting measurement. The availability of large amount of these measurements reduce poor measurement impact. In this paper, researchers explain radio range methods and their effect in position measurement. The well-known optimization algorithms of position estimation. The role of cooperative localization enables additional source for position parameters to enhance the accuracy of position estimated.

The term cooperative localization is common than relative position in almost research papers. The chapter is arranged in a following sequence: second section defines different range measurements. Third section explains the well-known cooperative localization algorithms. Fourth section summarizes some related works about cooperative localization. Fifth section introduces future researches and current challenges. Finally, section concludes some remarks.

BACKGROUND OF RANGE BASED MEASUREMENTS

This section explains different radio range to estimate the distance time or angle. Range based and range rate methods are subset of range methods. Range based methods consist of the angle of arrival (AoA), time of arrival (ToA), time difference of arrival (TDoA) and received signal strength indicator (RSSI), pseudo range and round time trip (RTT). Range rate method consists of Doppler Effect. All previous methods are affected by multipath effect, noisy environment and uncertainty measurements.

Time of Arrival (TOA) and Time Difference of Arrive (TDOA)

Figure 1 indicates TOA and TDOA. TOA represents one-way propagation model. The distance is measured as the time of the received signal as in below equation. The speed parameter is known for all vehicle nodes. TOA is represented as circle.

The center of circle is the receiver node. The trilateration is often used to know position. It requires at least three circles or three transmissions or three anchor nodes.

Figure 1. Time of arrival(a) and time difference of arrival (b)

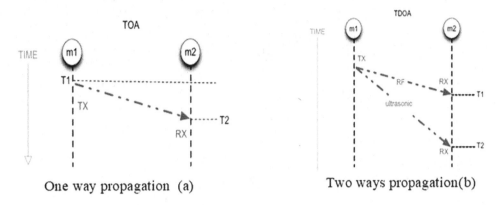

$$d_{ij} = T2 * v \qquad\qquad 2.1$$

Where v is velocity of light signal and T2 is time of received signal.

TDOA requires additional hardware to transmit ultrasonic signal. It is two-ways propagation model. therefore, it consumes more bandwidth. The distance is the difference time of received two different signals. As TOA, the position is also estimated by trilateration. The localization accuracy for TDOA is higher than TOA. These two methods require adjusting synchronization time. Practically, this is difficult in real environment. The distance is derived (Lingling Zhu et al, 2014):

$$d_{ij} = v_{Rf} * v_{Rx} * \left(t_{Rf} - t_{Rx} \right) / \left(v_{Rf} - v_{Rx} \right) \qquad\qquad 2.2$$

Round Trip Time

Figure 2 explains round trip time RTT that is a sum of signal travelling time t1 from transmitter to a receiver and received signal time t2 from receiver to transmitter. No synchronization is required. The drawback is the latency when receiver processes message and sends back acknowledgment. All vehicles should know latency time at advance. The drawbacks cause long latency as result from sequential transmission (Ahmed Abdel Wahab et al, 2013).

The distance is derived as shown in below equation:

$$RTT = \alpha * t1 + \left(1 - \alpha \right) * t2 \qquad\qquad 2.3$$

Where α is constant factor, t1 is transmitting time and t2 is received time.

Angle of Arrival

Angle of arrival (AOA)It requires hardware like antenna array or smart antenna array. The receiver node senses the direction of the received signal. It may require compass to change directions. Each node uses

Figure 2. Round trip time

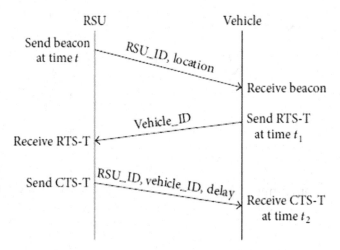

north direction and x- axes to know heading signal. Obscure position is assessed by triangulation. This provides high accuracy; however, it requires high computational time for signal processing of antenna arrays and large bandwidth (Ayman Naguib et al, 2013).

Received Signal Strength Indicator (RSSI)

The path loss model is a well-known propagation model. Distance can be assessed by RSSI. RSSI is influenced by path loss exponent. path loss exponent (n_p)represents the attenuation of the signal's power with the distance. The path loss exponent reflects the obstacles during signal travelling in environment area. There is an inverse relationship between RSSI and distance. It has Low localization accuracy than AOA (Francisco J. Ros et al, 2014). The received signal strength (RSSI) is calculated as follows:

$$P_r(d) = P_t(d_0) - 10n_p log_{i0}\left(\frac{d}{d_0}\right) + x_\alpha$$

2.4

Where $P_r(d)$ is the receiving signal power strength when the transmitter and receiver distance at d. $P_t(d_0)$ is transmission power at reference distance d0. n_p is pass loss exponent. Xά defines a shadowing effect. The distance is estimated as

$$d = d_0 * 10^{\frac{pr(d_0)-pr(d)}{10n}}$$

2.5

Almost research papers used RSS threshold to consider the distance estimated for location. It is experiment by different path loss exponent.

Pseudo Range

Pseudo range measurement is estimated between satellites and GPS receivers. Pseudo range consists of true distance, common errors and local error. Common error shares between receivers such as clock bias, ionosphere delay. Local error varies from receiver to another one such as receiver noise and multipath error (Kai Liu et al, 2014).

$$\rho_i^k = R_i^k + t_i + x^k + \varepsilon_i^k$$

2.6

Where R_i^k is true distance between satellite k and vehicle i, t_i is a receiver clock offset from the GPS time, common noise ε_i^k and non-common error x^i. Common error can be shared by nearby vehicles. Almost papers neglect non-common error however it consists of multipath effect. It causes far true position.

Table 1. Range based measurement

Range Method	Type of measurement	Pos	Cons
Time of Arrival (TOA)	Distance	Simple and easy to estimate	Synchronization problem. It is difficult with high dense network.
Time Difference of Arrival (TDOA)	Distance	Solve synchronization problem	large bandwidth and latency in processing time. Additional hardware device.
Received Signal Strength Indicator (RSSI)	Distance	No additional hardware device.	Adjust the pathloss model's parameters. They consume more time.
Angle of Arrival Angle (AOA)	Heading or direction of received signal	Robust measure against the noise.	Additional hardware devices
Pseudo range	Distance	Common error between nearby vehicle can be reduced.	Non-line of sight
Round time trip (RTT)	Distance	Solve synchronization problem	Latency

Table 1 discuss the drawbacks of range-based methods and compare between them in spite of advantages and disadvantages

Doppler Effect

Figure 3 indicates doppler effect that is the alter in recurrence wave for a mobile spectator relative to its source for instance a fire truck approaches, the sound increases more than normal level because the sound waves are more arrived. When the fire truck passes and moves absent, you listen a drop-in pitch since the wave peaks are less arrived. The Doppler effect is influenced by the clock floats additionally requires raise relative speed between the transmitter and the recipient. The advantage of Doppler shift is less influenced by multipath effect...etc. (Bo Xu et al, 2011).

Figure 3. Doppler effect

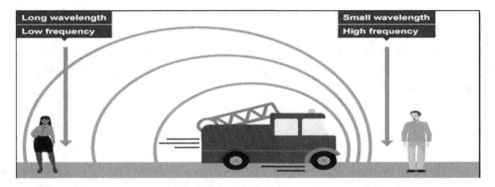

Dead Reckoning

It is also known as kinematic model. The obscure position depends on how distant a vehicle has moved from a last known position: given the heading, initial position and velocity as follows:

$$\begin{bmatrix} x_k \\ y_k \end{bmatrix} = \begin{bmatrix} x_{k-1} + l_k \cos(\theta_k) \\ y_{k-1} + l_k \sin(\theta_k) \end{bmatrix}$$ 2.7

where l is velocity or distance, θ the current heading and (x, y) are coordinates in the flat plane. k is a discrete time. Dead reckoning depends on the estimation of a set of custom sensors such as accelerometers, gyroscopes, compass and odometer. These sensors are low cost. Therefore, uncertainty measurements are high. (Ming-Fong Tsai et al, 2015). Its accuracy depends on initial position and dynamic state. DR is useful for small period time. DR causes accumulation error. Therefore, it combines with another localization method to overcome above limitations. It can be useful in indoor environment for small period time when GPS are unavailable (Skog et al, 2009).

Map Matching.

It is a mapping method for locate vehicle on electronic map (i.e. GPS / Dead reckoning) to get the genuine position of vehicles in a street boundary. Map matching methods can be classified into geometric map, topological map and advanced map (Lianxia Xi1 Quan Liu1 et al, 2007). Geometric map ignores the history data and connectivity information and the way of road construction. Geometric matching is divided into point to point, point to curve and curve to curve. point-to-point matching: Point is coordinated to the closest 'node' or 'shape point' of a road segment. It is simple to execute and exceptionally quick. Point-to-Curve matching: Figure 4 indicates distance that is evaluated from the point to each line. There are some of estimated positions p0, p1, p2, p3 which indicates the travelling direction from p0 to p3. There are two matching roads AB, BC. It is wrong to match p1, p2 to BE road. That result from non-considering history movement. Curve-to-Curve matching: Identify the candidate nodes or pairwise points construct line segment. It estimates the space from that curve to the curve of road network. The way axes which is nearest to the curve. it is taken as travel road. It is difficult to identify the closet road in case of two possible parallel roads like ABF and BCE. Pont to curve is outperforms curve to curve method.

Figure 4. Geometric map matching

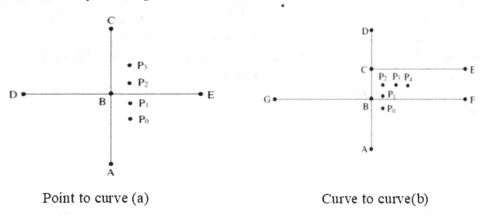

Point to curve (a)   Curve to curve(b)

Topology map matching uses additional information such as history data, connectivity information and velocity of vehicles. It consists of initial map function and map function. Initial map function uses geometric matching to find the closest street to GPS position. Determining all line segments that connected to this node. When new position is available, point to arc is performed. Map function: draw line segment between previous point and current point. Use distance and orientation of line to match street set. There are two methods for similarity: shortest distance from point to arc, intersection lines and orientation of the arc. Advanced map matching aims to reduce the error in position estimated and deals with the complexity of road network in urban area. Data fusion methods are used to reduce localization error in selected road

BACKGROUND OF COOPERATIVE LOCALIZATION ALGORITHMS

Different algorithms are assumed to minimize position errors for GPS or inertial navigation system (INS) or both. There are two types of cooperative localization algorithms in Figure 5. First, Optimization algorithms are used extensively in almost research papers. They achieve acceptable accuracy than GPS. Their accuracies are more related how to adapt noise measurement and priori position. They consume more computer resources that may cause some delay. This delay is not acceptable for critical applications. The multi-hop localizations are used extensively in localization of wireless sensor networks. Two types of nodes are anchor nodes and unknown node. Anchor nodes have knowledge of their location. Unknown nodes search for knowing their location with the help of anchors. The accuracy is related to

Figure 5. localization algorithms

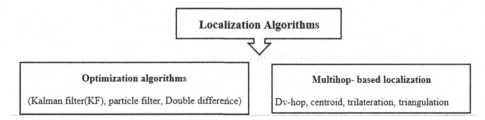

the density and distribution of anchor nodes. The multi-hop localization can be defined as GPS- free localization where a number of road side units spread along road to exchange the position with its vehicle neighbors. Unknown nodes use mathematical operation to estimate position such as centroid, DV-hop, trilateration…etc. It is a less time consumption than optimization algorithms. Their performance is affected by range radio and limited number of anchor nodes.

Localization error equals mean square error (MSE). It is the mean difference between estimated position and genuine position as follows:

$$\sigma_{pos} = \sum_{i=1}^{N} \sqrt{\frac{\left(\hat{x_{i,k}} - x_{i,k}\right)^2 + \left(\hat{y_{i,k}} - y_{i,k}\right)^2}{N}} \qquad 3.1$$

Where N is vehicle numbers, ($\hat{x_{i,k}}, \hat{y_{i,k}}$) is the estimated position and ($x_{i,k}, y_{i,k}$) is a genuine position.

Examples of well known optimization localization algorithms.

The Kalman Filter

(Drawil et al, 2010) The Kalman filter (KF) could be a well- known recursive filter calculation that gauges the current state of energetic framework from priori estimation and clutter information. Measurement and noise data follow Gaussian distribution. KF uses a pair-time priori and posteriori estimator i.e. $X_{t|t-1}$ is called the priori estimate of X_t, and $X_{t|t}$ is called the posteriori estimate of X_t. In general, KF enhances current GPS position of vehicle from priori estimated position and weighted error between actual position and estimated position. Vehicle begins moving from position X_K at time t_k. Its future position at time t_{k+1} equals the following equation:

$$x_{k+1} = AX_k + BU_k + w_k \qquad 3.2$$

$$z_{k+1} = HX_{k+1} + \hat{A_k} \qquad 3.3$$

Where x_{k+1} is future location, X_k is current location and U_k represents the mobility metric such as speed and direction. z_{k+1} vector represents measurement such as INS or GPS. A, B, H are transition matrix. The w_k, $\hat{A_k}$ are noisy data that follow Gaussian distribution with mean 0 and covariance matrix Q, R respectively. These noisy data can be represented as priori estimate $p_{k+1/k}$ and an aposteriori estimate errors $p_{k+1/k+1}$ covariance matrix. KF aims to minimize a priori estimate error $p_{k+1/k}$ that is evaluated as Kalman gain G where is estimated as follow:

$$G_{k+1} = p_{k+1/k} H^T \left(H p_{k+\frac{1}{k}} H^T + R \right)^{-1} \qquad 3.4$$

Then a priori and aposteriori error covariance can be defined as

$$p_{k+1/k} = A p_{k/k} A^T + Q \qquad 3.5$$

$$p_{k+1/k+1} = (1 - G_{k+1}H)p_{k+1/k} \qquad\qquad 3.6$$

KF in Figure 6 consists of prediction and update measurement phases. The figure explains the process and recursive nature of KF. At the beginning, the mobility metrics such as speed, and direction in X_k are used to estimate the next position $x_{k+1/k}$ and estimate a priori error covariance. In second step, the GPS receiver measurement is obtained and fused with the result of prediction step after calculating the Kalman Filter gain G. Aposteriori error covariance is required to provide filter in initial state and a priori error.

Figure 6. Flow chart of Kalman Filter

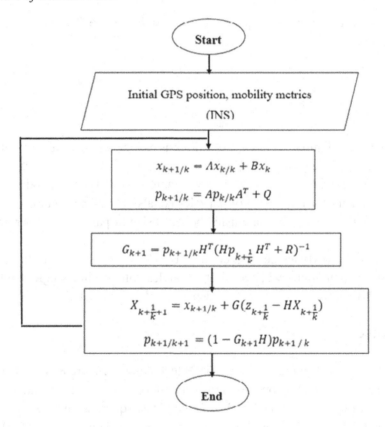

The nature of localization is nonlinear. The accuracy is more related with initial states and adjusted noise data in dynamic environment. KF doesn't give applicable results in location estimation. Extended Kalman filter (EKF) is proposed for nonlinear problem. It is assumed a mapping function for translating nonlinear problem to linear problem. The mapping function may cause losing measurement data. It is affected by outlier.

The Particle Filter

(Mohsen Rohani et al, 2015) The particle filter (PF) is another optimization algorithm for enhancing GPS position with the help of neighbor vehicles. It is commonly used with map matching.it is known as sequential Monto Carlo (SMC). SMC is based on factorizing function g(x) = g(x).Π(x) where x ϵR_x^n and Π(x) follows the probability density function (pdf)with Π(x) >=0 and $\int\Pi(x)dx = 1$. If number of samples N >>1 then the integral part equals the sample mean

$$I_N = \frac{1}{N}\sum_{i=1}^{N} f(x^i).w(x^i)$$

3.7

Where x={i=1...N} are autonomous samples, $w(x^i)$ is weight sample. The normalized weight sample is calculated as follows:

$$w(x^i) = \frac{w(x^i)}{\sum_{j=1}^{N} w(x^j)}$$

3.8

It begins in Figure 7 with initial set of GPS positions as particles, update the weight for each particle and resampling particle set frequently until maximum number of iterations reached. If the estimated position falls outside the road boundary, it will set weight to zero. Otherwise, update weights and position. There is an agreement for initial size of particles equals 1000. The accuracy of position is more related with initial set. there is direct relationship between size of particle, number of dimensions and time computation.

In resampling step, the particles get higher weights. They are more likely to be chosen and this causes the circumstance that after a whereas all the samples collapse in a single point. In this manner, the samples reduce differently and total genuine density can't be evaluated.

Double Difference

(Anas Mahmoud et al, 2015) Double difference (DD) technique in Figure 8 is an analytical tool which is defined as sequence of subtracting operation to accumulate error or increase the probability of more accurate candidates. It may be combined with weighted least square to increase accuracy of distance estimation. In general, GPS satellites orbit Earth at a nearly altitude of altitude of 20,200km. Pseudo-range common error or time synchronization bias can be shared by receivers. The ρ_i^k, ρ_j^f, ρ_i^k, ρ_i^f equals pseudo range between the two satellites k, f to two vehicles or receivers i, j respectively.

Signal is semi or full blocked from satellite f to receiver j as in figure. Double difference of pseudo ranges is sum of the difference between more satellites to the same more receivers. According to DSRC standard, receiver or vehicle j will get pseudo range of neighbor vehicle i. The double difference for two satellites k, f is calculated as follow:

$$DD^{f,k} = \sum_{s=k,m,n} \left|\Delta\rho_i^{sf} - \Delta\rho_j^{sf,k}\right|$$

3.9

Figure 7 Particle Filter

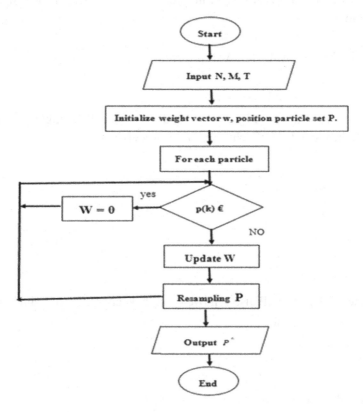

Figure 8. Pseudo range from two receivers i, j and two satellites k, f

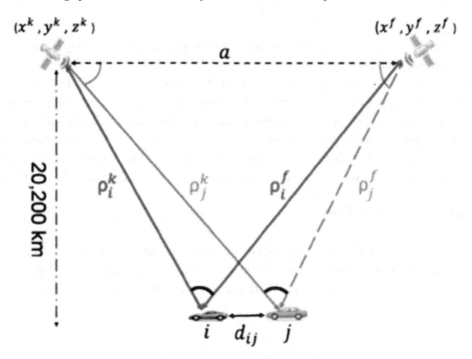

where s equals number of common visible satellites between two vehicles i and j. In more general form, it will compute as follows

$$DD^{f,k} = \left| \Delta\rho_i^{kf} - \Delta\rho_j^{kf,k} \right| + \left| \Delta\rho_i^{mf} - \Delta\rho_j^{mf,k} \right| + \left| \Delta\rho_i^{mf} - \Delta\rho_j^{mf,k} \right| \qquad 3.10$$

$\Delta\rho_i^{kf}$ is the difference between the pseudo range ρ_i^k and ρ_i^f. it is called single difference. This amount of difference removes the clock bias of vehicle i and the receiver's noise.

$$\Delta\rho_i^{kf} = \rho_i^k - \rho_i^f \qquad 3.11$$

$$= \left(R_i^k - R_i^f \right) + \left(\alpha^k - \alpha^f \right) + \left(\varepsilon_i^k - \varepsilon_i^f \right) \qquad 3.12$$

$$= \Delta R_i^{kf} + \Delta\alpha^{kf} + \Delta\varepsilon_i^{kf} \qquad 3.13$$

At the same manner, the $\Delta\rho_i^{mf}$ will also remove clock bias and noise of vehicle i. The $\Delta\rho_j^{kf,k}$ is difference between $\Delta\rho_j^{kf}$ and $\Delta\rho_j^{k}$ as follow:

$$\Delta\rho_j^{kf,k} = \rho_j^k - \rho_j^{f,k} \qquad 3.14$$

$$= \left(R_j^k - R_j^f \right) + \left(\alpha^k - \alpha^f \right) + \left(\varepsilon_j^k - \varepsilon_j^f \right) - \mu^{f,k} \qquad 3.15$$

$$= \Delta R_j^{kf} + \Delta\alpha^{kf} + \Delta\varepsilon_j^{kf} - \mu^{f,k} \qquad 3.16$$

After sequence subtraction operation between receiver j and other satellites, they remove the receivers clock bias and clutter from all the pseudo-ranges of vehicle j.

At the same manner, DD^{fn} and DD^{mf} can be derived. The error within the created pseudo-range collects three times for each twofold difference. Therefore, increasing the probability of error of the pseudo range generated by each of the common satellites. Pseudo range with minimum DD can be selected as more accurate pseudo range. The precision of DD is more subordinate on the inter- distance nearby vehicles. The minimum distance between vehicles about 20 m is preferable to approximately equivalent pseudo-range for invisible satellite. This method neglects the impact of non-common error.

Weighted Least Square Error

(Guohao Zhang et al, 2018) Weighted least square error uses alone or with optimization algorithm to increase the position accuracy. It searches for minimum error in inter-distance estimation. It also depends on linear relationship. Inter-distance r_{ab}. is calculated between vehicles a, b as follow:

$$r_{ab} = \left(H^T W H \right)^{-1} H^T W D_{ab} \qquad 3.17$$

W is a weight vector for each candidate. H, D are measurement data for input and output parameters.

Examples of well-known multi-hop localization algorithm. The common multi- hop localization in VANET are: Trilateration, cell of origin, centroid and weighted centroid.

Trilateration

(Tay, J. H. S et al, 2006) Trilateration in Figure 9 means that position of obscure node is the crossing point of three circles. The distances between anchor nodes and unknown node are the radii of circles with anchor centers location:

$$(x_i - x_u)^2 + (y_i - y_u)^2 = r_i^2 \; for \; i = 1, 2, 3 \qquad\qquad 3.18$$

Where (x_i, y_i) is anchor location i, r_i range to anchor i, (x_u, y_u): obscure node coordinates. Then deducting eq. 3 from equations 1 and 2:

$$(x_1 - x_u)^2 + (x_3 - x_u)^2 + (y_1 - y_u)^2 - (y_3 - y_u)^2 = r_1^2 - r_3^2 \qquad\qquad 3.19$$

$$(x_2 - x_u)^2 + (x_3 - x_u)^2 + (y_2 - y_u)^2 - (y_3 - y_u)^2 = r_2^2 - r_3^2 \qquad\qquad 3.20$$

Figure 9. Trilateration where A is anchor node and U is unknown node

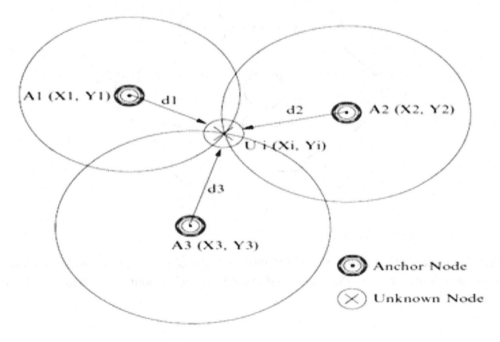

Rewriting the previous equation as a matrix and solving by least square error.

$$2\begin{bmatrix} x_3 - x_1 & y_3 - y_1 \\ x_3 - x_2 & y_3 - y_1 \end{bmatrix}\begin{bmatrix} x_u \\ y_u \end{bmatrix} = \begin{bmatrix} \left(r_1^2 - r_3^2\right) - \left(x_1^2 - x_3^2\right) - \left(y_1^2 - y_3^2\right) \\ \left(r_2^2 - r_3^2\right) - \left(x_2^2 - x_3^2\right) - \left(y_2^2 - y_3^2\right) \end{bmatrix} \qquad 3.21$$

Cell of Origin

In cell of origin (COO), position is determined by anchor point where owned the strongest signal received. precision is affected by density of anchor and distance estimated.

Centroid

(Shaoguo Xie et al, 2014) Centroid in Figure 10 means that position is determined by average location of anchor points.

$$x_{est}, y_{est} = \frac{\sum_{i=1}^{N} x_i}{N}, \frac{\sum_{i=1}^{N} y_i}{N} \qquad 3.22$$

Figure 10. Centroid method

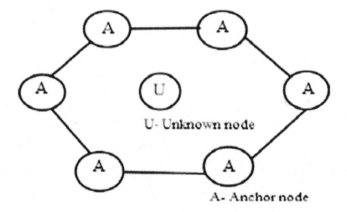

Weighted centroid (WCL) means that gives more weight to anchor points which are near to the localizing node. In both methods, Placement and number of anchor points play critical rule (Shaoguo Xie et al, 2014).

$$x_{est}, y_{est} = \frac{\sum_{i=1}^{N} w_i x_i}{\sum_{i=1}^{n} w_i}, \frac{\sum_{i=1}^{N} w_i y_i}{\sum_{i=1}^{n} w_i} \qquad 3.23$$

RELATED WORKS

This section introduces the previous work previous categories. V2V cooperative localization in Figure 11 means that combining GPS information, position of nearby vehicles via V2V communication.

Figure 11. v2v communication

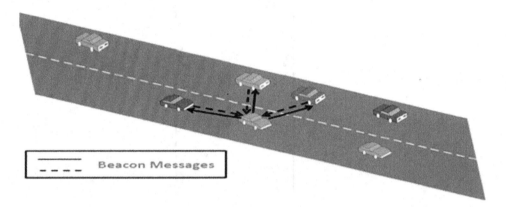

All vehicles are configured with GPS and on-board unit (OBU). Orange car exchanges GPS information between itself and its neighbors to enhance GPS location. It used one of the well- known optimization algorithms to enhance position estimated. GPS free localization requires fixed road side units that are installed on road sides. it utilizes V2I communication to estimate distance, direction, position. The information of road topology can enhance location accuracy by ensuring position coordinated lie inside road boundary such as lane number, road width, length road

(Chia-Ho Ou, 2012) authors proposed GPS free localization algorithm. Authors utilized V2I communication in Figure 12 where road side nodes deployed in two sides of roads. Each vehicle estimated the distance to RSU and angle.

Vehicles drive along straight street with a length L and a width W isolated into two lanes. Two RSUs Rl, Rr are installed on either side of the road at the middle position (xl, yl) and (xr, yr), respectively. Each vehicle estimates its range to a pair of RSUs via radio range transmission methods. vehicle decides its road heading basically by comparing the heading between its current movement vector v and the road heading. The angles are estimated for north and south headings as follow:

$$\theta_{v,n} = cos^{-1}\left(\frac{v.n}{\|v\|\|n\|}\right)$$
\hfill 4.1

$$\theta_{v,s} = cos^{-1}\left(\frac{v.s}{\|v\|\|s\|}\right)$$
\hfill 4.2

Figure 12. Two road side unit's Rr and Rl and two vehicle A, B

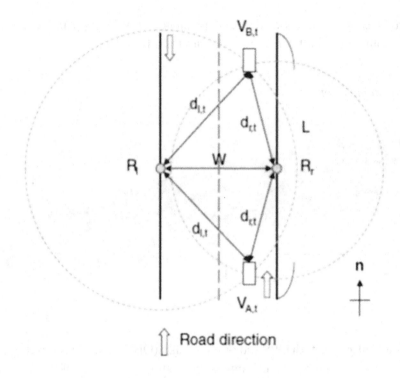

⇑ Road direction

Where n, s refers to north and south direction. If angle to north heading is less than angle to south heading $\Theta_{v,n} < \Theta_{v,s}$ then vehicle decides north heading as eq 4.1otherwise, it decides south heading. At time t, each vehicle had two possible positions related to two road side units $V_{A,t}$, $V_{B,t}$.

$$\left(x_{A,t}, y_{A,t}\right) = \left(\frac{x_r^2 - x_l^2 + d_{l,t}^2 - d_{r,t}^2}{2x_r - 2x_l}, y_l - \sqrt{-x_{A,t}^2 - x_l^2 + 2x_l x_{A,t} + d_{l,t}^2}\right) \qquad 4.3$$

$$\left(x_{B,t}, y_{B,t}\right) = \left(\frac{x_r^2 - x_l^2 + d_{l,t}^2 - d_{r,t}^2}{2x_r - 2x_l}, y_l + \sqrt{-x_{B,t}^2 - x_l^2 + 2x_l x_{B,t} + d_{l,t}^2}\right) \qquad 4.4$$

At next time t+1, vehicle receives second set of beacon messages. The possible locations for r vehicles are defined as $V_{A,t+1}$, $V_{B,t+1}$ like above equations 4.3 and 4.4. The genuine position of vehicle v is evaluated to the heading road and angle between v and direction. Each vehicle had chosen the nearest position by less angle. It is not applicable to estimate position in case of failure roadside unit, the position estimated by previous position. The accuracy of localization was related to number of roadside units' deployment. They represent high cost deployment. There is error in distance estimation as a result from radio range communication. Increasing speed of vehicles led to increase collision packet and density of vehicle.

(Ahmed Khattab et al, 2016) authors proposed GPS free localization algorithm in Figure 13 based on INS- Assisted single roadside. The algorithm was based on only one roadside. They deployed at the beginning, middle and last road. It consisted of four steps.

Figure 13. One side RSU: north RSUn, middle RSUi and south RSUs

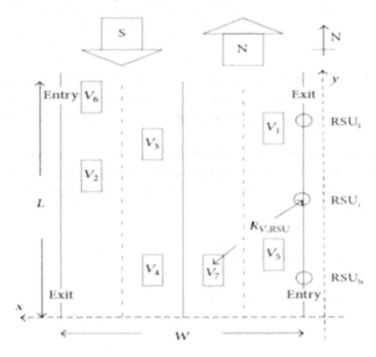

In first step, each vehicle estimated the direction after received two consecutive messages. Second step, vehicle calculates Y coordinate based on large distance to RSU.

$$y^- = L_{RSU} \mp R_{v,RSU} \qquad\qquad 4.5$$

Where L_{RSU} is y-coordinate of RSU, $R_{v,RSU}$ is distance between vehicle and RSU and sigh indicates driving direction. This equation is valid for large distance small road width. The distance $R_{v,RSU}$ is estimated based on two-way reciprocal time of arrival as follow:

$$R_{v,RSU} = \frac{(t_2 - t_1 - T)C + \Delta y}{2} \quad \Delta R > 0 \qquad\qquad 4.6$$

$$R_{v,RSU} = \frac{(t_2 - t_1 - T)C - \Delta y}{2} \quad \Delta R < 0 \qquad\qquad 4.7$$

Where ΔR is difference of radio range estimated after received beacon i and i+1. Δy equals $(t_2 - t_1)$ v, v is average speed of vehicle t1, t2 is time of receiving two successive beacon messages. Third step integrates the previous data with INS measurement to update Y, x coordinates. One method of KF or extended KF was used interchangeable in case of linear relationship (Y location) or non- linear relationship.

Fourth step was called lane boundary adjustment stage. This step aimed to guarantee **x** location that lied into roadside boundary. Lane boundary data were used instead of road boundary data to increase the accuracy of x coordinate. The estimated x coordinate can be summarized as follow:

$$x_k^- \begin{cases} 0, & \text{if } x_k^\wedge \le 0, \\ w, & \text{if } x_k^\wedge \ge w \\ L_{i-1} \le x_k^- \le L_i & \text{if } current\ lane = lane\ i \end{cases}$$

4.8

Where w is width of lane, L is boundary of lane i-1. Current lane is the average speed for M moving data. The drawbacks are summarized as high computation time, accumulation error from INS, multipath effect in radio range communication and poor performance in case of high density of vehicle. There is no metric to control large distance.

(Himan Zarza et al, 2016) authors proposed RSU/INS aided localization system (RIALS). Position in Figure 14 was estimated by integrated the information from RSU and inertial navigation system. Each vehicle maintained a queue. vehicle creates locus circle centered at the RSU with radius equal to the estimated range from the RSU i.e. TOA.

Figure 14. Several locus circles at RSU centers

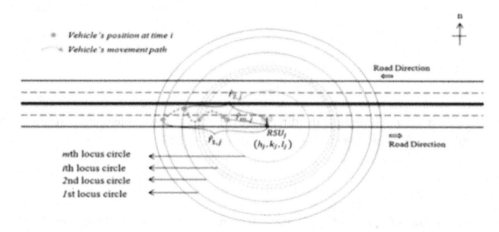

Each vehicle also maintained a queue with INS measurement data upon receiving two subsequent messages. Upon receiving four beacon messages, vehicle estimated position directly by least square methods. Length of queue impacted on the update information. Limited coverage area of a single RSU. Synchronization complexity and multipath effect were related to TOA.

(Alessio Fascista et al, 2016) authors proposed free GPS algorithm. The proposed algorithm used a smart antenna to estimate multi AOA. The position is estimated by kinematic model as equation 2.7. Author assumed constant velocity for all vehicles. The proposed algorithm consists of two stages: AOA estimations are computed by vehicle V for each signal received from RSU at time t=1…k. The AOA is nearly equaled as follow:

$$\theta_k = \arccos\left(\frac{||pv(t_k) - pc(t_k)||}{||pv(t_k) - p_R||} \right)$$

4.8

where pc(tk) is the cross point between the vehicle trajectory due period [tk, tk+1]. It considers the channel effects such as path loss, fading, shadowing as follow

$$\hat{\theta_i} = \hat{\theta_i} + e_i \qquad\qquad 4.9$$

Where e_i is the estimation error at time i =1..k. It follows Gaussian distribution with mean 0 and variance σ_i . Second phase, the AOA estimations and the RSU position (included in each beacon packet) are input variables for vehicle position method. Weight least square error is used to estimate the position as the minimum weight angle error estimated as follow

$$\hat{pv}(t0) = \arg min_{pv(t0)} \sum_{i=1}^{k} w_i \left(\hat{\theta_i} - \hat{\theta_j} \right)^2 \qquad\qquad 4.9$$

Where w_i is a weight for signal to noise ratio as follow

$$w_i \propto n_i = SNR_i sin^2 \hat{\theta_i} \qquad\qquad 4.10$$

The kinematic model is used to estimate position. It is more convenient to use signal to noise ratio as weight factor. Accuracy of position depended on distance to RSU, received signal strength, density of received packets that cause overhead communication and lose packet.

(Nasreddine et al, 2010) authors proposed free GPS algorithm. It was based on clustering approach. Cluster head selection phase aimed to select the first cluster head by waiting fixed time. Selected cluster head would be a center of network with known position (0, 0). Two neighbor vehicles were selected. RSSI was used to estimate distance between neighbor vehicle and selected cluster head. Cluster head used trilateration to estimate the position of previous three nodes. Backbone cluster heads were constructed where every selected cluster head selected other two cluster heads. Each unknown cluster head position used RSSI and trilateration to estimate position. Cluster head vehicle can be changed to maintain connectivity in case of failure cluster head. This localization accuracy was sensitive to selected neighbor vehicles. There was no mechanism to selected neighbor vehicles or cluster head. Accumulation error could be occurred in error position. RSSI was more sensitive to multipath effect. Proposed algorithm assumed low mobility model to increase opportunity to locate vehicle and to reduce position error.

(Maryam M. Alotaibi et al, 2014) authors proposed a distributed relative cooperative position algorithm (ReCOP). Recop in Figure 15 was v2v cooperative localization algorithm. Recop utilized V2V communication and clustering algorithm to reduce broadcast messages storm. The framework of Recop algorithm consists of three modules.

First module is partitioning module. Partitioning module divide the network into k clusters by utilizing kinematic information and radio range methods. Cluster head for each cluster was selected by minimum average distance.

Position module constructs local relative map for each cluster by cluster head node. The coordinate of any vehicle j (x_{kj}, y_{kj}) ^{tj} from the cluster head j at time tj, is computed as follow

$$x_{kj} = d_{kj}^- sin\left(\theta_{kj}^-\right) \qquad\qquad 4.11$$

$$y_{kj} = d_{kj}^- cos\left(\theta_{kj}^-\right) \qquad\qquad 4.12$$

Figure 15. Recop algorithm

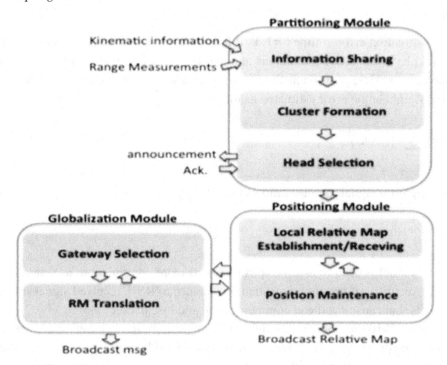

Where d_{kj}^-, θ_{kj}^- are distance and angle between vehicle j and cluster head k respectively. The distance and angle estimation follow Gaussian distribution with mean μ and variance σ. Position maintenance changes vehicle position estimation by utilizing vehicle trajectory. In other words, the orientation of distance of vehicle to cluster head is determined by its direction i.e. north, west, east and south. X co-ordinate is summation of previous distance, add to new distance and subtract from distance dedicated by origin node. Y coordinate equals new dedicated distance, and the distance dedicated by origin node subtract from past distance from CH. Globalization module consists of gateway selection and translating relative map. Vehicle is selected as gateway broadcasts beacon message to all nodes in the same zone with translated relative map. Translation relative maps means that views the relative map for each cluster from another relative map. The advantage of Recop utilizes cluster architecture for position estimation. Therefore, it attempts to reduce multipath effect and poor received signal strength that lead to increase the accuracy of inter- distance and angle. Accumulation error can be resulted by initial position and uncertainty environment. Recop ignored other parameter to clustering algorithm such as link quality, bandwidth consumption rate, communication period. In addition, simulation is applied to single lane and number of clusters is two clusters.

(Mohsen Rohani et al, 2014) authors introduced dynamic ground base station DGPS. All vehicles equipped with GPS. Therefore, all vehicles considered as dynamic base station. They used V2V communication to improve the estimated position. Each vehicle combined GPS information, INS measurement and nearby vehicles information. Vehicle estimated pseudo- range corrections (i.e. common error) and variance for its visible satellite as follow: Pseudo range correction $\Delta\rho_j^i$ was based on the difference between measured pseudo range ρ_j^i between vehicle i to satellite j and estimated distance D_j^i from vehicle i to the same satellite j as follow:

$$\Delta \rho_j^i = D_j^i - \rho_j^i \qquad\qquad 4.13$$

Vehicle estimates variance of estimated pseudo range correction from different sources i.e. nearby vehicle for the same satellite as follow:

$$(\sigma_j^i)^2 = H_{x_i^-} P_{x_{(i)}} H_{x_i^-}^T \qquad\qquad 4.14$$

$$H_{x_i^-} = \frac{x_j - x^{\wedge(i)}}{D_j^{\wedge i}}, \frac{y_j - y^{\wedge(i)}}{D_j^{\wedge i}}, \frac{z_j - z^{\wedge(i)}}{D_j^{\wedge i}} \qquad\qquad 4.15$$

Where $H_{x_i^-}$ is cosine direction and $(\sigma_j^i)^2$ represents the pseudo range correction trust level. It depends on variance of $D_j^{\wedge i}$ estimated distance for estimated position, its covariance matrix $P_{x_{(i)}}$ and satellite 's position. Each vehicle used EKF to minimize position error. The data dependent problem results from independent pseudo range correction and leads to over convergence. Vehicle estimates weight or variance for various autonomous pseudo range corrections for exactly one satellite. Vehicle chooses pseudo range correction with the least variance. Authors concern on clock bias error and inter distance between nearby vehicle. At each time, it takes variance of pseudo range correction and variance of inter distance. The proposed algorithm neglects multipath effect. It depends on EKF to reduce non-common error. It doesn't provide mechanism to evaluate nearby vehicle from its link quality or signal to noise ratio.

(Mohsen Rohani et al, 2015) it is an enhanced for previous work (Mohsen Rohani et al, 2014). Authors combine cooperative map matching with dynamic DGPS to get more position accuracy. Cooperative map matching means that vehicle exchanges its GPS position and pseudo range correction to allow other vehicles to map their position through road constraint. Therefore, they have the similar effect of common error. The vehicle uses particle filter algorithm to get the average and covariance matrix of position for distributing between vehicles. Non- common error is independent from vehicle to vehicle. If it is neglect, it will cause far true position. Vehicle can't apply road constraint of nearby vehicles. It will use weighted road map. The on-road points keep their previous weight and off-points road are weighted based on distance to road edge as follow

$$w_i^{'} = W\left(d_w, 0, \sigma_w^2\right) = w_i * e^{\frac{-d_w^2}{-2\sigma_w^2}} \qquad\qquad 4.16$$

Where d_w is the range between the i particle and the road edge, w_i is the previous weight of the particle and variance σ_w^2 includes non-common error as the norm of the diagonal elements of $p_n^{(i)}$ matrix

$$\sigma_w^2 = \left\| diag\left(p_n^{(i)}\right) \right\| + \sigma_{map}^2 \qquad\qquad 4.17$$

Where σ_{map}^2 is uncertainty of specific section on road. Position accuracy is related to quality of road map and measurement data.

(Gia– Minh Hoang et al, 2017) authors proposed new cooperative localization algorithm (CLOC) in tunnel environment. It combined measurement from V2V communication as virtual anchor nodes and

V2I communication as a fixed anchor node. In addition, measurement from inertial measurement unit and wheel speed sensor. Both were used in prediction mobility model but they suffered from accumulated error especially in long tunnel environment. The ultra-wide band (UWB) time of flight or RSS radio communication were used in V2V / V2I interchangeable. Particle filter used as data fusion to fuse all previous measurements and minimize error in estimated position. Vision system and lane boundary (i.e. digital map) identified the current road to verify position. Particle lied outside road constraint. It would be removed from particle sample. The advantage of this work was The UWB time of flight is more efficient than RSS. Massive RSU-RSSI deployed in two sides' road that yielded better performance. This performance was less than UWB. Short inter distance RSU- UWB yielded better localization accuracy. Drawbacks can be summarized as Authors didn't use all benefits of V2I communication. Large data set lead to high time computation. Position accuracy still related to inter distance RSU and number of RSU. Not all nearby vehicles were valid as virtual anchors.

(Lina Altoaimy & Imad Mahgoub, 2016) authors used weight centroid method for localization. The weight of vehicle i is estimated by summation of link quality LQD_i, heading and map information as follow:

$$w_i = \alpha * LQD_i + \beta * heading + \mu * Map_i \hspace{3cm} 4.18$$

Where α, β, μ are constant factors. The link quality is ratio between signal to noise ratio $SINR$ and distance d_i as follow:

$$LQD_i = \frac{SINR_i}{d_i} \hspace{4cm} 4.19$$

Signal to noise ratio is estimated as follow:

$$SINR_i = \frac{S}{I+N} \hspace{4cm} 4.20$$

Where S is received signal power, I is cumulative power of interfering signal and N is noise parameter. The heading can be determined by Manhattan mobility model. The heading has four different degree: $0°$, $90°$, $180°$, and $270°$. vehicles are going to east or west direction. They have heading $0°$ and $180°$ and the same y coordinates. Vehicles are going to north or south. They have heading $90°$ and $270°$ and the same x coordinates. Map factor gives higher weight for vehicles that are traveling on the same road, otherwise, it gives low weight for vehicles that are not going on the same road. Authors also use the fuzzy logic to estimate the weight via distance and heading information. Un-overlapped triangle membership function was used for fuzzification step. The parameters of membership function (MF) were estimated by experts. Low accuracy in distance estimation by of RSS. Authors didn't consider the concept of fuzzy boundary in membership function. There was a direct relationship between number of variables and number of rules.

(Pinar Oguz Ekim et al, 2016) authors suggested algorithm to solve GPS's non-line of sight. Authors used EKF to minimize error in position estimated. The input to EKF were TOA and kinematic model. The obtained position from EKF was enhanced by topology matching to select the road travelling. Heading information of selected road network is used to update motion vector. Suggested algorithm achieved high accuracy against GPS. EKF is a biased nonlinear model and requires adjusting measurement noise. This is difficult in dynamic system. In addition, multipath effect existed in radio range communication. Low cost INS sensors represented high uncertainty in motion measurement.

(Anas Mahmoud et al, 2015) authors proposed angle approximation (AA) to solve GPS' non line of sight problem. Vehicle should see at least four satellites. Large distance between satellite and vehicle could be represented as parallel lines. Nearby vehicles had nearly the same angle to satellites. Angle estimation was affected by multipath effect or couldn't estimate in NLOS condition. Aimed vehicle used angle of nearby vehicle. As the distance between nearby vehicles approached, aimed vehicle could get pseudo range of un-visible satellite and estimate artificial candidate pseudo range. Aimed vehicle uses total of the absolute value of the double differencing between all artificial candidate pseudo range and all other observed pseudo range from all communicated vehicles (ASODD). Some biased parameter could be removed. At the end stage, the ASODD consists of true range or distance and error in all generated pseudo range. The ASODD with less accumulated error were chosen to estimate position. The drawbacks could be summarized in localization accuracy related to density of vehicle, Multipath effect and noisy environment still exist and Less accuracy in tunnel environment. (LASSO) optimized measurement sparsification parameter. Drawbacks could be summarized as Membership function parameters were determined by experts. Authors ignored other parameters such as noisy environment or update time of measurement in weight variable.

(Mariam Elazab et al, 2015) authors proposed algorithm to enhance GPS position Vehicle used V2V communication to know some parameters such as position, heading and speed measurement. The distance is computed by round trip time. Vehicle neighbors replied with previous information and appended last time of updated previous information. Vehicle accepted message from nearby vehicle under a certain power level condition. Vehicle used 2D RISS (one odometer and one gyroscope) to update motion vector and position. Vehicle combined all previous information and executed extended Kalman filter to update position. Drawbacks could be summarized as time delay of RTT increased with the density of vehicles. Therefore, time computation increased with density of vehicles. It was based on good condition (i.e. LOS was available) to get GPS position.

(Guohao Zhang et al, 2018) authors proposed a novel v2v cooperative localization with double layers of consistency check (CC) in Figure 16. In each vehicle, the absolute position and pseudo range are obtained by GNSS. They are optimized by least square error.

The least square error is estimated as follow:

$$\Delta x = \left(H^T H\right)^{-1} H^T \Delta\rho$$

Where Δx denoted state vector that contains the clock bias between two types of satellites GPS system and BeiDou satellite. In addition, the pseudo range difference vector for two satellites as follow

$$\Delta x = \begin{pmatrix} \Delta r \\ \delta\rho_{rec} \\ \delta\rho^{BDS} \end{pmatrix} \qquad 4.21$$

Figure 16. A novel v2v cooperative localization with double layers

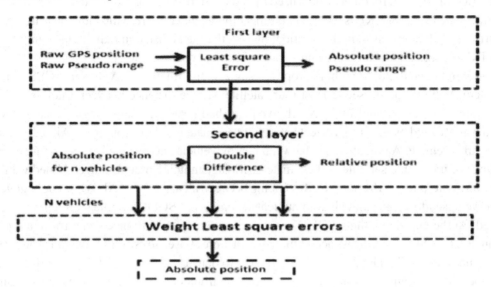

H is matrix measurement that consists of line of sight or distance from receiver to n satellites. $\Delta\rho$ equals pseudo range vector difference between estimations and prediction for n satellites. The consistency of measurement is evaluated by pseudo range residual $\hat{\varepsilon_{LS}}$ as follows:

$$\hat{\varepsilon_{LS}} = \Delta\rho - H.\Delta x \qquad\qquad 4.22$$

It is assist normalized with the sum of square error. The output of first layer is absolute position and associated pseudo range measurement. Second layer, the measurement of first layer is cooperating with other vehicle's measurement. The goal of second layer is removed inconsistency of surrounding vehicles measurements by double difference method. Using the least square for DD of pseudo range measurement and corresponding square error of relative position as follow:

$$\hat{\varepsilon_{DD}} = D - E.\Delta r \qquad\qquad 4.23$$

Where E equals difference LOS vector between reference satellite and other satellites. D is DD measurement between reference satellite and other satellites for two receivers i.e. common error between two receivers. Δr is relative distance or position between two receivers that is gotten by least square error. It is further optimized by sum of square error. Finally, the absolute and relative positions are combined by weight least square error to enhance absolute position. Position vector is position of vehicle as reference vehicle plus the relative position of reference vehicle and its surrounding vehicles. Weight equals average of pseudo range residual per estimations. Finally, it gets the optimized position matrix for all vehicles. The complexity of proposed algorithm becomes more complex with increasing number of vehicles. Weight is evaluated based on common error between receivers i.e. clock bias for no time synchronization

(Waqas Ahmed et al, 2018) authors propose local closed based V2I cooperative localization. It is assumed M anchor nodes along the road. Vehicle received the signal from anchor node within its range. Vehicle estimates the average received power. It is fed into closed local localization algorithm for position estimation as follow:

Vehicle i uses free space path loss model between itself to anchor node j. path loss and received signal strength is related as

$$z_T = L_{ij} + z_i\left(d_{ij}\right)$$
4.24

Where z_T is transmit power, L_{ij} is free path loss and $z_i\left(d_{ij}\right)$ is received signal strength of anchor j at distance d_{ij} as follow

$$z_{ij}\left(d_{ij}\right) = z_o\left(d_o\right) - 10n log10\left(\frac{d_{ij}}{d_o}\right) + n_{ij}$$
4.25

Where $z_o\left(d_o\right)$ is received signal at reference distance d_o, d_{ij} is distance between anchor j and vehicle i and n_{ij} is range error. The pathloss of vehicle i or difference of power as follow:

$$L_i(d_i) = z_T - z_i\left(d_i\right)$$
4.26

Where $z_i\left(d_i\right)$ is received power at distance d_i for vehicle i. The ratio between received signal strength and transmit power equals distance d_i.

$$\frac{\tilde{z}_T}{\tilde{z}_{ij}\tilde{L}_0} = d_i$$
4.27

The Euclidean distance between vehicle i to anchor j ϑ_{ij} equals the difference between their positions c_i, c_j respectively plus the range error n_{ij} as follow:

$$\vartheta_{ij} = \left\|c_i - c_j\right\| + n_{ij} = d_{ij} + n_{ij}$$
4.28

The received signal strength RSS based on distance estimated equals:

$$\frac{\tilde{z}_T}{\tilde{z}_{ij}\tilde{L}_0} - n_{ij} = \left\|c_i - c_j\right\|$$
4.29

Squaring both sides, it gets

$$\left(\frac{\tilde{z}_T}{\tilde{z}_{ij}\tilde{L}_0}\right)^2 - \left\|c_i\right\|^2 - \left\|c_j\right\|^2 = 2\frac{\tilde{z}_T}{\tilde{z}_{ij}\tilde{L}_0}n_{ij} - 2c_j^T c_i - n_{ij}^2$$
4.30

For simplicity consider $\|c_i\|^2$ as θ, and $\frac{\tilde{z_T}}{\tilde{z_{ij}}\tilde{L_0}}$ as θ_{ij}, it obtains

$$= -2\theta_{ij} + n_{ij} - n_{ij}^2 + 2c_j^T c_i$$

4.31

Solve the above equation by least square error to find estimated position $\hat{c_i}$ that equals

$$\hat{c_i} = G + k\theta$$

4.32

The proposed algorithm provides mathematical approach to evaluate the distance and then the position using RSS. Uncertainty environment will have negative impact on estimated distance and position. The soft computing such as fuzzy logic deals with uncertainty and provides more accurate estimation for distance and position.

(Susana B.Cruz et al, 2017) authors proposed neighbor-aided localization algorithm. It utilized two stages of Bayesian filter. An unscented Kalman filter (UKF) used for heading estimation and particle filter used for received signal strength RSS, velocity, GPS position and map matching. It consists of three stages: state equations, measurement equations and map restriction. In the first stage: state space model can be described as follow

$$x_0(k) = \left[x_0(k), y_0(k), s_0(k), h_0(k)\right]$$

4.33

Where $x_0(k), y_0(k)$ are the position coordinate of vehicle at time k, $s_0(k)$ is vehicle speed and $h_0(k)$ is vehicle heading from east to north direction. The state space model can be gotten by kinematic model as follow:

$$x_0(k) = x_0(k-1)Ts_0(k-1)cos\left(h_0(k-1)\right)$$

4.34

$$y_0(k) = y_0(k-1)Ts_0(k-1)sin\left(h_0(k-1)\right)$$

4.35

$$s_0(k) = \hat{s_0}(k) + w_{sk}$$

4.36

$$h_0(k) = h_0(k-1) + \Delta\hat{h} + w_{hk} .$$

4.37

Where time T equals time interval between k-1 and k, $+\Delta\hat{h}$ is the estimated heading during T, $\hat{s_0}$ is the average estimated speed during T and w_{sk}, w_{hk} are clutter for heading and speed estimations. clutter variables Gaussian distribution with zero mean and variance T σ_h^2 and Tσ_s^2. UKF is implemented for heading change.

Measurement equation: Z(k) represents vector of GPs position, RSS and velocity. RSS is formed by free space path loss model which it is based on distance between target vehicle v_0 position and its neighbors or mobile anchor nodes n_a in its range transmission. Due to uncertainty in GPS positions. The GPS position of neighbor anchors follow Gaussian distribution with average $\hat{x_a}(k)$ and standard deviation σ_a

at time k. It draws 100 particles for reducing cost computation. If GPS location information at individual vehicles are available, the likehood function can be estimated as follow:

$$p(z(k)|X(k))) = l_L\big(x_0(k)\big)l_\rho\big(x_0(k)\big)$$ 4.38

Where $l_L\big(x_0(k)\big)$ is the product of the probabilities of $x_0(k)$ being the current position of vehicle v_0 for each mobile anchor nodes.

Map restriction, for each particle, it decides if the position lies on road or not. outside particles will be removed. The remaining particles will be replicated to keep the number of particles according to higher weight. The authors use two different algorithms i.e. EKF and particle filter to deal with the uncertainty environment and road boundary. They will consume more computation resources. The results are more related to with initial values.

(Mohamed El-Cheikh Ali et al,2017) authors propose an enhanced schema for position estimation. It is based on roadside unit to get initial position and then is enhanced via cooperation among neighbors. Upon delivering the beacon packet from the farthest two neighbor RSU. Vehicle estimates distance to RSUs via TOA method and estimates the separation distance between two RSU d_{RR}. It computes its angle by

$$\alpha = cos^{-1}\big(\frac{d_{R1}^2 + d_{RR}^2 - d_{R2}^2}{2d_{R1} * d_{RR}}\big)$$ 4.39

Vehicle estimates its position based on kinematic model as follow:

$$x_v = d_{R1} * cos(\alpha)$$ 4.40

$$y_v = d_{R1} * sin(\alpha)$$ 4.41

It applies Kalman filter in which measurement matrix consists of kinematic information i.e. speed, heading and estimated position. Vehicle exchanges cooperative awareness message (CAM) with its neighbors. CAM contains position, heading, speed and acceleration. Vehicle estimates its distance to each neighbor using RSS. The distance between two vehicles at time t equals:

$$d_t^2 = \Delta x_{1-2,t}^2 + \Delta y_{1-2,t}^2$$ 4.42

Where $\Delta x_{i-j,t}^2 = (x_{i,t} - x_{j,t})^2$ and $\Delta y_{i-j,t}^2 = (y_{i,t} - y_{j,t})^2$. The speed vector is represented as pair (vx, v_y) then Δv_x and Δv_y are calculated as follow

$$\Delta v_x = \big(v_1 cos\theta_1 - v_2 cos\theta_2\big) * \Delta t$$ 4.43

$$\Delta v_y = \big(v_1 sin\theta_1 - v_2 sin\theta_2\big) * \Delta t$$ 4.44

Then

$$(x_{1,t-1} - x_{2,t-1})^2 = \left(\Delta v_x - \Delta x_{1-2,t} \right)^2 \qquad\qquad 4.45$$

$$(y_{1,t-1} - y_{2,t-1})^2 = \left(\Delta v_y - \Delta y_{1-2,t} \right)^2 \qquad\qquad 4.46$$

The distance d at time t-1is calculated as follow:

$$d_{t-1}^2 = \left(\Delta v_x - \Delta x_{1-2,t} \right)^2 + \left(\Delta v_y - \Delta y_{1-2,t} \right)^2 \qquad\qquad 4.47$$

$$d_t^2 = \left(\Delta x_{1-2,t} \right)^2 + \left(\Delta y_{1-2,t} \right)^2 \qquad\qquad 4.48$$

Vehicles don't change the lane frequently so Δv_y equals zero at almost time. There are two cases: first $\Delta v_y = 0$

$$\Delta x_{1-2,t} = \frac{d_t^2 - d_{t-1}^2 + \Delta v_x^2}{2 * \Delta v_x} \qquad\qquad 4.49$$

$$\Delta y_{1-2,t} = \pm \sqrt{d_t^2 - \Delta x_{1-2,t}^2} \qquad\qquad 4.50$$

Second case: $\Delta v_y \neq 0$

$$\Delta y_{1-2,t} = k - \alpha * \Delta x_{1-2,t} \qquad\qquad 4.51$$

Where k $= \dfrac{d_t^2 - d_{t-1}^2 + \Delta v_x^2 + \Delta v_y^2}{2 * \Delta v_y}$ and $\alpha = \dfrac{\Delta v_x}{\Delta v_y}$

And the dimension $\Delta x_{1-2,t}$

$$\Delta x_{1-2,t} = \frac{2k * \alpha \pm \sqrt{4 \left(k * \alpha \right)^2 - 4 * \left(1 + \alpha^2 \right) * \left(k^2 - d_t^2 \right)}}{2 * \left(1 + \alpha^2 \right)} \qquad\qquad 4.52$$

Authors combined two approaches for cooperative localization algorithm to enhance precision of estimated position. The accumulation error can be faced from initial position in case of failure RSU. The clutter estimation needs adjustment.

(Felipe Lobo et al,2019) Authors proposed cooperative vehicle localization improvement using distance information (CoVaLID) Algorithm.it is an improved for VANET location improve algorithm (VLOCI). It is aimed to improve GPS position by collected the GPS position error and also distance information.

It evaluates GPS error as function of GPS position and true position. It applies the triangle similarity measure. It mentioned that if two triangles participate coincident angles, the ratio of any related axes for two triangles are equaled. Finally, it estimates the distance between GPS's distance and Sensor's distance. EKF is used as data fusion to improve the GPS location via distance information only. CoVaLID helps to reduce GPS location error at rate 63%. It depends on triangle similarity to estimate the distance between nearby vehicles instead of range method to overcome the multipath effect and non-line of sight. There stills exist high uncertainty in sensor measurement and GPS. In addition, the loss of information is results from mapping function in EKF.

Table 2 and table 3 summarize the related works GPS free localization and v2v localization respectively. They discuss the advantages and drawbacks for each research paper in spite of range methods and data fusion to minimize the error in GPS position. Some research papers prefer using TDOA than TOA and RSSI. They also indicate to use digital map to bound coordinate system to boundary road. EKF is used extensively than KF as its ability to deal with nonlinear problem. Its mapping function may cause lose data. PF is used frequently with map matching techniques. It needs to initial large data set. Inertial navigation system or kinematic model is used frequently with any range measurement as attempt to overcome initial position problem. Finally. Some research papers attend to use RSU to get its position and attempts to evaluate amount of error in position or distance and angle measurements. These localization algorithms depend on V2I communication only. They achieve less localization accuracy than V2V communication. The hybrid approach consists of V2V and V2I communication that is called v2x communication. It achieves the best localization accuracy.

FUTURE RESEARCH DIRECTIONS

This section introduces the current challenges and future trends in cooperative localization. Cooperative localization faces the current challenges as follow:

1. Radio range measurement: the accuracy of radio range measurement is more related with cost of wireless devices. Time synchronization requires adjust clock for receiver and transmitter. It is difficult in dense network. Poor signals result from noisy and multipath effect.
2. Accumulation error: is resulted from an error in initial position. It leads to raise position error for neighbors.
3. Delay: results from using two or more optimization algorithms. It is critical for safety application.
4. Cost deployment: number of deploying RSU along the road represent high cost. It requires the vehicle inside the range of RSU. Digital map is used to align the coordinate to boundary road.
5. Dense mobile anchor nodes: is an alternative solution of road side unit. However, the distribution and the number of mobile anchor nodes are significant role in position estimation.
6. Throughput or overhead: all cooperative localization algorithms require more information to increase the opportunity of obtained well measurements. That means exchanges a lot of beacon messages. It consumes more bandwidth, more energy and lose packets. That leads to noisy measurements and reduce of number delivery packet ratio.

Table 2. GPS free localization

References	Range	Location Estimation method	Localization Accuracy (RMSE)	Pos	Cons
(Chia-Ho Ou, 2012)	TDOA	Trilateration	3.3 m free fault environment 5.5 m fault environment	TDOA is more accurate than RSSI. Position is estimated by 2 RSU.	It is less performance in high traffic density. it needs to evaluate against car following mobility model. Large bandwidth consumption. Accuracy relates to close distance to RSU
(Ahmed Khattab, et al 2016)	TDOA	KF for linear relation (Y -coordinate). EKF for nonlinear relation (x -coordinate).	1.82 m with noise σ 6m. 2.13 m to 1.68 m with decrease noise data 'sσ from 3 to 0 .5	It outperforms than using GPS/INS as result from combining KF and EKF. It depends on existence three RSU.	It is sensitive to large distance in y coordinate. Accumulation error is resulted from error initial position. It has high computation time.
(Himan Zarza, et al, 2016)	TOA	LSE	< 1m	speed changing has less impact than changing in traffic density.	It is sensitive to increase INS σ measurement error. Synchronization problem. update measurement rate is critical factor on localization accuracy. Accumulation error has negative impact.
(Alessio Fascista, et al, 2016)	-	Triangulation	< 1m	Triangulation is more accurate than Trilateration. It considers SNIR as weight for goodness degree of signal received level.	With large distance to RSU and noise measurement, the accuracy has more reduced. One RSU represents low cost and poor power signal received level.
(Nasreddine, et al, 2010)	RSSI	Trilateration	< 4m in low mobility. RNP reaches 92, 5% < 8m in high mobility and RNP reaches 73, 33%.	It uses cluster architecture.	It is sensitive to topology change. RSSI is more sensitive to noise environment and path loss model's parameters.
(Pinar Oguz Ekim, et al, 2016)	TDOA	EKF + map	NA	It uses map to bound location on road.	Lose measurement may accrued from mapping function. Accuracy relates to the accuracy of map.
(Mohamed El-Cheikh Ali, et al,2017)	RSSI/ TOA	KF/LSE	< 1m	It benefits from V2I to get good initial positions. Nearby neighbors' position is then utilized for raise accuracy.	The nature of localization is nonlinear. Synchronization problem. The accuracy relates with number of RSU and close RSU to vehicle. Multipath effect comes from v2v communication.
Waqas Ahmed, et al, 2018)	RSSI	WSE	-	RSSI doesn't require additional device. It depends on 4 existence RSU.	The accuracy is related to number of RSU. RSSI data needs more time for adjusting data noise. Localization is nonlinear nature.

Future work can be concluded as:

1. Reducing the energy consumption of localization process that will have positive effect in position parameter estimation.

Table 3. Localization based on v2v communication

References	Range	Location Estimation method	Localization Accuracy (RMSE)	Pos	Cons
(Maryam M. Alotaibi, et al, 2014)	RSSI	Kinematic model	Slight high over 1m	Cluster architecture	Accuracy has an opposite relation with traffic density and speed.
(Mohsen Rohani, et al, 2015)	Pseudo range	Map Matching + particle filter	9.17m to 2.93m.	Pseudo range error reduces with increased density.	Accuracy decreases with increased density. PF requires large initial data size. Uncertainty measurement has negative influence on localization accuracy.
(Gia– Minh Hoang, et al, 2017)	RSSI	particle filter	About 2 m	Hybrid approach V2X to solve the problem of accumulation error.	It represents high cost mechanism. It deals with uncertainty with high range cost.
(Lina Altoaimy and Imad Mahgoub, 2016)	RSSI	Weight Centroid	About 30m	It deals with uncertainty by fuzzy logic. SNIR is used as metric for link quality.	Increased traffic density and multipath have negative impact on accuracy. Centroid method has less influence in nonlinear problem.
(Anas Mahmoud, et al, 2015)	Pseudo range	ASODD	-	ASODD is simple and more efficient than KF.	The accuracy is related to the distance between nearby vehicles to minimize common error. Traffic density and multipath effect have negative impact on accuracy.
(Mariam Elazab, et al, 2016)	RTT	EKF	< 1m	Distance is estimated by RTT.	Velocity has an influence impact to reach to suitable number of neighbors and also power level. Latency results from RTT computation especially in critical application.
(Guohao Zhang, et al, 2018)	Pseudo range	LSE/DD	About 7m	DD method has influence impact to reduce the multipath effect.	The dependency of LSE method is not enough to improve absolute position. It still multipath effect has negative impact
(Susana B.Cruz, et al, 2017)	RSSI	Unscented KF / PF	About 6m to 9m	Unscented KF is more efficient than EKF in mapping function.	The accuracy is related with good initialization parameters. Its accuracy is less efficient when compared with KF and EKF. High computation time.
(Felipe Lobo, et al,2019)	RSSI	Similarity of the Triangles/ EKF	Reduction rate 63%, and 53%	Triangle similarity measure determines distance between nearby vehicles	It still multipath effect and accumulation error have negative impact. Lose measurement can occurred as result of mapping function.

2. The working on reducing overhead communication or increasing the packet delivery ratio to increase the opportunity of obtained well parameters.

3. Dealing with the uncertainty environment by utilizing the soft computing techniques to handle the uncertainty of measurements and to reduce computation resources.

4. Two or more radio range methods can have positive effect to overcome clock bias.

5. Hybrid approach combines V2V and V2I communications to overcomes the defects for each type of communication. That will reflect with positive impact on localization accuracy.

CONCLUSION

This chapter introduces cooperative localization algorithms in vehicular networks. The cooperative localization is an alternative solution for GPS' problems especially for non- line of sight and multipath effect. GPS is unavailable in all day-hours. V2V and V2I communications available during day hours. RSU represents high cost deployment than V2V communication. V2I communication solves less density vehicles and initial known position especially in highway scenario. X-coordinate is more evaluated frequently than Y-coordinate in V2I communication. It needs to adjust in spite of the boundary road. It will depend on the accuracy of digital map. V2V communication solves non-line of sight but multipath effect and poor received signal still exist. X-Y coordinate systems are evaluated in V2V communication. They are exchanged and enhanced via KF, particle filter and double difference. Radio range measurement consist of angle and distance estimations. It has drawbacks in time synchronization and poor signals. It may require high cost sensors and additional multi antenna smart to guarantee more accurate measurement. It will raise the price of vehicle. The chapter also introduces recent related work of cooperative localization. The cooperative localization based on multi-hop routing still in its infancy and need a lot of papers. The localization algorithms such as KF, particle filter, double difference, least square can't adjust noisy measurement in high dynamic system especially non-linear problem. Trilateration, centroid and weight centroid methods are not suitable for localization method in high dynamic system. In addition, it is based on density of anchor nodes.

REFERENCES

Abdel Wahab, A., Khattab, A., & Fahmy, Y. A. (2013). Two-Way TOA with Limited Dead Reckoning for GPS-Free Vehicle Localization Using Single RSU. In *Proceedings 13th International Conference on ITS Telecommunications (ITST)*, 244 -249. IEEE.

Ahammed, F., Taheri, J., Zomaya, A. Y., & Ott, M. (2012). VLOCI: Using Distance Measurements to Improve the Accuracy of Location Coordinates in GPS-Equipped VANETs. Institute for Computer Sciences, Social Informatics, and Telecommunications Engineering, 149–161.

Ahmed, W., Saeed, N., & Dost, M. S. B. (2018). *Localization of vehicular ad hoc networks with RSS based distance estimation. In Proceedings international conference on computing, mathematics, and engineering technologies*. IEEE.

Ali, M. E.-C., Artail, H., & Nasser, Y. (2017). An Intelligent Transportation Systems cooperative and roadside unit-aided schema for vehicular ad hoc networks. In Proceedings international conference on electrical and computing technologies and applications, 1-5. IEEE.

Alotaibi, M. M., Boukerche, A., & Mouftah, H. (2014). Distributed Relative Cooperative Positioning in Vehicular Ad-hoc Networks. In *Proceedings Global Information Infrastructure and Networking Symposium (GIIS)*, IEEE. 10.1109/GIIS.2014.6934255

Altoaimy, L., Mahgoub, I., & Rathod, M. (2014). Weighted localization in vehicular ad hoc networks using vehicle-to-vehicle communication. In *Proceedings Global Information Infrastructure and Networking Symposium (GIIS)*, 1-5, IEEE. 10.1109/GIIS.2014.6934270

Benslimane. (2005). Localization in Vehicular Ad Hoc Networks, In *Proceedings Systems Communications,* 19–25.

Cruz, S. B., Abrudan, T. E., Xiao, Z., Trigoni, N., & Barrosn, J. (2017). Neighbor-Aided Localization in Vehicular Networks. *Transactions on Intelligent Transportation Systems, IEEE, 18*(10), 2693–2702. doi:10.1109/TITS.2017.2655146

Drawil, N., & Basir, O. (2010). Toward Increasing the Localization Accuracy of Vehicles in VANET. In *Proceedings International Conference on Vehicular Electronics and Safety*, 13-18. IEEE.

Drawil, N. M., & Basir, O. (2010). Intervehicle-communication-assisted localization. Intelligent Transportation Systems. *IEEE Transactions on Intelligent Transportation Systems, 11*(3), 678–691. doi:10.1109/TITS.2010.2048562

Elazab, M., Noureldine, A., & Hassanein, H. S. (2015). Integrated cooperative localization for connected vehicles in urban canyons. In *Proceedings IEEE Global Communications Conference (GLOBECOM)*, 1-6. 10.1109/GLOCOM.2015.7417819

Fascista, A., & Ciccarese, G. (2016). A localization algorithm based on V2I communications and AOA estimation. *IEEE Signal Processing Letters*, 1–5.

Golestan, K., Sattar, F., Karray, F., Kamel, M., & Seifzadeh, S. (2015). Localization in vehicular ad hoc networks using data fusion and V2V communication. Computer Communications. Retrieved from www.elsevier.com/locate/comcom,1-12

Hoang, G.-M., Denis, B., Ḧarri, J., & Slock, D. T. M. (2017). Robust Data Fusion for Cooperative Vehicular Localization in Tunnels. In *Proceedings IEEE Intelligent Vehicles Symposium (IV)*, 1372-1377. 10.1109/IVS.2017.7995902

Jagadeesh, G. R., Srikanthan, T., & Zhang, X. D. (2004). A Map Matching Method for GPS Based Real-Time Vehicle Location. *The Journal of Navigation*, 57, 429–440.

Khattab, A., Fahmy, Y. A., & Abdel Wahab, A. (2016). High Accuracy GPS-Free Vehicle Localization Framework via an INS-Assisted Single RSU. *International Journal of Distributed Sensor Networks,* Hindawi Publishing Corporation, 1-16.

Lagraa, N., Yagoubi, M. B., & Benkouider, S. (2010). Localization technique in VANets using Clustering (LVC). *IJCSI International Journal of Computer Science,* 7, 4-9.

Liu, K., Lim, H. B., Frazzoli, E., Ji, H., & Lee, V. C. S. (2014). Improving Positioning Accuracy Using GPS Pseudo range Measurements for Cooperative Vehicular Localization. *IEEE Transactions on Vehicular Technology, 63*(6), 2544–2556. doi:10.1109/TVT.2013.2296071

Lobo, F., Grael, D., Oliveira, H., Villas, L., Almehmadi, A., & El-Khatib, K. (2019). Cooperative Localization Improvement Using Distance Information in Vehicular Ad Hoc Networks. *International Journal of Sensors,* 1-27. Retrieved from www.mdpi.com/journal/sensors

Mahmoud, A., Noureldin, A., & Hassanein, H. S. (2015). VANETs Positioning in Urban Environments: A Novel Cooperative Approach. In *Proceedings Vehicular Technology Conference (VTC)*, 1-7. IEEE. 10.1109/VTCFall.2015.7391188

Mautz, R. (2012). Indoor Positioning Technologies. Institute of Geodesy and Photogrammetry, Department of Civil, Environmental, and Geomatic Engineering, ETH Zurich.

Naguib, A., Pakzad, P., Palanki, R., Poduri, S., & Chen, Y. (2013). Scalable and Accurate Indoor Positioning on Mobile Devices. In *Proceedings International Conference on Indoor Positioning and Indoor Navigation*, 1-10. IEEE. 10.1109/IPIN.2013.6817856

Oguz-Ekim, P., Ali, K., Madadi, Z., Quitin, F., & Tay, W. P. (2016, November). Proof of Concept Study Using DSRC, IMU and Map Fusion for Vehicle Localization in GNSS-Denied Environments. In *Proceedings IEEE 19th International Conference on Intelligent Transportation Systems (ITSC)*, 841-846. IEEE.

Chia-Ho Ou (2012). A roadside unit-based localization scheme for vehicular ad hoc networks, *International Journal of Communication Systems, 27*, 135–150.

Rohani, M., Gingras, D., & Gruyer, D. (2014). Vehicular Cooperative Map Matching. In *Proceedings International Conference on Connected Vehicles and Expo*, 779-803. IEEE.

Rohani, M., Gingras, D., & Gruyer, D. (2015). A Novel Approach for Improved Vehicular Positioning Using Cooperative Map Matching and Dynamic Base Station DGPS Concept. *IEEE Transactions on Intelligent Transportation Systems*, 1–10.

Ros, F. J., Martinez, J. A., & Ruiz, P. M. (2014). A survey on modeling and simulation of vehicular networks: Communications, mobility, and tools. *Computer Communications, 43*, 1–15. doi:10.1016/j.comcom.2014.01.010

Sahasrabudhe, M. S., & Chawla, M. (2014). Survey of Applications based on Vehicular Ad-Hoc Network (VANET) Framework. [IJCSIT]. *International Journal of Computer Science and Information Technologies, 5*, 3.

Skog, I., & Handel, P. (2009). In-Car Positioning and Navigation Technologies—A Survey. Intelligent Transportation Systems. *IEEE Transactions on Intelligent Transportation Systems, 10*(1), 4–2. doi:10.1109/TITS.2008.2011712

Tay, J. H., Chandrasekhar, V. R., & Seah, W. K. G. (2006). Selective Iterative Multilateration for Hop Count-Based Localization in Wireless Sensor Networks. In *Proceedings 7th International Conference on mobile data management*, 152-152. IEEE. 10.1109/MDM.2006.139

Ming-Fong Tsai, Po-Ching Wang, Ce-Kuen Shieh ·Wen-Shyang Hwang, Naveen Chilamkurti, Seung-min Rho& Yang Sun Lee(2015).Improving positioning accuracy for VANET in real city environments. Springer Science+Business Media,1975–1995.

Xi, L., Liu, Q., Li, M., & Liu, Z. (2007, October). Map matching algorithm and its application. *International Journal of Computational Intelligence Systems*, 1-7.

Xie, S., Hu, Y., & Wang, Y. (2014). Weighted centroid localization for wireless sensor networks. International Conference on Consumer Electronics - China, 1-4. IEEE.

Xu, B., Shen, L., Yan, F., & Zheng, J. (2011). Doppler-shifted frequency measurement-based positioning for roadside-vehicle communication systems. Wireless communications and mobile computing, Wiley Online Library, 866-875.

Zarza, H., Yousefi, S., & Benslimane, A. (2016). RIALS: RSU/INS-aided localization system for GPS-challenged road segments. *Wireless Communications and Mobile Computing,* 1290–1305.

Zhu, L., Yang, A., Wu, D., & Liu, L. (2014). Survey of Indoor Positioning Technologies and Systems. *Communications in Computer and Information Science,* 400–409. Springer.

KEY TERMS AND DEFINITIONS

Absolute Position: position is determined by GPS or inertial navigation system.

Angle of Arrival: The receiver node senses the direction of the received signal.

Localization Error: is the difference between true position and estimated position.

Relative Position: is an alternative name of cooperative localization. It means that determined position with the help of nearby vehicle or roadside units.

Round Trip Time: is a sum of signal travelling time t1 from transmitter to a receiver and received signal time t2 from receiver to transmitter.

Time of Arrival: The distance is measured as the time of the received signal.

Time Difference of Arrival: The distance is the difference time of received two different signals.

Chapter 4
Intelligent Transportation System:
A Complete Insight

Parul Agarwal
 https://orcid.org/0000-0002-5051-3950
Jamia Hamdard, India

Syed Imtiyaz Hassan
 https://orcid.org/0000-0003-2453-9580
Maulana Azad National Urdu University, India

Jawed Ahmed
Jamia Hamdard, India

ABSTRACT

Today, the technology is moving at a fast pace and has also changed the pace at which the commuter is moving. No longer is the commuter ready to waste time and resources while travelling. This has led to a revolution in the transport sector. ICT, smart devices, and different enabling technologies make intelligent transport systems (ITS) a reality. If well implemented, they can save time and money, help to reduce the environmental threats, and also create business opportunities for many. Today's era is an era of revolution, technological advances, Internet, digitalization, mobile communications, big data, and an era of harnessing the potentials of Cloud Computing. Realizing the benefits of each of these and their utilization and need, a global potential for a powerful and less costly ITS has to be created. This chapter shall give a complete insight into the ITS: its history, components, benefits, issues, and challenges. It would also discuss the future that is in store for ITS but with a realization that the environment is not at stake.

DOI: 10.4018/978-1-7998-2570-8.ch004

INTRODUCTION

Intelligent Transportation System is smart and intelligent!! Smart and intelligent as it provides services to the users and makes a safer, smarter and a well-coordinated, innovated way of using the transport networks. (Whatis.com) defines it as the application of sensing, analysis, control and several communication technologies so as to improve mobility, safety and the efficiency for the benefit of the users. But, any of the application of intelligent transportation system should be environmental and economically sustainable as a solution.

"Intelligent transportation systems" applies information, communication and several sensor technologies to traffic, vehicles, and transportation and the infrastructure so as to provide real time information to the commuters to enable them to make better decisions. ITS aims to decrease the traffic congestion, decrease air pollution, improve safety, and improve energy efficiency. The recent developments of ITS emphasizes upon vehicle to vehicle communications.

HISTORY OF ITS APPLICATIONS IN THE WORLD

Technological advancements have led to the innovations in ITS. But, in 1939, at the World's fair held at New York, the visitors could witness the vehicles of the future, vehicles which could be controlled electronically, moved smoothly on the highways and the surface streets. Then, in 1960's as well as 1970's, an emphasis was laid on centrally monitored route guidance. Similar paths of planning, strategies were carried out in continents like Asia, Europe and North America. The evolution in transportation systems also led to the development of smart cities.

NEED FOR ITS

Smart cities needed a smart and a smooth flow of goods, people and services over a transport network. An increase in the population has led to an increase in vehicular traffic on the roads. This has led to several problems like traffic jams, increased accident rates, environmental threats and many more. Though we are advancing in several ways, but the villages, towns and even cities are lacking a proper road infrastructure, this problem being prevalent in the developing countries. Thus, to tackle the congestion on roads which leads to increased travel times, and industry costs, to provide a controlled guidance and support in the form of display boards, to make the transportation system more secure, user friendly and safer, the need for ITS grew. The greater the traffic jam, more is the smoke emitted from vehicles and greater the negative impact on the environment. ITS comes as a solution to all these hurdles. Truly, ITS can be described as a revolution in the transport sector to smoothen the way people commute and efficient ITS shall result in an improved life for the citizens of the country. Also, the intelligent transport market shall be driven by the need to improve safety of the commuters by reducing the road accidents. Growth in population and rise in the vehicular traffic dives the need for an effective traffic management system.

Digital era has led to a revolution in the way Information and Communication technologies (ICT) and its applications in every sector is being perceived today. Well, w.r.t. the intelligent Transport systems, it has now been extended from being just a transport information system to the extent that it can now control the traffic congestion, manage the traffic, devise policies, integrate various means and the supporting infrastructure, provide help and support through apps to the passengers by providing information about the best route, weather conditions, traffic density, alternate means, seat booking, pooling facility and so many more of the likes. But it must be noted that various factors like weather forecasting also play a role in the information chain as mentioned in (Sherry, 2001; Oakland, 2003; Keith, 2001).

LITERATURE SURVEY

Substantial research has been carried out in the past related to the Intelligent Transportation system, which has been extensively discussed in this section. In (Dia & Thomas, 2011), the authors discuss how neural networks based models can be used for automatic incident detection for arterial roads. The paper uses data obtained through probe vehicles and inductive loop detectors. They compare previous work and assess the performance based on a similar idea. The paper concludes by proposing the use of data fusion neural networks for incident detection. (Pal & Singh, 2011) developed an advanced travel information system by integrating WWW and GIS both and harnessed the benefits of these technologies. In (Hickman & Hanowski, 2011), safety monitoring was done by providing truck to the participating drivers. They drove the truck in a normal fashion where in one scenario, the feedback light of the on-board safety monitoring system were disabled but safety related events were recorded and in another scenario, the light was enabled to provide safety measures as feedback to the drivers. Travel assistance device was proposed in (Barbeau et. al, 2010), which helps the travelers in transit while they are using public transport means. This service provides real time audio-video support, which assists them by helping them to move out of the vehicle. New, customized itineraries can be created which would aid the authorized personnel to constantly monitor the traveler's location at real-time basis.

The advanced travelers information system has been discussed in (Zhang, Liao, Arentze, and Timmersans, 2011), where real time information or advice regarding navigation is provided to the travelers, especially when the means may alter between the public and the private transportation mode to decrease the congestion problem. In this paper, a generic transport-network model has been proposed for these types of applications. The approach used in this paper (Ramachandran and Devi, 2011) is to identify any ten critical accident spots and then identifying nearest support locations or buildings in form of hospitals, ambulances, and police station. Then, the algorithm based upon genetic approach finds the optimal route between the accident spot to the hospital. In addition, as the more prone accident spots have been identified, so safety measures are devised to combat the occurrence of accidents (Daniker, 2011).

In (Logi and Ritchie, 2001), the objective was to develop a knowledge based system for making decisions regarding traffic control plans to be executed post congestion. For this, two algorithms, one for congestion analysis and another for selecting control plans was developed. In (Faghri and Hammad, 2002), use and application of GPS for traffic management was analyzed. In (Hernandez et al., 2002), the authors propose a multi-agent architecture for an intelligent way of handling the traffic.

It was found that the GPS data was could be aptly used for calculating the travel time and delay and was much efficient than the normal practices. (Peng, 1997) discussed an Automatic Transit Traveler information system which was GIS based. Optimal route was suggested to the travelers between their source and destination. Since, not all bus stops maybe functional or open all day and night, so route considers this aspect for providing route information about the active and functional bus-stops. (Kumar, Singh and Reddy, 1999) also suggest an advanced traveler information system (ATIS), which was also GIS based. This paper proposed and developed a system for the Hyderabad city, India, and traveler assistance basic facilities in the city. (Hasnat, Haque and Khan, 2006) developed an ATIS targeted system using web and wireless communication technologies. It works at 2 levels, web based and SMS based. While the Web-based provided aid to the user in form of map and text, the SMS based received queries from users and responded to them by calculating the travel time for the users. For traffic system (Messelodi et al., 2009) to work efficiently, gathering road traffic data is crucial. This would be collected in form of Floating car data, as it is normally known as. This data refers to the data which would be continuously collected from a fleet of cars and would help monitor the traffic congestion on roads. This could be useful for updating the driver about using an alternate route in case of traffic congestion detection. In this paper, the user emphasizes on how the data can be collected from nearby vehicles and their sensors for updating the relevant information. Several other related works have been reported in (Chen et al., 2010; He and Zhang, 2009; Kejun, Yong, & Xiangwu, 2008; Molina, 2005; Mulay, Dhekne, Bapat, Budukh, and Gadgil, 2013; Ossowskiet. al, 2005; Xie and Hoeft, 2012).

In (Mariagrazia, Pia and Carlo, 2003), the authors suggest a real time-based optimization model that addresses traffic control in the urban areas. They also include the pedestrians and their issues as part of the model. In (Wenjie, Lifeng, Zhanglong, and Shiliang, 2005), the authors calculate the travel time required by a vehicle from a particular point to an intersection point using sensors. In (Queen, 2008), current flows on road can be monitored by data provided by the CCTV cameras installed besides the roads. In (Sharma, 2011), the authors propose a distributed network of vehicular and wireless sensors for getting an insight to traffic situation and for lowering the congestion. In (Kafi, Challal, Djenouri, Bouabdallah, Khelladi, and Badache, 2012) it has been proposed that by establishing communication between emergency cars and traffic lights, the response time can be decreased. In (Zhou, Cao, Zeng and Wu, 2010), depending on the density of traffic, waiting time of the vehicles, etc. parameters can be used to determine the length of green light. This adaptive traffic light control algorithm can be used to increase the throughput. In (Sinhmar, 2012), based upon the density of traffic measured using the IR sensors, the traffic lights are updated. In (Hussain, Sharma, Sharma and Sharma, 2013), a system based upon micro-controller placed at each junction is used for determining the traffic flow and to manage the traffic in an efficient manner. In (Srivastava, Sachin, Prerna, Sharma and Tyagi, 2012) the weight sensors have been used to determine the number of vehicles on road, and then analysis is done using a programmable logic controller.

In (Gambardella, 2003) ant colony optimization is used for determining an optimized route for transportation. This optimized path would reduce the traffic on roads. In (Ozkurt and Omci, 2009), neural networks and its advantages have been used for analyzing the traffic density and to calculate an optimized route. In (Malik, Yi and Hongchi, 2007), wireless sensors installed besides the roads detect the traffic density in real-time basis for conveying the information to the control station. In (Blessy, Devi and LaxmiPriya, 2013), radars and sensors are used to measure the traffic on roads and then the GSM service sense this information to the remote server, which in turn informs the nearby signal junction and other drivers, thus forming a chain like network of information flow. The delays caused by red lights leading to traffic congestion has been captured by minimizing the time settings of the traffic lights in accordance with the density of traffic using a graph. Optimal solutions to such delays have been extensively covered in papers depending on the approach used. In (Dey Samanta, Yang, Chaudhri, and Das, 2013; Samanta, Acharjee, Mukherjee, Das, and Dey, 2013; Samanta, Chakraborty, Acharjee, Mukherjee, and Dey, 2013; Chakraborty, Pal, Dey, Das and Acharjee, 2014).

In (Azura and Lai, 2010), a fuzzy based traffic controller system has been proposed and simulated using MATLAB, which identifies the traffic light time so that flow of traffic is smoothened by ensuring a low waiting time and delay time. In (Emad, Kareem, Jantan, 2011), not only was the traffic monitored using the minimized traffic lights but the streets were analyzed to identify whether they are empty or crowded and this is done using the video cams installed on the roads. In (Plackzec, 2011), the focus of the paper is on optimizing the traffic signals by laying stress on the movement of the emergency vehicles/ priority vehicles and traffic density and using these parameters to prevent traffic congestion. In (Dakhole & Moon, 2014), an ARM based traffic control system was designed. In (Park, Rilett, and Spiegelman, 2008), the authors have suggested a Markov chain-based estimator for ITS. Several other papers in the recent past have been proposed related to intelligent transport systems and have extensively discussed several issues related to it. They are mentioned in (Yan, yang and Ukkusuri, 2019; Aslam, Cheng and Cheshire, 2019; Zhang, Li, Yang, Cui, Li, and Qiaoet, 2018; Yap, Cats and Arem, 2018; Liu and Cheng, 2018; File, Legara, Monterola, 2018; He, Agard, and Trepanier, 2018; Anda, Erath and Fourie, 2017; Ghaemi, Agard, Trépanier, and Nia, 2017; Benenson, Elia, Rofé, and Geyzersky, 2017; Jánošíková, Slavík, and Koháni, 2017).

WORKING OF INTELLIGENT TRANSPORTATION SYSTEMS

Intelligent transport system comprises of a Traffic Management Centre (TMC) as a vital unit. The transportation authority is responsible for technically administering it. This unit has to be well organized and work in efficiency for the ITS to perform its functions appropriately. The job is to first collect the data, then its proper analysis and then performing the necessary traffic control functions. These main steps of this unit are mentioned below:

Data collection: Data is the most important aspect of any modern technology usage. Precise, prompt, accurate, and extensive data generated on the roads or otherwise in form of sensors, GPS based vehicle locators, cameras, video recorders, etc., needs strategic planning. These hardware devices form the basis of the transport system. The type of data fetched is the traffic density in form of number of vehicles at a particular location, the status of the lights functioning, surveillance, travel time, location of the vehicles, delays etc. The servers stored at the centre are connected to these devices.

Data Transmission: Real-time, rapid and correct information first is transmitted from the site to the centre and then after processing needs to be sent back to the travelers for decision making depending on the situation of their location. This information could be in the form of messages flashed on the electronic message sign boards, SMS, internet, cellular connectivity, radio links and infra red links.

Data Analysis: The data can be analyzed properly only if pre-processing on the data has been performed. This pre-processing could consist of data cleaning, error rectification, and data synthesis. Special software can be used for the rectification, which is then pooled for further analysis, and then this collected data is analyzed using the analytical techniques for prediction, incident detection, traffic management, congestion control, traffic information and so on and so forth.

Traveler Information: Traveler information or advisory sends appropriate updates in real-time about the traffic conditions to the traveler. This helps the traveler to make correct decision regarding the journey undertaken or to be undertaken.

APPLICATIONS OF INTELLIGENT TRANSPORTATION SYSTEMS

The following is a complete list of the components/ application areas of Intelligent transport systems. These have been discussed in (Singh & Gupta, 2015; Qureshi & Abdullah, 2013).

Advanced Traveler Information System (ATIS)

It is an area which has found recognition since about twenty to thirty years. Though, it geared up more in the American and European sub-continent but has off-late also been focused upon in the Asian as well as the African continent. As was discussed in (Peng, 1997), a GIS based ATIS was proposed, wherein an optimal route from a dedicated source and destination was provided to the traveler which could be covered by the traveler by walking, transfer, waiting and in-vehicle time. In addition, several other works have been proposed that have used GIS and other support technologies like web-based and SMS based services. Since, GIS is spatial based so provide an accurate spatial analysis based upon the data whereas WWW based analysis provides a real-time analysis of incident occurrence. ATIS can be accessed either through mobile phones or through personal computers.

Thus, as we have seen from the discussion, ATIS provides information to the drivers about the real time traffic, the routes and travel updates, directions about navigation, information about any delays caused due to weather conditions, traffic congestion, road repairs, congestion caused due to accident and so on. The information can be provided to the drivers about not only the road on which they are travelling but also about the surrounding roadways, and thus enables them to an optimal route update, its selection and its use in navigation thus, making the availability of the information on several platforms, both in vehicle and out-vehicle. This real time information availability involves three key steps: its collection, its processing and then the dissemination where different technology usage in form of hardware, platforms and actors is entailed.

Some of the advanced ATIS help to make the parking easier (Chai et. al., 2019), which indicate the drivers about the vacant spaces in the cities and also enables them to make advance reserved parking online. A few where this deployment has geared up is Singapore, Stockholm, San Francisco and others.

Advanced Traffic Management System (ATMS)

Traffic management systems mainly comprises of congestion control and is the most important branch of ATMS. Several papers have been written related to this system which include (Logi and Ritchie, 2001; Faghri and Hamad, 2002; Hernandez, Ossowski, and Serrano, 2002) and others. These papers have suggested the use of type 2 fuzzy model, GPS, and artificial intelligence techniques for managing the traffic.

The main objectives of ATMS includes the technologies that can connect the sensors, roadside equipment, message sign (variable or dynamic), cameras, and several other devices that let us detect any roadside hazards, dangerous weather conditions, mis-happenings etc. It focusses on Traffic control devices like the intelligent signals, message sign boards, ramp metering that inform the user about the traffic or highway updates. Several traffic operation centers rely on information obtained from several sources. An intelligent and adaptive traffic signal timing would enable the traffic signals to detect the number of waiting vehicles or vice-versa info flow using short range communications, which would smoothen the traffic flow and help to reduce congestion. Ramp metering are the traffic signals on entrance ramps that are free-way and they break up vehicles that enter the free-way thus reducing the disruptions to traffic flow and thus makes merging of traffic easier.

Advanced Public Transport Management System (APTMS)

Advanced Public Transport Management system involves steps targeted to public transport. (Molina, 2005) proposed a knowledge-based system targeted for public transport. This architecture served three purposes: diagnosis, prediction and planning. It was applied to Torino city in Italy and Vitoria in Spain. (Feizhou, Feizhou, Xuejun, and Dongkai, 2008) applied Genetic Algorithm along-with its hybrid approach for performing an optimal scheduling of vehicles public in nature on the basis of the operational environment.

(Hatem and Habib, 2009) propose a method for managing public transportation system by integrating RFID and the WSN approach. Using the RFID antennas, and monitor sensors, and ultra-high frequency tag at the entry and exit gates of bus stations, the identification of the bus is sent to a central computer. The information gathered through these means is then displayed using the LED boards, and is available to the passengers. This information is useful for scheduling and for managing the bus service.

Thus, to summarize, Advanced Public Transportation Systems includes applications like electronic fare payment that allows users to perform advance booking of seats and pay online for seat reservation or otherwise, an automatic vehicle location that enables the vehicles on transit to update about their location, thus enabling the traffic managers to form a real view status of assets in the public transport system. Thus, it would consist of a smart tacking app available on smartphones that allow the passenger to have information about the public transport means timetable, its precise location and so on.

Emergency Management System (EMS)

A life-saving system, it targets those areas that deal with emergency like situation and the steps that can be initiated to manage the traffic. This would typically include applications that can provide optimal route guidance in case of emergency. The most prone danger zones can be identified and fire services can be provided based upon this information. In addition, GIS based accident rescue systems for free-ways can be established. The purpose would be to warn about an accident and then its rescue plans can be devised. Areas prone to accidents can be identified using sensors and then rectifications as per can be done to reduce its occurrence. A detailed database of emergency services along with their locations using GIS can be prepared and broadcasted. Based on this, routes, closest facility available etc. can be tracked too. An in-vehicle electronic call feature lets passengers notify a control center about an accident or an emergency. Such kind of call could comprise of information like the place of accident/ location, vehicle identification, time and other similar data. This call would not only carry the voice but also data associated with an emergency. In case of severity the call could be auto generated, sensed by the sensors or could be manual by the occupants of the car.

Automatic Road Enforcement

Automatic road enforcement system would consist of cameras and vehicle-monitoring devices which can be used to detect those vehicles (cars, buses, level crossing vehicles) and so on, which disobey traffic rules. Tickets could be generated which would be given to the vehicles. Applications include:

- Speed cameras which identify those vehicles that cross the prescribed speed limits. Radars could also be used this offence.
- Red-light cameras can be used to identify those vehicles that cross a red-light/ stop light. This is necessary for smooth functioning of the traffic and to inculcate a sense of behavioral ethics and self-discipline.
- Bus lane cameras can be used to identify those vehicles that travel in the designated bus lanes which disrupts the traffic flow.
- Level crossing cameras identify those vehicles that cross the trains at grade in an illegal manner.

Variable Speed Limits Monitoring

A few of the recent jurisdictions have started the experimentation with using variable speeds relaxation depending on the density of the traffic, surrounding factors, and others. These factors can lead to better traffic management. An extensive discussion on the same is done in (Ackaah, Bogenberger, and Bertini, 2019).

Dynamic Traffic Light Sequence

A dynamic traffic light sequence (Khalid, Khateeb, Jaiz, Johari, Wajdi, and Khateeb, 2008) can be used using the RFID approach. An efficient algorithm, database, and enabling technology can be applied for a multi-vehicle moving in multi-lane areas. This system is like emulating the job of a traffic police personnel deployed on the lanes or roads.

A summary of the above broad applications is summarized below in Table 1.

Table 1. Summary of applications of ITS

Category	Services and applications
1. Traveller Information	Real time information of traffic which would typically include Pre- trip and on-trip driver information, Route guidance and its navigation, personal information service, parking related information, and Weather information service.
2. Traffic management	Typically includes traffic control means, traffic planning, traffic regulations, adaptive traffic signal controlling, message sign boards which include the variable/ dynamic ones, Demand management, incident management and infrastructure management.
3. Public Transport Management	Smart public transport tracking system, an automated schedule on display, shared transport management system, on demand responsive system, location tracking, arrival and exit times of modes of public transport based on delays or other factors, re-routing of these means in case of road blockage, etc.
4. Vehicle management system	Vehicle pre-clearance, collision avoidance, automated vehicle detection and operations, vehicle fleet management, safety readiness,
5. Emergency management system	Incident detection, hazardous zones detection, emergency services available and their locations, optimal route requirement in case of an emergency, etc.
6. Transportation pricing system	Electronic toll collection, congestion pricing, variable parking fees, fee base hot lanes etc.

ENABLING TECHNOLOGIES OF ITS

There is a range of ICT technologies that can be used for the development and growth of ITS. Table 2 given below gives a summary of these. This information has been extensively discussed in (Qi, 2008; Jarašꞏnienꞏ 2007);

Table 2. Summary of enabling technologies of ITS

S.No.	Category	Technology used
1	Data acquisition	Traffic detectors sensors which typically include radar, Live-visual images captured using the CCTV cameras which help the traffic control rooms to monitor the traffic and smoothen the flow, Video images detectors, automatic incident detection using various types of sensors, and weather monitoring devices, Sensors Inductive Loops, Microwave (RADAR), Infrared Beams, LIDAR, Vision-based Sensors, Acoustic scanning Laser and many others. This data acquisition can be applied for vehicle probing and automatic vehicle detection.
2	Data storage and Data processing	Information gathered using the data acquisition sources is then stored at data management centres. This data now needs to be sent for processing, verification, and then to be consolidated that becomes useful for operators. This can be performed using data fusion process. Compact Disc, Magnetic storage, Media Magnetic stripe cards, hard disks and data cartridges, smart cards. Data dictionaries, data fusion, Automatic Incident Detection (AID) (for data processing), Global positioning system too can be used for processing of data.
3	Data distribution	Computers (Desktop and laptop), Telephones, fax machines, television, and variable message signs (VMS), cathode ray tubes and LCD's, car radios, cellular telephones, and hand-held digital devices. The data and processed information can be used to improve the environmental condition, and improve safety and achieve efficiency.
4	Information utilization	Ramp metering can be used for flow control of vehicles that merge onto an expressway.
5	Information distribution	For distribution of information, various means such as the dynamic Message sign boards, Variable message sign boards on the roads, kiosks, Internet, etc. means can be used. These are useful for Handsets and Personal Digital Assistants and for in-vehicle information.
6	Location referencing	Electro-magnetic compasses, laser sensors, GPS, and digital map databases and several display technologies.
7	Communications	Optical fibre networks, Co-axial cables, fixed microwave links, transponders, cell phone receivers and networks, wireless or wire-line communications, Fibre optics, etc. These can be used for signal pre-emption, e-toll collection, parking management, and in-vehicles traveller information and in-vehicle signing, commercial vehicle operations (CYO),s parking management, e-toll collection (ETC), and beacon-based route guidance systems.

ITS has several advantages to offer to the users using any means of transport. These are discussed in the next segment.

BENEFITS OF ITS

ITS has numerous benefits to offer. As pointed out in ("Local Authority," 2014), the local authorities are under pressure, nevertheless, they realize that only the ITS can solve problems like congestion, air quality, congestion, better transport provisions, access to the public transport system) and many more. ITS also has the potential to increase the productivity of any city and shall lead to job creation. In addition, a minor effect of Autonomous Adaptive Cruise Control (AACC) on throughput, speed, and travel time was estimated in (Vanderschuren, Katwijk and Schuurman, 2000). In (Werf, Shladover, Miller, and Kourjanskaia, 2002), an advanced and co-operative cruise control system has been suggested. Several research on ("Evaluation of," 2010; Thomas, 2001) points out benefits that have been summarized and mentioned below.

- Lesser traffic congestion as usage and stress on using public transport means shall increase.
- Environment friendly as would in no way impact land, noise, water, rather would provide eco-friendly solutions in terms of electric vehicles and eco-friendly fuel options like CNG Compressed Natural gas).
- Acts as the entry gate for more economic growth and business profits in terms of companies developing even more smarter phones, their applications and portals.
- Usage of public transport can be eased by providing information like status of public mode, its real time location tracking and booking of seat in advance.
- Wastage of fuel usage reduced by finding the optimal route between the source of travel and the destination.
- Reduce the number of stoppage points and help reduce delays at the intersection points.
- Provide speed control means and improve it.
- Inculcate self-discipline by identifying the offenders (traffic rule violators).

And the list is endless...... But, like a coin has two sides to it, similarly ITS too has some issues associated with it. The next section deals with the same and then proposes a few solutions for them.

ISSUES AND SOLUTIONS OF ITS

Whether the developed countries or the developing countries, barring a few, a common vision on the roads is the construction of highways, broader roads, electronic message- sign boards, high rises, tall concrete structures which have come up in a few years. Sensors and cameras all around us, regular monitoring the traffic details using the ICT. All the apps, and the infrastructure required for maintaining the Intelligent Transport systems comes with its own baggage of environmental threats. It fails to provide a healthy and a sound community life. So, would we be perceiving the Intelligent Transport systems in say next 20 years needs to be understood by analyzing the constraints of the system? So, should we call the intelligent transport system really "Intelligent"? Well, unless the relationship between the people's and goods mobility is established fully with the social mobility, and the social impact analysis of the transport infrastructure is done, we really can't call the system "Intelligent". Stress on "well-being" has to be laid to understand the repercussions of the ITS.

Though, the intelligent system have the responsibility of not only reducing the pollution and congestion and many other advantages, it should be designed to analyze the social impact and also consider the social consequences which might be serious in nature like an economic setback, poor health, environmental issues, deprivation, premature deaths and casualties. The intelligent transport system must not only work at an upper level in terms of enhancing the traveler's experience in form of smart apps and facilities but should also cater to providing convenience to the common travelers. This can be done by providing an economically sound environment to people to enable them to walk between their source and destination, provide a smart and intelligent solution to the local transport modes and associated facilities and above all an environment where convenience and safety would matter. Motorcyclists, pedestrians, and cyclists amongst other categories of travelers are the most prone to get injured by accidents. But even for other types of travelers, the risk of injury varies in complexity, severity, and varies according to the age, behavioral mode, personal habits, the mode of transport used, and the roads on which we travel, their conditions, the area and its geographical aspects the traveler is traversing through and several more of the likes.

A major constraint lies as on today. Maybe the future initiatives need to devise ways where transport companies develop cargos which could carry the bicycles at a cheap cost for such areas which are prone to accidents. Or, rather, have some smart devices as part of wearable ones, which could guide them about the unruly traffic which might be approaching from the wrong side, develop apps that can guide the pedestrians and the cyclists about the navigation routes along some of the safest and less polluted routes. None of the smart initiatives has discussed the issues related to those commuters who are not the car-owners. We foresee an irony in any of these steps. The intelligent systems and its related technologies which require a lot of investment, in terms of money at-least, sadly, does not consider those sections of the society who are economically weak. Though not in all cases, but generally walking or cycling is taken up due to economic constraints and very less as a choice. But, solutions, policies, documents, fail to consider them and their concerns.

So, it is sad that the modern transport infrastructure has not been designed to cater to the needs of those travelers who are living and working around an area, rather is being designed and developed for those who are passing through them. No initiative in any of the intelligent transport system components is dealing with one of the most challenging issue and aspect of the modern transport system. Policies and concrete steps need to be undertaken to an aspect which though sounds simple, yet is connected with life and death of any traveler. Travelling is not just for leisure, but also for performing social, economic and professional needs, rather simply put, for sustainability. In several parts of the world, it has been seen that several smart structures which are a part of smart cities have come up but have not been built keeping the interests of the pedestrians. For example, in Atlanta's Buford Highway, is a multi-lane road, having no pavements, no junctions, no pedestrian crossings, for a long distance. It is a smart infrastructure built for vehicular traffic and not for the people walking on it or passing through it. With no safe access to the pedestrians for this highway, with either an option to walk along or to cross, the only option remains is to risk their lives to achieve this.

How far these smart and intelligent transport systems can deal with the air quality improvement, vehicle emissions from particularly diesel vehicles, is a critical issue. A critical analysis and impact assessment of effect of the type of air we breathe, the environment we live in, the black smoke we inhale daily while commuting, and to add to that the introduction of several e-infrastructure becomes necessary. Several people of all ages are dying because of these factors, and we are sure that this is not the aim of smart cities. What about the corporate giants involved in designing smart technologies, the urban designers, the architects, the town planners, municipalities, and the likes who are using sophisticated technology to design and develop cities all around the world, to enable co-existence of good living, and an efficient travelling experience actually doing to critically understand these issues?

The need of the hour is to propose and develop a "sharing economy" based business models to enhance the commuter's travelling experience and emphasize on a local travel. Several such sustainable solutions related to the transport sector have been discussed in (Agarwal and Alam, 2018). Sharing economy (Rouse, 2013) refers to the economic and social systems that provide shared access to services, and goods. Generally, they make use of technologies like the smart phones, social media to create online peer to peer trading networks that can replace the traditional supply-chains. For example, Ebay trades second-hand commodities, Uber and Ola connects the passengers with the drivers. But a similar "sharing economy" model is missing in the Transport sector. Independently, many companies related to it are providing services to the commuters but a cost-effective, shared business model is yet to be proposed, adopted and implemented.

The future lies in capturing the essence of intelligent transport system usage in the realization of health benefits of walking, cycling, developing techniques to realize the role of traffic in decreased air quality and in its improvement. Another innovation of the current era is the self -driving car. Though, the advantages associated with it cannot be under-estimated, but the space they occupy on the road is the same as our traditional or even the modern cars. So, are they providing a means of congestion or mere convenience? They behave like human drivers do. Drive by choosing the best route, which we all do these days. They are able to recognize the distance between car-car to avoid collisions, and so on. But aren't these advantages restricted to an individual and depict selfish interests rather than societal interests?

Space forms an important aspect as on today when, large housing and corporate offices are coming up rapidly and that too on the "green land". These green pastures could be used effectively to inhale "pure air", to walk, to play, to exercise and relax. We need to realize the relation between space, transport and the total well-being to harness the best of advantages that the future intelligent system is supposed to provide to us. Henry Ford, the person who invented the first mass- produced automobile once said "If I had asked people what they wanted, they would have said faster horses."

An important part of "Intelligent Transport system" that is missing is the identification of stake-holders of this system, their views and opinions and developing smart technologies accordingly. These stake-holders include the developers, companies, town planners, architects, designers, and most importantly representatives using varied means of transport. Their issues need to be addressed. Their well-being needs to be considered. The smart technology should be smart in every aspect in the best possible way.

Energy, mobility, health, well-being should be collectively addressed. Thus, the major constraint of the current smart system is lack of respect for the cross- disciplinary insights into the needs of each and every-one of us who gets affected by wrong, incomplete policies, poor planning, political pressures, lack of good transit means, lack of smart local transportation, lack of sensitivity of right to breathe fresh air, and many more that have gripped the current "Intelligent Transportation System".

FUTURE OF ITS

Several predictions, estimations, management as well as control methods related to mobility and ITS, need to be performed in real time based upon the information gathered from the sensors. The present scenario related to ITS comes with a baggage of problems like variables possessing parametric relationships which are yet to be understood, huge volume of incomplete data, and several other constrains (Kickuchi, 2009) and goals which need a formal understanding and clarity.

Artificial intelligence (AI) has been recently adopted in developing a robust ITS. The reason for the same lies in the fact that AI possess the capability in knowledge building and can perceive and analyze the data collected from the sensors, and ease the process of achieving our goals (Russel and Norvig, 2009). These reasons have facilitated its adoption for ITS and mobility. The recent application of AI is in the use of machine learning algorithms, neural networks, Bayesian networks and the support vector machine. The recent development of deep learning techniques that make use of mapping between inputs and the outputs through multiple hidden layers, its processing and exhaustive training through the deep learning models has the potential to take the ITS to a new level in terms of its usage and utility. They can be best suited for addressing the transportation problems owing to the constraints listed above.

Deep learning brings the best results when the data is massive and through its deep techniques and models can be used to address the parametric relationships mentioned earlier. ANN's and SVM both can be adopted for incident detection (Shrinivasan, Sanyal and Sharma, 2007; Yuan and Cheu, 2003; Xiao and Lio, 2012), state forecasting as discussed in (Fu and Rillet, 2000; Ye, Szeto and Wong, 2012), for traffic control (Ghanim and Lebdeh, 2012) and for behavioural analysis (Chong, Abbas, Flintsch, and Higgs 2013).Similarly, SVM which deals with supervised models which analyze the input data and perform an accurate classification of scenarios, are capable of accident prediction (Sun and Sun, 2017; Ni, Huang and Zheng, 2015).

Several other problems that can be solved using SVM are mentioned in (Zhang and Liu, 2009; Zhang and Xe, 2008). Bayesian on the other hand, is not data driven solely, rather are statistical models which work upon the probabilities of the control variables. In the ITS context, Bayesian networks can be used to solve transportation problems listed in (Zhu, Qu and Jin, 2017; Li et. al., 2016) but are best suited for traffic forecasting (Castillo et. al, 2018; Zhu et. al., 2016) and for accident/ incident detection (Hossain and Muromachi, 2012; Gregoriades and Mouskos, 2008).

In future, ITS and ITS enabled technologies shall not work for individual vehicles, rather shall work for connected vehicle (Zhu and Ukkusuri, 2018) to vehicle set-up with the infrastructure. The vehicles shall communicate amongst themselves in the future. This would enhance the usage of ITS. But, this can be achieved only because of advancements in ICT and the sensing technologies. This also leads to the installation and usage of Vehicle automation and the communication systems (VACS) in vehicles. They can improve safety, convenience, comfort, emissions in these connected vehicles (Diakaki, 2015) and has its potential in achieving the traffic efficiency by maintaining traffic control (Zhu and Ukkusuri, 2015; Roncoli, Papageorgiou, and Papamichail, 2015; Roncoli, Papageorgiou, and Papamichail, 2015; Roncoli, Papageorgiou, and Papamichail, 2016). In near future, say in the coming decade, the major players on the road shall be both regular human-piloted vehicles (RHV's) (Levin and Boyles, 2016; Levin and Boyles, 2016; Stern et al.; Talebpour, and Mahmassani, 2016) and connected automated vehicles. Thus, both RHV's and CAV's shall soon share the road traffic with a positive impact in terms of reduced traffic, better traffic control and improved network performance. As discussed in (Diakaki, 2015), VAC'S shall create changes in the behavior of traffic flow by responding to adaptive and cooperative adaptive cruise control systems.

Pedestrian users on the road are the most vulnerable among the lot. Their safety is important. ITS has to contribute in some manner by developing methods to look into this. But the urban setup is quite complex owing to less reactive time by the drivers to respond to situations. So, the current efforts have to focus on the development of advanced driver assistance systems based pedestrian protection systems. Pedestrian safety can be improved by solving pedestrian and traffic collisions through vehicle to pedestrian communication technologies.

The initial modeling of improving traffic on the road or finding the best and the shortest route from the source to the destination, by suggesting the travelling salesman problem or the Prim's algorithm are gone. This technique was then substituted by the development of apps like the Google maps and using GPS for navigation. The future lies in using ICT, smart devices, and infrastructure, the transportation has been connected beyond just physical boundaries. Today it occupies space in the form of cyber, physical, human, and social aspect (Xiong, Zhu, Liu, Dong, Huang, Chen, Zhao, 2015). And it is with respect to these spaces that ITS occupies, lies its future. The data collected for analysis and prediction is not just the sensor generated data, rather it should also consider the public perceptions gathered from sources like the social networks to properly understand the status and performance of any city's transportation system. The data generated from these sources should be monitored and well managed in the future ITS. Natural language processing (NLP) algorithms can be effectively used to extract useful information and used effectively for accurate analysis. NLP should be able to detect social events and capture the sentiments in public comments which might help in detecting traffic issues (its extent and severity) and can be used for improving the problems based scenarios. Particularly, the comments are spatially and temporally based so can capture the problems accurately. In addition, cognitive computing models can be used to infer the network connectivity in future. Also, owing to the fact that RHV's and CAV's shall define the future traffic on roads, but the constraint that the characteristics of both differ from each other substantially, so a mixed flow environment of these vehicles has to be critically analyzed.

Well, a lot has been done, but a lot more constructive and effective steps are in store for "Intelligent Transport Systems". The future would also include controlling and managing the drones that are being predicted the future transport means.

CONCLUSION

We need to develop feasible, socially and environmentally sound solutions to harness the full potential of Intelligent Transport systems. The steps involved if carefully undertaken shall surely help to achieve sustainability and thus one of the 2030 sustainability goals can be met. The stakeholders are the programmers, the government, the policy makers, the passengers, civic and transport authority representatives who shall play a major role in this. The drivers too, if involved, have a pivotal role because assistance in the form of lane guidance, collision warning and alert monitors can help avoid accidents. Any new initiative should comprise of the body where representatives of each of the above stated stakeholders become a part. The sensitivity to the problems faced by each shall surely improve upon the way things are looked at and worked upon. The future lies in new innovations in this area which shall be ruled by electric vehicles, drones, eco-friendly fuel alternatives and more.

REFERENCES

Ackaah, W., Bogenberger, K., & Bertini, R. L. (2019). Empirical evaluation of real-time traffic information for in-vehicle navigation and the variable speed limit system. *Journal of Intelligent Transport Systems*, 23(5), 499–512. doi:10.1080/15472450.2018.1563864

Agarwal, P., & Alam, A. (2018). Use of ICT for Sustainable Transportation, in *Proceedings of International Conference on Future Environment and Energy*, 150(1), pp. 1-7.

Anda, C., Erath, A., & Fourie, P. J. (2017). Transport modelling in the age of big data. *International Journal of Urban Sciences*, 21(1), 19–42. doi:10.1080/12265934.2017.1281150

Aslam, N. S., Cheng, T., & Cheshire, J. (2019). A high-precision heuristic model to detect home and work locations from smart card data. *Geo-Spatial Information Science*, *22*(1), 1–11. doi:10.1080/1009 5020.2018.1545884

Azura, C. S., & Lai, G. R. (2010). MATLAB simulation of fuzzy traffic controller for multilane isolated intersection. *International Journal on Computer Science and Engineering*, *2*(4), 924–933.

Barbeau, S. J., Winters, P. L., Georggi, N. L., Labrador, M. A., & Perez, R. (2010). Travel assistance device: Utilizing global positioning system-enabled mobile phones to aid transit riders with special needs. *Intelligent Transport Systems*, *4*(1), 12–23. doi:10.1049/iet-its.2009.0028

Benenson, I., Elia, E. B., Rofé, E., & Geyzersky, D. (2017). The benefits of a high-resolution analysis of transit accessibility. *International Journal of Geographical Information Science*, *31*(2), 213–236. do i:10.1080/13658816.2016.1191637

Blessy, A., & Devi, H., R., & LaxmiPriya, C. (2013). An automatic traffic light management using vehicle sensor and GSM model. *International Journal of Scientific and Engineering Research*, *4*(6), 2354–2358.

Castillo, E., Menendez, J. M., & Cambronero, S. S. (2008). Predicting traffic flow using Bayesian networks. *Transportation Research Part B: Methodological*, *42*(5), 482–509. doi:10.1016/j.trb.2007.10.003

Chai, H., Ma, R., & Michael, H. (2019). Search for parking: A dynamic parking and route guidance system for efficient parking and traffic management. *Journal of Intelligent Transport Systems*, *23*(6), 541–556. doi:10.1080/15472450.2018.1488218

Chakraborty, S., Pal, A. K., Dey, N., Das, D., & Acharjee, S. (2014). Foliage Area Computation using Monarch Butterfly Algorithm. In *2014 International Conference on Non-Conventional Energy*, Kalyani, India: IEEE. 10.1109/ICONCE.2014.6808740

Chen, S., Chen, F., Liu, J., Wu, J., & Bienkiewicz, B. (2010). Mobile mapping technology of wind velocity data along highway for traffic safety evaluation. *Transportation Research Part C, Emerging Technologies*, *18*(4), 507–518. doi:10.1016/j.trc.2009.10.003

Chong, L., Abbas, M. M., Flintsch, A. M., & Higgs, B. (2013). A rule-based neural network approach to model driver naturalistic behavior in traffic. *Transportation Research Part C, Emerging Technologies*, *32*, 207–223. doi:10.1016/j.trc.2012.09.011

Dakhole, A. Y., & Moon, M. P. (2014). Design of intelligent traffic control system based on ARM. *The Journal of VLSI Signal Processing*, *4*(4), 37–40.

Daniker, V. M. (2009). Visualizing real time and archived traffic incident data. In *Proceedings of the 10th IEEE International Conference on Information Reuse and Integration*, 206–211, IEEE Press: Piscataway

Dey, N., Samanta, S., Yang, X. S., Chaudhri, S. S., & Das, A. (2013). Optimisation of scaling factors in electrocardiogram signal watermarking using cuckoo search. *International Journal of Bio-inspired Computation*, *5*(5), 315–326. doi:10.1504/IJBIC.2013.057193

Dia, H., & Thomas, K. (2011). Development and evaluation of arterial incident detection models using fusion of simulated probe vehicle and loop detector data. *Information Fusion*, *12*(1), 20–27. doi:10.1016/j. inffus.2010.01.001

Diakaki, C., Papageorgiou, M., Papamichail, I., & Nikolos, I. (2015). Overview and analysis of vehicle automation and communication systems from a motorway traffic management perspective. *Transportation Resource part A*, *75*, 147–165. doi:10.1016/j.tra.2015.03.015

Emad, I., Kareem, A., & Jantan, A. (2011). An intelligent traffic light monitor system using an adaptive associative memory. *International Journal of Information Processing and Management*, *2*(2), 23–39. doi:10.4156/ijipm.vol2.issue2.4

(2010). Evaluation of the public health impacts of traffic congestion: A health risk assessment, Harvard Center for Risk Analysis. *Environmental Health*, *9*(65). Retrieved from http://www.ehjournal.net/content/9/1/65

Faghri, A., & Hamad, K. (2002). Application of GPS in Traffic Management Systems. *GPS Solutions*, *5*(3), 52–60. doi:10.1007/PL00012899

Feizhou, Z., Xuejun, C., & Dongkai, Y. (2008). Intelligent Scheduling of Public Traffic Vehicles Based on a Hybrid Genetic Algorithm. *Tsinghua Science and Technology*, *13*(5), 625–631. doi:10.1016/S1007-0214(08)70103-2

Fille, E., Legara, T., & Monterola, C. P. (2018). Inferring passenger types from commuter eigentravel matrices. *Transportmetrica B. Transport Dynamics*, *6*(3), 230–250. doi:10.1080/21680566.2017.1291377

Fu, L. P., & Rilett, L. P. (2000). Estimation of time-dependent, stochastic route travel times using artificial neural networks. *Transportation Planning and Technology*, *24*(1), 25–48. doi:10.1080/03081060008717659

Gambardella, L. M. (2003). Ant colony optimization for ad-hoc networks. In *The first MICS workshop on routing for Mobile Ad-Hoc Networks*. Zurich, Switzerland.

Ghaemi, M. S., Agard, B., Trépanier, M., & Nia, V. P. (2017). A visual segmentation method for temporal smart card data. *Transportmetrica A: Transport Science*, *13*(5), 381–404. doi:10.1080/23249935.2016.1273273

Ghanim, M. N., & Lebdeh, G. A. (2015). Real-time dynamic transit signal priority optimization for coordinated traffic networks using genetic algorithms and artificial neural networks. *Journal of Intelligent Transport Systems*, *19*(4), 327–338. doi:10.1080/15472450.2014.936292

Gregoriades, A., & Mouskos, K. (2013). Black spots identification through a Bayesian networks quantification of accident risk index. *Transportation Research Part C, Emerging Technologies*, *28*, 28–43. doi:10.1016/j.trc.2012.12.008

Hasnat, M. A., Haque, M. M., & Khan, M. (2006). GIS Based Real Time Traveler Information System: An Efficient Approach to Minimize Travel Time Using Available Media. Retrieved from www.bracu.ac.bd

Hatem, B. A., & Habib, H. (2009). Bus Management System Using RFID In WSN, in the *proceedings of European and Mediterranean Conference on Information Systems*, Abu Dhabi, UAE. Academic Press.

He, L., Agard, B., & Trépanier, M. (2018). A classification of public transit users with smart card data based on time series distance metrics and a hierarchical clustering method. *Transportmetrica A: Transport Science*, 1–20.

He, Z., & Zhang, Q. (2009). Public Transport Dispatch and Decision Support System Based on Multi-Agent. *In the proceedings of Second International Conference on Intelligent Computation Technology and Automation*, Zhangjiajie, China.

Hernandez, J. Z., Ossowski, S., & Serrano, G. A. (2002). Multiagent Architectures for Intelligent Traffic Management Systems. *Transportation Research Part C, Emerging Technologies*, *10*(5-6), 473–506. doi:10.1016/S0968-090X(02)00032-3

Hickman, J., & Hanowski, R. J. (2011). Use of a video monitoring approach to reduce at-risk driving behaviors in commercial vehicle operations. *Transportation Research Part F: Traffic Psychology and Behaviour*, *14*(3), 189–198. doi:10.1016/j.trf.2010.11.010

Hossain, M., & Muromachi, Y. (2012). A Bayesian network based framework for real-time crash prediction on the basic freeway segments of urban expressways, *Accident Analysis and Prevention*, *45*, 373–381. PMID:22269521

Hussain, R., Sharma, S., Sharma, V., & Sharma, S. (2013). WSN applications: Automated intelligent traffic control system using sensors. *International Journal of Soft Computing and Engineering*, *3*(3), 77–81.

Jánošíková, L., Slavík, J., & Koháni, M. (2014). Estimation of a route choice model for urban public transport using smart card data. *Transportation Planning and Technology*, *37*(7), 638–648. doi:10.1080/03081060.2014.935570

Jarašūnienė, A. (2007). Research into Intelligent Transport systems: Technologies and efficiency. *Transport*, *22*(2), 61–67. doi:10.3846/16484142.2007.9638100

Kafi, A. M., Challal, Y., Djenouri, D., Bouabdallah, A., Khelladi, L., & Badache, N. (2012). A study of wireless sensor network architectures and projects for traffic light monitoring. In *Proceedings International Conference on Ambient Systems, Networks and Technologies*, 543–552. 10.1016/j.procs.2012.06.069

Keith, J. (2001). Video Demystified: a handbook for the digital engineering, 3rd edition. Eagle Rock, VA: LLH Technology Publishing.

Kejun, L., Yong, L., & Xiangwu, L. (2008). Emergency Accident Rescue System in Freeway Based on GIS, in the *proceedings of International Conference on Intelligent Computation Technology and Automation*. Academic Press.

Khalid, A. S., Khateeb, A., Jaiz, A. Y., Johari Wajdi, F., & Khateeb, A. (2008). Dynamic Traffic Light Sequence, Science Publications. *Journal of Computational Science*, *4*(7), 517–524. doi:10.3844/jcssp.2008.517.524

Kikuchi, S. (2009). Artificial intelligence in transportation analysis: Approaches, methods, and applications. *Transportation Research Part C, Emerging Technologies*, *17*(5), 455. doi:10.1016/j.trc.2009.04.002

Kumar, P., Singh, V., & Reddy, D. (1999). Advanced Traveler Information System for Hyderabad City. *IEEE Transactions on Intelligent Transportation Systems*, *6*(1), 26–37. doi:10.1109/TITS.2004.838179

Levin, M., & Boyles, S. (2016). A multiclass cell transmission model for shared human and autonomous vehicle roads. *Transportation Research*, *62*(part C), 103–106.

Levin, M., & Boyles, S. (2016). A cell transmission model for dynamic lane reversal with autonomous vehicles. *Transportation Research Part C, Emerging Technologies*, *68*, 126–143. doi:10.1016/j.trc.2016.03.007

Li, D., Miwa, T., & Morikawa, T. (2016). Modeling time-of-day car use behavior: A Bayesian network approach. *Transportation Research Part D, Transport and Environment*, *47*, 54–66. doi:10.1016/j.trd.2016.04.011

Liu, Y., & Cheng, T. (2018). Understanding public transit patterns with open geodemographics to facilitate public transport planning. *Transportmetrica A: Transport Science*, 1–28.

Local Authority Guide to Emerging Transport Technology, the Institution of Engineering and Technology and ITS (UK), 2014. Retrieved from http://www.its-uk.org

Logi, F., & Ritchie, S. G. (2001). Development and Evaluation of a Knowledge-Based System for Traffic Congestion Management and Control. *Transportation Research Part C, Emerging Technologies*, *9*(6), 433–459. doi:10.1016/S0968-090X(01)00002-X

Malik, T., Yi, S., & Hongchi, S. (2007). Adaptive traffic light control with wireless sensor networks. In *Proceedings of IEEE Consumer Communications and Networking Conference*, pp. 187–191, Las Vegas, NV: IEEE.

Mariagrazia, D., Pia, F. M., & Carlo, M. (2003). Real time traffic signal control: application to coordinated intersections. In IEEE International Conference on Systems, Man and Cybernetics, vol. 4, 3288-3295. Washington, DC: IEEE.

Messelodi, S., Modena, C. M., Zanin, M., De Natale, F. G. B., Granelli, F., Betterle, E., & Guarise, A. (2009). Intelligent extended floating car data collection. *Expert Systems with Applications*, *36*(3, Part 1), 4213–4227. doi:10.1016/j.eswa.2008.04.008

Molina, M. (2005). An Intelligent Assistant for Public Transport Management. In *Proceedings of International Conference on Intelligent Computing*, LNCS 3645, 199-208, Hefei, China: Springer.

Mulay, S. A., Dhekne, C. S., Bapat, R. M., Budukh, T. U., & Gadgil, S. D. (2013). Intelligent City Traffic Management and Public Transportation System. *International Journal of Computer Science Issues*, *10*(3), 46–50.

Ni, D., Huang, H., & Zheng, L. (2015). Support vector machine in crash prediction at the level of traffic analysis zones: Assessing the spatial proximity effects. *Accident; Analysis, and Prevention*, *82*, 192–198. doi:10.1016/j.aap.2015.05.018 PMID:26091769

Oakland, S., & Follower, R. (2003). *Statistical process control* (5th ed.). Cornwall, UK: MPG Books Limited.

Ossowski, S., Hernandez, J. Z., Belmonte, M. V., Fernandez, A., Garcıa-Serrano, A., Perez-de-la-Cruz, J., ... Triguero, F. (2005). Decision Support for Traffic Management Based on Organizational and Communicative Multiagent Abstractions. *Transportation Research Part C, Emerging Technologies*, *13*(4), 272–298. doi:10.1016/j.trc.2005.07.005

Ozkurt, C., & Camci, F. (2009). Automatic traffic density estimation and vehicle classification for traffic surveillance systems using neural network. *Mathematical and Computational Applications, 14*(3), 187–196. doi:10.3390/mca14030187

Pal, S., & Singh, V. (2011). GIS Based Transit Information System for Metropolitan Cities in India. In *Proceedings of Geospatial World Forum*, (pp. 18-21), Hyderabad, India.

Park, E. S., Rilett, L. R., & Spiegelman, C. H. (2008). A Markov Chain Monte Carlo-Based Origin Destination Matrix Estimator that is Robust to Imperfect Intelligent Transportation Systems Data. *Journal of Intelligent Transport Systems, 12*(3), 139–144. doi:10.1080/15472450802262364

Peng, Z. R. (1997). A Methodology for Design of a GIS-Based Automatic Transit Traveler Information System. *Computers, Environment, and Urban Systems, 21*(5), 359–372. doi:10.1016/S0198-9715(98)00006-4

Placzek, B. (2011). Performance evaluation of road traffic control using a fuzzy cellular model. In *6th International Conference on Hybrid Artificial Intelligence Systems*, (59-66), Wroclaw, Poland. 10.1007/978-3-642-21222-2_8

Qi, L. (2008). Research on intelligent transportation system technologies and applications. In Proceedings *Power Electronics and Intelligent Transportation System*. IEEE. doi:10.1109/PEITS.2008.124

Queen, C., M., & Albers, C. J. (2008). Forecasting traffic flows in road networks: a graphical dynamic model approach. 1-24.

Qureshi, K. N., & Abdullah, A. H. (2013). A Survey on Intelligent Transportation Systems. *Journal of Scientific Research, 15*(5), 629–642.

Ramachandran, N., & Devi, G. (2011). Accident Emergency Response and Routing Software (AERARS) Using Genetic Algorithm. *International Journal on Computer Science and Engineering, 3*(7), 2835–2845.

Roncoli, C., Papageorgiou, M., & Papamichail, I. (2015). Traffic flow optimization in presence of vehicle automation and communication systems — part I: A first-order multi-lane model for motorway traffic. *Transportation Research Part C, Emerging Technologies, 57*, 241–259. doi:10.1016/j.trc.2015.06.014

Roncoli, C., Papageorgiou, M., & Papamichail, I. (2015). Traffic flow optimization in presence of vehicle automation and communication systems – part II: Optimal control for multi-lane motorways. *Transportation Research Part C, Emerging Technologies, 57*, 260–275. doi:10.1016/j.trc.2015.05.011

Roncoli, C., Papamichail, I., & Papageorgiou, M. (2016). Hierarchical model predictive control for multilane motorways in presence of vehicle automation and communication systems. *Transportation Research Part C, Emerging Technologies, 62*, 117–132. doi:10.1016/j.trc.2015.11.008

Rouse, M. (2013). Sharing economy. Retrieved from https://searchcio.techtarget.com/definition/sharing-economy

Russell, S., & Norvig, P. (2009). *Artificial Intelligence: A Modern Approach* (3rd ed.). New Jersey: Prentice Hall.

Samanta, S., Acharjee, S., Mukherjee, A., Das, D., & Dey, D. (2013). Ant Weight Lifting Algorithm for Image Segmentation. In *Proceedings IEEE International Conference on Computational Intelligence and Computing Research*, Enathi, India: IEEE. 10.1109/ICCIC.2013.6724160

Samanta, S., Chakraborty, S., Acharjee, S., Mukherjee, A., & Dey, N. (2013). Solving 0/1 Knapsack Problem using Ant Weight Lifting Algorithm. In *Proceedings IEEE International Conference on Computational Intelligence and Computing Research*, Enathi, India: IEEE. 10.1109/ICCIC.2013.6724162

Sharma, A., Chaki, R., & Bhattacharya, U. (2011). Applications of wireless sensor network in Intelligent Traffic System: A review. In *Proceedings 3rd International Conference on Electronics, Computer Technology*, Kanyakumari, India: IEEE. 10.1109/ICECTECH.2011.5941955

Sherry, L. (2001). *Report on non-traditional traffic country methods* (p. 85748). Tucson, AZ: Tanque Verde Loop Rd.

Singh, B., & Gupta, A. (2015). Recent trends in intelligent transportation systems: A review. *Journal of Transport Literature*, 9(2), 30–34. doi:10.1590/2238-1031.jtl.v9n2a6

Sinhmar, P. A. (2012). Intelligent traffic light and density control using IR sensors and microcontroller. *International Journal of Advanced Technology & Engineering Research*, 2(2), 30–35.

Srinivasan, D., Sanyal, S., & Sharma, V. (2007). Freeway incident detection using hybrid fuzzy neural network. *IET Intelligent Transport Systems*, 1(4), 249–259. doi:10.1049/iet-its:20070003

Srivastava, M. D., Prerna Sachin, S., Sharma, S., & Tyagi, U. (2012). Smart traffic control system using PLC and SCADA. *International Journal of Innovative Research in Science Engineering and Technology*, 1(2), 169–172.

Stern, R. E., Cui, S., Monache, S. L., Bhadani, R., Bunting, M., Churchill, M., . . . Work, J. B. (2017). Dissipation of stop-and-go waves via control of autonomous vehicles: field experiments, [On-line]. Retrieved from https://arxiv.org/abs/1705.01693

Sun, J., & Sun, J. (2016). Real-time crash prediction on urban expressways: Identification of key variables and a hybrid support vector machine model. *IET Intelligent Transport Systems*, 10(5), 331–337. doi:10.1049/iet-its.2014.0288

Talebpour, A., & Mahmassani, H. S. (2016). Influence of connected and autonomous vehicles on traffic flow stability and throughput. *Transportation Research Part C, Emerging Technologies*, 71, 143–163. doi:10.1016/j.trc.2016.07.007

Thomas, D. (2001). Expanding Infrastructure: the ITS option, *20th South African Transport Conference*, Pretoria, South Africa.

Vanderschuren, M., van Katwijk, R., & Schuurman, H. (2000). Increase of the Highway Capacity without additional infrastructure. In *Proceedings of the Conference on Technology Transfer in Developing Countries, Automation in Infrastructure Creation*. Pretoria, South Africa.

Vanderschuren, M., van Katwijk, R., & Schuurman, H. (2000). Increasing the Highway Capacity without Additional Infrastructure. TNO Netherlands Organization for Applied Scientific Research and Transport Research Centre. Delft, The Netherlands.

Wenjie, C., Lifeng, C., Zhanglong, C., & Shiliang, T. (2005). A realtime dynamic traffic control system based on wireless sensor network, parallel processing. *In Proceedings International Conference on ICPP Workshops*, pp. 258–264.

Werf, J. V., Shladover, S. E., Miller, M. A., & Kourjanskaia, N. (2002). Evaluation of the Effects of Adaptive Cruise Control on Highway Traffic Flow Capacity. *Transportation Research Record: Journal of the Transportation Research Board, 1800*(1), 78–84. doi:10.3141/1800-10

Xiao, J., & Liu, Y. (2012). Traffic incident detection using multiple-kernel support vector machine. *Transportation Research Record: Journal of the Transportation Research Board, 2324*(1), 44–52. doi:10.3141/2324-06

Xie, G., & Hoeft, B. (2012). Freeway and Arterial System of Transportation Dashboard. *Transportation Research Record: Journal of the Transportation Research Board, 2271*(1), 45–56. doi:10.3141/2271-06

Xiong, G., Zhu, F., Liu, X., Dong, X., Huang, W., Chen, S., & Zhao, K. (2015). Cyber-physical social system in intelligent transportation, IEEE/CAA. *Journal of Automatica Sinica, 2*(3), 320–333.

Yan, F., Yang, C., & Ukkusuri, S. (2019). Alighting stop determination using two-step algorithms in bus transit systems. *Transportmetrica A: Transport Science, 15*(2), 1522–1542. doi:10.1080/23249935 .2019.1615578

Yap, M., Cats, O., & Arem, B. V. (2018). Crowding valuation in urban tram and bus transportation based on smart card data. *Transportmetrica A: Transport Science*, 1–20.

Ye, Q., Szeto, W., & Wong, S. C. (2012). Short-term traffic speed forecasting based on data recorded at irregular intervals. *IEEE Transactions on Intelligent Transportation Systems, 13*(4), 1727–1737. doi:10.1109/TITS.2012.2203122

Yuan, F., & Cheu, R. L. (2003). Incident detection using support vector machines. *Transportation Research Part C, Emerging Technologies, 11*(3–4), 309–328. doi:10.1016/S0968-090X(03)00020-2

Zhang, J., Liao, F., Arentze, T., & Timmersans, H. (2011). A multimodal transport network model for advanced traveler information systems. *Procedia: Social and Behavioral Sciences, 20*, 313–322. doi:10.1016/j.sbspro.2011.08.037

Zhang, T., Li, Y., Yang, H., Cui, C., Li, J., & Qiao, Q. (2018). Identifying primary public transit corridors using multi-source big transit data. *International Journal of Geographical Information Science*, 1–25. doi:10.1080/13658816.2018.1554812

Zhang, Y., & Liu, Y. (2009). Traffic forecasting using least squares support vector machines. *Transportmetrica, 5*(3), 193–213. doi:10.1080/18128600902823216

Zhang, Y., & Xe, Y. (2008). Travel mode choice modeling with support vector machines. *Transportation Research Record: Journal of the Transportation Research Board, 2076*(1), 141–150. doi:10.3141/2076-16

Zhou, B., Cao, J., Zeng, X., & Wu, H. (2010). Adaptive traffic light control in wireless sensor network-based intelligent transportation MATLAB. In *Vehicular Technology Conference Fall* (pp. 1–5). IEEE.

Zhou, M., Qu, X., & Jin, S. (2017). On the impact of cooperative autonomous vehicles in improving freeway merging: A modified intelligent driver model-based approach. *IEEE Transactions on Intelligent Transportation Systems*, *18*(6), 1422–1428.

Zhu, F., & Ukkusuri, S. (2015). A linear programming formulation for autonomous intersection control within a dynamic traffic assignment and connected vehicle environment. *Transportation Research*, *55*(Part C), 363–378.

Zhu, F., & Ukkusuri, S. (2018). Modeling the proactive driving behavior of connected vehicles: A cell-based simulation approach. *Computer-Aided Civil and Infrastructure Engineering*, *33*(4), 262–281. doi:10.1111/mice.12289

Zhu, X. Y., Yuan, Y. F., Hu, X. B., Chiu, Y., & Ma, Y. L. (2017). A Bayesian network model for contextual versus non-contextual driving behavior assessment. *Transportation Research Part C, Emerging Technologies*, *81*, 172–187. doi:10.1016/j.trc.2017.05.015

Zhu, Z., Peng, B., Xiong, C. F., & Zhang, L. (2016). Short-term traffic flow prediction with linear conditional Gaussian Bayesian network. *Journal of Advanced Transportation*, *50*(6), 1111–1123. doi:10.1002/atr.1392

Chapter 5
Novel Congestion Control Model for Maintaining Quality of Service in MANET

Mamoon Rashid

School of Computer Science and Engineering, Lovely Professional University, Jalandhar, India

Aabid Rashid

School of Electronics and Communication Engineering, Shri Mata Vaishno Devi University, Katra, India

Sachin Kumar Gupta

School of Electronics and Communication Engineering, Shri Mata Vaishno Devi University, Katra, India

ABSTRACT

This chapter is related to quality of service in the network. The congestion is the factor which affects quality of service in the network. The AODV is the routing protocol used to establish path from source to destination. To maintain quality of the service, novel approach is proposed. The technique of back propagation is proposed in this work for the congestion avoidance in the network. The back propagation algorithm calculates changes of congestion on each node in network. The node with the least chances of congestion is selected for path establish from source to destination. The proposed approach is implemented in network simulator version 2 and results are analyzed in terms of throughput, packet-loss, delay, and load. It is analyzed that network throughput is increased, packet-loss, delay, and load is reduced in the proposed methodology as compared to state-of-art.

DOI: 10.4018/978-1-7998-2570-8.ch005

INTRODUCTION TO MOBILE AD HOC NETWORKS

In the last few years, the demand for mobile computing has been increased to a very large extent because of the enlargement of economical and effortlessly obtainable wireless equipment's. Therefore, in the present scenario, a number of investigators have made several researches in the area of ad hoc networks. Inside MANETs, the nodes present in the wireless range of one another interact in a direct manner (Soundararajan et al. 2012). The nodes depend on one another in order to transmit information amid nodes existing beyond the broadcasting range and this result in the generation of multi-hop situations. Different nodes provide aid in the transmission of data packets form source to target.The MANET is generated according to the prerequisite of the customer and it does not require any kind of accessible framework or different types of permanent stations inside it (Tang et al 2002). The MANET can be described as an independent arrangement of mobile hosts (MHs) which uses wireless connections for links. The network produced in MANET is in the structure of a random communication table utilized for numerous functions. A single hop cellular network system in which base stations exists and uses wireless communication for the information transmission is totally dissimilar from these kinds of systems. These networks consists wired arrangements and set base stations in order to provide communication amid two movable sensor nodes. These networks are described as infrastructure less kind of networks. As nodes can move freely anywhere in the system, therefore an unpredictable alteration occurs in the topology of these kind of networks. The ad hoc networks are peer-to-peer multi-hop mobile wireless networks. These networks use store-and-forwards method for the transmission of information packets with the help of intermediary nodes. The information about the alteration of network topology should be provided to other nodes. According to the movement of mobile hosts, this information is restructured or detached.

Figure 1 depicts that it is not possible for all mobile hosts to be present within the coverage area or range of one another. In a case when entire mobile hosts are nearer and exist within the radio range, then problems related to routing do not occur. In any case, absurd quantity of energy should be provided in genuine conditions for the completion of connectedness. The attention should be given to different other problems such as battery life span and dimensional readopting present in this kind of network. The existence of symmetric and asymmetric associations is one more kind of issue existing within these kinds of networks. Several protocols consider symmetric associations in conjunction with the associative radio range. The MH3 and MH1 lie within the radio range of one another as described by the figure. In these networks, symmetric types of interaction associations exist. This supposition is made applicable although it is not achievable as the execution of routing is extremely difficult in asymmetric systems. Since the breakdown of these associations is very much probable, therefore the identification of such paths is possible which prevents the occurrence of asymmetric associations. For the whole mobile hosts, equal amount of abilities and duties occur inside the symmetric associations. The issue of symmetric and asymmetric associations is one of the most important issues present inside the MANETS. The other main concern of MANETs is the existence of different mobility prototypes of dissimilar nodes. The movement factor of some mobile hosts is large which other nodes are motionless. The mobility and order of mobility of a mobile host cannot be forecasted easily (***Lochert et al 2007***). The MANETs are extremely decumbent towards intrusions and untrustworthy as well because of their altering nature. The adopted routing method is leading branch of any network. Every node should cooperate with other nodes too in conjunction with its individual appropriate performance. The MANET can experience different kinds of safety intrusions or attacks. Therefore, the identification of a safe and reliable continuous route is necessary for MANETs.

Figure 1. Overview of MANET

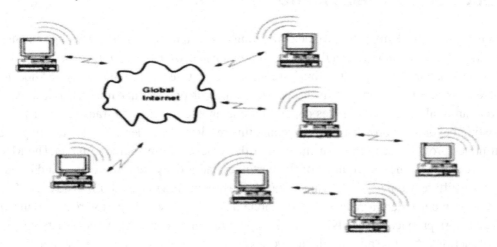

Types of MANET's

The different kinds of MANETs are:

Vehicular Ad hoc Network (VANET): The idea of MANET was used for the designing of Vehicular ad hoc networks. This network presents an effectual interaction in order to provide communication with the roadside components (Venkatasubramanian et al. 2010).

Internet Based Mobile Ad hoc Networks (IMANET): Different kinds of internet protocols such as TCP/UDP and IP are sustained in this kind of wireless ad hoc arrangement. Internet Based Mobile Ad hoc Network uses a network-layer routing protocol for the generation of paths in automatic manner. These paths are generated for the linkage of movable nodes.

Intelligent Vehicular Ad hoc Networks (INVANET): Artificial intelligence is utilized in highly accidental prone areas for getting a control over the unanticipated proceedings such as connection vehicle collision and catastrophes.

Flying Ad hoc Network (FANET): The flying ad hoc networks implanted in altered inflight vehicles are utilized for the gathering of information from distant regions with the help of movement and connectedness features.

Characteristics and Features of MANETs

The ad hoc networks comprise quality properties which creates difference amid them and wired networks. Different kinds of pioneering manners are used for the implementation of network performance. Several significant features of MANETs are described below:

Wireless Medium: These networks involve time-anecdotal exposure and an asymmetric transmission property which makes the communication possible amid different nodes through a wireless mean. This arrangement is less trustworthy and extremely decumbent towards attacks than wired arrangements.

Dynamic Topologies: The nodes are free to move randomly in this kind of network at different velocities. Therefore, an arbitrary and erratic alteration in the network topology occurs at different time periods.

Infrastructure less Network: As these networks are infrastructure less kind of networks, therefore these networks perform all operations autonomously (Chen, K et al. 2004).

Power Management: Since stationary nodes do not exist in these networks, therefore batteries are provided in the form of power sources. During the creation of systems and protocols for these kinds of networks, the power control should be the major area of attention.

Peer-to-Peer Nature: This arrangement does not comprise stationary nodes which are allocated with several predefined services. Thus the protocols should be redesigned and these stout networks should manage the dispersed dynamic topologies for the disseminated situations which involve peers. For the controlling of different properties, the novel methods should be generated different from the methods utilized in wired systems. This will result in the proper functioning of the network. IEEE 802.11 is the frequently implemented standard used for the wireless arrangements largely inside the physical and data-link layer of the networks.

Limited Computing and Energy Resources: As the ability of battery is not as much along with the little dimension, heaviness and price of the tool, thus the calculating memory of power and given disk dimension are restricted as well.

Limited Service Coverage: The service execution for wireless equipments is extremely difficult as compared to the wired networks due to the obtainable tools, the remoteness amid two mechanisms and the restrictions of network situations (Belkadi, M et al. 2010). As a result, MANETs face numerous restraints.

Higher Interference Results in Lower Reliability: The infrared signals face obstruction from the sunshine and warmth sources. A number of substances and resources are present which can provide protection or soak up these obstructions. But this situation is not faced by radio signals as they cannot be obstructed. Though, the electrical equipment's can deduce them. The communication may be of broadcast character while whole equipment's are possibly interfering with one another. Multipath leads to self-interference as well.

Highly Variable Network Conditions: Hindrance results in the origin of superior information loss rates. The mobility of consumer causes recurrent extrication. An alteration is seen in the channel during the movement of consumers. The established energy can be reduced according to the remoteness (S. F. 2010).

Limited Bandwidth: The wireless links are less capable in comparison with the infrastructure-based networks. Additionally, as compared to the utmost broadcasting rate of radio waves, the throughput of wireless infrastructures is fewer in case of manifold access, noise, desertion and intrusion.

Architecture of MANET

The MANET architecture is divided into three major branches of Enabling Technologies, Networking and Middleware & Application and is shown in Figure 2.

Figure 2 Layered Architecture of MANET

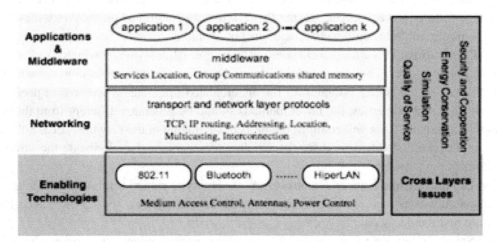

1. **Enabling Technologies:** The enabling technologies are classified according to their exposure range. This classification is described as:

    BAN (Body Area Network): The genuine coverage area of Body Area Network is around 1 meter. This network provides connectedness amid wearable processing equipment's (Dukkipati, N et al. 2005).

    PAN (Personal Area Network): The Personal Area Network provides a coverage area of approximately 10 meters. This network provides connectedness amid the movable and fixed equipment's.

    WLAN (Wireless Local Area Network): The coverage area of Wireless Local Area Network lies within the range of 100 to 500 meters. This kind of coverage range can be used to connect single building or a cluster of buildings.

2. **Networking:** The primary processes of the majority of networking protocols present inside the MANET should be redesigned for the generation of self-arranging, vibrant, unbalanced and end to-end interaction. The attainability of one-hop broadcasting assistance is the major aim of networking protocols. Therefore, peer-to-peer trustworthy aids are produced within these networks from source to target. The recognition of recipient inside the system is imperative for the repetition of peer-to-peer interaction. The location service maps the recipient position in a vibrant way in order to give the location in the network.

3. **Middleware & Application:** In the exploitation of ad hoc techniques, various wireless mechanisms have been determined. The ad hoc networking functionalities are utilized in several situations like during urgent situations, tragedy resurgence and for the atmosphere observation as well. The individuality of MANET is utilized in different private applications such as PAN, business applications, learning applications and rule administration processes. As the middleware is totally relied on the applications required for the handling of desired services, thus it does not remain present in the mobile ad hoc infrastructure schemes.

Applications of MANET

The operation of MANETs is reasonably simple because these networks do not require any infrastructure for interaction. These networks are installed frequently primarily in the military applications and crisis survival applications. Though, these networks are in great demand because of their features. But at the same time, these networks require more growth inside a number of business functions. Several areas in which MANETs have been utilized are given below:

Military Services: The military services are one of the most frequently identified areas in which MANETs have been utilized. In these areas a permanent infrastructure or framework cannot be provided because of which these networks can be installed easily. The MANETs can make communication possible within extremely fewer time periods in such areas. The movable nodes act as army in these kinds of networks. Therefore, the network is connected in a case when soldiers or nodes are moving around. The mobile ad hoc networks provide this type of aid for link (Zhai, H et al. 2005). Some other military applications include the synchronization of the military plans and the soldiers inside the battleground. For example, if a message is mandatory to be conveyed by the army head to its soldiers, the accessibility of safe and trustworthy routing protocol can provide aid for this.

Emergency Services: The crisis services are necessarily essential during the occurrence of natural tragedies while whole interaction framework is in confusion. In this condition, speedy restoration of communication is imperative. These networks are capable for the generation of framework within some weeks.

Education: The MANETs are also installed in learning organizations as well either for the creation of implicit classrooms or providing aid in summits or lectures with the help of ad hoc infrastructure provided to the consumers included.

Sensing and Gaming: The sensor network is a particular kind of ad hoc network in which mobility of nodes is not an issue. Though, the main issue is the battery energy present inside the sensors. In a sensor network, every sensor comprises a transceiver, a minute micro-controller and an energy resource entrenched inside all sensors. These sensors relay the data from other equipment's for the transmission of information to a middle observer. The sensors are generally organized in regions in order to sense the important data from the nearby regions. These sensors generate an ad hoc network in order to gather the essential data. In order to analyze the behavior of patients inside the hospitals or meetings, climate conditions for forecasting cyclones, the sensors existing inside them can move freely in different areas (Lochin et al. 2010).

Personal Area Networking: For the exchange of information data amid each other, the Personal Area Network (PAN) is produced. In this network, numerous equipment's like laptops, cellular phones etc. are connected for the generation of a network. Though, the area of coverage is extremely minute in these kinds of networks. This kind of application can be utilized for providing ad hoc messaging in different areas.

BACKGROUND

Yefa Mai et.al (2018) proposed a new scheme named cognition control AODV which is used to manage the proposed routing conditions. The table entry will significantly increases the package delivery rate when the package drop rate will be reduced and the implementation causes package overhead. Large numbers of simulations were conducted on the NS3 simulator. These experiments and simulations compares the results between the AODV and the proposed CCAODV based five different parameters. Yadav et al. (2016) presented a survey on the existing congestion techniques. The nodes present in MANET having dual behavior and they behave as a routers as well as computing devices. It has limited bandwidth and its changing topology leads to the problem of congestion in MANETs. The detection of congestion is quite difficult in wireless networks due to several reasons behind the packet drop. Khan, M et al. (2016) designed a new algorithm by making use of combination of Ad-hoc on Demand Distance Vector (AODV) and Cross layer design approach. This approach is also known as Congestion Control AODV (CCAODV). This avoids the links break within the MANET and the received signal strength is used as cross layer design parameter. This protocol creates the strong and stable route by using signal strength of node. Rathore et al. (2016) proposed an ACO based multipath congestion control approach in which depending upon the load in dynamic networks; the queue can be varied. Although, an alternative path is provided by AOMDV for balancing load in the networks, it cannot be applied in all the scenarios. For transmitting the data, multiple paths are provided by AOMDV. Soelistijanto et.al (2014) presented that for supporting the functionalities of MANETs, different versions of TCP have been proposed. Within the opportunistic networks, these versions are however, not much effective due to which different approaches are needed here. Courcoubetis et al. (2017) stated that a basic issue related to the minimization of background traffic was present during the scheming of congestion or jamming handling protocols. This effect helped in the attainment of standard throughput in the specified time but this showed least impact on small TCP flooding. Kumar, H et al. (2014) provided a brief review of mobile ad hoc networks. In these networks, nodes were deployed in random manner. These networks did not comprise any centralized manager because of which nodes could leave or join the network according to their wish. Congestion was the most imperative constraint which occurred due to the unavailability of network reserves.

NOVEL CONGESTION CONTROL SCHEME

A mobile ad-hoc network is the network which comprises movable nodes. These nodes are circulated in random fashion. These networks do not have any centralized control. These networks are also named as infrastructure less kind of networks because of the motion of nodes. In this study, the network is created in a totally dissimilar way. Within these networks, no framework remains present and the operating cost of these networks is extremely valid. In this network, IEEE 802.11 Wi-Fi protocol is utilized to provide the interrelated amenities of low level ad hoc network. These networks can function either independently or along with the larger networks for providing links. A client can make it feasible for the other client to be linked anywhere in the whole world. These networks can be organized for different applications such as debacle management and military applications. In these networks, devices can be linked with each other at any place during any time period without the need of any permanent framework. The network topology of mobile ad-hoc networks can be altered at all time without requiring any centralized control because of their dynamic nature. Because of their infrastructure less arrangement, the entire nodes in the network are dispersed in random manner within the network. The nodes of the network use the similar arbitrary access wireless tunnel through which this network employs itself in the multi hop forwarding. The movable nodes in the network act like routers for information transferring. In this network, no permanent infrastructure remains available for the nodes that is infrastructure of the nodes keep on changing with the passage of time. Therefore, this network needs routing protocols for the transferring of information packets. The data routing-protocols choose the optimal route from base station to target. The routing protocols which do not collect network data for the formation of route are identified as proactive routing-protocols. The topology tables are preserved on every node in the network for the routing of information. The entire routing data is upheld within the routing tables. This routing table is upgraded with the alteration of network topology. Different routing protocols have been formed under this class through the use of link state routing. There routing information is amended within each routing table in various routing protocols. These routing protocols maintain several tables. This kind of protocols do not perform well in the big and extremely dynamic networks as whole network requires amendment after the departure of some node from the network. This procedure increases the utilization of bandwidth which results in the increased overhead within the routing table. Several issues identical to quality of service occur within the mobile ad-hoc network because of the altering nature of network routing. In these networks, overcrowding occurs when information forwarding rate is higher in comparison with the information receiving rate. In this study, the approach of neural networks is presented for the avoidance of overcrowding within the network. The neural network approach computes the fault on every node and node having minimum fault is chosen for information sending. The back propagation algorithm is trained from the earlier practice and provides novel standards. The back propagation algorithm utilizes input node number and their buffer volume. It will compute the real value of the overcrowding on a meticulous node.

x=n w=n

$$\text{Actual Value} = å \ xnwn + bais \tag{1}$$

x=0 w=0

The real value of overcrowding is computed through equation number 1. The fault is computed by the subtraction of desired value from the real value

$$\text{Error} = \text{Desired Value} - \text{Real Value} \tag{2}$$

The movable node having minimum fault is chosen as the most appropriate node for the route formation. Advancement is presented in the AODV routing protocol for the prevention of overcrowding within MANET. The nodes having slightest fault, least amount of hop count, and highest sequence number are utilized by the AODV routing protocol for the establishment of path. The step by step procedure used in this work is shown in Figure 3.

EXPERIMENTAL RESULTS AND DISCUSSION

This investigative study is relied on the prevention of congestion within mobile ad hoc networks. The neural networks are utilized for the improvement of AODV routing protocols. The performance of presented AODV protocol is compared with the obtainable AODV routing protocol for the formation of route. The simulation factors are described in Table 1.

The network is organized with various movable nodes as demonstrated by the Figure 4. The source and target nodes are described for information sending.

Figure 3. Step procedure of novel congestion scheme

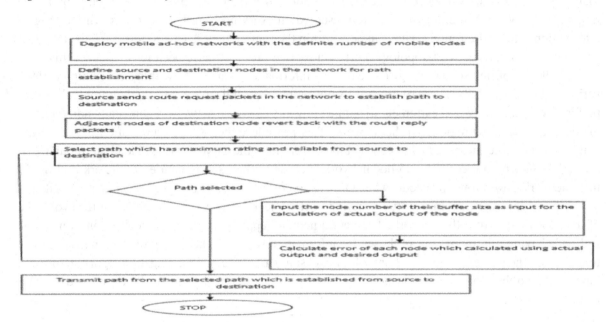

Table 1. Simulation parameters

Parameters	Values
Propagation Model	Two Ray
Antenna Type	Omi directional
Number of Nodes	28
Queues	Priority Queue
Area	800*800 meters
Standard	802.11

Figure 4. Network deployment with movable nodes

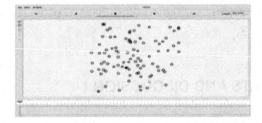

The information sharing nodes are determined within the network as illustrated in Figure 5. These nodes are named as source and destination nodes. At this instant, the source node floods the route request massage in the network for the creation of route amid source and target or destination node.

Figure 5. Path establishment process

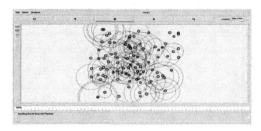

The nodes which send route request messages will respond back with the reply messages as depicted by the Figure 6. The most suitable routes are discovered. With the help of these routes, the source nodes receives message.

Figure 6. Acknowledgment of request messages

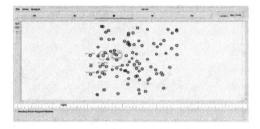

The source node gets reply back messages from different nodes present in the network as depicted by the Figure 7. The routing algorithm chooses the finest route amid source and destination or target node in terms of minimum hop count and highest sequence number.

Figure 7. Establishment of optimal path

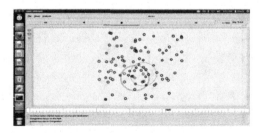

The source node starts the transmission of information towards the destination via the finest route as described by the Figure 8. The overcrowding occurs in the chosen route because of the high rate of information transportation within the network and this results in packet loss.

Figure 8. Congestion in the selected path

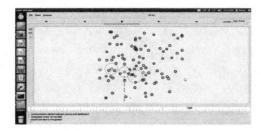

The neural network approach is implemented within the network as depicted by the Figure 9. This approach computes fault on every node. The node having highest rating is selected as the most suitable node for data forwarding.

Figure 9. Application of proposed technique for network congestion

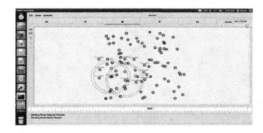

The neural network approach is implemented in the network for the assortment of nodes having minimum probabilities of overcrowding as described by the Figure 10. The chosen finest route is revealed with the help of red color and it comprises minimum congestion probabilities.

Figure 10. Selection of congestion free path

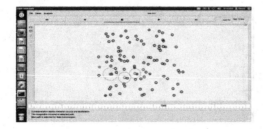

A comparison amid proposed technique and existing AODV protocol is performed on the basis of packet loss within the network as demonstrated by the Figure 11. The above figure describes the packet loss of proposed method. The amount of nodes involved is denoted on x-axis while amount of packets are represented on the y-axis.

Figure 11. Packet loss comparison of proposed technique and AODV

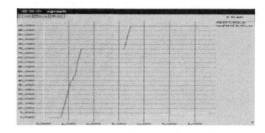

The proposed and accessible protocols are compared on the basis of network throughput as shown in Figure 12. In the presented method, neural networks are utilized along with AODV protocol which decreases the probabilities of congestion because of which network throughput is improved at a stable rate.

Figure 12. Throughput comparison of proposed technique and AODV

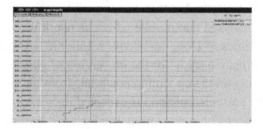

The end to end delay of the presented and accessible algorithm is compared for the performance scrutiny as demonstrated by the Figure 13. It is scrutinized that the delay of the presented algorithm is smaller than the accessible algorithm.

Figure 13. Average end to end delay comparison

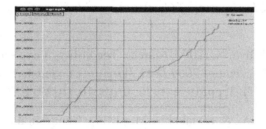

The network load of existing and proposed is compared for the performance analysis in Figure 14. It is analyzed that load of the existing technique is high as compared to proposed technique.

Figure 14. Network load comparison of proposed technique and AODV

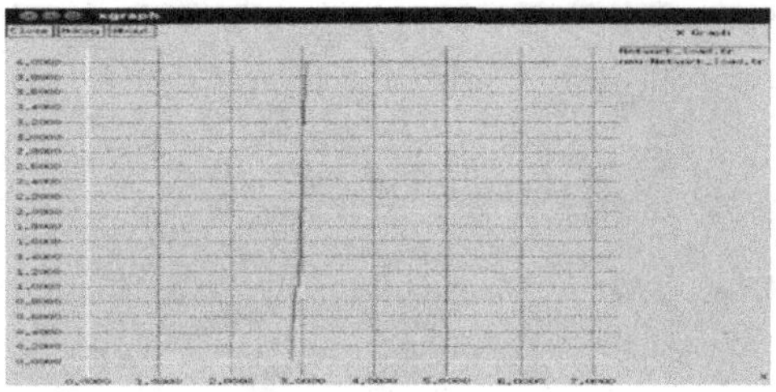

CONCLUSION

The reactive routing protocols do not utilize the pre-defined information of network for the formation of route. The route request messages are sent by the source node for the formation of route towards destination. The nodes having necessary data will reply back to the messages. In order to choose the finest route from one point to other point, several parameters are determined. The performance of these kinds of routing protocols is relatively higher than the proactive routing protocols by means of some of parameters. In this study, it is analyzed that mobile ad-hoc network is a decentralized kind of network because of which high probabilities of clogging occurs within the network. The neural network technique is presented in this investigative study for the prevention of congestion within the network. The back propagation approach computes the upcoming potentials from the existing data for the prevention of clogging or congestion. The presented method is executed in Network Simulator 2. The simulation outcomes demonstrate an enhancement in network throughput and lessening in packet loss.

REFERENCES

Alam, F. (2011). Node Feed-Back Based Tcp Scheme For Mobile Ad-Hoc Network. *Computer Science & Telecommunications, 31*(2).

Belkadi, M., Lalam, M., M'zoughi, A., Tamani, N., Daoui, M., & Aoudjit, R. (2010). Intelligent routing and flow control in manets. *CIT. Journal of Computing and Information Technology, 18*(3), 233–243. doi:10.2498/cit.1001470

Chen, K., Nahrstedt, K., & Vaidya, N. (2004, March). The utility of explicit rate-based flow control in mobile ad hoc networks. In *Proceedings 2004 IEEE Wireless Communications and Networking Conference (IEEE Cat. No. 04TH8733)*, 3, pp. 1921-1926. IEEE. 10.1109/WCNC.2004.1311847

Courcoubetis, C. A., Dimakis, A., & Kanakakis, M. (2017). Congestion Control for Background Data Transfers with Minimal Delay Impact. *IEEE/ACM Transactions on Networking, 25*(5), 2743–2758. doi:10.1109/TNET.2017.2710879

Dukkipati, N., Kobayashi, M., Zhang-Shen, R., & McKeown, N. (2005, June). Processor sharing flows in the internet. In *Proceedings International Workshop on Quality of Service* (pp. 271-285). Berlin, Germany: Springer.

Khan, M. (2016, December). Cross layer design approach for congestion control in MANETs. In *Proceedings 2016 IEEE International Conference on Advances in Electronics, Communication and Computer Technology (ICAECCT)* (pp. 464-468). IEEE. 10.1109/ICAECCT.2016.7942633

Kumar, H., & Singh, P. (2014, February). TCP congestion control with delay minimization in MANET. In *Proceedings International Conference on Information Communication and Embedded Systems (ICICES2014)* (pp. 1-6). IEEE. 10.1109/ICICES.2014.7033929

Lochert, C., Scheuermann, B., & Mauve, M. (2007). A Survey on Congestion Control for Mobile Ad-Hoc Networks Wiley. *Wireless Communications and Mobile Computing, 7*(5), 655–676. doi:10.1002/wcm.524

Lochin, E., Jourjon, G., Ardon, S., & Sénac, P. (2010). Promoting the use of reliable rate-based transport protocols: the Chameleon protocol.

Mai, Y., Rodriguez, F. M., & Wang, N. (2018, January). CC-ADOV: An effective multiple paths congestion control AODV. In *Proceedings 2018 IEEE 8th Annual Computing and Communication Workshop and Conference (CCWC)* (pp. 1000-1004). IEEE.

Rahman, K. C., & Hasan, S. F. (2010). Explicit rate-based congestion control for multimedia streaming over mobile ad hoc networks. *International Journal of Electrical & Computer Sciences IJECS-IJENS, 10*(4), 28–40.

Rathore, S., & Khan, M. R. (2016, November). Enhance congestion control multipath routing with ANT optimization in Mobile ad hoc Network. In *Proceedings 2016 International Conference on ICT in Business Industry & Government (ICTBIG)* (pp. 1-7). IEEE. 10.1109/ICTBIG.2016.7892721

Soelistijanto, B., & Howarth, M. P. (2013). Transfer reliability and congestion control strategies in opportunistic networks: A survey. *IEEE Communications Surveys and Tutorials, 16*(1), 538–555. doi:10.1109/SURV.2013.052213.00088

Soundararajan, S., & Bhuvaneswaran, R. S. (2012, May). Multipath load balancing & rate-based congestion control for mobile ad hoc networks (MANET). In *Proceedings 2012 Second International Conference on Digital Information and Communication Technology and its Applications (DICTAP)* (pp. 30-35). IEEE. 10.1109/DICTAP.2012.6215393

Tang, K., Obraczka, K., Lee, S. J., & Gerla, M. (2002, July). Congestion controlled adaptive lightweight multicast in wireless mobile ad hoc networks. In *Proceedings ISCC 2002 Seventh International Symposium on Computers and Communications* (pp. 967-972). IEEE. 10.1109/ISCC.2002.1021789

Venkatasubramanian, S., & Gopalan, N. P. (2010). A Quality of service architecture for resource provisioning and rate control in mobile ad hoc networks. International Journal of Ad hoc [IJASUC]. *Sensor & Ubiquitous Computing, 1*(3), 106–120. doi:10.5121/ijasuc.2010.1309

Yadav, S., & Singh, D. (2016, March). A survey on congestion control mechanism in multi-hop wireless network. In *Proceedings 2016 3rd International Conference on Computing for Sustainable Global Development (INDIACom)* (pp. 683-688). IEEE.

Zhai, H., Chen, X., & Fang, Y. (2005, March). Rate-based transport control for mobile ad hoc networks. In *Proceedings IEEE Wireless Communications and Networking Conference, 4*, (pp. 2264-2269). IEEE.

Chapter 6
Open Threads–Enabled Mesh Networks in Vehicles for Real-Time Traffic Monitoring

Parul Choudhary
Teerthanker Mahaveer University, India & Bharati Vidyapeeth's Institute of Computer Applications and Management, New Delhi, India

Rakesh kumar Dwivedi
Teerthanker Mahaveer University, Moradabad, India

Umang Singh
Institute of Technology and Science, Ghaziabad, India

ABSTRACT

The exponential increase of traffic on roads has led to numerous disastrous consequences. These issues demand an adaptive solution that ensures road safety and decreases the traffic congestion on roads. New paradigms such as Cloud computing and internet of things are aiding in achievement of the inter-communication among the vehicles on road. VANETs are designed to provide effective and efficient communication systems to develop innovative solutions but are restricted due to mobility constraints. This chapter proposes an IP-based novel framework composed of open threads integrated with VANETs exchanging information to create a mesh network among vehicles. This novel Open Threads-based infrastructure can help in achieving a more economical, efficient, safer, and sustainable world of transportation which is safer and greener. This chapter also discusses and compares various thread-enabled microcontrollers by different vendors that can be utilized to create a mesh network.

DOI: 10.4018/978-1-7998-2570-8.ch006

INTRODUCTION

In current global scenario, traffic management demands utmost efficiency to manage the ever-expanding number of vehicles on roads along with their maneuvering. This exponential increase in population has resulted in an alarming rise in the number of on-road vehicles leading to disastrous human, environmental and economical consequences (Fussler, Schnaufer, Transier, & Effelsberg, 2007). According to (Priyanka & Dhonde, 2017), it is expected that the worldwide count of on-road vehicles, both passenger and commercial, shall cross 2 billion by 2035. This huge number of vehicles shall lead to many grave consequences like heavy traffic congestion, air pollution, high fuel consumption and consequent economic issues, to name a few (Zeadally, Hunt, Irwin, & Hassan, 2010). This shall also result in alarming rise in the number of road accidents. According to World Health Organization (Anand, 2013), more than 1.3 million people die out of road accidents annually. Increased road congestion is also resulting in wastage of crucial human wasted by people behind the wheel.

All above issues demand a feasible, economic solution to control several transport-related problems and their consequences. The solution must enable mechanisms to improve on-road safety as well as security of both vehicles as well as passengers. One plausible solution could be to build streets and highways with much higher capacities to accommodate the increased count of vehicles and thus reduce traffic congestions. However, due to certain space limitations on the expansion of roads, this solution proves to be costly and building of new infrastructure is time taking. A better alternative would be utilization of existing infrastructures in a smart and efficient manner. This could be done by utilizing the current capacity of streets and highways optimally to reduce congestion and thus, ensure better traffic management.

In order to combat the issues and improve the efficiency, safety and security of the transportation system, intelligent mechanism need to be designed (Nellore & Hancke, 2016). Optimal traffic control and management has been the primary subject of researchers for a long time for the design, development and deployment of cost-efficient solutions (Engineering, 2015). Significant changes are expected to be seen in the transportation system in the near future. The fulfilment of the ever-increasing requirements of vehicles and passengers can be done with the help of new paradigms like Cloud Computing, Internet of Things, etc. (Rizwan, Suresh, & Rajasekhara Babu, 2017). These advancements in computing technologies have led to the innovation of devices capable of wireless communication and having processors embedded in them. The devices offer virtual intelligence via a new concept of Internet of Things (IoT) thus, ensuring a safe and manageable environment (Yu, Sun, & Cheng, 2012).

VANETs have been the prime topic of research for over a decade in both academia and industry. VANETs facilitate wireless communication between on-road vehicles and other vehicles or with other roadside infrastructures. This communication is achieved by forming a dynamic ad-hoc network in which vehicles present at the current instant on road act as nodes. On-road vehicles communicate through their On-Board Units (OBUs) to broadcast their data to all the connected vehicles' OBUs as well as to RoadSide Units (RSUs) embedded in other equipment on road (Elumalai, Murukanantham, & Technology, n.d.). The information is exchanged continuously between vehicles and fixed base stations across roads via these units. In case, a direct data exchange is not possible between an OBU and an RSU, the information is relayed to other vehicles using a multi hop transmission strategy till it reaches its destination RSU.

Several additions to VANETs have been proposed over the years such as inter-vehicular, vehicular-Internet, vehicular-personal devices (Ho, Leung, Polak, & Mangharam, 2007). Each of the variant tries to handle some of the issues faced by VANETs including those of limited processing capacity. It is difficult for VANETs to efficiently evaluate the large amounts of information gained from continuously moving dynamic vehicles. By enhancing the VANET communication system using robust units and IP based connectivity to the Internet, we can improve their processing capacity to a great extent (Indra & Murali, 2014). In this context, the concept of vehicular ad-hoc networks is evolving with mesh networks through open threads. It is an industry-wide IPv6 protocol suite for IoT, based on IEEE 802.15.4-2006 radio and the IETF RFC 6LoWPAN standard (Sailhan et al., 2007).

This manuscript is further divided as follows: Section I introduces the issues and possible solutions for traffic congestion. Section II elaborates on the mitigation of traffic congestion using VANETs as a tool to manage traffic congestion. Section III focuses on the need for open threads with VANETs. Section IV highlights the framework required to create mesh network using open thread in VANET enabled vehicles. Section V concludes the study by laying down the future challenges to be worked upon for the implementation of the novel Open Threads based framework.

VANETs TO MANGE TRAFFIC CONGESTION

VANETs are being widely applied for providing solutions for the severe traffic issues due to heavy number of vehicles on road (Umang & Choudhary, 2018). Proper traffic management shall curb the repercussions of prolonged traffic congestion on road. This section has been divided into two parts. The first subsection discusses the issues and possible solutions for traffic congestion. The second subsection focuses on mitigation of traffic congestion using advanced technologies.

Traffic Congestion

Heavy traffic congestion is a resultant of the rise in world's population and thus, a huge increase in the number of vehicles (Parul & Umang, 2015). With this flaring count of vehicles streaming on the existent limited capacity streets and highways, the issue of traffic congestion is bound to occur on such a vast level. A great amount of money is spent by the Government's to curb the issue of congestions as well as meet the increase in demand of fuel (Nidhi & Lobiyal, 2012). This exponential rise in traffic congestion on roads has also given a step up to several environmental issues at the global level including air pollution, heavy fuel consumption and expenditure. Global warming has these escalating vehicle numbers as one of its prime contributors. The Carbon dioxide (CO_2) emissions by the vehicles have also maximized in proportion to their count (Kshirsagar & Sutar, 2015).

Researchers have been proposing solutions that could help maintain a proportion between the speed of vehicles and their fuel consumption rate along with balancing the CO_2 emissions to save the environment. Several curves have also been designed over the decades depicting the same (Mohamed, 2013). It has been observed, that for any vehicle, the amount of CO_2 emissions rises as well as its fuel consumption rate gets higher during the times when the speed of the vehicle is lower than the average travelling speed i.e. £ 40 km/hr when there are lot of stops in between the driving. The frequent engine idling during a journey also pays a contribution for the same. Furthermore, it showed that any vehicle's CO_2 and Greenhouse gases emissions can be alleviated by providing smoother trips on road which includes fewer stop and go points as well as smaller stopping times. All of these outcomes can be achieved by lowering the amount of traffic congestions during a vehicle's journey (Geroliminis, Karlaftis, & Skabardonis, 2009).

One possible solution could be to build new streets and highways with much higher capacity in order to accommodate the booming vehicle count. However, the expansion of roads come with certain limitations on the space availability as well as the excruciating time and cost investment. Additionally, research on ŏnding alternative efŏcient fuels demands much higher time and effort for it to become a reality. A much more economical and efficient solution is provided through advanced paradigms of Intelligent Transportation System (ITS), Internet of Things (IoT) and Vehicle ad hoc Network (VANET). Processor-embedded devices working with wireless technologies to offer a safe and manageable environment works as a new concept of Internet of Things and VANETs (Aliyu et al., 2018). These approaches along with their advantages and disadvantages are discussed in next subsection.

Advanced technologies

A Vehicular Adhoc Networks (VANETs) is a subclass of Wireless Ad hoc Networks (WANETs) or Mobile Adhoc Networks (MANETs), aimed to form an on-road communication system for interaction among vehicles acting as nodes(Alam, Saini, Ahmed, & El Saddik, 2014). The communication system is engineered to work in two modes:

Vehicle-to-Vehicle (V2V)

In V2V mode, a vehicle's OBU is used to exchange information with another vehicle's OBU. This is an OBU to OBU interaction.

Vehicle-to-Infrastructure(V2I)

In V2I mode, a vehicle's OBU communicates with the RSU of any roadside infrastructure. The information may have been relayed from several V2V exchanges to finally reach the RSU.

The communication system is supported by the Federal Communication Commission (FCC) which has allocated frequencies for the wireless communications. In order to provide DSRC for communication in VANETs, IEEE has worked on the Wireless Access in Vehicular Environments (WAVE) standard, or IEEE 802.11p. DSRC is a communication service at a frequency range from 5.850 to 5.925GHz operating in public and private safety.

In a VANET, an Ad hoc network is formed with a wide communication range. Every vehicle within the transmission range acts as a node, and can serve for the role of a sender, a receiver or a network router dynamically (Karnadi, Mo, & Lan, 2007). Despite of no dependency on any fixed network infrastructure, in order to enhance the inter-vehicle communication of VANETs, few base stations at the roadside are provided to act as the fixed nodes in the networks i.e. RSUs. VANETs work as a self-organizing network with each node relaying the information to other OBUs and RSUs. OBUs are also attached with GPS systems to fetch the accurate position of vehicles on-road. These locations are often the requirement for several protocols and applications based on VANETs (Tonguz, Wisitpongphan, Bai, Mudalige, & Sadekar, 2007).

Communications within the network for effective operations is done through exchange of two types of messages:

Cooperative Awareness Messages

These messages are exchanged between the nodes in order to get acquainted with the current state of their neighboring nodes in terms of their presence, geographical position and movements. These messages are broadcasted periodically on the control channel so as to receiveup to date status. Service announcements are also communicated to/from the nodes. These types of messages are also known as BeaconsA.

Event-Driven Emergency Messages

These messages are transmitted from a node to its neighboring nodes during times of an emergency. These are used make the nodes aware about any abnormality with the normal routine. They can also be used to alert the nodes of any dangerous situation detected by the network.

Another system known as, Intelligent Transportation System (ITS) has emerged to combat the issue of traffic congestion(Taleb et al., 2007). ITS incorporates the network-based information such as vehicular networks and wireless sensor network, as well as the electronic technologies such as sensors and cameras with transportation technologies to design a solution.

NEED FOR OPEN THREADS WITH VANETS

VANETs form an ad-hoc network with on road vehicles acting as mobile nodes that are connected to and disconnected from the network based on their position and the joining network's coverage range. However, a vehicular ad hoc network is considered to be a restricted network suffering from mobility constraints(Alba, Luna, & Toutouh, 2008). These constraints are affected by the number of connected node vehicles and are triggered due to heavy traffic congestions, obstructing buildings with tall size along with bad conduct by drivers. All these factors affect the processing capability of VANETs thus, taking a toll on their performance(Lèbre, Mouël, Ménard, Dillschneider, & Denis, 2014). Furthermore, the incapacity of VANETs to analyze and process the global information collated from all the nodes of a network serve as another limitation. Nonetheless, VANETs are best fitted to be used for short term applications. VANETs are also well suited for collision prevention or road hazard control notifications services and other small-scale services(Raw, Kumar, & Singh, 2013).

Contrarily, the networking of vehicles and their proper management in terms of road conditions, level of traffic congestion, pollution levels along with safety services for vehicles are the technological visions incorporated by mesh network through open threads. A global network of vehicles in cities offering multiple services to the connected vehicles and associated humans can be developed using open threads.

An IP-based infrastructure can be composed of open threads integrated with VANETs exchanging information. This infrastructure can help in achieving a more economical, efficient, safer and sustainable world of transportation which is safer and greener. The current market holds a hatful of 802.15.4 network technologies that can serve in the implementation of mesh networks. However, they pose severe problems such as negligible usability, incapability to work with IPv6 communications, requirements for high power, single point of failure, to name a few. All these reasons stood in the way of mesh networks with open threads becoming a success (Rzepecki, Iwanecki, & Ryba, 2018).

Furthermore, all the above-mentioned reasons also triggered the development of another innovative networking technology called Thread. Threads were aimed for low power and secure 802.15.4wireless mesh networks. Moreover, with the help of Thread, a node is allowed to join the best-fitmesh network from the neighboring networks and network managers are permitted to allot a node to a speciðc mesh without disturbing the application's regular workflow (Sailhan et al., 2007).

Thread General Characteristics

The support for IPV6 addresses along with bridging to other IP networks at a low cost is provided by the Thread Stack (Unwala, Taqvi, & Lu, 2018). The stack also provides optimization for low-powered or battery-packed operations and wireless communication between devices. Other general characteristics of Thread are as follows:

1. **Easy Installation Setup and Operation:** The Thread Stack is capable of supporting numerous network topologies. Installation process is simple and can be easily done by using either a smartphone, a tablet or a computer. Authorization for joining the network is achieved by the use of product installation codes. Forming or joining a network follows simple protocols that make the systems be able to self-configure and be capable to solve any routing issue that may occur.

2. **Secure:** Unauthorized devices are not allowed to join the network. Furthermore, all types of communications are encrypted and secure. Network layer security is provided and can be extended to Application layer. Advanced Encryption Standard (AES) encryption scheme is used along with latest authentication schemes used in the smartphone-era for encryption of all Thread networks. This provides a much stronger security as compared to other wireless standards evaluated by the Thread Group.

3. **Optimal for Small as Well as Large Home Networks:** Optimization of network operation on the basis of the expected use is kept in mind while designing the Network layer, for it to work on home networks with size of numerous to hundreds of devices.

4. **Scalable:** A single Thread network falls short to handle all the system, application and network requirements at the time of large commercial installations. For this, the Thread Domain Model facilitates scalability of up to tens of thousands of thread devices in a single deployment by using a combination of different connectivity technologies such as Thread, Ethernet, Wi-fi and thus, the ability to manage larger commercial installations.

5. **Extended Range:** Usually, the range provided by devices is just enough to cover a normal home. This range can be further extended up to a significant point with the use of designs with power amplifiers and these are readily available. More immunity against interference is achieved by using distributed spread spectrum at the Physical Layer (PHY). The range can further be extended to a much greater extent so as to cover several mesh subnets. For this, a backbone is provided by the Thread Domain model to let multiple Thread networks communicate with each other. This type of communication and range is required during large commercial installations.

6. **No Single Point of Failure:** All operations are secured and have reliability even in case of failures or loss of individual devices. The Thread Stack is responsible for such fault tolerance and reliability.

7. **Low Power Consumption:** Under normal battery conditions, devices are capable to provide a rich user experience using efficient communication. Because of their low power consumption, the devices can survive and operate efficiently for several years on AA type batteries using suitable duty cycles.

8.   **Cost-Effective:** Multiple vendors are giving chipsets which are well-suited with software stacks and economically priced for huge deployment. These are designed to give very low power too.

A TYPICAL THREAD NETWORK

9.   Border Router

Border Router is responsible for connecting the Thread network to Internet and to other neighboring networks. Commissioning and management of routers also come under the duties of border router.

10.   Router

Router has the task of joining of the network to other networks. The routing of information within the network also come under the responsibilities of router.It also provides security services in the network.

11.   Router Enabled End Devices (REED)

Router Enables End Devices (REED) refer to those end devices which are not routers but can upgrade to one if required by the network.

12.   Sleepy end devices

Sleepy end devices cannot communicate directly with other devices. The communication path for these end devices is only through their parent router.
Figure 1 shows a typical thread network with border router (BR), Router (R) and end devices (E).

THREAD DOMAINS

The Thread Domain Model facilitates for multiple Thread Networks to integrate with each other seamlessly. It also provides a smooth interface to all the non-Threaded IPv6 networks. Furthermore, the Thread Domain model has its major benefit by making devices flexible enough to join and be a part of any Thread Network which is available and has been configured with a common Thread Domain. Thus, at times of network size or data volume being scaled up, the use of Thread Domain Model resulted in severe minimization of all manual reconfigurations and further reduction in the need for manual network planning which usually incurred heavy costs.

Figure 1. Thread network

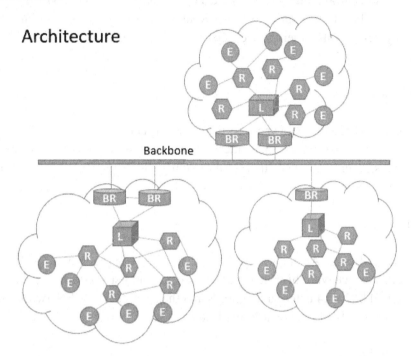

THREAD ROLES OVERVIEW

The type and configuration of a Thread network join process are used to determine the role portrayed by the participant devices of a Thread network. Thread Commissioning is another name for a Thread network join process. The following section describes the various types of roles that can be played by the Thread devices in a network.

1.   Joiner

The Joiner is the device which does not possess network credentials and thus, human administrator is required to add it to a commissioned Thread Network. This role cannot be combined with another role in one device and requires the intervention by a Thread interface in order to operate.

2.   Joiner Router

The Joiner Router is a device which is one radio hop away from the Joiner. It may be an existing Thread router or a Router-Eligible End Device (REED) i.e. an end device which is not a router but can upgrade to one if required. Unlike Joiner, the role of Joiner Router allows the portraying device to be combined in any device with other roles except the Joiner role. Joiner Router also requires a Thread interface to perform.

3.   Leader

The Leader acts as a central arbiter of network conðguration state. It is the only distinguished device in any Thread Network Partition. Similar to Joiner Router, the role of Leader also allows the device to be combined in any device with other roles except the Joiner role. The Leader also requires a Thread interface to perform.

4.   On-mesh Commissioner

The role of an On-mesh Commissioner comes to play during certain collapsed cases and is a combined role wherein the Commissioner has a 15.4i interface and possesses the Thread Network Credentials. An On-mesh Commissioner is always both a Commissioner and its own Border Agent. Furthermore, it may also be a JoinerRouter.

5.   Native Border Agent

The role of a Native Border Agent portrayed by a device serving the role of Border Agent for a Native Commissioner. A device with this role needs to have only an IEEE 802.15.4 radio with it to bridge between the unsecured 802.15.4 external neighbors and the secured Thread Network. Also, the role of a Native Border Agent can be served by a Joiner Router.

6.   Native Commissioner

The role of a Native Commissioner is given to either a Commissioner or a candidate Commissioner that possesses the interface same as the one used by the mesh. This same interface would be an IEEE 802.15.4 radio, in the case of Thread. But, as compared to an On-mesh Commissioner, the Thread Network credentials are not possessed by a Native Commissioner.

THREAD STACK

Thread can be defined as an open networking standard based on IP and designed to function for connected home appliances. It is based on the IEEE 802.15.4 MAC and physical layer operating at 250 kbps in the 2.4 GHz band. A simple protocol is used by a Thread for forming of the network along with its joining and its maintenance are simple. Figure 2 shows the layers of Thread stack(Gonzalez, Gonzalez, & Ferré, n.d.).

IEEE 802.15.4

The physical layer and Media Access Control (MAC) layer of the Open System Interconnect(OSI) model are defined by IEEE 802.15.4 standard. Various data rates are offered by the standard including250kb/s,40kb/sand 20 kb/s. Star, mesh and peer-to-peer operations are the major operations for which the standard is being used. Good data transfer reliability is assured because of the used protocol being a full handshake. Furthermore, the standard facilitates low power consumption and provides support for low

Figure 2. Thread stack

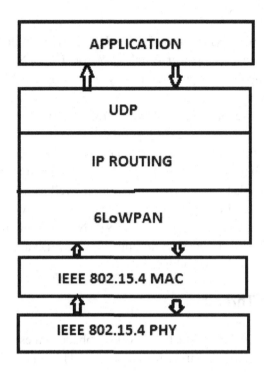

latency devices. The standard functions at several frequencies including the one in 2.4 GHz ISM band with 16 channels, in 915MHz ISM band with 10 channels and in European868MHzbandwith1channel.

Each layer is assigned different responsibilities which are described in the following subsection.

1.   Physical layer

The physical layer is responsible for packet transmission and reception over the physical medium. The distribution of packets is done with the activation and deactivation of radio trans-receiver. The strength or quality of a received packet is calculated by performing Link Quality Indication in the physical layer. It is implemented using energy detection (ED), SNR or a combination of both. Clear channel assessment is done using techniques such as energy detection above ED threshold, Carrier Sense only and carrier sense with energy above threshold.

2.   Network layer

To estimate the received power within the bandwidth of a channel, a technique called Receiver energy detection is used. Channel selection is performed by the network layer using this technique.

3.   MAC layer

The responsibilities of the MAC layer in 802.15.4 standard are contention management of data, error correction, channel acquisition and addressing.

6LoWPAN

A simple network facilitating wireless connectivity for devices with limited power that conform to the IEEE 802.15.4 standard is called a Low power Wireless Personal Area Network (LoWPAN). LoWPAN is a low-cost network. The computational power, memory and energy availability is limited in the devices getting connected to the network.

An adaptation between IP layer and 802.15.4 MAC layer is served by incorporatingIPv6 over Low-power Wireless Personal Area Networks (6LoWPAN) layer.

Fragmentation of packets occurs when moving from IP layer to 802.15.4 MAC layer. The fragmented packets are then reassembled into IPv6 format during the reverse passing from 802.15.4 MAC layer to IP layer. Low powered devices that are mostly battery run as well as have a low bandwidth and small packet size requirement are a good fit for 6LoWPAN. The physical layer has a maximum size of 127 bytes. Star and Mesh topologies are supported by 6LoWPAN. Furthermore, 6LoWPAN offers numerous data rates including 250 kbps for 2.4 GHz, 40 kbps for 915 MHz and 20 kbps for 868 MHz which is also supported by IEEE 802.15.4 physical layer.

Mesh Network of Open Thread

Radio systems are made more reliable by Mesh Networks Embedded mesh networks since they allow the relaying of message from radios to other intermediate radios. This means, in case a node is not able to directly send a message to another node, then the message is relayed through one or more intermediary nodes by the embedded mesh network. Constant connection and maintenance in the mesh is ensured by preserving of routes and connectivity within the network by all the router nodes in the Thread Stack.

An upper limit of 64 router addresses is maintained within the Thread network with the inability of all addresses being used simultaneously. Addresses belonging to deleted devices can also be reused. The router eligible devices, also known as sleepy end devices within a mesh network, do not perform routing for other devices. Instead, all these devices have a router as their parent to which they send their messages. The parent router is then responsible for performing routing of all its child devices.

Routing and Network Connectivity

At a point of time, a maximum of 32 routers can be active within the Thread network. Next-hop routing based on the routing table is used by the routers to transfer messages. Up-to-date paths to any router in the network are stored in the routing table which is maintained by the Thread Stack. This ensures constant connectivity and availability of updated paths to all the connected routers. The routing cost from one router to another is shared amongst routers in a compressed format using Mesh Link Establishment (MLE).

Mesh Link Establishment (MLE)

The periodic multicasting by a node of the estimated quality of links to its neighboring nodes is achieved with the use of Mesh Link Establishment (MLE) protocol. It allows for dynamic configuration of nodes and ensures security of radio links. Link reliability is estimated efficiently with the detection of unreliable links before configuration and thus, eliminating the need for two-way message exchanges. Single hop link local unicasts and multicasts are performed between routers to transport MLE messages. Link and path cost information of all neighboring routers is encapsulated in single-hop MLE advertisement packets which are exchanged periodically between all routers in a Thread network. The path cost information to any other router present in the network is updated via these messages by all the routers.

Dynamic selection of the next most suitable route to the destination is performed by the router if an already used route becomes no longer usable. This dynamic selection also helps the routers to find any dropped off routers on the Thread network. Link margin is defined as the relative signal in dB received above the noise ñoor. The link cost on incoming messages from the neighboring devices is the basis for calculation of the link quality in each direction. Furthermore, the incoming link margin is then mapped to a link quality from 0 to 3. The MLE advertisement message contains the one-way link quality within it. Once the MLE unicast response has been received, the nodes can then calculate the two-way link quality. The MLE outlines link conðguration, parameter dissemination, neighbor detection in the specification. Furthermore, Type-Length-Value (TLV) command formats to network formation and maintenance with address solicitation and router management included is also defined within the specification.

Low-power802.15.4 networks mostly use Route Discovery and Repair On-demand route discovery. Since devices broadcast route discovery requests through the network, this results in an increased network overhead and puts a load on the bandwidth thus, on-demand route discovery is costlier as compared to route discovery. One-hop MLE packets are exchanged within the Thread stack and these packets include cost information to all other routers in the network. The on-demand route discovery is no longer a requirement since all the routers are provided with up-to-date path cost information to any other router in the network. The route to the destination which is the next most suitable in line is selected by the routers in case of the current route being no longer usable. The high bits of the child's address are used to evaluate the router address of its parent in order to perform routing to child devices. After figuring out the device's parent router, the task of determining the path cost information and next hop routing information for that device is covered. The MLE single-hop messages are used to circulate any changes concerning the route cost or the network topology within the network. The link quality between two devices is used to decide the routing cost between them. The quality of link in each direction is determined by the link margin coming from the adjoining device on incoming message. Moreover, this incoming Received Signal Strength Indicator (RSSI) is mapping from 0 to 3 according to its link quality. Value 0 in this mapping, specifies unknown cost. When a new MLE message is received from a neighbor, then either router makes a new entry for this device or it has already a neighbor table entry for the device. Once the entry has been made or discovered, the newly received incoming cost from the neighbor, contained within the MLE message is updated corresponding the neighbor's entry in the table. Additionally, these MLE message give the updated routing information for other routers which is updated in the routing table. The maximum number of active routers in network is decided by the amount of routing and cost information which can that can be fitted into a single 802.15.4 packet. This limit is currently set to 32 routers.

ROUTING

IP routing is the mechanism used to forward packets in routing devices. The routing information about the network addresses and the suitable next hop is stored in a routing table. In order to get the routes to address present on the local network, Distance vector routing is used. Routing could be done on local network or off network as described in the following subsections.

1. For a local network, the high order 6 bits of the 16-bit address are used to define the router desti-nation. To forward the packets to the destination is the responsibility of the routing parent and is done based on the remainder of the 16-bit address.

In case of an off-network routing, the Router Leader is notified by the Border Router about the pre-fixes it serves, and this information is then distributed within the MLE packets as network data. This network data includes the prefix date with 6LoWPAN context along with the Border Routers, SLAAC or DHCPv6 server for that prefix. The suitable SLAAC or DHCP server corresponding to an address is contacted in case a device is to configure the address using that prefix. Moreover, a list of routing serv-ers which are incorporated within the network data are 16-bit addresses of the default Border Routers.

Furthermore, in a commercial space with a Thread Domain model, the router leader of the Domain Unique Prefix is notified by the serving Backbone Border Router, an indication of the mesh being a part of the larger Thread domain. For this, the prefix data, 6LoWPAN context, and the border router ALOC is included with the network data. Though there are no SLAAC or DHCPv6 flags set for this prefix set, but the address assignment follows the stateless model. Service and server TLVs indicating the "backbone" service capability of this border router are also present.

The registration of a device's Domain Unique Address (DUA) with the BBR ensures the capability for duplicate address detection. A device's DUA never changes during its lifetime in a Thread domain. Thus, enabling migration across different Thread networks in a single domain and ensuring routing by respective BBRs across multiple Thread networks. Standard IPv6 routing technologies including IPv6 Neighbor Discovery (NS/NA as per RFC 4861) and Multicast Listener Discovery (MLDv2 as per RFC 3810) are used over the backbone.

A designated Leader is responsible for allowing router-eligible devices to upgrade to routers or down-grade from routers to router-eligible devices. The assignment and management of router addresses using CoAP also comes under the duties of a Leader. However, periodic advertisement of all the information contained in this Leader is done to the other routers. In case of the exit of the Leader from the network, auto-election of leader (one without user intervention) amongst the remaining routers is done. The handling 6LoWPAN compression or expansion and addressing to off network devices are the responsibilities of Border Routers. In addition, handling of MPL with IP-in-IP encapsulation and decapsulation for larger scope multicasts going into and out of the mesh comes under the duties of Backbone Border Routers.

Joining a Network

Two types of joining methods are allowed by Threads and they are outlined in the subsections below.

1. By using an out-of-band method for sharing of commissioning information directly with a device. By using this information, a device can be steered to the proper network.
2. By establishing a commissioning session between a joining device and a commissioning applica-tion on a smartphone, tablet, or the web.

Network Discovery

Network Discovery determines the availability of 802.15.4 networks within the radio range and is used by a joining device. All the channels are scanned and issued an MLE discovery request. It then awaits the MLE discovery responses. The 802.15.4 MLE discovery response comprises of a payload along with network parameters: Network Service Set Identifier (SSID), extended PAN ID and other values indicating whether the network is accepting new members and if it supports native commissioning or not. Already commissioned devices do not require Network Discovery since they are aware of the channel and extended PAN ID for the network. With the help of the commissioning material provided, these devices get attached to the network.

MLE Data

After being attached to a network, a device further requires a variety of information in order to be able to participate in the network. Several services are offered by MLE to already joined networks including transmitting a unicast to a neighboring device for requesting network parameters and updating of link costs to neighbors. A challenge response is conducted by MLE for newly joined device for the purpose of setting security frame counters. The sending and receiving of MLE link configuration messages ("link request", "link accept", and "link accept and request") are supported by all devices. The following information can be transmitted or configured using MLE exchange:

1. The 16-bit short and 64-bit EUI 64 long address of neighboring devices
2. The information regarding the capabilities of any device, including determination of whether it is a sleepy end device or not and further, its sleep cycle.
3. In case of a Thread Router, its neighbor link costs
4. Security material and frame counters between devices
5. Routing costs to all other Thread Routers in the network
6. Collection and distribution of Link Metrics about various link configuration values

CoAP

Constrained Application Protocol (CoAP) as defined in RFC 7252 is a specialized transport protocol. CoAP is meant to be used with constrained nodes and networks with low power. Several features provided by CoAP are described in the following subsection.

1. Provision for a request-response based interaction model between endpoints of an application
2. Inbuilt service and resource discovery support
3. Inclusion of key concepts of the web like URLs
4. Support for configuration of mesh-local addresses and multicast addresses needed by devices when used in Thread
5. Used for management messages so as to to get and set diagnostic information along with other network data on active Thread routers

DHCPv6

As defined in RFC 3315, DHCPv6serves as a client-server protocol for configuration management of devices present within the network. Data is requested from DHCP server using UDP by DHCPv6. Configuration of Network Addresses as well as Multicast Addresses is performed by DHCPv6. With its use, Duplicate address detection can be skipped due to assigning of short addresses by the server. Furthermore, assigning of addresses based on the prefix provided by Border Routers is done with the help of DHCPv6.

SLAAC

As defined in RFC 4862, Stateless Address Autoconfiguration (SLAAC) is a mechanism that allows a prefix to be assigned by a Border Router which is followed by a router deriving the last 64 bits of its address. The IPv6 stateless autoconfiguration mechanism, promotes minimal manual configuration of routers and no additional servers. In addition, the stateless mechanism allows hosts to auto generate their addresses by combining locally available as well as router advertised information.

SECURITY

Threads must be secured against over-the-air (OTA) attacks since they are wireless networks. Furthermore, Threads are also connected to the Internet and thus, there's a need for security against Internet Attacks. Thread Network security is crucial since numerous applications are being developed for Threads which will serve a broad spectrum of uses that demand long periods of unattended operation and low power consumption. A network-wide key is used by Thread for encryption at the Media Access Layer (MAC). IEEE802.15.4-2006 standard authentication and encryption also requires this network-wide key. Protection against over-the-air attacks originating from outside the network is provided by IEEE 802.15.4-2006 security. The network-wide key could be revealed in case of compromise of any individual node. That is why other forms of security are also applied within the Thread network. Within a Thread network, frame counters are exchanged between the nodes and their neighbors using an MLE handshake. Via these frame counters, Threads are secured against replay attacks.

For the security of end to end communication, any internet security protocol is permitted to the application by Thread. Randomizing of mesh-wide IP address and the MAC extended IDs is done to conceal the actual addresses. During the initial stages of join phase, the stock EUI64 assigned to the node is used as its source address. For the rest of the phases, its two-byte node ID based address or one of its randomized addresses serve as the node's source address. Thus, once a node is joined to a network, the EUI64 cannot be used as its source address.

The security of Network management is also vital. For this purpose, a Thread network management application is run on the internet-connected device. In case of new devices that are not already a part of the network, a secure Datagram Transport Layer Security (DTLS) connection must be established with a Thread Border Router. This connection establishment requires a management passphrase associated with each Thread network. After the connection of a management application with the Thread network, new devices are allowed to be added to the network.

FRAMEWORK FOR DEPLOYMENT OF MESH NETWORK IN VEHICLES THROUGH OPEN THREAD

VANET based wireless mesh networks help in increasing the throughput of traffic by dynamic updating of current on-road traffic information. This further aids in reducing carbon emissions and optimize energy consumptions in a smart city. Mesh Network among VANET enabled vehicles also ensures the safety of the occupants of vehicles by providing on-time delivery of traffic and other vehicle-related information such as the speed and position of other vehicles, real-time over the wireless mesh network to a central monitoring station. Open Threads have been the prime topic in research in both academia and industry. The challenge of creating a mesh network via open threads has been extended to IoT and Autonomous cars

A mesh network can be defined as a network topology that facilitates nodes to relay the data for the network. The transmission and receipt of data is coordinated by all the mesh node of the network. Numerous redundant paths for communication within the network are provided by Open Threads via VANETS. These paths make the network robust in case of link failure by automatic routing of messages onto alternate paths. Self-configuring and self-correcting are the properties of Mesh Networks. Currently, Microcontrollers with special purpose mesh routers and compatibility with Open Threads are being offered by companies.

The network efficiency can be further improvised by forming local mesh networks using open threads. With the help of these these local networks, data from connected devices or IoT enabled devices can be transmitted within the network without use of Internet. Data could also be exchanged with mobile phones which come in the vicinity of the mesh. In case of autonomous cars, mostly the data is to be transmitted and processed within the car itself. Or the autonomous cars may need to communicate with other cars nearby and vice versa. Open Threads offer their services best in situations where vehicles need to communicate within a mesh network without laying the burden on Internet bandwidth.

Vehicles equipped thread device will gather traffic-related data like speed, location, and direction of travel, weather conditions and other related information of vehicle that is useful can be deposited locally in the vehicle and sent across the wireless mesh network to a central monitoring station. This information is broadcasted wirelessly to the nearby vehicles which warns drivers of the approaching vehicles.

To attain communication among vehicles, auto manufactures need to include thread enabled microcontroller in vehicles and roadways must be are installed with wireless mesh network equipment's to establish connectivity among the vehicles which is able to send messages to vehicles moving at speeds up to 80 MPH or exceeding. There are different vendors that support open thread compatible chipsets. Some of them are listed below which can be used in VANET enabled vehicles to implement mesh network.

Nordic Semiconductor nRF52811

This microchip supports Bluetooth 5.1 and other protocols essential for IOT with numerous applications. It has many digital peripherals and interfaces like PDM, PWM, UART, SPI and TWI. It has 64MHz CPU with very low energy consumption and flexible system to manage power. The radio of this chip supports open thread and has 4 dBm TX power. Figure 3 shows the microcontroller.

Figure 3. Nordic semiconductor nRF52811

Nordic Semiconductor nRF52833

The nRF52833 is multiprotocol SoC that supports Bluetooth 5.1, 105°C temperature qualification, along with a generous amount of memory and much wide multiprotocol system. It is an ideal microchip for both commercial and industrial applications with robust coverage. Works both in analog and digital interfaces. Figure 4 shows the microcontroller.

Figure 4. Nordic semiconductor nRF52833

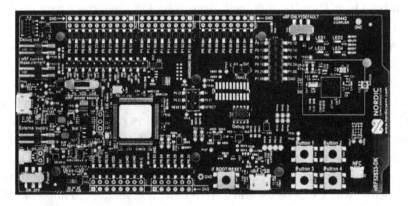

Nordic Semiconductor nRF52840

The nRF52840 SoC is highly flexible and advanced microchip which caters for ultra-low power wireless applications. It is equipped with a 32-bit CPU with 1 MB flash and 256 kB RAM available on the chip. Figure 5 shows the microcontroller.

Figure 5. Nordic semiconductor nRF52840

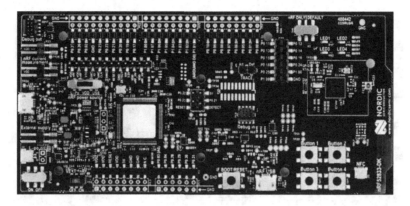

Silicon Labs EFR32MG12

EFR32MG12 system on chip can be connected with IOT devices and saves energy too. It supports both 2.4GHz 802.15.4 Zigbee and Thread networks. It's benefits of a powerful amplifier, hybrid MCU features and highly energy efficient makes it a powerful device for high performance systems. Figure 6 shows the microcontroller.

Figure 6. Silicon Labs EFR32MG12

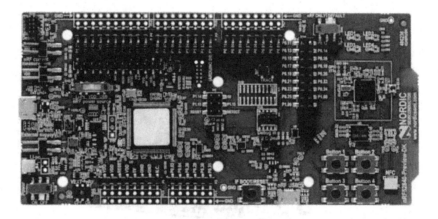

Silicon Labs EFR32MG21

EFR32MG21 has better processing power, enhanced RF performance with low current in accordance with improved levels of security which would be required for IoT products in future. It is a 2.4 GHz chip supporting Zigbee, Thread and Bluetooth mesh applications. Figure 7 shows the microcontroller.

Figure 7. Silicon labs EFR32MG21

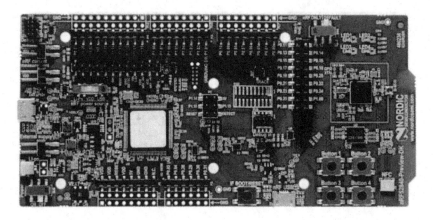

Texas Instruments CC1352

CC1352 microcontroller supports low energy Bluetooth, WiFi, Thread, ZigBee, 802.15.4 and host MCUs. It allows reuse of code as our requirements change. Its kit gives complete development environment and supports programming and debugging. Figure 8 shows the microcontroller.

Figure 8. Texas instruments CC1352

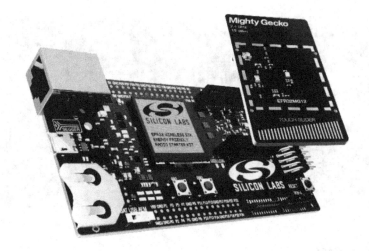

Texas Instruments CC2538

CC2538 system on chip is wireless microcontroller that commands security in complex network stacks and applications. It's 32KB on-chip RAM and up to 512KB on-chip flash enables it to get easy connections to the board. It also provides a powerful debugging system for smooth development. Figure 9 shows the microcontroller.

Figure 9. Texas instruments CC2538

CASCODA CA-8211

CASCODA CA-8211 is a highly efficient transceiver modem with sensitivity of 105dBm which is exceptionally best with low-power deployment. It supports Thread and has a adaptable interface. Figure 10 shows the microcontroller.

Figure 10. CASCODA CA-8211

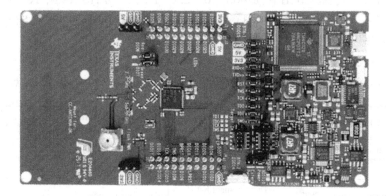

NXP KW41Z

The KW41Z is dongle with ultra-low-power and single-chip device that is highly integrated. It has low energy Bluetooth and enhanced RF connectivity which makes it portable target applications. Figure 11 shows the microcontroller.

Figure 11. NXP KW41Z

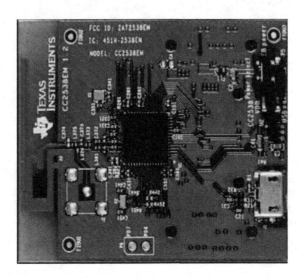

SYNOPSYS Design Ware Wireless Transceiver IP for Thread

The Design Ware Wireless Transceiver IP for Thread is compact and low power microcontroller that support connectivity between Thread, Bluetooth or Zigbee networks.

Table 1 compares all the above microcontrollers in terms of thread certification, hardware and their contribution in commercial usage. Nordic Semiconductor and silicon labs microcontrollers are good choice to be used in vehicles in terms of both cost and efficiency. However, Texas Instruments code reusability enhances its use in vehicles. These microcontrollers state a feasible solution in forming a mesh network via open thread in VANET enabled networks.

Table 1. Comparison of microcontrollers that support open thread in mesh network

Sr.No.	Name Of Microcontroller	Hardware	Complete/Limited Support Thread	Certified	Contribution
1	Nordic Semiconductor nRF52811	System-on-chip (SoC)	Complete Support	No	Active
2	Nordic Semiconductor nRF52833	Development Kit	Complete Support	No	Active
3	Nordic Semiconductor nRF52840	Development Kit, Dongle	Complete Support	Yes	Active
4.	Silicon Labs EFR32MG12	Development Kit	Complete Support	Yes	Active
5.	Silicon Labs EFR32MG21	Development Kit	Complete Support	No	Active
6.	Texas Instruments CC1352	Development Kit	Complete Support	Yes	Active
7	Texas Instruments CC2538	Development Kit	Complete Support	Yes	Active
8.	CASCODA CA-8211	Transceiver Modem	Complete Support	Yes	Non-Active
9.	NXP KW41Z	Dongle	Complete Support	No	Non-Active
10.	SYNOPSYS Design Ware Wireless Transceiver IP for Thread	Wireless Transceiver IP	Complete Support	Yes	Non-Active

CONCLUSION

This manuscript highlights why the current as well as the conventional solutions for on-road traffic management have proved inefficient despite volumes of work in this domain using varied VANETs enabled frameworks. We also analyze how VANETs are suitable for real-time traffic management and road safety. Due to its mobility constraint, a new framework is required. Recently, Open Threads have been used as a viable solution for establishing effective mesh networks. However, this mechanism has never been researched for creating mesh networks among VANET-enabled vehicles. In this manuscript, we first propose an Open threads enabled mesh network for real-time traffic management of VANET enabled vehicles. The feasible microcontrollers for implementing the same have been discussed in above sections. The actual implementation of the proposed framework built on the same is being worked upon at the time of this writing and shall soon be introduced in another work. However, before finalizing the implementation details of the same we need to evaluate many implementation challenges like selection of appropriate generic microcontroller suitable for every vehicle type. Furthermore, testing of the underlying algorithm for real-time traffic management using the selected microcontroller shall need a lot of effort.

REFERENCES

Alam, K. M., Saini, M., Ahmed, D. T., & El Saddik, A. (2014). VeDi: A vehicular crowd-sourced video social network for VANETs. In *Proceedings - Conference on Local Computer Networks, LCN, 2014-November,* 738–745. 10.1109/LCNW.2014.6927729

Alba, E., Luna, S., & Toutouh, J. (2008). Accuracy and Efficiency in Simulating VANETs. *Communications in Computer and Information Science, 14,* 568–578. doi:10.1007/978-3-540-87477-5_60

Aliyu, A., Abdullah, A. H., Kaiwartya, O., Cao, Y., Lloret, J., Aslam, N., & Joda, U. M. (2018). Towards video streaming in IoT Environments: Vehicular communication perspective. *Computer Communications, 118,* 93–119. doi:10.1016/j.comcom.2017.10.003

Anand, A. (2013). Performance evaluation of vehicular ad hoc network (VANET). *Using, 3*(2), 25–33.

Choudhary, P. (2015, March). A literature review on vehicular Adhoc Network for intelligent transport. In 2015 2nd International Conference on Computing for Sustainable Global Development (INDIACom) (pp. 2209-2213). IEEE.

Choudhary, P. (2018). Analyzing virtual traffic light using state machine in vehicular ad hoc network. *Advances in Intelligent Systems and Computing, 638,* 239–245. doi:10.1007/978-981-10-6005-2_25

Elumalai, P., Murukanantham, P., & Technology, I. (n.d.). *Reliable Data Dissemination for Car Safety Application in VANET.* 1–62.

Engineering, C. (2015). *Review on Intelligent Traffic Management System Based on VANET.* 2001–2004.

Fussler, H., Schnaufer, S., Transier, M., & Effelsberg, W. (2007). Vehicular ad-hoc networks: from vision to reality and back. In *Proceedings 2007 Fourth Annual Conference on Wireless on Demand Network Systems and Services,* 80–83. 10.1109/WONS.2007.340477

Geroliminis, N., Karlaftis, M. G., & Skabardonis, A. (2009). A spatial queuing model for the emergency vehicle districting and location problem. *Transportation Research Part B: Methodological, 43*(7), 798–811. doi:10.1016/j.trb.2009.01.006

Gonzalez Gonzalez, H., & Ferré, R. V. (n.d.). *Títol: Study of the protocol for home automation Thread.*

Ho, I. W. H., Leung, K. K., Polak, J. W., & Mangharam, R. (2007). Node Connectivity in Vehicular Ad Hoc Networks with Structured Mobility. In *Proceedings 32nd IEEE Conference on Local Computer Networks (LCN 2007)*, 635–642. 10.1109/LCN.2007.22

Indra, A., & Murali, R. (2014). Routing Protocols for Vehicular Adhoc Networks (VANETs). *RE:view, 5*(1).

Karnadi, F. K., Mo, Z. H., & Lan, K. C. (2007). Rapid generation of realistic mobility models for VANET. In *Proceedings IEEE Wireless Communications and Networking Conference, WCNC*, 2508–2513. 10.1109/WCNC.2007.467

Kshirsagar, N., & Sutar, U. S. (2015). *An Intelligent Traffic Management and Accident Prevention System based on VANET, 4*(7), 2013–2015.

Lèbre, M.-A., Le Mouël, F., Ménard, E., Dillschneider, J., & Denis, R. (2014). *VANET Applications: Hot Use Cases.* Retrieved from https://arxiv.org/abs/1407.4088

Mohamed, S. A. E. (2013). Smart Street Lighting Control and Monitoring System for Electrical Power Saving by Using VANET. *International Journal of Communications, Network, and System Sciences, 6*(8), 351–360. doi:10.4236/ijcns.2013.68038

Nellore, K., & Hancke, G. P. (2016). *Traffic Management for Emergency Vehicle Priority Based on Visual Sensing.* doi:10.339016111892

Nidhi, & Lobiyal, D. K. (2012). *Performance Evaluation of Realistic Vanet Using Traffic Light Scenario.* Retrieved from https://arxiv.org/abs/1203.2195

Priyanka, S., & Dhonde, S. (2017). VANET System for Traffic Management. *International Journal of Innovative Research in Computer and Communication Engineering, 5*(5), 9689–9693. .0505167 doi:10.15680/IJIRCCE.2017

Raw, R. S., Kumar, M., & Singh, N. (2013). Security Challenges, Issues and their Solutions for VANET. [IJNSA]. *International Journal of Network Security & Its Applications, 5*(5). doi:10.5121/ijnsa.2013.5508

Rizwan, P., Suresh, K., & Rajasekhara Babu, M. (2017). Real-time smart traffic management system for smart cities by using Internet of Things and big data. *Proceedings of IEEE International Conference on Emerging Technological Trends in Computing, Communications and Electrical Engineering, ICETT 2016.* 10.1109/ICETT.2016.7873660

Rzepecki, W., Iwanecki, L., & Ryba, P. (2018). IEEE 802.15.4 thread mesh network - Data transmission in harsh environment. *Proceedings - 2018 IEEE 6th International Conference on Future Internet of Things and Cloud Workshops, W-FiCloud 2018*, 42–47. 10.1109/W-FiCloud.2018.00013

Sailhan, F., Fallon, L., Quinn, K., Farrell, P., Collins, S., & Parker, D., ... Huang, Y. (2007). Wireless mesh network monitoring: Design, implementation and experiments. *GLOBECOM - IEEE Global Telecommunications Conference.* 10.1109/GLOCOMW.2007.4437816

Taleb, T., Sakhaee, E., Jamalipour, A., Hashimoto, K., Kato, N., & Nemoto, Y. (2007). A stable routing protocol to support ITS services in VANET networks. *IEEE Transactions on Vehicular Technology, 56*(6 I), 3337–3347. doi:10.1109/TVT.2007.906873

Tonguz, O., Wisitpongphan, N., Bai, F., Mudalige, P., & Sadekar, V. (2007). Broadcasting in VANET. *2007 Mobile Networking for Vehicular Environments, MOVE,* 7–12. doi:10.1109/MOVE.2007.4300825

Unwala, I., Taqvi, Z., & Lu, J. (2018). Thread: An IoT protocol. In *Proceedings IEEE Green Technologies Conference, 2018-April,* 161–167. 10.1109/GreenTech.2018.00037

Yu, X., Sun, F., & Cheng, X. (2012). Intelligent urban traffic management system based on cloud computing and internet of things. *Proceedings - 2012 International Conference on Computer Science and Service System, CSSS 2012,* 2169–2172. 10.1109/CSSS.2012.539

Zeadally, S., Hunt, R., Irwin, A., & Hassan, A. (2010). *Vehicular ad hoc networks (VANETS): status, results, and challenges.* doi:10.100711235-010-9400-5

Chapter 7
A Review on the Role and Importance of Congestion Control for Traffic Optimization in Vehicular Ad–Hoc Networks

Harjit Singh
Guru Kashi University, India

Vijay Laxmi
Guru Kashi University, India

Arun Malik
Lovely Professional University, India

Isha Batra
Lovely Professional University, India

ABSTRACT

Vehicular Ad hoc Networks (VANets) are designed to provide reliable wireless communications between high-speed mobile nodes. To improve the performance of VANets' applications, and make a safe and comfort environment for VANets' users, Quality of Service (QoS) should be supported in these networks. The delay and packet losses are two main indicators of QoS that dramatically increase due to the congestion occurrence in the networks. Indeed, due to congestion occurrence, the channels are saturated and the packet collisions increase in the channels. Therefore, the congestion should be controlled to decrease the packet losses and delay, and to increase the performance of VANets. Congestion control in VANets is a challenging task due to the specific characteristics of VANets such as high mobility of the nodes with high speed, and high rate of topology changes, and so on.

DOI: 10.4018/978-1-7998-2570-8.ch007

INTRODUCTION

Vehicle ad hoc network (VANET) are used to perform wireless communications within vehicle settings by Intelligent Transport Systems (ITSs). By decreasing road accidents, road jams and fuel consumption, VANET are intended to create a reliable and secure atmosphere for the customers. By means of vehicle communications and the exchange of data on environment, VANET users can be notified about dangerous situations (Zhu et al, 2016). VANET are a form of ad hoc network for mobile applications (MANets). The VANET cars are comparable to the MANets' mobile nodes. Although VANET possess most features of MANets, VANET have certain distinctive features, such as high mobility, high rate of change in topology and a high network density, etc (Sanchez et al, 2014). Basically, VANET is suggested to provide safety data, action groups and organisations for infotainment. The safety and growth organisation requires consistent data and this data can have a bearing on fundamental choices. Clear and practical safety tools are the notable problem of passing on VANET without attempting to be subtle. Without safety, a VANET scheme is fully accessible to distinct ambush, e.g. inciting fake warnings and also disguising licensed warnings which then speed up mismanagement. This makes the safety sector a real concern in the construction of such organisations. VANET is of paramount significance as they tend to be involved in the main company arrangement of the unique framework development. Vehicles are the larger piece of each and all center point, that is ready to mold self-handling frameworks, whose safety standard is small and which are some part of the framework that could be effectively trapped most unprotected. VANET advancements are limited to a large extent, with a wide range of requirements being passed on for customers, companies, for example, toll courts, guide boards and law pre-requisites (Zhang et al, 2018). Once again, the maliciousness in life and assets could be finished in an incredible degree without anchoring such frameworks, which enables the safety structures to send and recognize traffic data competently, for example incidents, continued development information or a ground condition. In this respect, the appropriate coordination framework with the elements stated in advance should be established. This control structure should ensure that the VANETS section is consistent and powerful. The features of VANETS are not utilized by the existing guiding traditions, which are generally anticipated for MANET. With regard to turf, the manufacturer must believe of the fact that the cars move at unequivocal velocity in distinct respects. Solitary correspondence associations may not be durable in such a component frame, and the directives that regularly move are uncertain.

Congestion takes place on the channels where the nodes competing to obtain the channels are saturated with these channels. Indeed, the amount of channel collisions improves the congestion in the network by raising the car density. Congestion improves delays and losses in packets (particularly for security emails) leading to a performance mitigation of VANET. Quality of service (QoS) should be endorsed in order to ensure reliability and security of vehicle communications and enhance VANET efficiency. It is an efficient means to promote QoS by controlling congestion. By managing congestion, time and packet loss and subsequently improving the efficiency of VANET, a safer and more trustworthy environment is provided for VANET customers.

The congestion control strategies differ from the congestion control strategies suggested for MANets because of their particular features. Congestion can be managed in VANET by tuning the speed, tuning the transmission energy, determining the dispute window size and the AIFS (Arbitration Interframe Spacing), and priorizing and scheduling messages. The congestion is regulated via VANET. Congestion control strategies in VANET however face issues, including large delays in transmission, unfair use of resources, inefficient use of bandwidth, overhead communication and overhead computing. Therefore, new strategies for controlling congestion in VANET, especially in situations critical to which safety message should be transferred without any significant delay and packet losses, should be developed in view of these problems.

Vehicular Ad-Hoc Network

VANET is another tried-and-tested frame condition that looks for a chance to enroll for the future. Vehicles with remote communications and workstation hubs will quickly be out of the city, and this will alter the way they travel. The progress of the expanded amount of cars is equipped with remote handsets to speak to several cars and to structure an outstanding class of distant frameworks or VANETS. Exceptionally named distant frames need to be able to develop themselves and themselves as a consequence of the unavoidable development of the adaptable structure. Adaptable hosts have to extend and send the message through the frame by using distinct hosts which are supported as switches for sending the message through all parts of the frameworks to a replacement host or a number of hosts which are not within the sender's reach. The flexible host must use it in unpredictable mode to send messages for any messages to be accepted. In order to update the drivers ' prosperity and to offer room to nature, message should be sent to cars through car trades for unmistakable reasons. VANETS brings hundreds of prospective outcomes to fresh requirements that will not just make the movement enjoyable anyway. It would be much harder to touch the foundation at the end or get aid. By adding distant correspondence and information boundaries, VANETS is very evident. The cars can be turned into a structure for companies like us used to working in our workplaces or homes. The potential of VANETS is highly obvious. VANETS are regarded to be an off-shot of MANETS; they, of course, also show features. In addition, VANETS from different views are comparable to MANETS. Both frames, for instance, are versatile multi-hop frameworks that have topological components (Mouchine et al, 2018).

Figure 1. VANET structure

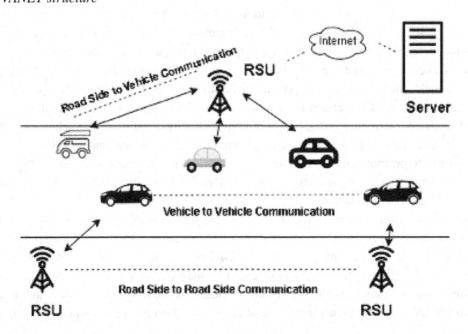

Difference Between VANET and MANET

Without the need for a system, MANET and VANET both work quickly. No central substance and hubs over the framework are available. Whatever the versatile frameworks of MANET and VANET, there are a number of complications between them, for example, the movability case of VANET center points is intended to continue along certain routes (lanes) and not sporadically from that point forward. This gives VANETS a playback over MANETS as it is predictable the convenience case of VANET center points.

MANETS are portrayed as frequently as possible by compulsory, low battery and ready-to-use cut-offs. VANETS have no such repressions, on the other hand. The cars can easily be opened with sufficient threshold and high ready power. In addition, similar vehicles have sufficient battery power to promote long-lasting communication (Singh et al, 2015). A differentiation in replacement is considerably ready VANETS topology, because cars can move at high speeds. This shortens the lifespan of correspondence between the centre.

Applications of VANETS

VANET can be ordered in subsequent classes

1. VANET offers flexible customers a ubiquitous system. In order for moving vehicles to be more and more profitable. You can send your messages throughout the framework without much stretching.
2. The Smart Transport System (ITS) allows a viable vehicle to communicating with a vehicle. ITS includes various orders such as a pleasant monitoring of development, movement control streams, externally hindered convergence and expectations of effect.
3. Order from Solace enables explorers to talk to different vehicles and to use the Web, which improves travelers ' comfort. In order to download music, send messages, view movies etc, VANET, for example, gives the web system to the vehicle center points while progressing.

Characteristics of VANETS

VANET is a MANET application, however it possesses its very own unquestionably shortenable qualities:

- **High Mobility:** In VANETS, center points move quickly. This makes it difficult to imagine the position of a central point and to protect center point insurance.
- **Changes in Network Topology Rapidly:** The circumstance of the center point changes occasionally because the high center point versatility and autonomous speed of the vehicles change. Sort the topology in VANETS along these lines will normally change as often as it can be expected in the circumstances.
- **Unlimited Network Size:** For one town, a few urban networks, or for countries, VANET can be made. Includes a topography-unbound measurement in VANET.
- **Frequent Data Exchange:** The unusually assigned nature of VANET is centered on data gathered from interchange cars and roadside equipment. Since then, the exchange of data between the center points is continuously increasing.

- **Wireless Communication:** For the distant situation, VANET is anticipated. Center points are connected and the data is exchanged using distant techniques. Therefore, in correspondence some safety exercise should be regarded.
- **Time Critical:** In order to decide on the central point and take similar action, the data in VANET must be moved to the center points on time. Time Critical.
- **Sufficient Energy:** The points at VANET have no substance and no resources to count. These VANET licenses allow the use of methodologies, such as RSA, ECDSA and unlimited transmission control.
- **Better Physical Protection:** Physically better guaranteed are the VANET center points. As such, the exchange of VANET facilities and the consequences of establishment attacks are increasingly hard.

Challenges in VANETS

VANETS views join rapid center progress, constant change in topology, brief life of membership, in particular with the multi-skip approaches and shadows in the urban area (Singh et al, 2014) . These features corrupt the implementation, essentially for an extremely named framework, of certain increasing topological guiding traditions. This is due to the need to maintain a route from source to destination, but as a consequence of coherent topological modifications the route slides rapidly. Implementation of VANET guiding traditions depends on a range of parameters such as adaptability shows, driving conditions and many others, so drawing up a competent tradition of coordination for conditions in VANET is a huge test. In addition, a productive VANET guiding tradition should tackle problems such as dense areas such as overload growth, tiny frame thickness, wet nature, lengthy distances, dormancy, etc.

Congestion Control

The vehicles should issue messages intermittently to report different vehicles about their circumstances, for example, speed, situating and heading. Every vehicle furnished with specialized gadgets will be a hub in the Vehicular Ad Hoc Network (VANETs) and permit to get and send different messages through the remote correspondence channels. This system will give wide assortment of administrations, for example, Intelligent Transportation System (ITS). The wellbeing application is a standout amongst the most vital application in ITS. For instance, if a vehicle identifies traffic sticking, it will illuminate other neighboring vehicles about this traffic circumstance. The traffic messages must be conveyed to each neighboring hub with no deferrals. Presently traffic Congestion is the significant issue in VANET that has happened in view of not quickly leeway of onwards traffic.

By and large, in each system, there are a few assets that are shared between the clients of the system contending to secure those assets. Modifying the information rate utilized by every client is basic to control the system stack and keep the channel over-burden. At the point when the bundles touch base to a switch hub and the switch can't forward them, the switch drops the new parcels, though these bundles expended a lot of assets for landing to this hub. One of the principle reasons, which brings about dropping the bundles by the switch hubs, is the congestion. Without a doubt, when the limit of the system is not exactly the systems stack, the bundles are dropped because of the Congestion event in the systems. The throughput of the system altogether diminishes because of the system congestion. In this way, Congestion control ought to be performed to keep the congestion event and increment the fruitful conveyance of information in the systems. What's more, controlling the congestion improve the transmission capacity use, responsiveness, and decency utilization of system assets. Congestion in the correspondence direct outcomes in bundle drops, throughput decrease and debasement of channel quality. Along these lines, congestion control plans are important to manage the traffic level at a worthy dimension.

RELATED WORKS

The Emergency Message Broadcast mechanism for collision avoidance (Zhu et al, 2016) is suggested in Urban VANET. A handshake mechanism has been developed to secure and quickly transmit messages to traffic-rich metropolitan regions. During sending the emails traffic can be decreased by preventing the packet sending failure. The handshake mechanism was intended by taking into account the quality and features of the highways. A hand-shaking mechanism for acknowledging the receiving response from several recipients is not feasible. That is why the RBEN / CBEM protocol is used to send emails quickly in urban highways without delivery of packets. In urgent texts the RBEM / CBEM mechanism is used only. The tall buildings and trees in the metropolitan regions create the signal transmission block, which allows multiple hop transmissions in the region. The MAC layer is used without recognition for the wide emergency cast of emails. Some cars are chosen for the retransmission as relay nodes and others as normal node for broadcasting the signal. Electronic maps vehicles recognize data and support its one-hop neighbours. Since the range is regarded as equal for all cars, the message can be quickly communicated. Thus, the message is transmitted quickly by RBEM/CBEM handshake protocol.

It is suggested to provide the VANET new tree-based Double-based Broadcast Protocol (Ahmad et al, 2012). The tree-based DCB protocol has been intended in VANET to achieve elevated packet delivery and decrease congestion. This method uses the tree-based framework to forward highly deliverable packets. During the messages broadcast it utilizes the set packet length percentage. Trees use the method of the shortest path. Construct a tree to select the parent node, taking into account the node that has a big amount of child nodes. The method is based on only one source node for traffic control and elevated overhead control. The tree structure thus helps to increase the elevated shipping percentage of packets with a set packet length.

The (Zhu et al, 2016) method for the control of congestion is suggested by decreasing the amount of VANET texts. The primary principle of the congestion control technique suggested in the ad hoc vehicle network is to utilize the current network resources and to prevent node overheads and network interfaces. However, it faces a lot of difficulties, such as frequent change in topology and node density etc., following up on the above points, a method has been suggested for controling unnecessary congestion by decreasing the amount of transmission emails in VANET. Each node comprises a table next to it to compare and discard comparable emails. This comparison is done using the database request and uses the queue or the queue.

In (Martinez et al, 2009) VANET proposes a mechanism to prevent accident-based communications and control congestion. This mechanism has been suggested in order to decrease accidents on the highways by considering vehicles as mobile nodes. This mechanism is used to prevent collisions through the Ad-Hoc vehicle network, where vehicles are deemed to be wireless routers. The main equipment used in this system is the on-board unit and the application unit. Furthermore, it checks that the message has already been received to decrease head control and also prevents message duplication. The air bag system is used to minimize accidents and the GPS module to inform the driver. This mechanism therefore alerts drivers quickly and efficiently about the accidents to occur.

The Adaptive Congestion Control for Safety Messages Transmitted to VANET is suggested under (Kolte et al, 2014). Many mechanisms for congestion control have been suggested but there is no system for resolving the issue correctly. The congestion monitoring mechanism is employed in this article to send emergency messages to the suitable receivers without delay and without traffic. The intelligent transport system has been created for vehicle safety on the road side for the cars which communicate in their own right. And this only utilizes wireless media. One is a beacon message here and the other a event driven message. Beacon messages are the status messages used to alert others to their situation and velocity. Messages motivated by events are the messages sent when the car is in an unusual state.

In (Bazzi et al, 2015) The suggestion has been included in the new VANET Congestion Control Approach. A increasing requirement of VANET has resulted in congestion in automotive communication and in the handling of a large number of vehicle requests and reactions. This paper provides a unique technique for controlling VANET congestion using easy congestion detection methods at an early stage. This change was made with the AODV protocol. The SUMO, MOVE, NS2 simulation is used to perform these methods. Researchers include maximum parameters, optimum use of channels and effective signal transmission. It obviously states that, regardless of car size, road type, velocity and driver features, the congestion control has been enhanced. The traffic jams can be avoided from stuck in traffic since the congestion has been identified at its previous point.

In (Cao et al, 2017) VANET proposes to control the potential of transmitting data rates for channel congestion mitigation. This article seeks to enhance road safety, provide fresh communication facilities and improve road users ' effectiveness. Because of bad strength and congestion of the radio channel, most of VANET are scalable. The majority of work on congestion monitoring generally relies on power control transmitting, whereas the transmission rate is not covered.

The aim is also to compare the transmission power control and the data rate control. The comparison demonstrates that the latter outperforms the former in different test scenarios, and that in a localized group of cars in particular the channel is involved.

The theoretical model for VANET network congestion management is presented in (Roy et al, 2015). This document provides a congestion control model for the future deployment of the VANET network. This model is based on the RED algorithm, but changes have been made to choice ranges and signals have been considered over network nodes.

The new VTL and VANET-based traffic monitoring mechanism is suggested in (Kumar et al, 2015). It addresses congestion management by using the traffic light to reduce congestion and carbon emissions.

For VANET, a Virtual Traffic Light (VTL) dynamic traffic control technique was suggested.

Each car can convey its intention to continue and share this "will" and associated traffic information at an intersection with traffic light. Number of simulation studies with the SUMO traffic simulator were carried out on various situations using NS3. The outcomes show the solution's viability in decreasing time to wait and enhancing traffic efficiency (Sahncez et al, 2014).

In (Gomez et al, 2016) VANET proposes an effective control of congestion in security messages. VANET's main objective is to ensure road safety. In order to accomplish this, vehicles use two kinds of safety messages. They are regular security messages for status data exchange and event-driven messages for the transmission of urgent messages. Both messages use the same control channel, resulting in congestion when many cars on the network restrict messages that affect safety circumstances driven by the case. This offers little security and in order to solve this issue research, distinct approaches are suggested by restricting the beacon bandwidth usage below the limit and messages driven by high priority events are reserved for ideal results using a distinct bandwidth control system.

In (Mondal et al, 2014) The VANET Strategy is suggested for dynamic and distributed channel congestion control. The control of congestion is a major study problem ensuring secure and reliable mobile vehicle communication in VANET. It contains secure and insecure messages between the cars. The purpose of this article was to dynamically regulate channel congestion where the data transfer rate is lowered between cars as texts.

This is a strategy* where only true cars may use the accessible network funds and the aggressors are thus withdrawn leading to dynamic channel control.

In (Mughal et al, 2010) It is suggested to use Empathy for VANET Congestion Control Approach. The document launched a fresh approach to VANET congestion control with a fresh model based on the techniques of hop-by-hop congestion control. The issue is modelled by means of a restricted programming and the result is solved in comparison to hop by hop strategy. This implies an interesting notion of empathy. When the packet count is very big, this empathic strategy demonstrated its effectiveness. It insists that many neighbors share bandwidth and avoid congestion for nodes.

Research Gap

The congestion control methodologies in remote systems can be additionally ordered into two general gatherings including start to finish and bounce by-jump techniques. At last to-end methodologies, just the correspondence streams among senders and collectors are considered. The start to finish techniques are not reasonable for controlling Congestion in VANETS on the grounds that, in these systems, the middle of the road hub setting (for example the crashes, impedances, and transmission issues) are not considered. In the jump by-bounce procedures, be that as it may, the limit of moderate hubs is considered.

The bounce by-jump systems are reasonable for controlling Congestion in VANETS because of the dynamic idea of these systems and the confinements identified with the capacity and calculation limits of the vehicles. The bounce by-jump techniques can locally control the Congestion for an explicit subset of hubs in the VANETS. Be that as it may, the use of these systems in VANETS present a few drawbacks. These methodologies create correspondence and calculation overheads. These methodologies are likewise not adaptable when the quantity of transmissions increments in the systems. In this manner, it is important to propose new systems considering the particular qualities of VANETS, for example, high portability, high rate of topology change, high thickness. In the accompanying, Congestion control techniques in VANETS and a portion of their arrangements are examined.

PROBLEM FORMULATION

Vehicular Ad hoc Networks (VANETS) are intended to give solid remote interchanges between fast portable hubs. So as to enhance the execution of VANETS ' applications, and make a safe and solace condition for VANETS' clients, Quality of Service (QoS) ought to be upheld in these systems. Congestion is a vital component that may result in corruption of QoS in VANETS. Congestion happens when the systems stack surpasses the limit of the systems. The congestion builds the bundle misfortune and postponement, and diminishes the throughput by soaking the diverts in the high-thickness systems. The deferral and parcel misfortunes are two primary markers of QoS that drastically increment because of the congestion event in the systems. In fact, because of congestion event, the channels are immersed and the bundle impacts increment in the channels. Hence, the Congestion ought to be controlled to diminish the parcel misfortunes and delay, and to build the execution of VANETS.

Congestion control in VANETS is a testing assignment because of the explicit attributes of VANETS, for example, high versatility of the hubs with fast, and high rate of topology changes, etc. Congestion control in VANETS can be completed utilizing the systems that can be arranged into rate-based, control based, CSMA/CA-based, organizing and planning based, and half breed methodologies. The congestion control procedures in VANETS face to a few difficulties, for example, unjustifiable assets use, correspondence overhead, high transmission delay, and wasteful data transmission usage, etc. Along these lines, it is required to grow new systems to adapt to these difficulties and enhance the execution of VANETS.

PROPOSED WORK METHODOLOGY

The methodology of the proposed algorithm for Congestion Control in VANETS can be represented by the following flow diagram

Step 1: To study the different types of congestion control schemes in VANET and identifying the drawbacks and weaknesses of the existing congestion control schemes.

Step 2: To design an efficient and secure congestion scheme in VANET by taking into account the drawbacks and weaknesses of the existing congestion control schemes.

Step 3: Identifying that whether the proposed scheme offers security without effecting the performance of network or not.

Step 4: Comparing the proposed congestion control scheme with the existing one on the basis of packet delivery ratio, throughput, delay, and communication overhead.

Step 5: Evaluating and validating the performance of the proposed scheme on the basis of packet delivery ratio, throughput, delay, and communication overhead.

Figure 2.

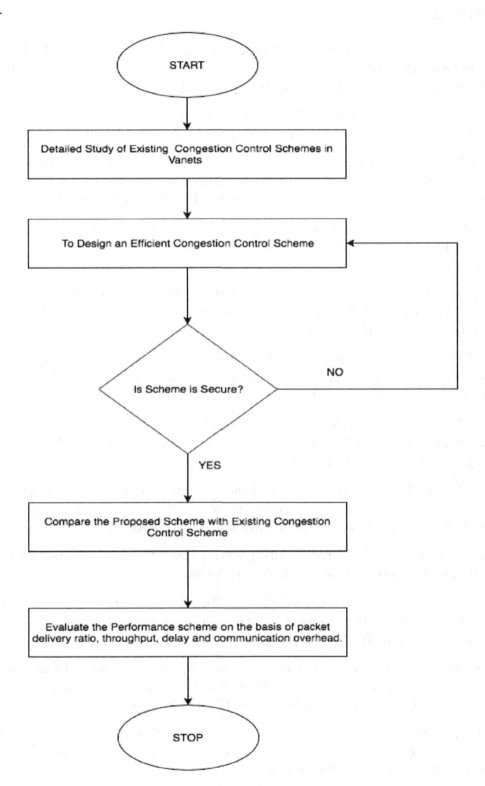

REFERENCES

Ahmad, A., Doughan, M., Mougharbel, I., & Marot, M. (2012, June). A new adapted back-off scheme for broadcasting on IEEE 1609.4 control channel in VANET. In 2012 The 11th Annual Mediterranean Ad Hoc Networking Workshop (Med-Hoc-Net) (pp. 9-15). IEEE.

Bazzi, A., Zanella, A., & Masini, B. M. (2015). An OFDMA-based MAC protocol for next-generation VANETs. *IEEE Transactions on Vehicular Technology, 64*(9), 4088–4100. doi:10.1109/TVT.2014.2361392

Cao, Z., Shi, K., Song, Q., & Wang, J. (2017). Analysis of correlation between vehicle density and network congestion in VANETs. In *Proceedings 2017 7th IEEE International Conference on Electronics Information and Emergency Communication (ICEIEC)*, pp. 409-412. IEEE. 10.1109/ICEIEC.2017.8076593

Gómez, A. A., & Mecklenbräuker, C. F. (2016). Dependability of decentralized congestion control for varying VANET density. *IEEE Transactions on Vehicular Technology, 65*(11), 9153–9167. doi:10.1109/TVT.2016.2519598

Kolte, S. R., & Madankar, M. S. (2014). Adaptive congestion control for transmission of safety messages in VANET. In *Proceedings 2014 International Conference for Convergence of Technology (I2CT)*, pp. 1-5. IEEE. 10.1109/I2CT.2014.7092177

Kumar, P., Kataria, H. S., & Ghosh, T. (2015). Congestion control approach by reducing the number of messages in VANET. In 2015 4th International Conference on Reliability, Infocom Technologies, and Optimization (ICRITO) (Trends and Future Directions), pp. 1-5. IEEE. 10.1109/ICRITO.2015.7359297

Martinez, F. J., Cano, J.-C., Calafate, C. T., & Manzoni, P. (2009). A performance evaluation of warning message dissemination in 802.11 p based VANETs. In *Proceedings 2009 IEEE 34th Conference on Local Computer Networks*, pp. 221-224. IEEE.

Mondal, A., & Mitra, S. (2014). Dynamic and distributed channel congestion control strategy in VANET. In *Proceedings 2014 International Conference on Advances in Computing, Communications, and Informatics (ICACCI)*, pp. 1697-1703. IEEE. 10.1109/ICACCI.2014.6968382

Mouhcine, E., Khalifa, M., & Mohamed, Y. (2018). Solving Traffic Routing System using VANet Strategy Combined with a Distributed Swarm Intelligence Optimization.

Mughal, B. M., Wagan, A. A., & Hasbullah, H. (2010). Efficient congestion control in VANET for safety messaging. In *Proceedings 2010 International Symposium in Information Technology (ITSim)*, vol. 2, pp. 654-659. IEEE. 10.1109/ITSIM.2010.5561609

Roy, A., & Chakraborty, J. (2015). Communication based accident avoidance and congestion control mechanism in VANETs. In *Proceedings 2015 International Symposium on Advanced Computing and Communication (ISACC)*, pp. 320-327. IEEE. 10.1109/ISACC.2015.7377363

Sanchez, J. F., & Cobo, L. A. (2014). Theoretical model of congestion control in VANET networks. In *Proceedings 2014 IEEE Colombian Conference on Communications and Computing (COLCOM)*, pp. 1-6. IEEE. 10.1109/ColComCon.2014.6860400

Singh, H., Bala, M., & Kumar, M. Performance Analysis of Zrp Star and Dsr Using Blackhole Attack Under Vanet's.

Singh, H., Bala, M., & Kumar, M. Performance Evaluation of Zrp Star and Dsr under Vanet's. IOSR Journal of Computer Engineering (IOSR-JCE) e-ISSN: 2278-0661.

Singh, Y., & Sharma, A. (2012). A new tree-based double covered broadcast protocol for VANET. In *Proceedings 2012 Ninth International Conference on Wireless and Optical Communications Networks (WOCN)*, pp. 1-3. IEEE. 10.1109/WOCN.2012.6331905

Zhang, W., Aung, N., Dhelim, S., & Ai, Y. (2018). DIFTOS: A Distributed Infrastructure-Free Traffic Optimization System Based on Vehicular Ad Hoc Networks for Urban Environments. *Sensors (Basel)*, *18*(8), 2567. doi:10.339018082567 PMID:30082595

Zhu, W., Gao, D., Foh, C. H., Zhao, W., & Zhang, H. (2016). A collision avoidance mechanism for emergency message broadcast in urban VANET. In *Proceedings IEEE 83rd Vehicular Technology Conference (VTC Spring)*, pp. 1-5. IEEE. 10.1109/VTCSpring.2016.7504057

Chapter 8

A Relative Study About Mobile Ad–Hoc Network (MANET):
Applications, Standard, Protocols, Architecture, and Recent Trends

Preety Khatri

Institute of Management Studies, Noida, India

Priti Rani Rajvanshi

Institute of Management Studies, Noida, India

ABSTRACT

This chapter includes a relative study of mobile ad-hoc networks (MANET), vehicular ad hoc networks (VANET), and Flying ad-hoc networks (FANET). The approaches and protocol applicable to MANET are equally applicable to VANET or FANET. Authors discuss several emerging application and the future trends of MANET, VANET, and FANET. The common attacks on ad hoc networks are also introduced. The chapter enhances the overall concepts relative to MANET, VANET, and FANET. Authors compare mobile ad-hoc networks (MANET), vehicular ad hoc networks (VANET), and flying ad-hoc networks (FANET) in all aspects with the help of several examples. The chapter includes a relative and detailed study of mobile ad-hoc networks (MANET), vehicular ad hoc networks (VANET), and Flying ad-hoc networks (FANET).

INTRODUCTION

Several Nodes in Wireless Environment managed with distributed authority to form a wireless ad-hoc network. Categorization of this network is depending upon the position permission, assignment intentions, user and connections. The wireless connection can be set up directly between computers it means it is a temporary network having computer -to -computer connection. There is no requirement to connect to a Wi-Fi router between them. The specifications to define network ad-hoc is non dependency of fixed or planned framework of network like access points works for infrastructure wireless networking, routers in

DOI: 10.4018/978-1-7998-2570-8.ch008

connected or predefined networks. The extemporaneous way of connecting nodes is a form of connected networks consist of Flying ad-hoc networks (FANET), Mobile ad-hoc networks (MANET) (Abusalah, Khokhar & Guizani, 2008) and vehicular ad hoc networks (VANET). In last few years, there has been growth in the field of MANET, FANET & VANET and these ad-hoc networks are growing day by day in the field of research and development.

Through the medium of wireless routers or nodes and interim network can be setup spontaneously to transfer the data between nodes . This ad hoc network can be operated without strict top-down network administration, For example, the network nodes like mobile phones, digital cameras, laptop and so on. MANET is the new developing and evolving techniques that allows everyone to transfer their information over infrastructure-less environment irrespective of their geographical location and this is the reason sometimes MANET is also known as "infrastructure less network". MANET attracts a large number of real world application areas and these are the areas where networks topology changes very fast (Govindaswamy, Blackstone & Balasekaran, 2011). But since last few years, lots of researchers are working on and trying to remove the main problems occurred in MANET or example computational power, limited bandwidth, security, battery power and so on. MANET become more exposed to the threads if we follow the same security solutions that are used to protect present wired network. geographical location, that's why it is sometimes referred to as an infrastructure less network.

As we know that VANET is subgroup of MANET. To create a mobile network technology, VANET works with automobile industry products like car and so on. The function of VANET is to allow automobiles to connect with the help of wide range of network. It converts every two wheeler or four wheeler automobile product. Main aim is to provide communication between vehicles and also established and maintains an efficient and safe transportation. As the vehicles are increasing, day- by- day so the chances of accidents has also increased. So to reduce the chances or possibilities of accidents, there is requirement to make our vehicles intelligent and this is the reason of adding the feature in vehicle by VANET. Vehicular ad-hoc network (VANET) originate several challenging standpoint as compared to MANET because of fast topology changes and high movability of nodes in VANET.

FANET is an ad-hoc network which is also related to air floating nodes and these nodes can be operated distantly and can fly independently (Murthy & Manoj, 2004). FANET is a separate type of MANET with various common infrastructural design convictions. FANET is a class of Unmanned Air Vehicle (UAVs) and these UAV's interact without any requirement of access point (Muller, 2012). But in between the classes of Unmanned Air Vehicle (UAVs), and these have to be linked in satellite. UAVs can be operated distantly and also can fly independently. Similarly like an autopilot, the UAVs work without human help. Earlier, UAVs were mostly used for military applications or operations because these were simple remotely piloted aircraft (Kumar, Basavaraju & Puttamadappa, 2008). However, in recent years, the UAVs operate without any pilot and the use cases for civil applications are increasing day by day e.g., non-military security work, policing and firefighting and so on. According to the earlier technology single-UAV system is commonly used, however according to new challenges that are by using a class of small UAVs has been added some leverage to the ad hoc networks (Sahingoz, 2014). However, the multi-UAV systems (Govindaswamy et. al, 2011) have one of the most important design issues is the communication and have some limited challenges also. FANETs are used very often in systems as the systems are more capable and can be applied and solve various problems. So, we can say that these networks have some additional advantages as compared to their traditional ad hoc networks as the unmanned systems are used to communicate in different zones (Zhang Jacob, 2003).

In This chapter we will discuss about detailed study of MANET, VANET, and FANET (Abusalah et. al, 2008) . This chapter also discuss about what are the protocols as well as approaches which are applicable to MANET is equally applicable to VANET or FANET. We will also discuss about several upcoming use cases with the latest agendas of MANET, VANET and FANET. The common attacks on ad hoc networks also introduced. Mainly this chapter enhances the overall concepts relative to MANET, VANET and FANET (Sahingoz, 2014). We will also discuss the comparison between MANET, VANET, and FANET in all aspects with the help of several examples. We will also study about the earlier technologies which were used in ad hoc networks and now days, since few past years, how ad hoc networks are growing day by day. All the above-mentioned networks are the best in their areas according to their features, but out of them (in MANET, VANET and FANET) which one is the best and what are the failures of these ad hoc networks, architecture design, vulnerabilities etc. These types of issues will be discussed in this chapter. In last of this chapter, we will discuss about the future scope of ad hoc networks. So, we can say that in this chapter we will discuss about the relative and detailed study of MANET, VANET, and FANET.

MANET is a temporary network consists of grounded mobile nodes and these are working self-organized wireless network and communication. In case of any tragic condition in which the conventional ways of communication are not available or not in condition to provide services. In that situation MANET (Mobile Ad hoc Network) play a very vital part to develop and maintain communication. Sensors, camera and several other devices are the sources to collect information for grounded mobile nodes to help MANET.

These mobile nodes in MANET connect together wireless network and communication with all other mobile nodes and did not use any pre-established infrastructure (Abusalah et. al, 2008) . These mobile nodes collect all the data and then multi hop way is used to transmit this data to base station. MANET establishes a very economical and can be made very fast whenever and whenever it is required because of no dependency on pre-established infrastructure of communication. There are several issues with the working of MANET as:

- No fixed topology
- Limited or low bandwidth
- No centralized control
- Unstable communication channel
- Security threats to the nodes
- Limited processing power and memory
- Lack of association between grounded mobile nodes
- Limited availability of resources
- Vulnerable
- Shared channel of communication on radio waves

Figure 1. Relationship between MANET, VANET and FANET

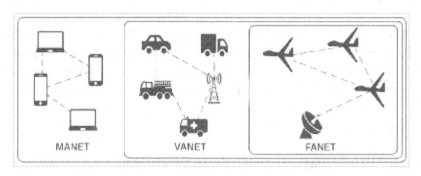

A MANET can serve lots of requirements and these requirements are not served by traditional physical infrastructure-dependent networks. Like: cellular network offloading provided by MANETs. But the network offloading may be critical for example: if these are large number of customers which are using the network and at a point the network capacity has been exceeds, causing interruptions or lags in service. Temporarily diverting traffic from traditional network infrastructure is also done by MANET to reproduce service. This ad-hoc network also added some features like information dissemination and communication capabilities which are applied in the areas that permanently or temporarily do not have well-organized communication infrastructure. For example: rural areas, areas having very less economic resources, post-natural disasters areas etc. The main advantage of MANET is Proximity-based applications (Lee, Gahng-Seop, Zhang & Campbell, 2000). The various applications of MANETs employ the co-location of nodes which is used to find opportunities and provide services like parking availability, which results for social and environmental benefits.

APPLICATIONS OF MANET

With the progress in wireless communication ad-hoc networking achieving some importance as well as it also extends the portable devices and also having a large number of applications for example: commercial sector, military and private sectors etc. These networks have some features like where the customers can exchange information irrespective of the geographical position. These networks allow to easily add or remove devices from the network or to maintain connections to the network. MANET doesn't require fixed infrastructure whereas mobile network does. So we can say that the area of MANET applications is very vast and dynamic (Kumar et. al, 2008).

Sensor Networks

Sensor network is a collection of small sensors and these networks has been used to discover a large number of areas like: pollution, pressure, temperature, toxins etc. Every sensor has a very limited capability, so to forward data to a central computer, each have to rely on others. These sensors are prone to loss or failure. So we can say that sensor networks has very vast area which is used to measure environmental conditions like sound, pollution levels, temperature, wind speed, humidity, direction, pressure etc.

Personal Area Network (PAN)

Personal Area Network also an important application area of MANET (Luo, Lu, Bharghavan, Cheng & Zhong, 2004). The interconnection between different mobile devices like cellular phone, laptop etc. is done with the help of Personal Area Network. It can extend its capability to networks like GPRS, WLAN etc. PAN is the wide area of MANET for the future perspective in mobile computing.

For Military Operations

Ad-hoc networks have vast area in the field of military purpose (Murthy et. al, 2004). With the help of networks, it provides short term as well as fast establishment of military deployments and communications in the unknown environments. Ad-hoc network technology is used for military purpose like to provide networks in between vehicles, soldiers etc.

Rescue Operations During Emergency:

MANET also has overcome the area of security as well as safety of people during emergency. It provides networks for communication in areas having no wireless support.

Disaster Management Support

MANET also provides support during disaster management by providing the communication networks.

Law Enforcement

During law enforcement operations, ad-hoc networks provide fast and secure communication.

Commercial Use

There are various applications related to MANET. Commercial use also the main application area of ad-hoc network and these are used for enabling communications like in business areas, seminars, conferences, exhibitions etc.

ROUTING PROTOCOLS

In ad-hoc networks there are variety of routing protocols has been used in ad-hoc networks. It is the most essential part of research issue in MANET, FANET as well as in VANET (Belding-Royer & Toh, 1999). But during fundamental research it must deal with some disadvantages like power failure, high error rates, low bandwidth, and problem during movement of nodes etc.

By using routing protocol, it reduces the signalling overhead and also provides end-to-end data delivery. As we know that FANET networks are very complex so it has a vast impact on the optimal routing protocol but it is the area of research till now (Bekmezci, Sahingoz & Temel, 2013). These optimal routing protocols like swarm-based routing protocols, topology-based routing protocols, position-based routing protocols etc. In the case of topology-based routing protocol, IP addresses are used to forward data packets (on optimal path) with the help of existing link information. The topology-based routing also establishes the optimal route between all types of communicating nodes. This type of topology has been further classified as reactive routing hybrid routing and proactive routing as shown in Figure 2. To improve FANET performance, these routing protocols has been used. the performance has been increased in terms of minimize delay, increase throughput, consumption of resources etc (Belding-Royer et. al, 1999).

Figure 2. Different types of routing protocols

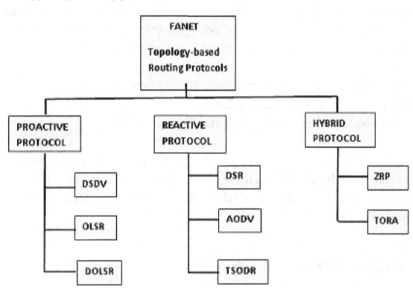

Proactive Routing Protocols (PRPs)

The PRPs are also known as active or table-driven routing protocols and in these types of protocols, routing table which is moderated on continual basis and these tables placed and stored on each UAV. So this storage shows the whole topology of the network. Thus, for transmitting data packets, the routing paths can be available when required (Muller, 2012). These protocols consist of the most updated information about the routes. So to maintain proper information regarding network, they introduces additional signalling overhead and due to these additional signalling, the controlled messages are transmitted without any need. The disadvantage of these protocols is that these are not suitable for large network.

Destination-Sequenced (DSDV)

DSDV's routing protocol is based on the Bellman–Ford–Moore algorithm. In this type of protocol, each UAV must be aware everything about all of the other UAVs and these UAVs must be connected to the network, so that it receives updated routing information (Lee, Roye & Perkins, 2003). In these types of protocols, routing tables are updated periodically, which results in routing loops. For maintaining the updated routing tables, these protocols also add sequence numbers with the help of data packets. These protocols are simple to apply and use as compared to other protocols, which benefits the data transmission among all the UAVs is loop-free. But the main disadvantage of these protocols is that extra signalling overhead issue in case of data transmission.

Optimized Link State Routing (OLSR)

OLSR's protocol (Singh & Verma, 2014). is the most routing protocols for FANET system (Muller, 2012). In this protocol system the routing paths are continuously updated in the routing table. So for data transmission path, when it is required, the protocol finds the path to all the possible destination UAVs. This protocol consists of a packet having collection of messages which are used to maintain communication UAVs. This unique packet consists of various type of messages:

1.   A message to control topology (to maintain topological information)
2.   A message HELLO, to find neighbouring UAVs
3.   The message related to multiple interface declaration on UAVs.

As shown in Figure 3 it displays the multipoint relay (MPR) mechanism in OLSR and this represents the MPR selection with the help of UAV and these MPR have the impact on no. of MPRs. The signalling overhead will reduce, in case if the number of MPRs shrinks. If the distance is greater, then DOLSR is selected for data transmission.

Figure 3. Multipoint relay (MPR) mechanism in OLSR

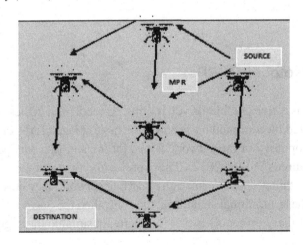

Reactive Routing Protocols (RRP)

RRP's also known as passive routing or on-demand protocols (Gerla, Lee & Su, 2000). *RRP's* used to maintain and discover the routing path in the network. For this, it maintains routing table, which updates the information regarding data to be send. The updating will be reflected in the routing table if and only if in case of the availability of data. During routing through these protocols, these are two types of messages are generated:

1. **RouteRequest:** This message generated from the source node and extends uotp all UAV's which are adjacent to the source.. This RouteRequest message uses the flooding process which is used to find out the optimal route.
2. **RouteReply Messages**: This message generated when reply message is received by UAV's.

Dynamic Source Routing (DSR)

DSR's protocol is very reactive in nature, it means this protocol is suitable for wireless mesh network. As like in reactive routing protocols, the source establishes the connection with target for routing path, similarly, DSR also establishes the same connection during routing path, but when required. Basically, this is based on the two factors:

1. **Route Discovery:** As the name suggests, this message represents to find out the route. The UAV's which are initiated through the source, have to find out the best route until the destination has been reached.
2. **Route Maintenance:** Maintenance between route has to be required only when there is some problem occurs between links.

Ad-Hoc On-Demand Distance Vector (AODV)

AODV's routing (Royer & Perkins, 1999) is very reactive in nature. Similar features like DSR, it maintains paths which are from source to destination. To avoid network congestion, AODV protocol allocates the time slots to packet transmissions (Lee et. al, 2003). There are three phases in routing protocol:

1. **Route Discovery:** This represents to find out route. In case if a source UAV sends the packet, so that message has been required.
2. **Packet Transmitting:** Without routing loops, it does the packet transmission and forward packet over a determined path,
3. **Route Maintaining:** This is the phase which represent maintenance between route to be required if some problem has been occurred between routes. This works same like in DSR protocol. It is required only when link failure occurs.

Time-Slotted On-Demand Routing (TSODR)

TSODR's protocol is mostly used for FANETs. It works in similar way (in case of time-slotted) like AODV (Royer et. al, 1999). TSODR sends packets in allocated time slot (Gerla et. al, 2000) This protocol provides better bandwidth and routing protocol in allocated time silce. It also avoids collisions among packets and data transmission.

Hybrid Routing Protocols (HRP)

HRP's (Wang, Chuang, Hsu & hung, 2003) *consist* of proactive as well as reactive routing protocol methods.

Reactive Routing Protocol: These protocols have been used to find out optimal route, which is very effective. This protocol also has advantage that it overcomes end-to-end delay. It has also some feature that shows that inner-zone routing is also possible and executed with the help of this protocol.

Proactive Routing Protocol: To control a large amount of messages the proactive routing protocol has been used. The large problem overhead has been overcome in this routing protocol.

Zone Routing Protocol (ZRP)

ZRP's based on the routing of "zones" which has been used for different types of mobility patterns of UAVs (Zhang et. al, 2003). These protocols have two types of routing:

Intrazone Routing: Intrazone routing is carried through proactive routing. The data packet routing is done with intrazone routing.

Interzone Routing: The interzone routing has been carried through reactive routing. The optimal path finding is done with interzone routing.

Temporarily Ordered Routing Algorithm (TORA)

TORA has been used for multi-hop networks as well as for proactive routing. These protocols maintain the acyclic graph (directed) from source to destination. Based on the directed acyclic graph, the multiple paths have been created from source to destination and these paths have been used to transmit the packets. For data packet transmission, this routing protocol used the top-down approach. It means the data packets have been transmitted from top UAVs to lower UAVs.

As shown in below table, this displays about the comparative study of topology-based routing protocols.

Table 1. Comparative study of topology-based routing protocols

Routing Protocol	Protocol Type	Topology Size	Communication Latency	Route Updates	Bandwidth Utilization	Signaling Overhead
DSDV	Proactive	Small	Low	Periodic	Minimum	Large
OLSR	Proactive	Small	Low	Periodic	Minimum	Large
DOLSR	Proactive	Small	Low	Periodic	Minimum	Large
DSR	Reactive	Large	High	On Need	Maximum	Small
AODV	Reactive	Large	High	On Need	Maximum	Small
TSODR	Reactive	Large	High	On Need	Maximum	Small
ZRP	Hybrid	Both	Low	Hybrid	Medium	Average
TORA	Hybrid	Both	Low	Hybrid	Medium	Average

Figure 4. MANET architecture

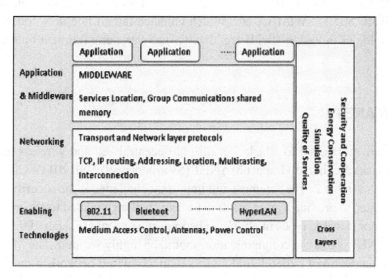

MANET ARCHITECTURE

As shown in the above figure 4, this displays about the MANET architecture (Swarnapriyaa, Vinodhini, Anthoniraj & Anand, 2011). It is divided into three layers:

- **Application & Middleware:** it is the first layer of MANET architecture. In this layer, the application and middleware which provide service location, group communications shared memory.
- **Networking:** This is the second layer of MANET architecture (Xiang, Wang & Yang, 2011). In this layer, the transport and network layer protocols which are used for IP routing, addressing, multicasting, interconnection etc. The main aim of network protocols is to develop to end-to-end reliable services and this transmission between sender and receiver.
- **Enabling Technologies:** This is the below most layer in the architecture. It consist of antennas, medium access control, power control etc. Based on the coverage area, these technologies are further classified as:
  - **PAN (Personal Area Network):** This network runs around an individual person and also connects mobile services through the network. The PAN network having the communication range is up to 10 meters.
  - **BAN (Body Area Network):** This network works on the pattern same like PAN, but as in case of PAN, it runs around an individual person whereas Ban runs around wearable devices. The normal range is 1-2 meters. This network is used to connect the devices wearable also.
  - **HiperLAN:** this network is used to provide an infrastructure or ad-hoc wireless with small radius and low mobility. There are different components of HiperLAN are: physical layer, link adaption, data ink control layer, convergence layer. This network supports isochronous traffic with low latency.
- **Cross Layers:** MANET architecture consists of various layers which are used to manage the architecture. These layers also provide some responsibilities for example to conserve the energy, to provide better quality service etc.

- • **Middleware and applications:** There are various middleware and applications like WIFI, Bluetooth, IEEE 802.11, WIMAX etc. Which enhance the ad hoc networking applications and ad hoc technologies in various fields e.g. disaster recovery, environment monitoring, emergency services etc.

ATTACKS IN MANET

MANET systems are more open to attacks because of decentralized and wireless medium then wired network several attacks are there to impact MANET (Swarnapriyaa et. al, 2011). Classification of these attacks shown in below table 2. The foremost and important challenge is the security of Wireless as-hoc networks. The first step to provide a good solution for any challenge related to security is to find out and understands the major possible types of attacks. The important point for secured transfer of any data or information in MANET is that the communication should be highly secured. The MANET will become more vulnerable to any kind of cyber/digital attacks than any wired network if there is no mechanism of shared wireless communication medium and non availability of central coordinator. MANET can be affected by several kinds and numbers of attacks. Some attacks categorized in the table as below:

Table 2. Different attacks in MANET

Different security Layer of MANET	Attacks in MANET
Application Layer	Unsuspected, unreliable code
Transport Layer	To hijack the session, flooding
Network Layer	Spoofing problem, grey, worm and black hole
Data Link Layer	To analyze and monitor the traffic

In MANET, the layout of these attacks are divided as active and passive attacks as described in below figure-

Figure 5. Different types of attacks in MANET

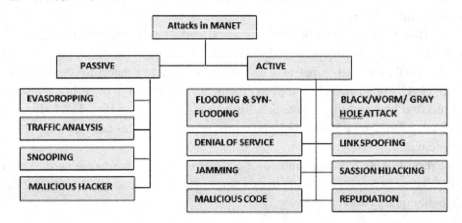

- **Passive Attack:** To access information of traffic not by insulating any wrong information however the intrusion will be performed by various types of continuous monitoring on specific networks. To perform an impactful attack, it will assist the attacker to provide the path of the network which is going to be attacked and to access all the information. Some passive attacks are categorized as eavesdropping, traffic analysis and snooping, malicious hacker.
    - **Eavesdropping:** Here, the attacker is also called eavesdropper. The secret information is being watched by the nodes continuously. Confidential information can be like password, public key, location, private key and so on. Then malicious nodes follow the footsteps of this node and the information will be accessed by the attacker.
    - **Traffic Analysis:** In traffic analysis attack is the major key areas for attackers are pattern of traffic and the data packets. This attack can also be in the category of active attack because of destroying the nodes.
    - **Snooping:** This type of passive attack is very similar to eavesdropping but with a difference as it is not only get access during the transmission but snooping also involve the basic observation of e-mails on any other user's system or even snooping what anyone is typing on their system. To access anyone else's information illegally is called Snooping.
    - **Malicious Hackers:** This type of passive attack adapt snooping as a technique to check continuously about the login information, interpret e-mail communication, key strokes, view passwords, any private communication and transmission of any confidential information. Snooping has both aspects positive and negative it depends upon its use by its user.
- **Active Attack:** The active attack can be performed by two ways either by modifying transmitted data or unethical access to network resources. Active attacks can be of further two types internal or external. In external attack the attack is caused by the node of external network whereas internal attack is caused by the internal node of the same network. Types of active attacks are explained below-
    - **Flooding and SYN-Flooding Attack:** These types of attacks have focus is to degrade the performance of the transmission network either by overuse the resources of nodes, like battery backup, disturb the routing operations or by wasting the resources of network like bandwidth, it will flood the network and result will be wastage of battery power and bandwidth and lead to denial-of-service (Lee & Gerla, 2000). SYN-Flooding attack is also having same technique as in flooding to attack on networks. In these types of active attack the invader generates several TCP connections which are half opened to the node on which the attack is going to be happened. These connections never complete the communication and that also lead to denial-of-service.
    - **Denial of Service Attack:** This type of active attacks follows the technique to destroy the complete information of route from the routing table and then focus on destroying all the operations of MANET.
    - **Jamming:** In this type of active attack there are two extremes one is positive as it helps to protect the authorized packets of information to be received by any other nonauthorized node. Jammer is the main resource in this attack which works on the transmission signals along with the threats to the security. It is also one of the types of DOS attack which starts after sensing the rate of communication between two nodes.

○ **Malicious Code Attacks:** In this attack the victim node can be user application and operating system as both the parties are involved in the communication and transmission. This attack involves viruses, spywares, Trojan horses, worms, intruders and so on. These malicious and unwanted pieces of codes affect the working of network and make it allow the abrupt operations in all the cases.

○ **Black/ Worm/ Gray hole Attack:** These three attacks majorly focus on the routing in the MANET. In case of black hole attack if invader found any request then a suspicious node mislead the traffic and drop it in the temporary area in the network by just showing that it has the fresh and shortest path, which even does not exist in reality. In the case of wormhole attack, it will work as a tunnel in between two attacks which are collaborative. This tunnel interrupts the routing via routing control messages. Invader once senses a packet at a location in the network send them to another location via tunnel. Wormhole attack is perilous as it can lead to damage without the information of the network. In case of gray hole attack, one is by showing itself a verified route from source to target place and another is by misleading packets to reach the wrong destination with some possibility.

○ **Link Spoofing Attack:** Link spoofing attack on MANET the invader or unwanted node spread a forged hyperlink with other receipts other than neighbourhood to interrupt the operations in routing of network. The invader then modifies the information or traffic data of routing and performing any other types of denial-of-service attack.

○ **Session Hijacking:** Session Hijacking attack of MANET it start searching for the sessions which are newly established and not so protected then destroy those sessions. This attack is also called address attack. The invader intrude into IP address of node which is going to be attacked, extract sequence number belongs to that node which is going to be hijacked and execute many denial-of-service attacks. It starts intruding into the confidential data starting from public key, private key, login information, passwords till all other information of nodes and networks.

○ **Repudiation Attacks:** Repudiation attack of MANET the major concern on the participation in the communication partially or fully (Yap, Liu, Tan & Goi, 2015). This attack creates denial participation on behalf of the victim nodes. Because of which packet security is not so sufficient via encryption and decryption and firewalls that are used at different layers of communication network.

COMPARATIVE STUDY

As from the above discussion, there are various FANET protocols (Bekmezci, 2013). Below given in table 3, which represents the comparison among basic routing protocols in FANET based on some major criteria.

• **Main Idea:** The routing information is static means whereas, in case of Proactive protocol the main idea is based on table driven protocol. On demand protocol (Lee et. al, 2003). comes under reactive protocol.

Table 3. A comparative study of FANET protocols based on some major criteria

TYPES OF PROTOCOLS				
Criteria	Static Protocols	Proactive Protocols	Reactive protocols	Hybrid Protocols
Main Idea	Static table	Table driven protocol	On demand protocol	Combination of proactive and reactive protocol
Operation	Fixed mission	Dynamic mission	Dynamic mission	Dynamic mission
Route	Static	Dynamic	Dynamic	Dynamic
Complexity	Less	Moderate	Average	Average
Popularity	Least	Medium	Medium	Best
Bandwidth Utilization	Best possible	Least possible	Best possible	Moderate
Failure Rate	High	Low	Low	Very Low
Convergence Time	Quicker	Slower	Mostly fast	Medium
Fault Tolerance	Missing	Missing	Missing	Mostly Present
Memory Size	Extensive	Extensive	Least memory	Medium memory
Topology Size	Small	Small	Large	Small & Large
Communication Latency	Less	Less	High	High
Signaling Overhead	Missing	Existing	Existing	Existing

- **Operation:** Operation in static protocol is fixed whereas in other protocols the operation is dynamic. Most protocols were used as a part of military operations. These protocols can be used for military as well as in civilian operations.
- **Route:** Routes are static for static protocols whereas these are dynamic for other protocols (Lee et. al, 2003).
- **Complexity:** In static protocol, complexity is comparatively low, whereas in reactive and hybrid protocols, complexity is average.
- **Popularity:** Static protocols are easy to understand but these are least popular as compared as compared to other protocols. The hybrid protocol is most popular as compared to other protocols.
- **Bandwidth Utilization:** Transmission capacity in static and reactive protocols is best as compared to other protocols. Transmission capacity for reactive protocol is source driven, so their bandwidth utilization capacity is very less.
- **Convergence Time:** The hybrid protocols required average time to converge the network whereas static protocols provide very fast convergence time for the network. The reason is that static protocol finds the route in the best possible way and very fast.
- **Fault Tolerant:** Fault tolerance is missing in static, proactive and reactive protocols. Whereas it is present in hybrid protocols. There are some routing methods which have fault tolerance mechanism which is used to find best optimum routes.
- **Memory Size:** There is less memory space in reactive protocols whereas large memory space is there in case of hybrid protocols. Large memory space is required in proactive protocols.
- **Topology Size:** It is the best use of static as well as proactive protocols for small network. But there is requirement of large network then reactive and hybrid protocol is best.

- **Communication Latency:** The Reactive and hybrid protocols have higher latency as compare to static and proactive protocol because reactive and hybrid protocols required time for route discovery.
- **Signalling Overhead:** Signalling overhead is present in proactive, reactive and hybrid protocols whereas it is absent in the static protocol. For example to request a route, reply messages, these are present in these protocols. But this is absent in static protocol.

To measure the performance between MANET protocols some of the measuring criteria has been followed:

- **Throughput:** Throughput defines that at specific period of time, how many data packets has been received.
- **Packet Delivery Fraction:** It defines that ratio of packets received by destination with packet sent by source.
- **Routing Load:** It defines the ratio of no. of routing packets transmitted with no. of packets received.
- **End-to-End Delay:** It defines what is the time taken to transmit packets from source to the destination.

Below given some of the comparison between some of these protocols based on these parameters:

Figure 6. Comparison between Routing protocols in terms of speed

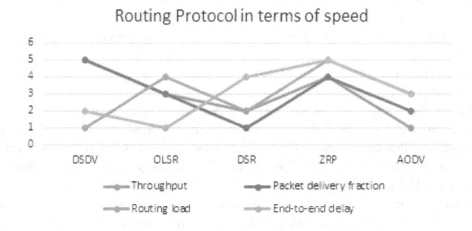

Figure 7. Comparison between Routing protocols in terms of network density

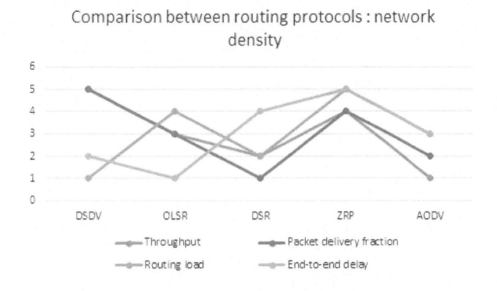

Figure 8. Comparison between Routing protocols in terms of pause time

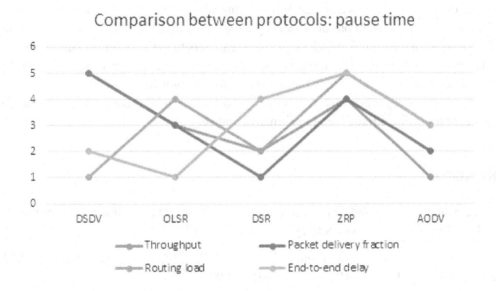

CONCLUSION AND FUTURE SCOPE

The future of ad- hoc networks provides the vision like: anywhere, anytime available network and it's having cheap communication. In today's scenario, the general aim in MANET is about larger scalability and protocols. There is requirement of higher frequency, which needs improvement in bandwidth and capacity of the network. Another challenging issue in future will be large scale ad hoc networks because ad hoc networks have smaller, cheaper and are more capable forms.

Figure 9. Comparison between Routing protocols: overall ranking

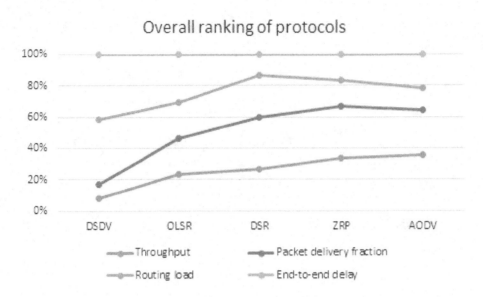

In the field of mobile computing, a large evolution has been driving towards mobile communication, where mobile devices form self-organising, self-creating wireless network which is known as MANET. MANET are more susceptible to physical security threats as compared to hardwired or fixed networks. MANETs, VANETs and FANETs which helps the researchers to the maximum. This chapter emphasis on several protocols, emerging application and the future trends of ad hoc networks. The nodes in ad-hoc networks will be cheaper and also available in various forms (Murthy et. al, 2004). So overall, the use of ad hoc networks is still years away, so we can say that in this field, there is large amount of research and implementation will continue being imaginative and very active.

REFERENCES

Abusalah, L., Khokhar, A., & Guizani, M. (2008). A survey of secure mobile ad hoc routing protocols (pp. 78–93). IEEE Communication: Surveys & Tutorials, IEEE.

Bekmezci, S. O., Sahingoz, O. K., & Temel, Ş. (2013). Flying ad-hoc networks: A survey. *Ad Hoc Networks*, *11*(3), 1254–1270. doi:10.1016/j.adhoc.2012.12.004

Belding-Royer, E., & Toh, C. (1999). *A review of current routing protocols for ad-hoc mobile wireless networks*(pp. 46-55). IEEE Personal Communication magazine.

Gerla, M., Lee, S., & Su, W. (2000). *On-Demand Multicast Routing Protocol (ODMRP) for Ad Hoc Networks*. Retrieved from draft-ietfmanet-odmrp-02.txt.

Govindaswamy, V., Blackstone, W., & Balasekaran, G. (2011). Survey of Recent Position Based Routing Mobile Ad-hoc Network Protocols (pp. 467-471). *Proceedings of 2011, UKSim, 13th International Conference on Modelling and Simulation*. 10.1109/UKSIM.2011.95

Kumar, S., Basavaraju, T., & Puttamadappa, C. (2008). *Ad-hoc Mobile Wireless Networks Principles, Protocols, and Applications*. New York: Auerbach Publications.

Lee, J., & Gerla, M. (2000). AODV-BR: Backup routing in Ad Hoc networks. *Proceedings of IEEE, WCNC*. 10.1109/WCNC.2000.904822

Lee, S., Gahng-Seop,, A., Zhang,, X.,, & Campbell,, A. (2000). INSIGNIA: An IP-based Quality of Service Framework for Mobile Ad-hoc Networks (pp. 374-406). Journal of Parallel and Distributed Computing8.   Scalability study of the ad hoc on-demand distance vector routing protocol (pp. 97-114). *International Journal of Network Management, 13*.

Luo, H., Lu, S., Bharghavan, V., Cheng, I., & Zhong, G. (2004). *A Packet Scheduling Approach to QoS Support in Multi-hop Wireless Networks* (pp. 193-206). International Journal of Mobile Networks and Applications.

Muller, M. (2012). Flying Adhoc Network. In *Proceedings of the 4th Seminar on Research Trends in Media Informatics*. Institute of Media Informatics, Ulm University.

Murthy, C., & Manoj, B. (2004). *Ad-hoc Wireless Networks Architectures and Protocols* (p. 07458). Upper Saddle River, NJ: Prentice Hall.

Royer, E., & Perkins, C. (1999). Multicast Operation of the Ad Hoc On Demand Distance Vector Routing Protocol (pp. 207-218). *Proc. ACM/IEEE MobiCom*.

Sahingoz, O. (2014*).* Networking models in flying Ad-hoc networks (FANETs): Concepts and challenges (pp. 513-527). *Journal of Intelligent & Robotic Systems*.

Singh, K., & Verma, A. (2014). Applying OLSR routing in FANETs. In *Proceedings International Conference on Advanced Communication Control and Computing Technologies* (pp. 1212-1215). IEEE. 10.1109/ICACCCT.2014.7019290

Swarnapriyaa, U., Vinodhini, A. S., & Anand, R. (2011). Auto Configuration in Mobile Ad Hoc Networks (pp. 61-66). In *Proceedings of the National Conference on Innovations in Emerging Technology*.

Wang, Y., Chuang, C., & Hsu, C., & Hung, C. (2003). Ad hoc on-demand routing protocol setup with backup routes (pp. 137-141). In *Proceedings of ITRE, International Conference on Information Technology, Research, and Education*.

Xiang, X., Wang, X., & Yang, Y. (2011). Supporting Efficient and Scalable Multicasting over Mobile [IEEE Transactions on mobile computing.]. *Ad Hoc Networks*, 544–550.

Yap, W., Liu, J., Tan, S., & Goi, B. (2015). On the security of a lightweight authentication and encryption scheme for mobile ad hoc network. *International Journal of Security and Communication Networks*.

Zhang, X., & Jacob, L. (2003). *Multicast Zone Routing Protocol in Mobile Ad Hoc Wireless Networks*. Proc. Local Computer Networks.

Chapter 9
A Taxonomy of Sybil Attacks in Vehicular Ad– Hoc Network (VANET)

Nirbhay Kumar Chaubey
https://orcid.org/0000-0001-6575-7723
Ganpat University, India

Dhananjay Yadav
https://orcid.org/0000-0001-5166-2133
Gujarat Technological University, India

ABSTRACT

Vehicular ad hoc networks (VANETs) are a class of ad hoc networks in which vehicle communicate with each other to show the traffic situation and any mishappening on the road. VANET is vulnerable to a number of attacks due to its infrastructure-less nature. One of these attacks is the Sybil attack. Security of data dissemination in VANET is very crucial, otherwise any mishappening can occur on road. Sybil attack is very difficult to be defended and detected, especially when it is launched by some conspired attackers using their legitimate identities, and this has become a growing research interest in VANETs in past few years. This chapter studies various dimension of VANETs including its structure, communication architecture, security issues, and critical review of technique to detect Sybil attacks.

INTRODUCTION

Vehicles on the road have been increased tremendously in last few decades, this resulted in heavy traffic on road. Due to increased traffic on road, probability of road accidents and other fatalities also increases very rapidly. Vehicular Ad-hoc Networks (VANETs) is a network which play an important role in providing road safety and security of people by enabling instant communication between vehicles, provide a quick relief in case of accidents and also to monitor vehicles about rash driving and over speeding. In VANET one vehicle can pass messages to other connected vehicle so that the other vehicle can know in

DOI: 10.4018/978-1-7998-2570-8.ch009

advance about traffic situation and other fatalities on road. The people in VANET can use entertainment services through which they can play audio and video etc. There are certain security risks which are serious concern about the safety and security of people. The highly dynamic environment of VANET due to change of their positions rapidly, they move in and out of range so quickly appears to be challenging and it becomes very difficult to establish a reliable end-to-end communication path to maintain efficient data transfer. Message delivery time is also a major concern in VANET. Security of data dissemination in VANET is crucial otherwise any mishappening can occur on road. Authors in this chapter highlights the key security issues of VANET and discussed state of art detection algorithms for Sybil attack.

VANET Structure

VANET structure has major components include Application Unit (AU), On Board Unit (OBU) and Roadside Unit (RSU) in providing communication. AU & OBU are devices which are attached with vehicles while RSU placed alongside the road and helpful in providing internet services. (Kumar Karn & Prakash Gupta, 2016).

Application Unit (AU): This unit is responsible for providing communication inside vehicles. It helps in monitoring driver about fatigue or drowsiness. The AU can be connected to the OBU through a wired or wireless connection.

Figure 1. VANET architecture

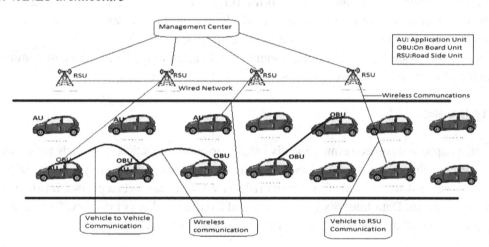

On Board Unit (OBU): It is a wave device mounted on-board in a vehicle and responsible for exchanging information between vehicles and roadside unit (RSU). The major functions of OBU in VANETs are ad-hoc and geographical routing, wireless radio access, network congestion control, reliable message transfer and data security.

Road Side Unit: The road side unit (RSU) is fixed along the road side or in a particular locations such as junctions or parking areas which is helpful in providing messages to vehicles in the vicinity (Saini, Alelaiwi, & El Saddik, 2015). It has radio frequency, high power, and long-range antenna to access a wireless medium. RSU is responsible for forwarding data packets to OBUs in its range and other RSUs. It Works as a gateway to provide Internet connectivity to OBUs.

Communication Architecture of VANET

The Communication Architecture is based on the various components in VANET. The communication type can be categorized into four types (i) In-vehicle communication (ii) Vehicle-to-vehicle (V2V) communication (iii) Vehicle-to-road infrastructure (V2I) communication and (iv) Vehicle-to-broadband cloud (V2B) communication (Liang, Li, Zhang, Sun, & Bie, 2015).

- **In-Vehicle Communication:** It provides intravehicular communication. The device called application unit (AU) is responsible for this. In-vehicle communication system can detect a vehicle's performance and especially driver's fatigue and drowsiness, which is critical for driver and public safety.
- **Vehicle-to-Vehicle (V2V) Communication:** This provides inter vehicular communication and it helps in providing data exchange platform for the drivers to share information and warning messages to expand driver assistance.
- **Vehicle-to-Road Infrastructure (V2I) Communication:** It provides communication between vehicle and roadside unit. This enables real-time traffic/weather updates for drivers and provides environmental sensing and monitoring.
- **Vehicle-to-Broadband Cloud (V2B) Communication:** This provides communication between vehicle and management centre through roadside unit. In this communication system, vehicles may communicate via wireless broadband mechanisms such as 3G/4G. The broadband cloud may include information about traffic and monitoring data, as well as infotainment communication which will be useful for active driver assistance and vehicle tracking.

Security Issues

Imagine what happens if someone intentionally breaks the communication or spreads wrong message in VANET wherein vehicles rely on shared messages. It creates a huge risk of safety, security of people and increases accidents risk on the road. The security risks in VANETs can be categorised into (i) Availability (ii) Authentication (iii) Data Integrity (iv) Privacy and Confidentiality (v) Privacy, Confidentiality and Integrity (vi) Authentication and Integrity (vii) Authentication and privacy.

Availability

Availability means network must be available to all nodes at all time. In this security issue, a legitimate node is unable to deliver messages to other nodes due to unavailability of network. Also the malicious node can drop or intercept the original message so that it cannot reach to legitimate node. The main security attacks in this type are denial of service attack, black hole attack and spamming attack etc.

Denial of Service Attack: In this type of attack, attacker jams the main communication medium by flooding the network so that the network is no more available to legitimate user and the communication breaks (Parmar, Astt, & Prof, 2015).

Figure 2. Denial of service attack

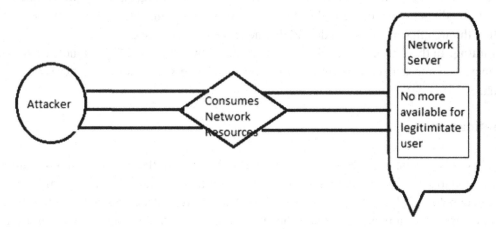

Figure 2 denotes that the attacker creates heavy load in the network by sending spam messages which consumes network resources and network becomes unavailable for communication amongst other legitimate vehicles.

Black Hole Attack: In Black Hole attack, a malicious node pretends to have an optimum route for the destination node and indicates that packet should route through this node after transmitting the fake routing information. The impact of this attack is that the malicious node can either drop or misuse the intercepted packets without forwarding those (Namarpreet & Aman, 2015).

Figure 3. Blackhole attack

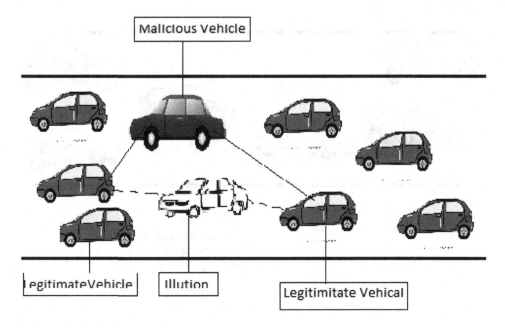

In the above figure 3, the malicious vehicle affects the routing algorithm by pretending himself as an optimum node between source and destination. So the communication starts between source and destination through this malicious node and that node drop the message.

Spamming: In this attack the attacker consumes the network bandwidth and increase the transmission latency. The attacker sends spam messages for which users may not have interested (Yousef Al-Raba'nah, 2015).

Authentication

If a vehicle wants to communicate with other vehicle in the network then first this must be authenticated to become able to send messages in the network. The legitimate vehicle also must verify the authenticity of vehicle before replying to each message that they receive. If the message that that they receive doesn't come from the authenticate vehicle then they simply discard that message (Abdelmagid Elsadig & Fadlalla, 2016).

Masquerading: In this type of attack the attackers try to fool other vehicle in the network by simply changing their identity (Khelifi, Luo, Nour, & Shah, 2018). The attacker tries to pose itself like an ambulance or other VIP vehicle. By seeing this other vehicle slowdown their speed and give way to attacker. The attacker performs this attack to take advantage of less traffic for himself on the road. The other vehicles easily give him way on road.

Figure 4 shows masquerading attack, wherein malicious vehicle poses himself as an ambulance. The legitimate vehicles thinks that there is an ambulance coming behind so they slow down their speed and give way to attacker.

Figure 4. Masquerading attack

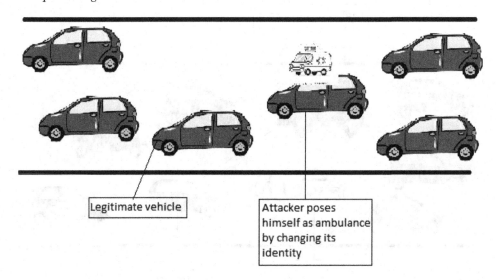

Bogus Information Attack: In this attack the attacker passes false information to misguide other vehicles in the network (Namarpreet & Aman, 2015). The attacker passes fake information in network like non-existent traffic as high traffic, accident happens with the reality though there is no accident happens.

GPS Spoofing: A malicious node utilizes the GPS satellite simulator to produce signals which are stronger than the actual satellite signals, tending to deceive vehicles to accept the false position information. This attack is related to physical devices (Khelifi et al., 2018).

Data Integrity Attack

It refers to accuracy and reliability of data. Like other attacks the attacker does not prevent legitimate user to access data or steal data. Data integrity ensures that the data could not be altered or modified intentionally by attacker. The main attacks included in this type of category are as given below.

Timing Attack: In this attack the messages delayed with some time. When a malicious vehicle receives any message in network then they keep this message to themselves for some time and then send the messages. The messages are delayed with some time and it is termed as timing attack.

Figure 5. Timing attack.

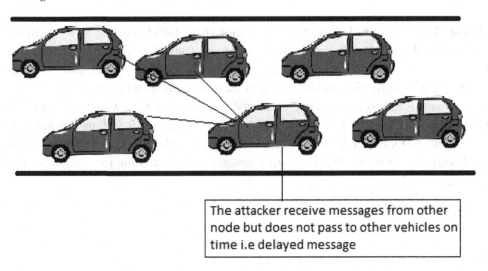

The attacker receive messages from other node but does not pass to other vehicles on time i.e delayed message

Social Attack: In this attack, the attacker tries to irritate the other driver in network by passing unethical and immoral messages in VANET. The main objective of the attacker is to annoyed the driver by passing such kind of messages. After getting such type of messages the driver reacts in annoyingly(Ajay Rawat, Santosh, Sharma; Rama, 2014). They get disturbed. It effects the driving of the vehicle which indirectly creates the problem in the network.

PRIVACY AND CONFIDENTIALITY

In VANET's the term confidentiality refers to the confidential communication. In a group no one except the group members are able to decrypt the messages that are broadcasted to every member of the group. Privacy means that an eavesdropper is impossible to decide whether two different messages come from the same vehicle (Parmar et al., 2015). The main aim in this is to provide confidential communication without piercing the veil of legitimate user. The main attacks in this category are as given below.

Impersonation attack: In this type of attack, the attacker poses himself as a trusted vehicle in the network and asks for sensitive information. If any member vehicle shares his, her information, then the malicious vehicle is able to hack his account or identity (Parmar et al., 2015).

Privacy, Confidentiality and Integrity

Privacy is a state in which a person or group conceal themselves so that they were not disturbed by other. The data or information they keep themselves cannot be seen or accessed by others.. Confidentiality means protecting data from unauthorized viewing and access and Integrity means protecting data from unauthorized changes so that data reliability can be maintained. There are certain security attacks which cause privacy, confidentiality and integrity issues of data. The main attack to this category is as given below.

Man in the Middle Attack: In this attack, a malicious node puts himself in between the two communicating nodes in such a way that the legitimate nodes are unaware of the presence of this malicious node. The malicious node then secretly makes modification or alteration in communication of the legitimate nodes. To make any modification and alteration in messages, the attacker must be efficient enough to intercept the messages between parties and as a consequence injecting new ones. Unencrypted wireless access point is the most vulnerable point to be the victim of such attack (Ahmad, Adnane, Franqueira, Kurugollu, & Liu, 2018). Figure 6 illustrate that legitimate vehicles are communicating with each other and the malicious vehicle intercepts, alter their messages secretly without the awareness of others.

Figure 6. Man in the middle attack

Authentication and Integrity

There are certain security attacks which creates authentication and integrity issues in VANET. The main attack to this category is tunnelling attack described here.

Tunnelling Attack: In this attack, when a vehicle passes through a tunnel then the GPS signals disappears temporarily, and at that time attacker has possibility to inject false information before leaving the tunnel (Irshad ahmad, Sumra, Sellappan, Abdullah, & Ali, 2018). The vehicle passes from a tunnel and when entering into the tunnel it injects wrong information to other vehicle about position described in Figure 7.

Figure 7. Tunnelling attack

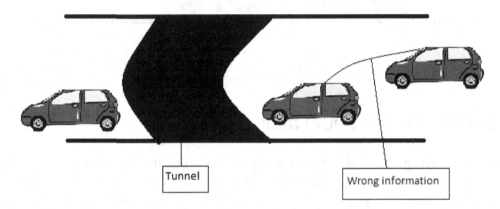

AUTHENTICATION AND PRIVACY

Authentication to verify the data as it comes from a genuine and truthful source or not and privacy to keep the data secretly so that no one except authorised person can see the data and access it. The main attack to this category Sybil attack is described here.

Sybil Attack: In this attack the malicious vehicle transmits multiple messages with different ID's to the other vehicles. In this way other vehicles on road feel that these messages are coming from different vehicles, so there is a high traffic further on road and hence they divert their route. The malicious vehicle enforces other vehicles to change their route. The legitimate vehicles can be in trap as they diverted their route without knowing the intention of malicious vehicle and any mishappening can occur to them. The main task of the attacker in this attack is to provide an illusion of multiple vehicles to other vehicles and to enforce them to choose alternate route and to leave the road for the benefits of the attacker. This task is done by sending multiple messages with different id (Hezam Al Junaid, Syed, Mohd Warip, Fazira Ku Azir, & Romli, 2018).

Figure 8 illustrates Sybil attack in VANET wherein malicious vehicle transmits multiple messages from different ids and creates an illusion about the presence of large number of vehicles on the road. Major issues of Sybil attack are (i) People in VANET are forced to divert their route by creating illusion of presence of multiple vehicles (ii) They can be in trap as they have diverted the route with the intention of other people and (iii) After diverting the route any mishappening can happen to them like robbery etc.

Figure 8. Sybil attack

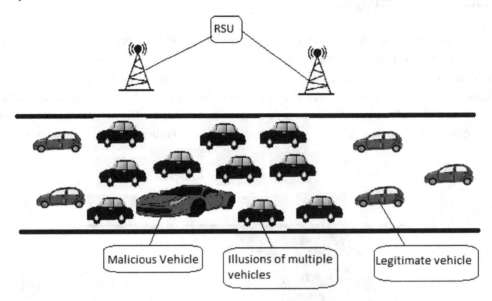

METHODS TO DETECT SYBIL ATTACK

Many researchers have proposed algorithms and approaches to detect Sybil attack in VANET. Based on the research work done until now, Sybil attack detection algorithms can be categorized into various types. Earlier researchers used cryptography approach to detect Sybil attack but other approaches are also used like Reduced Signal Strength Indication (RSSI), Data Mining, Machine learning and the approaches based on speed and position of the vehicles. The approaches to detect Sybil attack are (i) Cryptography based (ii) RSSI (iii) Position and speed of vehicles (iv) Data Mining and (v) Machine Learning.

Cryptographical Approach: Initially cryptographic techniques were used in VANET to detect the Sybil attack. Researchers used public key cryptography technique to provide secure communication among vehicles. This technique is used to authenticate the vehicle as the message is coming from the authentic source. The vehicles in VANET are first registered with RSU (Roadside Unit) and get a certificate id. Only vehicles with this certificate id are eligible to communicate in VANET. Different researchers have used different approaches to secure the communication and to detect the Sybil attack in VANET.

In 2011 a research paper with title "Efficient detection of Sybil attack based on cryptography in VANET" published (Rahbari & Jabreil Jamali, 2011). The authors in this paper use the cryptographic approach to detect the Sybil attack. They have used the public key authentication method to verify the vehicle. Without verification, the vehicle cannot send any message. The sender uses the authentication key and encryption method to send the message. Receiver verifies member authenticity by signature verification.

In 2014, other researchers proposed a session key based certification method (ravi prakash, 2014) to detect Sybil attack in VANET. First of all, vehicles id and master key is registered on VANET server. After that an anonymous identity of vehicle is created in local VANET and then validated by the main VANET server. The vehicle then uses this local id for communication in VANET. The vehicle which wants to send any information in VANET he has to concatenate his master key with his id. First the local id is verified in VANET and only after successful verification of id, the vehicle can proceed further and session is created. Otherwise their access is denied. In the next step based on its private key, vehicle will create its public key to send on local server and based on this public key local server will create its own public key. Local server then performs XOR operation to both public keys to generate a hash value. Now this hash value is multiplied with session key to generate the session certificate. The local server then saves id, expiration time and session certificate into its database for future use. Now suppose vehicle A wants to communicate to vehicle B then vehicle A has to send its message with its id, expiration time and session certificate to vehicle B. Vehicle B then concatenates its id and session certificate and send it to the local server. The local sever verifies the expiration time, id and session certificate with its database and then authenticate vehicle B to communicate with vehicle A. If certificates are not verified then vehicle is detached from the network.

(Mittal & Ahlawat, 2016) uses the authentication method for vehicle to detect the Sybil attack. The authors use two approaches to detect the Sybil attack. In first attempt they verify the neighbouring vehicle and in second step they verify the speed of vehicles. The RSU stores all the information about the vehicle. When a vehicle enters in network it sends hello message to RSU. Then RSU verifies its identity and sends an id to authenticate the vehicle and then store its neighbouring information. RSU has all information related to vehicle. It also defines the speed of vehicle. If vehicle changes its identity and send any message in network, then first RSU checks the adjacent node information of the vehicle and if information is same with other node then it is a Sybil attack as two vehicles in the network cannot have the same information. If information is not same with other vehicle then speed of vehicle is compared with threshold value (a fixed value in network). If speed of vehicle is less than the threshold value then the vehicle is a legitimate vehicle otherwise it is a Sybil vehicle.

In 2018, another cryptography approach proposed to detect the Sybil attack (Panchal & Singh, 2017). In this technique, author detected the Sybil attack by identifying trust of vehicles. The vehicle's information is stored on server of RSU. When new vehicle enters in range of RSU it sends a Hello message to RSU. The RSU then updates the number of vehicles in VANET with their identity. Trust value for each vehicle is calculated based on source, destination and intermediate hop. Trust value is based on the number of intermediate nodes between source and destination. When any vehicle enter into VANET then it sends a hello message to RSU. The RSU then certifies the vehicle by providing an id to it, and then discover its entire neighbour based on the information that it possesses. Based on the neighbouring information it computes its trust value. To detect Sybil attack, trust value of vehicle is compared with threshold value (a fixed value). If trust value of vehicle is less than threshold value than that vehicle is marked as real vehicle and if trust value is greater than the threshold value then the vehicle is termed as Sybil vehicle.

Received Signal Strength Indication (RSSI) Based Approach

RSSI is a measurement of power present in received radio signal. As the distance increases the signal strength gets weaker and the data rate decreases which leads to lower overall data throughput. Signal strength is used in received signal strength indicator which indicates how well a radio station can hear the remote client radio station. RSSI has no absolute value. The IEEE 802.11 standards specify that its value can scale from 0 to 255. The manufacturers of chipset can use their own value based on standards. For example, CISCO uses 0 to 100 scale and Atheros uses 0 to 60 scale. RSSI does not need any additional hardware requirement to determine the location of nodes as it is available in almost all Wi-Fi nodes. Based on these concepts of received signal strength indication, researchers have proposed several algorithms to detect the Sybil attack. RSSI technique is also used by researchers to detect the Sybil attack in VANET. In 2017, authors proposed reduced signal strength-based indication (RSSI) localization mechanism to identify Sybil attack in VANET (Garip, Kim, Reiher, & Gerla, 2017). In this technique mobile nodes are used to localize another mobile node and then it adjusts itself based on the heterogeneous interference levels in the environment.

In the year 2018, researchers proposed a technique based on signal strength to detect Sybil attack in network (Singh & Kaur, 2018). In this approach RSU stores the vehicles information, RSU broadcast ICMP (internet control message protocol) message in the network. The vehicles after receiving ICMP message send their signal strength information to RSU. RSU collects all information and shares it with all. When vehicle changes its identity or enter into the network, they have to send a hello message to RSU. The RSU then checks the neighbouring information to verify its authenticity. If signal strength is different with other vehicle then the vehicle is legitimate and can starts communication in the network but if signal strength is same with other adjacent node, RSU sends control packet in network to monitor the node. After receiving control packet the vehicle in network starts watching adjacent nodes. The vehicle which is malicious is detached from the network.

In year 2019, authors proposed a technique to detect Sybil attack without the use of RSU and base station (Yao et al., 2019). Authors also used the approach of RSSI (Reduced signal strength indication). Voiceprint algorithm by allowing it to conduct detection on Service Channel (SCH) to shorten observation time is improved and furthermore, they have extended voiceprint with change-points detection to identify those illegitimate nodes performing power control. The main stages in this algorithm (voiceprints) are collection, comparison and confirmation.

Position and Speed Based Approach

This technique is based on the position of vehicle in VANET and their speed. The position of vehicles with neighbouring vehicles is determined to check the attack. It is assumed that in case of high traffic the speed of vehicles is low and in case of low traffic the speed of vehicles is high. Based on this concept researchers proposed some algorithms to measure the speed of vehicles and after determining the speed of vehicle they try to detect the Sybil attack.

In recent year authors proposed to detect Sybil attack with the help of RSU and event manager.(Baza et al., 2019). When RSU encounters a vehicle, sends a proof of location to vehicle. These proofs of location called trajectories are used for identification of vehicle. When a vehicle reports certain events like accident or high traffic on road then he has to show his trajectories. These trajectories are then compared with the RSU with help of event manager. The event manager then verifies all the trajectories and group the vehicle based on similarity between the trajectories. At very first instance, event manager identifies similarity between trajectories and with overlapped trajectories it groups the vehicles. In this way it detects the Sybil attack.

In year 2019, authors published a research paper in which they considered that if traffic is high than speed of vehicle is low and if traffic is low than the speed of vehicle is high (Ayaida, Messai, Najeh, & Boris Ndjore, 2019). Based on this consideration authors performed the Sybil attack detection by comparing the actual speed of vehicle with estimated speed and the given threshold speed in VANET. If the difference between actual speed and the estimated speed is higher than the threshold then there can be the possibility of Sybil attack. In the next step to confirm Sybil attack the vehicle broadcasts a notification message to its neighbours. If no confirmation is received after a custom duration then it is neglected otherwise if another vehicle correspond to the same conclusion then it is a Sybil attack.

In year 2017 researchers proposed an algorithm based on position of neighbouring nodes using dynamic certificate generation techniques to detect the Sybil attack in VANET (Sharma, Saroj, Chauhan, & Saini, 2017). The malicious node which creates fake identities, all has same physical properties. Any vehicle which detects multiple nodes with same physical property put them into suspected vehicle. Each vehicle in the network creates list of suspected nodes of vehicles. After that one of the nodes becomes the coordinator and compares all the suspected nodes. After comparison for each vehicle, coordinator generates a Sybil node list (SNL) and a message and broadcast it to all neighbour vehicles.

In year 2019, researchers proposed a hybrid algorithm to detect a Sybil attack (Hamdan, Hudaib, & Awajan, 2019). This hybrid algorithm is a combination of P2DAP (privacy preserving detection of abuses of pseudonyms method) and footprint algorithm. P2DAP works better in case of increase number of vehicles and footprint method works better in increase of speed of vehicles. In this approach each vehicle receives deployment information from RSU, then RSU check the average speed of vehicles on road. If it is less than the threshold than the footprint algorithm runs. The attack is detected by link tag of each vehicle generated by different RSU. If link tags have no similarity than there is no attack otherwise there is a Sybil attack. In P2DAP approach RSU divides the vehicle in course grained group. If in this group, two vehicles share the same key than a suspicious event occur and RSU send this report to DMV. It then divides the vehicle into fine course group. If still the vehicle are in same fine grained group than there is a Sybil attack.

In year 2019, authors proposed an algorithm to detect the sybil attack(Ayaida, Messai, Wilhelm, & Najeh, 2019). This technique has various steps in detection mechanism. In first step neighbours list is updated, second step number of neighbours are computed, third step algorithm is used to estimate the speed of vehicle whereas in fourth step Sybil attack is detected by using the above three steps and then calculating the difference between the actual speed of vehicle with estimated speed and then comparing with threshold speed. If difference between the actual speed and the estimated speed is greater than the threshold speed then it is detected as Sybil attack and message is broadcasted in the network.

Data Mining Based Approach

There are various data mining algorithms helpful in prediction, categorization and classification of data.

Few researchers use this data mining technique to find the driving pattern and to detect Sybil attack. A research paper (Dutta & Chellappan, 2013) presented in 2013 uses the clustering approach to detect the Sybil attack in network. They have used the approach of clustering to detect the Sybil attack in network. The authors in this research paper find the clusters of vehicles for detection of attack. Their idea is based on the concepts that vehicles can't be always in same clusters for long duration due to road friction, vehicle signalling and characteristic, human factors like driver's fatigue, inherent randomness in drivers behaviour, lane changing etc. Hence if it is found that some group of vehicles are staying in same cluster for longer duration then it is verified to detect the Sybil attack.

In 2017, authors (Gu, Khatoun, Begriche, & Serhrouchni, 2017) proposes a technique based on nearest neighbour algorithm for detection of Sybil attack. When a vehicle enters in network, it sends its information to RSU. RSU then assigns unique id to each vehicle. The vehicles then discover their neighbour and share this information with RSU. Each vehicle are then categorised into different groups based on the similarity in their driving patterns. If same driving pattern found in any group then it is verified because two vehicles cannot have same driving pattern in same group. After verification malicious vehicle is termed as Sybil and it is detached from the network.

In year 2017, (Shipra & Kashyap, 2017) proposed a hybrid algorithm to detect the Sybil attack in VANET. This hybrid algorithm is a combination of two algorithms. First, they have used the fuzzy algorithms to create relationship between the attributes and the labels based on the objective function. In second step they use K means (in k mean algorithm k centroids are identified and then every data point is allocated to any of the cluster) algorithm that computes mean value of distances between vehicles, and based upon these two algorithms they detected the Sybil attack. To calculate objective function they have used the formula $ff=åw1.Ri+w2.Ej+w3.Di$, where Ri is the range of the source node Ej are the residual energy of the target nodes and Di is the distance between the source and the target node. The distance between the nodes is calculated using the Euclidian distance formula which is given by $Di=Ö((x1-x2)^2+(y1-y2)^2)$

In year 2019, authors (Bedi, Singh, & Devi, 2019) proposed KNN (K Nearest Neighbour) a non-parametric method for classification and regression, first K objects are taken and then their distance is measured and based upon their distance the objects are classified in different groups algorithm to detect the Sybil attack. First of all they have assigned each vehicle a unique id and then they compute the position of each vehicle. Based on the position of each vehicle they group the vehicle in each cluster. If two vehicles having same id present in any cluster then there is a Sybil attack as in network.

Machine Learning Approach

Machine learning is an application of Artificial Intelligence (AI) in which machine learns itself with experience and take decision accordingly. In machine learning certain computer programs are used to access data and this data is further used by machine to learn itself and take decision accordingly. Figure 8 depicts machine learning algorithms categorised into supervised learning, unsupervised learning and reinforcement learning. In supervised learning classification and regression task are performed, in classification algorithms, neural network, decision tree and support vector machine (SVM) are used for prediction whereas in regression, logistic regression, support vector regression (SVR) and gaussian process regression (GPR) are used. The main tasks performed in unsupervised learning are clustering and dimension reduction. For clustering k means, spectrum clustering and dirichlet process (DP) algorithms are used for getting results. Locally linear embedding (LLE), Manifold learning and isometric feature mapping (ISOMAP) are the main algorithms which are used in dimension reduction. Policy learning task is performed in reinforcement learning where Q learning algorithm is used to show the results and is mainly used in resource management routing.

Reinforcement learning algorithms are mostly used in VANET for predicting traffic and detecting security attacks. Authors in (Pinto, Lachowski, Pellenz, Penna, & Souza, 2018) classify the received signal strength data to detect the spoofing attack in wireless sensor networks. The authors in (Chandre, Mahalle, & Shinde, 2019) used the machine learning approach for intrusion detection in wireless sensor networks.

In 2019, researchers (Sujatha & Anita, 2019) proposed a hybrid algorithm to detect the Sybil attack using machine learning approach. Authors collect the data set from experimental test beds, and then load the data in the central sink system for training and testing, 70% training data and 30% as testing data are used. After selecting training and testing data, RSSI, number of neighbours, distance and energy threshold value are set first, then researcher applies fuzzy rule set to select the selection cluster head based on energy. After applying fuzzy rule network training is performed with set of input values and threshold values to detect the Sybil attack.

Figure 9. Category of algorithm (Ye. et al., 2018)

Category	Tasks	Algorithms	Applications
Supervised learning	Classification	Neural networks, decision Tree, SVM	Intrusion/fault/anomaly detection
	Regression	Logistic Regression, SVR, Gaussian process for regression	Throughput prediction, channel parameter estimation
Unsupervised learning	Clustering	K-means, spectrum clustering, Dirichilet process	Congestion control, hierarchical routing
	Dimension reduction	Manifold learning, LLE, ISOMAP	Data aggregation
Reinforcement learning	Policy learning	Q-learning	Resource management, routing

SUMMARY

Table 1 provides brevity of methods along with approaches to detect the sybil attack.

Table 1. Summary of main methods used to detect sybil attack in VANETs

Sr.No	Main Methods	Basic approach	Findings
1.	Cryptography	Encryption, decryption, static certificates, dynamic certificates	Complexity is more Creates high network overhead in vanet
2.	RSSI	Single signal strength, multiple signal strength, Voiceprint algorihm	Totally dependent on signal strength. Noise and inference are major issues
3.	Data Mining	KNN algorithm	Based on prediction of vehicles driving pattern
4.	Position & speed of vehicles	Determine the number of neighbours and compare the speed of vehicle with threshold speed	For each vehicle neighbouring information has to be stored. It is also complex and creates network overhead
5.	Machine Learning	Reinforcement learning	Used for traffic prediction. Spoofing etc.

CONCLUSION

This chapter classified various attacks in VANETs and analysed existing solutions to detect sybil attack of VANETs. It is observed that machine learning technique is more efficient for detecting Sybil attack in VANETs. The approaches like RSSI, Cryptography and neighbouring vehicles position creates network overheads as these algorithms continuously running in VANET to store the vehicles information.

REFERENCES

Abdelmagid Elsadig, M., & Fadlalla, Y. A. (2016). VANETs Security Issues and Challenges: A Survey. Indian J*ournal of Science and Technology, 9(28),* 1–8. doi:10.17485/ijst/2016/v9i28/97782

Aggarwal, A., Gandhi, S., Chaubey, N., & Jani, K. A. (2014, February). Trust based secure on demand routing protocol (TSDRP) for MANETs. In Proce*edings 2014 Fourth International Conference on Advanced Computing & Communication Technologies (pp.* 432-438). IEEE. Retrieved from https://ieeexplore.ieee.org/xpl/articleDetails.jsp?arnumber=6783493

Ahmad, F., Adnane, A., Franqueira, V. N. L., Kurugollu, F., & Liu, L. (2018). Man-in-the-middle attacks in vehicular ad-Hoc networks: Evaluating the impact of attackers' strategies. S*ensors (Switzerland), 18(11),* 4040. doi:10.339018114040 PMID:30463282

Ayaida, M., Messai, N., Najeh, S., & Boris Ndjore, K. (2019). A Macroscopic Traffic Model-based Approach for Sybil Attack Detection in VANETs. *Ad Hoc Networks, 90*(February), 0–12. doi:10.1016/j.adhoc.2019.01.010

Ayaida, M., Messai, N., Wilhelm, G., & Najeh, S. (2019). A Novel Sybil Attack Detection Mechanism for C-ITS. In *Proceedings 2019 15th International Wireless Communications & Mobile Computing Conference (IWCMC)*, 913–918. doi:10.1109/iwcmc.2019.8766572

Baza, M., Nabil, M., Bewermeier, N., Fidan, K., Mahmoud, M., & Abdallah, M. (2019). *Detecting Sybil Attacks using Proofs of Work and Location in VANETs*. 1–15. Retrieved from https://arxiv.org/abs/1904.05845

Bedi, R., Singh, B., & Devi, M. (2019). Position Depended Sybil Attack Detection using Efficient KNN technique with Clustering. *International Journal on Computer Science and Engineering*, 7(2), 266–272. doi:10.26438/ijcse/v7i2.266272

Chandre, P. R., Mahalle, P. N., & Shinde, G. R. (2019). Machine Learning Based Novel Approach for Intrusion Detection and Prevention System: A Tool Based Verification. *Proceedings - 2018 IEEE Global Conference on Wireless Computing and Networking, GCWCN 2018*. 10.1109/GCWCN.2018.8668618

Chaubey, N. K. (2016). Security Analysis of Vehicular Ad Hoc Networks (VANETs): A Comprehensive Study. *International Journal of Security and Its Applications*, 10(5), 261–274. doi:10.14257/ijsia.2016.10.5.25

Dutta, N., & Chellappan, S. (2013). A Time-series Clustering Approach for Sybil Attack Detection in Vehicular Ad hoc Networks. In *Proceedings VEHICULAR 2013: The Second International Conference on Advances in Vehicular Systems, Technologies, and Applications*, (February), 35–40.

Garip, M. T., Kim, P. H., Reiher, P., & Gerla, M. (2017). *INTERLOC: An interference-aware RSSI-based localization and sybil attack detection mechanism for vehicular ad hoc networks*. 1–6. doi:10.1109/ccnc.2017.8013424

Gu, P., Khatoun, R., Begriche, Y., & Serhrouchni, A. (2017). K-Nearest Neighbours classification based Sybil attack detection in Vehicular networks. In *Proceedings of the 2017 3rd Conference on Mobile and Secure Services, MOBISECSERV 2017*. 10.1109/MOBISECSERV.2017.7886565

Hamdan, S., Hudaib, A., & Awajan, A. (2019). Detecting Sybil attacks in vehicular ad hoc networks. *International Journal of Parallel Emergent and Distributed Systems, 34*, 1–11. doi:10.1080/17445760 .2019.1617865

Hezam Al Junaid, M. A., Syed, A. A., Mohd Warip, M. N., Fazira Ku Azir, K. N., & Romli, N. H. (2018). Classification of Security Attacks in VANET: A Review of Requirements and Perspectives. *MATEC Web of Conferences, 150*, 1–7. 10.1051/matecconf/201815006038

Khelifi, H., Luo, S., Nour, B., & Shah, S. C. (2018). Security and privacy issues in vehicular named data networks: An overview. *Mobile Information Systems, 2018*, 1–11. doi:10.1155/2018/5672154

Kumar Karn, C., & Prakash Gupta, C. (2016). A Survey on VANETs Security Attacks and Sybil Attack Detection. *International Journal of Sensors, Wireless Communications and Control, 6*(1), 45–62. doi:1 0.2174/2210327905999151103170103

Liang, W., Li, Z., Zhang, H., Sun, Y., & Bie, R. (2015). Vehicular ad hoc networks: Architectures, Research issues, Challenges, and trends. *International Journal of Distributed Sensor Networks, 2015(1)* (1), 1–11. doi:10.1155/2015/745303

Mittal, P., & Ahlawat, D. (2016). Sybil Node Detection Using Neighbourhood Information Passing. *International Journal of Computer Science and Mobile Computing, 5*(8), 230–240.

Namarpreet, K., & Aman, A. (2015). A review on security issues in VANET. *International Journal of Advanced Research in Computer Science, 6*(2), 161–165.

Parmar, U., & Singh, S. (2015). Overview of Various Attacks in VANET. *International Journal of Engineering Research and General Science, 3*(3), 120–125.

Panchal, A., & Singh, D. D. (2017). Segregation of Sybil Attack using Neighbouring Information in VANET. *Iarjset, 4*(6), 172–180. doi:10.17148/IARJSET.2017.4631

Pinto, E. M. D. L., Lachowski, R., Pellenz, M. E., Penna, M. C., & Souza, R. D. (2018). A machine learning approach for detecting spoofing attacks in wireless sensor networks. In *Proceedings - International Conference on Advanced Information Networking and Applications, AINA*. 10.1109/AINA.2018.00113

Prakash, R., & Kamal, S. (2014). Improved session key-based certificate to detect sybil attack. *IJERT, 3*(5), 116–119.

Rahbari, M., & Jabreil Jamali, M. A. (2011). Efficient Detection of Sybil attack Based on Cryptography in Vanet. *International Journal of Network Security & Its Applications*. doi:10.5121/ijnsa.2011.3614

Rawat, ASantosh, S., & Rama, S. (2014). Vanet: Security Attacks and Its Possible Solutions. *Journal of Information and Operations Management, 3*(1), 301–304. doi:10.100713398-014-0173-7.2

Roweis, S., & Saul, L. (2000). Nonlinear dimensionality reduction by locally linear embedding. *Science, 290*(5500), 2323–2326. doi:10.1126cience.290.5500.2323 PMID:11125150

Saini, M., Alelaiwi, A., & El Saddik, A. (2015). How close are we to realizing a pragmatic VANET solution? A meta-survey. *ACM Computing Surveys, 48*(2), 1–40. doi:10.1145/2817552

Saul, L., & Roweis, S. (2003). *Think globally, fit locally: Unsupervised learning of nonlinear manifolds.* JMLR.

Sharma, A. K., Saroj, S. K., Chauhan, S. K., & Saini, S. K. (2017). Sybil attack prevention and detection in vehicular ad hoc network. In *Proceeding - IEEE International Conference on Computing, Communication, and Automation, ICCCA 2016,* (April), 594–599. 10.1109/CCAA.2016.7813790

Shipra, D., & Kashyap, R. (2017). *DETECTING SYBIL ATTACK USING HYBRID FUZZY K-MEANS ALGORITHM IN WSN., 5*(2), 1560–1565.

Singh, K., & Kaur, H. (2018). Evaluation of proposed technique for detection of Sybil attack in VANET. *International Journal of Scientific Research in Computer Science and Engineering, 6*(5), 10–15. doi:10.26438/ijsrcse/v6i5.1015

Sujatha, V., & Anita, E. A. M. (2019). FEM-hybrid machine learning approach for the detection of sybil attacks in the wireless sensor networks. *International Journal of Innovative Technology and Exploring Engineering.*

Sumra, I., Sellappan, P., Abdullah, A., & Ahmad, A. (2018). Security issues and Challenges in MANET-VANET-FANET: A Survey. *EAI Endorsed Transactions on Energy Web, 5*(17), 1–6. doi:10.4108/EAI.10-4-2018.155884

Tenenbaum, J., de Silva, V., & Langford, J. (2000). A global geometric framework for nonlinear dimensionality reduction. *Science, 290*(5500), 2319–2323. doi:10.1126cience.290.5500.2319 PMID:11125149

Yao, Y., Xiao, B., Wu, G., Liu, X., Yu, Z., Zhang, K., & Zhou, X. (2019). Multi-Channel Based Sybil Attack Detection in Vehicular Ad Hoc Networks Using RSSI. *IEEE Transactions on Mobile Computing, 18*(2), 362–375. doi:10.1109/TMC.2018.2833849

Ye, H., Liang, L., Li, G. Y., Kim, J., Lu, L., & Wu, M. (2018). Machine Learning for Vehicular Networks: Recent Advances and Application Examples. *IEEE Vehicular Technology Magazine, 13*(2), 94–101. doi:10.1109/MVT.2018.2811185

Yousef Al-Raba'nah, G. S. (2015). Security Issues in Vehicular Ad Hoc Networks (VANET): A survey. *International Journal of Sciences & Applied Research, 2*(4), 50–55.

Chapter 10

Data Science in Vehicular Ad-Hoc Networks

Ananthi Govindasamy

Department of Electronics and Communication Engineering, Thiagarajar College of Engineering, India

S. J. Thiruvengadam

Thiagarajar College of Engineering, India

ABSTRACT

Vehicular Ad-hoc Networks (VANET) is a mobile ad-hoc network in which vehicles move rapidly through the road and topology changes very frequently. VANET helps to provide safe, secure, and more comfort travel to travelers. Vehicles intelligence is an important component in high mobility networks, equipped with multiple advanced onboard sensors and contain large volumes of data. Datascience is an effective approach to artificial intelligence and provides a rich set of tools to exploit such data for the benefit of the networks. In this chapter, the distinctive characteristics of high mobility vehicular ad-hoc networks are identified and the use of datascience is addressing the resulting challenges. High mobility vehicular ad-hoc networks exhibit distinctive characteristics, which have posed significant challenges to wireless network design. Vehicle traffic data, and road traffic future condition data are analyzed and incorporated to enhance the VANET performance. VANETs technologies are useful to efficiently model and reliably transmit big data.

INTRODUCTION

The use of communication equipment in VANET is that the vehicles are used to pass the messages from the vehicle to another vehicle called as vehicle to vehicle communication. By means of vehicle to roadside infrastructure, vehicle can pass the messages to roadside unit. A vehicle collects traffic safety information by means of V2V and V2R communications in VANET to drivers for secured driving. In order to realize this technique, IEEE 802.11p standard is proposed in VANET known as Dedicated Short-Range Communication system (DSRC) explained by Hassnaa Moustafa., & Yan Zhang (2009).

DOI: 10.4018/978-1-7998-2570-8.ch010

Intuitively, radio resource allocation for vehicular ad-hoc networks employ device to device communications to support vehicle to vehicle transmission in cellular systems described by the Cheng, Yang and Shen (2015). In future, vehicles are equipped with a sensor, engine control units, radar, lidar and cameras, to help the vehicle observe the traffic environment in real time. The system collects, generates, stores and communicate huge traffic data referred as mobile big data explained by Cheng et al. (2017).

Sensors are placed inside a vehicle to measure the speed, acceleration and distance from other vehicles. Global Positioning System receiver is used for finding the position of vehicles and provides navigation services. Interfacing system is applicable for human interaction in a system.

Sensors are placed in roadside access points used to detect real time events, collect and process the information and deliver the traffic information. Data gathering is the major research area in VANET. Road traffic flow conditions, unusual traffic behavior, traffic density for irregular structure of road geometry in VANET is to be analyzed. Hence, Data science is the major research area in VANET is used to predict the traffic condition in earlier stage.

Data science comprises many fields such as data preparation, data aligning, data cleansing, data capturing, problem solving, programming, mathematics and statistics. By using certain algorithm in data science and machine learning tool one can insight extract traffic data in VANET published by the authors Xu et al. (2018). Data modeling and production of data processes can be designed using prototypes, algorithms and predictive models. This chapter addresses the use of data science in Vehicular Ad-hoc Networks.

VEHICULAR AD-HOC NETWORKS

The number of moving vehicles in VANET is limited in road topology; one can easily expect the position of the vehicle in future. If more vehicles are present in VANET, the challenge here is to provide sufficient computing, communication and sensing capabilities to provide power for supporting the functions.

The nodes or vehicles in VANET are dynamic in nature, usually at very high speed and update its position continually. The link between the vehicles will be disconnected frequently due to the high mobile dynamic networks topology and that will be extended to the entire road network.

Each Vehicle in VANET consists of onboard unit and access units. The connection between onboard unit and access unit is wired or it may be wireless connection. This domain is called as vehicle domain unit. In another domain, each vehicle consists of on board unit and roadside unit. On board unit is treated as a mobile node and roadside unit is called as static node. This domain is called as ad-hoc domain unit. Roadside units are connected to the internet by means of gateways. Roadside units are connected by means of multihop communication.

TYPES OF VEHICLE COMMUNICATION

In-vehicle communication: detect vehicle performance.

Vehicle to vehicle communication: shares the information among vehicles

Vehicle to roadside unit communication: informs traffic flow in real time, weather condition, environmental information

Vehicle-to-broadband cloud (V2B) communication: access wireless broadband systems for vehicle tracking.

Onboard Equipment: consists of Global Positioning System, Trusted Component, Sensors and OBU. Liang et al. (2017) explained the concept of central processing unit in each vehicle uses communication protocol and a wireless transceiver is used for transmission of data between vehicles and vehicles to roadside units.

Road Side Equipment: collects real time traffic information from roadside unit and informs to the moving vehicles.

WAVE Standard (Wireless Access in Vehicular Environments)

WAVE is a complex IEEE 802.11p standard used to pledge fast reliable exchange of secured messages. This standard is allotted 75MHz spectrum band in DSRC at 5.9GHz in vehicular environments. The transmitter block is given in figure 1 uses scrambled binary data and is given to the convolution encoder for forward error correction concept is specified by the authors Jiang and Delgrossi (2008). 2/3 and ¾ coding rates are generated using patterns called as puncturing. The binary data encoder output is passed through the two-step permutation algorithm used in interleaver. The complex data symbols are generated using quadrature phase shift keying modulation and quadrature amplitude modulation (16 QAM and 64 QAM) based on the standard given. The complex data symbols are converted from serial to parallel form for transmission. Four pilot tones are used and the complex data symbols are verified along with subcarriers. Inverse fast Fourier transform is to convert frequency domain data into time domain data. Then it is parallel to serial converted and the cyclic prefix is added to eliminate the effect of multipath propagation. In signal field, Orthogonal Frequency Division Multiplexing (OFDM) symbols are represented, this OFDM symbols are combined with the preamble considered as a packet and is transmitted to the radio channel.

Figure 1. Transmitter

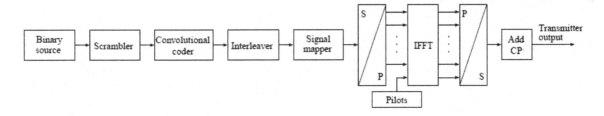

Channel

The frequency selective time variant channel consists of delay line tapped model and additive white Gaussian noise (AWGN) is added in the receiver. The discrete convolution has been performed between the transmitted signal and Channel Impulse Response. The channel impulse response is measured using 3D ray optical modelling and is measured using stochastic channel models. The channel impulse response is restructured for each sample period T= 0.1μs. The output of the signal is given as the input of the receiver block given in figure 2.

Figure 2. Channel models

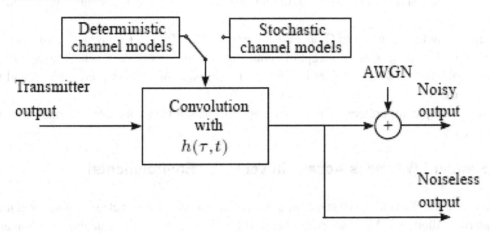

Receiver

Receiver consists of two parts namely preamble field processing, signal decoding and data fields. The structure of the receiver is represented in figure 3. Preambles are used to achieve frequency synchronization such as coarse and fine synchronization respectively. The preambles size can either be short or long preambles.

The received signal is given to the receiver block. The received signal is equalized and is decoded to retrieve the transmitted information based on payload size and data rate. The OFDM symbols are decoded in the data field. Cyclic prefix is removed in the receiver. The OFDM symbols are converted from serial to parallel form and by using 64-point FFT, frequency domain representation takes place. Subsequently, channel estimation takes place.

The complex data symbols are converted to binary data using log likelihood principle. It is given to interleaver, Viterbi decoder and descrambler. Bit error rate and packet error rates are considered using transmitted data and receive data.

Figure 3. Receiver

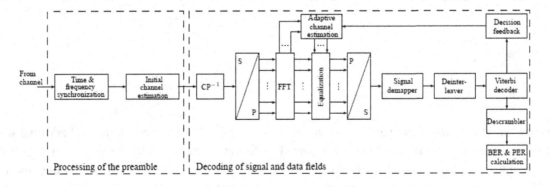

Theoretical Analysis for Vehicular Channels

Novel Vehicular system model is to be created and have a significant impact on Line of Sight environment in vehicular ad-hoc networks in vehicle to vehicle channels are to be analysed. A closed form expression for Bit Error Rate (BER) of the different Received Signal Strength Indicator (RSSI) measurements is to be derived.

Deterministic Channel Models

The complex baseband representation of ray optical channel model is given by

$$h(\tau,t) = \sum_{k=1}^{N(t)} a_k(t) e^{j(2\pi f \tau_k(t) + \phi_k(t))} \delta(\tau - \tau_k(t)) \tag{1}$$

where the kth multipath amplitude $a_k(t)$, a delay $\tau_k(t)$ and phase shift $\phi_k(t)$ at time t. $N(t)$ is the number of multipath components.

Stochastic Channel Models

- **VTV:** Vehicle to Vehicle -Expressway oncoming (EO)
- **VTV:** Vehicle to Vehicle -Urban canyon oncoming (UCO)
- **VTV:** Vehicle to Vehicle -Expressway same direction with wall (ESDWW)
- **RTV:** Roadside to Vehicle -Suburban street (SS)
- **RTV:** Roadside to Vehicle -Expressway (E)
- **RTV:** Roadside to Vehicle -Urban Canyon (UC)

The above techniques are characterized by a LOS component and multipath components. Multipath components represent a delay value, maximum Doppler shift and the line of sight Doppler component. The Doppler frequencies are at the speeds of 120 or 140km/h in physical layer simulations of high mobile propagation scenarios. Since this model is non stationary in nature, modelling vehicular channels are an important research issue described by the authors Mecklenbra uker et al. (2011).

DATA SCIENCE

Data science is a technique which uses algorithms, processes and systems to extract traffic information from traffic datasets.

Big Data

Big data is the research area used to predict real time traffics (Voorhees, 2013) by studying huge amount of data.

NEED FOR BIG DATA IN VANET

Different sensors are placed in vehicles and roads to collect weather conditions, vehicle conditioning and response of the drivers due to the change in traffic condition and send the traffic data in VANET. The developing models in VANET helpful for predicting road conditions and driver behavior that leads to secure roads. Big data techniques described by bedi & Jindal (2014) are useful in VANET to collect huge traffic data for improving the traffic management processes.

Nan Cheng et al. (2018) described the concept of big data analysis in VANET using onboard GPS equipment placed in each vehicle, gathers the data from neighboring vehicles by means of other onboard GPS units placed in that vehicles and sends the vehicles information data.

VANET THZ CHANNEL MODELING

The factors influencing the Vehicular terahertz channel modeling is that channel geometry of vehicular channels, vehicle motion, the directivity of the antenna and radiation pattern of weather conditions. The received signal in each vehicle is given by

$$r(t) = \text{Re}\left\{\left(x_I(t) + jx_Q(t)e^{j2\pi f_c t}\right)\right\} \tag{2}$$

Equation (2) represents the received vehicle signal consists of multiple copies of the transmitted vehicle signals with different attenuations and delays. f_c is the transmission frequency. The pass band signal is given by,

$$h_{PB}(t) = \sum_{l=0}^{L-1} a_l \delta(t - t_l) \tag{3}$$

$h_{PB}(t)$ is the baseband channel. L is the multipath components. a_l represents loss and t_l denotes the delay respectively. The vehicular channel is given by

$$h(t) = \sum_{l=0}^{L-1} a_l e^{-j2\pi f_c t_l} \delta(t - t_l) \tag{4}$$

Consider line of sight component in Equation (4), L=1, Equation (4) becomes

$$h(t) = a_f e^{j\theta} \delta(t - t_o) \tag{5}$$

Where a_f is the line of sight component amplitude, θ is the phase; t_0 is the terahertz wave propagation delay. It is noted that in THz vehicular channels, if directional antennas were used, the antenna misalignment, loss due to frequency dependency and frequency dispersion index a_f. The vehicular channel consists of specular and diffused components in a static environment are given by

$$m_l = a_l e^{-j2\pi f_c t_l} = s_l + d_l \tag{6}$$

$$s_l = \sigma_{s_l} e^{(j2\pi f_c \cos(\theta_l) + \varphi_l)} \tag{7}$$

$$d_l = \sigma_{d_l} \frac{1}{\sqrt{M_l}} \sum_{m=1}^{M_l} b_m e^{(j2\pi f_c \cos(\theta_m) + \varphi_m)} \tag{8}$$

where σ_{s_l} is the amplitude of the specular component; θ_l is the angle of arrival component; and φ_l is the phase of the specular component, respectively. σ_{d_l} is the amplitude of the diffused component; M_l is the number; b_m is the amplitude; θ_m is the angle of arrival component; and φ_m is the phase of the signal of the diffused component, respectively. The values of σ_{s_l} and σ_{d_l} are assumed to be unity in ideal case. It is concluded that in the absence of line of sight component, the distribution of channel is Rayleigh under angle of arrival assumption. If line of sight signal is considered, Rice and Nakagami distributions are modelled in vehicular channels. The Path loss is given by

$$PL = PL_0 + 10n \log_{10}(d) + M \tag{9}$$

where PL0 is the path loss, n is the path loss exponent, d is the transmitter and receiver separation; and M represents misalignment factor related with antenna gain.

VEHICULAR THZ WAVE CHANNEL SIMULATION USING NYUSIM SIMULATOR

Channel parameters:

RF bandwidth: 800MHz
Frequency: 100GHz
Transmitter-Receiver separation distance: 10-500 meters
Transmit power: 30dBm
Transmit and receive array type: Uniform Linear array

Simulation of Power delay profile is given in figure 4.

VEHICLE TRAFFIC BIG DATA

Apache Hadoop

It is the most popular Big Data framework. It is a project with an open source code managed by the Apache Software Foundation. This platform is used for distributed calculations based on traffic data. The storage capacity in this platform is petabytes of data of information. Hadoop increases the speed of data processing performance grows in accordance with the increase of data storage space.

Figure 4. Power delay profile from NYUSIM simulator

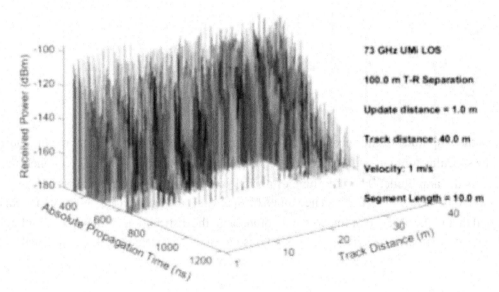

DEEP LEARNING ALGORITHM: STACKING DILATED CONVOLUTIONAL AUTOENCODERS

The training samples of vehicular traffic dataset numeric vectors are in the form of library called as pcap files is considered as a raw data given to the input of dilated convolutional autoencoder deep learning block. Dilated convolutional autoencoder is given in figure 5.

Figure 5. Dilated convolutional autoencoder

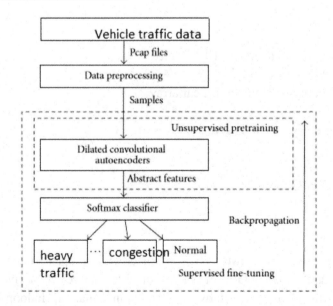

Types of Training:

- ◦ Unsupervised pretraining
- ◦ Supervised fine tuning

In unsupervised pretraining process, dilated convolutional autoencoders train a set of features of huge volumes of unlabeled traffic datasets. The learned unlabeled datasets are improved using supervised fine-tuning process given in figure 6 using the back-propagation algorithm and we can use rare labeled data for training. Figure 7 shows the convolutional neural network without using dilated convolutions without pooling layers. It is observed that one convolution layer is given in figure 7 from a convolutional autoencoder. SoftMax classifier is to perform classification to extract dataset features.

Figure 6. Fine tuning process

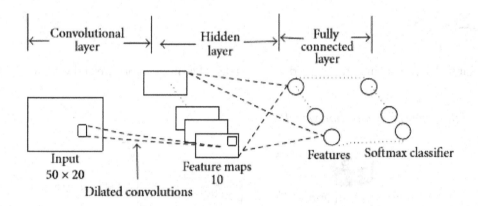

Figure 7. Dilated convolutional autoencoder

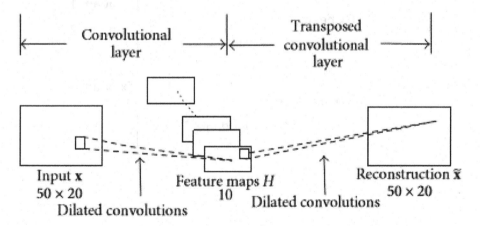

The traffic dataset is given to the feature maps are given to the activation function

$$h^k = f\left(xW^k + b^k\right)$$ (10)

Where x is the traffic dataset input is in the form of two dimensional numeric vector, W^k is the weight matrix, bk is the bias term, $f(\times)$ is the kth feature map. Rectified linear unit is used as an activation function. The output of the hidden layer are mapped by means of transposed convolution.

$$x^\sim = f\left(\sum_{k\in H} h^k W^k + b^\sim\right)$$ (11)

H is a set of feature maps. The mean square error of the dilated convolutional encoder is to minimize the input and reconstruction vectors. The mean squared error is given by,

$$L\left(x, x^\sim\right) = \frac{1}{n}\sum_{i}^{n}(x_i - x_i^\sim)2$$ (12)

Vehicular network database creation is done using deep learning algorithm and vehicular traffic data.

Figure 8. High speed communication vehicle

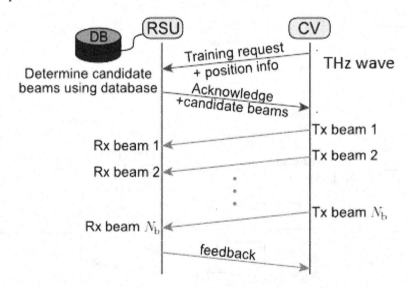

TIMING DIAGRAM

Algorithm

1. Each vehicle sends the request beam position to the roadside unit and sends its current position based on localization sensors.
2. Roadside unit acknowledges the list of beam pairs for training by establishing the database using communication vehicles position.
3. The training has been done using deep learning dilated convolutional autoencoder algorithm.
4. The roadside unit feeds back the best beam to the vehicle and high-speed Terahertz wave communications begin.
5. Upon request, the roadside unit uses the position information informs the database.
6. Roadside unit determines the best beam from the database sends the best link to the vehicle.
7. Roadside unit sends acknowledgement also.

CONCLUSION

In this book chapter, data science in VANET is discussed in a detailed manner. The fundamentals of VANET and characteristics, standards are explained. Dilated convolutional autoencoder deep learning algorithm is useful for training the traffic datasets in VANET. The traffic datasets are taken in real time using GPS, Onboard equipment and localization sensors placed in vehicle as well as roadside sensors. A methodology for traffic requisition in VANET in real time traffic has been analyzed. This chapter is useful for finding the traffic flow in VANET to provide secure roads.

REFERENCES

Bedi, P., & Jindal, V. (2014). Use of Big Data Technology in Vehicular Ad-Hoc Networks. In *Proceedings of. IEEE ICACCI*, 1677–83.

Cheng, N., Lyu, F., Chen, J., Xu, W., Zhou, H., Zhang, S., & Shen, X. S. (2018). Big Data Driven Vehicular Networks. *IEEE Network*, *32*(6), 160–167. doi:10.1109/MNET.2018.1700460

Cheng, X., Fang, L., Hong, X., & Yang, L. (2017). Exploiting mobile big data: Sources, features, and applications. *IEEE Network*, *31*(1), 72–79. doi:10.1109/MNET.2017.1500295NM

Cheng, X., Yang, L., & Shen, X. (2015). D2D for intelligent transportation systems, A feasibility study. *IEEE Transactions on Intelligent Transportation Systems*, *16*(4), 1784–1793. doi:10.1109/TITS.2014.2377074

Jiang, D., & Delgrossi, L. (2008). IEEE 802.11p: Towards an International Standard for Wireless Access in Vehicular Environments, *IEEE Vehicular Technology Conference*, 2036–2040.

Liang, L., Peng, H., Li, G. Y., & Shen, X. (2017). Vehicular communications: A physical layer perspective. *IEEE Transactions on Vehicular Technology*, *66*(12), 647–659. doi:10.1109/TVT.2017.2750903

Mecklenbrauker, C. F., Molisch, A. F., Karedal, J., Tufvesson, F., Paier, A., Bernadó, L., ... & Czink, N. (2011). Vehicular Channel Characterization and Its Implications for Wireless System Design and Performance. *Proceedings of the IEEE, 99*(7), 1189–1212.

Moustafa, H., & Zhang, Y. (2009). *Vehicular Networks: Techniques, Standards, and Applications*. Boca Raton, FL: CRC Press.

Voorhees, A. M. (2013). A general theory of traffic movement. *Transportation, 40*(6), 1105–1116. doi:10.100711116-013-9487-0

Xu, W., Zhou, H., Cheng, N., Lyu, F., Shi, W., Chen, J., & Shen, X. (2018). Internet of vehicles in big data era, *IEEE/CAA Journal of Automatica. Sinica, 5*(1), 19–35.

Chapter 11
Efficient Encryption Techniques for Data Transmission Through the Internet of Things Devices

Deena Nath Gupta

ⓘ https://orcid.org/0000-0001-6323-411X

Jamia Millia Islamia, India

Rajendra Kumar

Jamia Millia Islamia, India

Ashwani Kumar

United College of Engineering and Research, India

ABSTRACT

A secure environment is needed to communicate without any information leakage. From large devices having UPS to small devices having a battery, the parameter about security changes over time. Researchers need to work in three basics of security: (1) Mutual authentication between devices, (2) Strong encryption methodology for transmission, and (3) Secure storage environment with anytime availability. The IoT-enabled devices demand a lightweight secure environment. In this chapter, authors are concerning on all three points, i.e. Mutual authentication between devices, Strong encryption methodology for transmission, and Secure storage environment with anytime availability. Authors study some of the methods related to lightweight mutual authentication, lightweight cryptography, and local storage techniques; will talk about different issues in the field of secure communication, secure transmission, and secure storage; and will try to find out some research gap with a possible countermeasure.

DOI: 10.4018/978-1-7998-2570-8.ch011

COMMUNICATION IN THE INTERNET OF THINGS ENVIRONMENT (INTRODUCTION)

Communication is an important part of our life. It is necessary for the growth and development of an individual as well as for the growth and development of the whole society. Researchers are working hard to design an efficient methodology for secure communication. Three things are very important in order to formulate an efficient communication methodology: (1) language knowledge and understanding of the sender, (2) language knowledge and understanding of the receiver, (3) strong and unbreakable secure communication medium.

The need of the present time is not only the communication between machines and humans but also one need strong security for the communication between machines and machines (i.e. M2M communication). In the scenario of the Internet of Things, almost all objects of the real world are communicating. These communications are done through sensors without or hardly any human intervention. A large number of sensors are deployed everywhere for sensing and actuation purposes. The increasing number of sensors and end devices are prone to attack easily and hence author need a next level of the secure algorithm but at the same time a lightweight one.

Machine to Machine Communication (M2M), Cyber-Physical System (CPS), Vehicular Area Network (VANET), Body Area Network (BANET) and likewise terminologies are a subset of the Internet of Things (IoT) (Atzori, Iera, & Morabito, 2010). Figure 1, the 3-TIER architecture of Body Area Network (Source: Internet), is illustrating an architecture that is meant for a typical body area network used by doctors. One can see a three-tier communication here. Many sensor devices are placed on different part of the body to get different readings according to their need.

Figure 1.

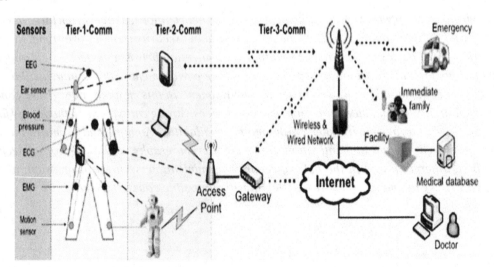

In all these types of networks the communication has to be done in three ways: (1) communication between end devices and local sensors, (2) communication between local sensors and cluster head sensor, (3) communication between cluster head sensor and processing unit. The number of end devices and sensors are very large and hence designer needs a strong mechanism to ensure the confidentiality, integrity, and authentication of participating devices. Because every device is communicating, they should be smart enough to send and receive the signals, to store some data, and to actuate. Highly complex algorithms are meant only for the devices working on UPS such as the desktop PC. Programmers need the algorithms having less complexity yet a similar level of security for mobile devices, such as laptop PC or PDA or cellular communication devices (Khan, Khan, Zaheer, & Khan, 2012). Similarly, for RFID Tags or Internet of Things devices, researcher needs lightweight secure algorithms or ultra-lightweight secure algorithms. The devices used in the Internet of Things framework are very less powered (equipped with a tinny battery) and hence, one cannot impose long algorithms over them. In the Internet of Things, the algorithms with lesser gate requirements are considered good for use. Achieving a similar level of security with less gate equivalent (GE) is the main challenge for the security algorithms of Internet of Things devices. The Gate Equivalent (GE) value is calculated by dividing the complete area of the circuit by the area of a basic NAND Gate (Maimut & Ouafi, 2012).

TRADITIONAL COMPUTING AND INTERNET OF THINGS (KEY CHALLENGES)

Change is the law of nature. No one can deny the new requirements of the coming generation. This is the time to shift from traditional computing environment to a new Internet of Things environment where each and every seen object of the earth is going to be connected via the internet. As researchers are growing, many old boundaries need to be rescaled.

Huge number of devices needs strong mechanism for their identification. In the Internet of Things, researchers mainly are using a large number of sensors to collect the data from different geographical location. These sensors are small and having very less power, so researchers may see a quick replacement for them. Unique name for each device is then required to differentiate among different sensors. A well planned naming and identity management system is required that can actively assign and manage unique identity for such a huge number of objects (Robshaw & Williamson, 2015).

Internet of Things is the unification of different technologies. Two sensors may be built by two different manufacturers by using different standardization. There is a need to provide an interoperable platform so that the information from one device will communicate to another device seemingly. It will also guaranty the accessibility of a device.

No nearby device should be able to read the communication of other devices. In cryptography, researchers mainly focus on information privacy. The number of devices is large and also they are in close proximity to each other, so a side-channel attack may possible. Also one may produce itself as a neighbouring node. Information leakage in any form should be protected (Singh, Tripathi, & Jara, 2014).

Limited availability of spectrums is also a problem with a large number of wireless communications. Spectrums should be allocated dynamically in order to meet the demands of the Internet of Things devices because devices in the Internet of Things may need the communication channel, not at the same time.

CRYPTOGRAPHY IN ITS LIGHTWEIGHT VERSION

Internet of Things (IoT) is the combo of three orientations: Object-oriented, Network-oriented, and Logic-oriented. A statement is issued by CASAGRAS (COORDINATION AND SUPPORT ACTION FOR GLOBAL RFID-RELATED-ACTIVITIES AND STANDARDIZATION) consortium – "A global infrastructure to connect mechanical and logical objects is known as the Internet of Things." Wireless Identification and Sensing Platform (WISP) have been used to measure different physical quantities such as temperature in a certain environment (Gubbi, Buyya, Marusic, & Palaniswami, 2013). The workflow of the Internet of Things can be defined as: Physical object sensing, identification of machine, communication of information then take action, and at last results of action invoked. Chonggang wang and Mohamoud Daneshmand suggested the Internet of Things as a CPS (cyber-physical system). A cyber-physical system can be seen as a network of networks where the collection of raw data should be done with utmost care.

Many architectures of the Internet of Things have been suggested and from them, Cisco's seven-level model is the most famous. Earlier researchers are having a three-level model that consists of the wireless sensor networks as physical level, cloud servers as network level, and applications. After that, there comes a five-level model which includes edge nodes at level-1, object abstraction at level-2, service management at level-3, service composition at level-4, and applications at level-5. The currently used Cisco's seven-level model consists of edge nodes at level-1, communication at level-2, edge computing at level-3, data accumulation at level-4, data abstraction at level-5, applications at level-6, and users and centers at level-7. Mainly used devices to identify and/or collect the information from objects are RFID, 2D-barcode, and infrared sensors, and IEEE 802.15.4. The transmission technologies used in the Internet of Things arena are 3G (third generation), UMTS (Universal Mobile Telecommunications Service), Wi-Fi (Wireless Fidelity), Bluetooth, Infrared, and Zigbee etc. The service-oriented architecture consists of the application at level-1, service composition at level-2, service management at level-3, object abstraction at level-4, and trust, privacy and security management at level-5 (CHONGGANG et al., 2013).

Lightweight cryptography is a security system that is made for constrained devices. While making any lightweight algorithm, the main focus is on its hardware implementation. The required logic gate to run any program is termed as Gate Equivalent. The lower the GE, the lighter the algorithm is. In table 1, a comparison of some well-known ciphers is given in terms of Gate Equivalent.

On the other hand, while working on codes researchers try to make them as small as researchers can, without compromising the security. The software in this mechanism should be compatible with the tiny OS used in small battery-operated devices. As researchers progress in automation and start including the devices from our daily life, the concern for their security also risen (IHS Technology, 2016).

To provide adequate security to these devices the concept of lightweight cryptography emerged. Some advancement from our traditional block and stream ciphers includes the concept of shift operations. In the process of lightweight security system design, authors mainly use the concept of low computing overhead, pre-image resistance (one-way) and second pre-image (key-pair) resistance hash functions and pseudorandom number generators that include the concept of non-linear feedback shift registers. Lightweight cryptography is important to save the energy and storage of devices. A grain level of detailing about lightweight cryptographic primitive is given in figure 2, Lightweight Cryptographic Primitives.

It is very useful for low-power embedded systems, machine to machine (M2M) communication, radio frequency identification (RFID)s tags, nanotechnology, sensors, and smart networks (Papers, 2019). Two of the main components used in cryptographic security algorithms are hash functions and random

Table 1. A comparison of some well-known ciphers is given in terms of gate equivalent

Cipher	Key Bits	Block Bits	GE
PRESENT-80	80	64	1570
PRESENT-128	128	64	1886
AES	128	128	3400
HIGHT	128	64	3408
MCrypton	96	64	2681
DES	56	64	2309
DESL	56	64	1848
DESXL	184	64	2168
Hummingbird	128	16	2159
Trivium	80	1	2580
Trivium X 8	80	8	2952
Trivium X 16	80	16	3166
Grain	80	1	1450
Grain X 8	80	8	2756
Grain X 16	80	16	4248
MICKEY	128	1	5039
Pandaka (16,6)	96	16	760
Pandaka (32,6)	192	32	1520

Figure 2.

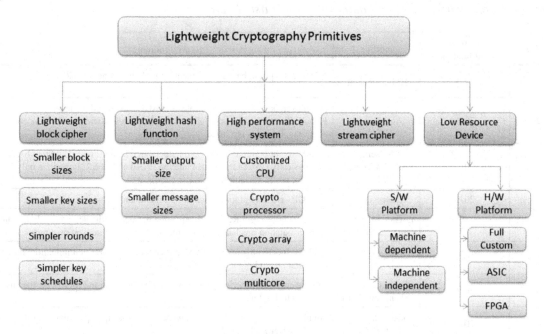

number generators. Authors will see each of them in greater detail. Internet of Things is one of the very famous concepts in computer science industry having a strong root. Ubiquitous computing needs scalability to be fit in the Internet of Things environment. As of now, authors are facing some issues while communication between two devices. Authors know that any secure communication needs to handle three basic things (1) transmission time, (2) storage requirement, and (3) security threat; authors will talk about challenges in all three aspects in brief.

Mutual Authentication for the Internet of Things Devices

Mutual authentication works on the session layer (level-5) of Open Systems Interconnection OSI model. Internet of Things basically unites different cultures. Heterogeneous working environments work together to form a system where anyone can send any type of data. A central mechanism is required that will be responsible for the communication between two different end systems. The transparency of received data should be maintained so that one knows the working of the central system. While working with different environments a mutual consent is required (Chien, 2007).

As authors are moving towards lightweight cryptography, a lightweight version of mutual authentication protocol is much needed. Working on the Internet of Things is like creating a whole new world. A parallel system will build to work on every aspect of computing, i.e., communication, storage, and actuation. Communication is an important part of any system. This is the source of information. Information that makes the system works.

So this communication should be secure. A sense of security can be achieved by authenticating both the parties mutually. Many works have been done in advance. Table 2 enlists some of the work done by different authors to achieve secure mutual authentication.

Table 2. Different works on mutual authentication is listed here

Sl. No.	Year of Publication	Author	Methodology
1	1998	Hoffstein et. al.	NTRU encryption, based on elementary probability theory and polynomial algebra.
2	2006	Anshel et. al.	A lightweight key agreement protocol AAGL and coined the term E-multiplication, a one-way function that improves efficiency. The concept of Algebraic Eraser is also used.
3	2010	L. Kulseng, Z. Yu, Y. Wei, and Y. Gyan	A lightweight communication and holdership transfer for RFID system based on Physically UNCLONABLE Function (PUF) and LFSR. It requires only 784 gates for 64-bit variables.
4	2013	Peeters et. al.	IBIHOP - requires at least 3 scalar multiplications to tag.
5	2014	L. Gao, M. Ma, Y. Shu, and Y. Wei	An ultra-lightweight RFID authentication protocol with cyclic redundancy check and permutation mechanism to overcome the de-synchronization attack.
6	2015	Lu et. al.	An ECC based authentication system that requires scalar multiplication, hash computation, and point addition.
7	2016	C. Jin, C. Xu, X. Zhang, and F. Li	Elliptic curve cryptography based Mutual Authentication Protocol on the basis of RFID technology.
8	2017	Akanksha Tewari, and B. B. Gupta	An ultra-lightweight protocol that works on bitwise manipulation and produces very low overhead.

Oscillating circuit, communication channel, and the controller is all that need to compose a reader. Radiofrequency is used to transfer energy to the tags from the reader. Tags are of three types; active, semi-passive, and passive.

Reader and Tag Authentication

There are some frequency variances also on tags, namely: low-frequency, high-frequency, and ultra-high-frequency. Reader and tag both are fit-out with the antenna through which they send or receive the signals. A serious security threat in this regard is the tag cloning where an attacker may get all the information about a tag and may produce its clone. If the identifier of both the tags will be the same, it will be impossible for one to differentiate. The ill-fitted tag may cause any harm to the system that is why the mutual authentication and verification is important. Mutual authentication process includes tag recognition, mutual verification, and key update (Chakraborti, Chattopadhyay, Hassan, & Nandi, 2018). Radiofrequency System Identification framework is depicted in figure 3, Radiofrequency System Identification framework and Single tag certification process.

Figure 3.

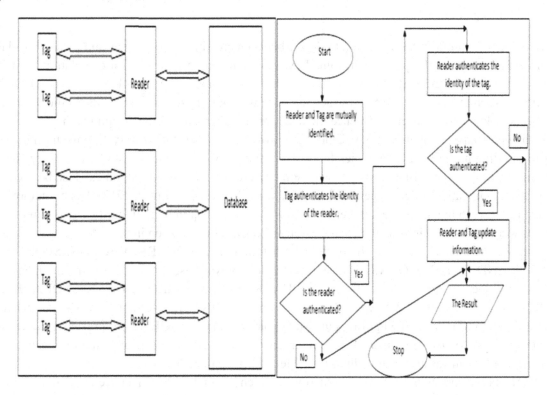

Hash Designs Used in Internet of Things Framework

Hash calculations are mainly used for security, for example, code authentication. Because of this only feature, Hash calculations are widely used in cryptography. The development of Hash calculations are no way different from the development of secure key calculations. As the computer industry progressed, researchers tried for lightweight hash design. As these designs affect the hardware implementation, the community decides some criteria for lightweight hashing, i.e., if the algorithm takes nearly 2000 GE (Gate Equivalent) then only authors will term them as lightweight (Guo, Peyrin, & Poschmann, 2000). A comparison of earlier hash designs having Gate Equivalent above 5,000 is given in table 3.

Table 3. A comparison of earlier hash designs having gate equivalent above 5,000

Digest	Hash	Gate Equivalent	ASIC
512-bit digest	Cube Hash (SHA-3)	7630 GE	0.13 μm
128-bit digest	Feldhofer & Wolkerstorfer (MD-5)	8001 GE	0.35 μm
160-bit digest	O'Neill (SHA-1)	6122 GE	0.18 μm
256-bit digest	Yoshida et. al. (MAME Composition)	8100 GE	0.18 μm

To achieve lower Gate Equivalent, a trade-off between creating new schemes and reusing available schemes (according to the power-constrained system) is much needed. A hash calculation is mainly determined by the count of state bits and the length of functional and control logic used in a ROUND function. To achieve the low size and low power constraints of tinny devices the focus should be on state size because logic size does not influence the total area requirements of the design much.

Unlike pervasive computing, tinny devices can work on 64 or 80-bit security. Sponge hash is a new way of building hash functions in which the internal state S of t bits consists of C-bit capacity and the r-bit bit rate (t = c + r), is first initialized with some fixed value. Sponge function can also be used as a message authentication code (Berger, D'Hayer, Marquet, Minier, & Thomas, 2012). Hence, authors use sponge function to minimize the number of memory registers requirement in hardware. A comparison of Lightweight Hash Designs that are using Sponge Construction is given in table 4.

Some of the already designed lightweight hash functions are QUARK, PHOTON, SPONGENT, GLUON, AND Hash-One. QUARK's design methodology was based on Grain (a stream cipher) and KATAN (a block cipher). Three instances of QUARK exists, those are U-QUARK, S_QUARK, and D-QUARK. Next is SPONGENT, which is based on PRESENT-type permutation. Unlike QUARK, SPONGENT produces fixed-length output. Many variants of SPONGENT are present and they can be referred to as SPONGENT-n/c/r. Where n,c,r denotes the hash size, capacity, and rate respectively (Manayankath, Srinivasan, Sethumadhavan, & Megha Mukundan, 2016).

PHOTON is also a sponge-based construction in which a matrix with 8-bit entries is used to represent the internal state. PHOTON uses AES like fixed key permutation. 12 rounds of Add Constants, Sub Cells, Shift Rows, and Mix Column Serial are used just like in AES.

Table 4. A comparison of lightweight hash designs that are using sponge construction

Digest	Hash	GE (Gate Equivalent)	ASIC (Application-Specific Integrated Circuit)
64-bit digest	Bogdanov et. al. DM-Present 2008	1600 GE (LW)	0.18 µm
64-bit digest	KECCAK 2010	2520 GE (LW)	0.13 µm
64/ 80/ 112 bit digest	U/ D/ S QUARK (CHES-2010)	1379/ 1702/ 2296 GE (LW)	0.18 µm
80/ 128/ 160/ 224/ 256 bit digest	PHOTON (CRYPTO-2011)	865/ 1122/ 1396/ 1736/ 2177 GE (LW)	0.18 µm
80-bit digest	SPONGENT (CHES-2011)	1329 GE (LW)	0.13 µm
80-bit digest	GLUON	2799 GE (LW)	0.18 µm
80-bit digest	Hash-One	1006 GE (LW)	0.18 µm

In figure 4, Hardware implementation of PHOTON Hash Function, an illustration of photon hardware is shown. From (Guo, Peyrin, & Poschmann, 2011) you can get the full detail about Round Constant, Internal Constant, Add Constant, S-box, States, and Mix Collam Serial. GLUON is inspired by F-FCSR-v3 and X-FCSR-v2 (both are stream ciphers). A word ring FCSR that include the main shift register and a carry register is used to design GLUON.

Figure 4.

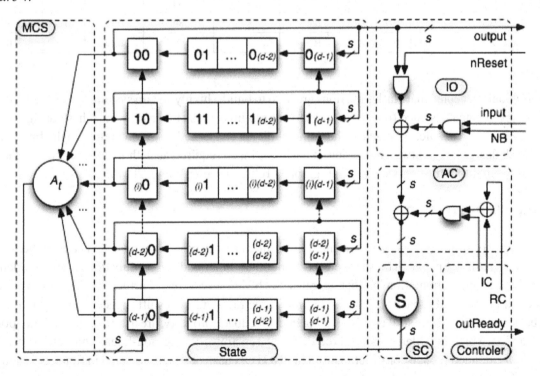

Two NFSRs of sizes 80 bits and 81 bits are used in Hash-One. Hash-One uses the sponge state of 161-bits. 324 rounds of state updates needed in the absorption of first and last message bits whereas only 162 required for intermediate message bits. Squeezing phase need only one round of state updates. Hash-One uses shift registers to reduce complexity.

The hash function should be tested for statistical randomness, collision resistance, strict avalanche criteria (SAC), linear span test and coverage test. In strict avalanche criteria for a particular S-box, whenever single bit in input is changed, every bit in output must change with probability 0.5. Collision resistance means that it should be difficult to get two messages with the same hash value. The coverage test output a given function f through examining the elements of the output set taken from a subset of its domain (Bussi, Dey, Biswas, & Dass, 2016). A comparison of Lightweight Hash Designs on the basis of the number of cycles is given in table 5.

Table 5. Comparison of lightweight hash designs on the basis of the number of cycles

Hash function	N	C	R	Preimage	Collision	Second Preimage	Process (μm)	Area (GE)	Cycles
Hash-One	160	160	1	160	80	80	0.18	1006	324/162
Hash-One	160	160	1	160	80	80	0.18	2130	14/7
SPONGENT	176	160	16	144	80	80	0.13	1329	3960
SPONGENT	176	160	16	144	80	80	0.13	2190	90
D-QUARK	176	160	16	160	80	80	0.18	1702	704
D-QUARK	176	160	16	160	80	80	0.18	2819	88
PHOTON	160	160	36	124	80	80	0.18	1396	1332
PHOTON	160	160	36	124	80	80	0.18	2117	180
GLUON	160	160	16	160	80	80	0.18	2799	50

It is widely accepted that Hash Functions are used to build a highly secure system. Two of its features, namely pre-image resistance (one-way) and second pre-image resistance (kay-pair) hash design, make this function unbreakable. As much as the vulnerability is concerned, everyone relies on the functionality of hash designs. A lightweight version of hash was much required as authors moved towards the era of a lightweight to ultra-lightweight cryptography (Tehranipoor & Wang, 2012).

Sponge Construction

To work on constrained devices, a new method to calculate the hash is generated. The new method of performing hash is Sponge. The sponge used to build an input and output function of variable length using fixed-length permutation "f" that operates on "b" number of bits. Further "b" (the width) can be divided in bit rate and capacity. "b = r + c" bits. Three registers, two shift registers having non-linear feedback property and one shift register having linear feedback property, are used to construct the sponge construction which is updated using three different functions having non-linear chaeacteristics. The process of extended sponge construction used in PHOTON hash design is depicted in figure 5, Extended Sponge Construction used in PHOTON hash design.

Figure 5.

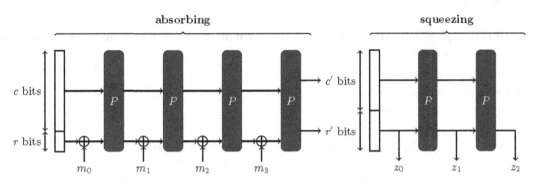

Two steps are there in the construction of Sponges where the first is absorbing phase and second is squeezing phase. In the first phase, "r bits" of the state and the "r bit" input message blocks are XORed. In the second phase, the first "r bits" of the state are returned as output blocks. Authors can design a permutation "f" on "b = r + c bits" to build the sponge function F(f, pad,r) with domain Z_2* and codomain Z_2^* (Avoine & Oechslin, 2005).

The input and output size is arbitrarily long in a sponge and hence this construction is used for a hash function, stream cipher or a MAC design. The output of a sponge is taken as the first I bits which requested. The absorbing function ABSORB (f, r) takes a string P as input with |P| multiple of r. the output of this function is the state obtain after absorbing P. From the state at starting authors truncate ℓ bits; this is done via squeezing phase. For Z = sponge [f, pad, r](m, ℓ), authors have: P = M || pad[r] (|M|), S = ABSORB [f, r] (P), Z = SQUEEZE [f, r] (s, ℓ). Authors can't get back P from s or s from Z, this is the beauty of sponge constructions, and it preserves backward secrecy.

Pseudo-Random Number Generators

A simple but efficient method for generating a pseudo-random number generator is called Blum Blum Shub (BBC) after the names of its three inventors; the generator is illustrated in figure 6, Blum Blum Shub (BBC) Pseudo Random Number Generator. BBC uses quadratic residue congruence, but it is a pseudo-random bit generator instead of a pseudo-random number generator, it generates a sequence of bits (0 or 1) (Junod, 1999). Below figure shows the idea of this generator.

Figure 6.

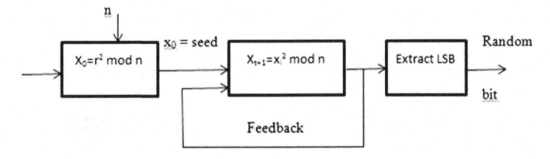

The following shows the steps:

1. Select two large prime numbers y and z in the form of 4a+3, where a is an integer (both y and z are congruent to 3 modulo 4).
2. Calculate the modulus b = y X z.
3. Choose a random integer c which is co-prime to b.
4. Calculate the seed as $x_0 = c^2 \bmod b$.
5. Generate the sequence as $x_{t+1} = x_i^2 \bmod n$.
6. Extract the LSB of the generated random integer as the random bit.

Random numbers are of much importance because of their uses in confidential key generation. A type of challenge-response methodology may also be created by using random numbers. They are also helpful in the nonce-based authentication system. By using a nonce, authors can secure our devices from any type of hardware attack. Small battery-operated devices are very much in need of the algorithms that can work on shift operations and can produce a desirable level of security. To some extent, one can use a hash function and other encryption methods but pseudo-random number generator is a major security component for small battery-operated devices (Peris-Lopez, Hernandez-Castro, Estevez-Tapiador, & Ribagorda, 2009).

To generate truly random numbers based on a physical source (some well-known methods are: thermal noise ZENER diode and radioactive decay). However, they are inefficient in terms of aggregating many physical resources. On the other hand, pseudo-random number generators can be generated mathematically by using some functions such as Linear Congruential Generators (LCG) and Linear Feedback Shift Registers (LFSR) (Ali Eljadi & Taha Al Shaikhli, 2014). Only for illustration purpose, authors are showing the logic gate implementation of a well-known cipher Warbler in figure 7, the logic gate implementation of Warbler. If you are interested in full detail, you may refer (Mandal, Fan, & Gong, 2016).

Figure 7.

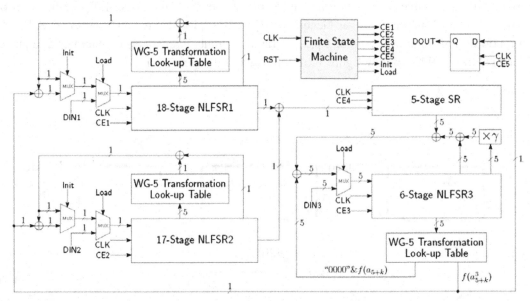

In cryptography, authors use LFSRs very often to perform shift operations because of its efficiency and simplicity in terms of implementation. To check this distribution, authors perform a test that focuses on the existing non-randomness in the generated PRNG binary sequences. According to NIST, the frequency test should be done first because it reveals the non-uniformity of a sequence. It gives the proportion of 0's and 1's for the entire sequence. This should be approximately equal for the truly random sequence. This is very useful in the case of the challenge-response mechanism between small battery-operated devices. Authors can't use the complex data encryption methods or large hash functions for these devices (Melia-Segui, Garcia-Alfaro, & Herrera-Joancomarti, 2010).

Different lightweight pseudorandom number generator (PRNG) for EPC Class-1 Generation-2 (EPC C1 Gen2) RFID (GS1, 2013) tags tested under NIST (Rukhin, Soto, & Nechvatal, 2010) specification is given in table 6.

Table 6. Different lightweight pseudorandom number generator (PRNG) for EPC Class-1 Generation-2 (EPC C1 Gen2) RFID tags tested under NIST specification

Statistical Behavior	EPC Specification(standard)	Melia-Segui et. al.	Warbler	LAMED	J3Gen	Chen et. al.	AKARI-1 and AKARI-2
Probability of a single sequence (after analyzing 30 million 16-bit sequences)	$0.8 / 2^{16} < P(j) < 1.25 / 2^{16}$	$0.9 / 2^{16} < P(j) < 1.09 / 2^{16}$	$0.9409 / 2^{16} < P(j) < 1.0693 / 2^{16}$	$0.96 / 2^{16} < P(j) < 1.05 / 2^{16}$	$0.8 / 2^{16} < P(j) < 1.25 / 2^{16}$	$0.8 / 2^{16} < P(j) < 1.25 / 2^{16}$	$0.8 / 2^{16} < P(j) < 1.25 / 2^{16}$
Probability of simultaneously identical sequences (per ten thousand tags)	shall be less than 0.1%	Almost 0 (zero)	approximately 2^{-45}	0.000157	0.0383%	0.0026%	less than 0.1%
Probability of predicting a sequence (after 10 ms)	Shall not be predictable with a probability greater than 0.025%.	.000036%	2^{-16}	$2^{-11.77}$	Shall not be predictable with a probability greater than 0.025%.	Shall not be predictable with a probability greater than 0.025%.	Shall not be predictable with a probability greater than 0.025%.

Random Oracle

In 1993, Bellare and Ragaway proposed a new model named Random Oracle. Random oracle is a computational model based on a mapping function that maps each possible question to a random answer from the output domain. This model acts as the interface between cryptographic theory and cryptographic practices. It is having applications in many areas of cryptography such as Hash calculations and RNGs (Canetti, Goldreich, & Halevi, 2000). Some of the main points of this model are:

1. It produces a fixed-length digest from a new message having variable length input.
2. If there is already a digest existing for some message, this does not calculate a new one.
3. The messages themselves can pick their existing digest from the record.

An interesting correlation between random oracle and pigeonhole principal or birthday paradox occurs, that is, there should be less number of digests in contrast to the number of messages received. This model says that collision is a reality. However, a test is conducted by using four birthday problems for preimage, second preimage, and collision attack.

There are two steps in designing a cryptographic protocol: the first one is to design an ideal system for all parties who have access to the true random function and also proving the security. In the next step, the cryptographic hash function is replaced by random oracle for all parties. The only ideal system was implemented before the discovery of the random oracle method. In Random Oracle methodology, it is not expressed how to implement the design on the ground level. When the ideal system is implemented, it is clear about security, but in the random oracle model, it is not clear when cryptographic hash function replaces by a theoretical black box or a random oracle. In order to replace the random oracle for maintaining the security firstly identify the property of random oracle methodology to show a minimal formulation called correlation intractability (Maurer, Renner, & Holenstein, 2004). It is said that if a system's security relies on correlation intractability, the machine can be secure. Further, it is also said that digital signature and public key encryption are secure because these system's security is based on the random oracle model.

Cryptographic systems have a set of parties modeled based on probabilistic polynomial. For the security purpose, one should specify the opponent abilities. The abilities of the opponent include the computational power to communicate with other parties. The triumph of the opponent and all parties are defined by the predetermined polynomial-time ground of the application's universal view. If the system is secure, the opponent and all parties have a negligible probability of success. Random oracle model operates among all parties and opponents are interacting with each other with the help of oracle queries output by a single function. When implementing an ideal system that does not have access to a theoretical black box or a random oracle, authors first need to implement random oracle for the aspect of an ideal system. If the standard model is procure, the random oracle model will also be procure. One should replace the fixed-function into oracle then the ideal system will be converted into a real system and oracle machine will be converted into a globally accepted machine in a natural manner. When implementing this function authors should know about the behaviour of the opponent in an ideal system. In this case, it is perfectly ok that if the ideal system is secure, the random oracle will return only with negligible probability.

In the system set up phase, all the functions and descriptions are available for all parties. These functions are used instead of the random oracle model. These functions are given for variable input length although applying by any user or opponent. Implementation of an ideal system follow some security parameter, these parameters are available for all concern including the opponent. In this phase evaluation of the function replace oracle call to an interactive theoretical black box oracle machine by the corresponding query. These systems (functions) are called implementation by a functioning ensemble. Correlation intractability is good for implementation of random oracle and it should be unreasonable to find an input to the function that has a rare connection with the corresponding output. To implement this property authors may require desorption of the function and find an order of pre-image with their image to satisfy some given relation under the function. If it is difficult to find an order of pre-image with their image under the random oracle model satisfy the relation, it will be considered as good function (Paper & Nielsen, 2002).

Implementation of theoretical black box or random oracle methodology, for the purpose of security, should be taken as a non-guarantee. For security reason, there is no structure in this model. A generic attack may be possible. Random oracle model may produce a negative result because the random oracle model provides the input of its choice.

Ran stated that if programmers assume only logical object the result may come negative. A generic attack can be seen when programmers give the input of their own choice to the random oracle illustrating some mathematical function. When applying reverse engineering, if ignoring the computational theoretic reality that when the code of the program is running, unexpected behaviour found. The author constructs a non-CS proof for a random oracle model. These proofs are exercised to verify a polynomial-time variable within a time-bound by the fixed polynomial. If applying the CS proof in encryption and signatures those are assured in the theoretical black box or random oracle model but not in the physical world. After getting a result from the theoretical black box or random oracle methodology, if it does not sound good with respect to the natural assumption of implementation of the the theoretical black box or random oracle, these negative outcomes have no effect on security.

In the core of this cryptographic application, authors may found many protocols related to networking. Almost all components are responsible for the security of an application and this is the best way to analyze multiple units. This analysis can be represented in a convinsing way with many details that are beside the point to the security. It is said that many details may be left outside the model by a cryptographic application. Such as, assume a delivery message is communicated between two machines i.e. one machine write the value to another machine. When authors are satisfied with explaining and analyzing the security of the protocol in the abstract model, we believe the proposed methodology is good. It is said that if a perfect ruling is secure and feasible then there exists a secure implementation. If one wants to explain and analyze the security of the protocol in the ideal model then he/she should perform some changes outside the model and make sure that the resulting execution is secure. Authors suggest that if an ideal hash calculation is available authors should implement the cryptographic protocol on it. There are many algorithms designed for the security of protocols in complexity based modern cryptography among them random oracle model seems to be an efficient protocol as no attack against it is known (Pointcheval & Stern, 1996).

True Random Number Generator

Pseudorandom number generator (PRNGs) works perfectly in the case of a secure key generation process for cryptographic algorithms. However, these take their input from a truly random source known as True Random Number Generator (TRNGs). It is said that PRNGs are prone to attack and anyone by using some mathematics can guess the next number because these are software. On the other hand, TRNGs are produced by some mechanical workforce and hence are not predictable.

The random number generator is a very crusial cryptographic attribute used for key generation and authentication protocols. The random number generators are used in a digital computer simulation program. There are two varients of random number generator used in the cryptographic applications. The true random number generator is totally based on a physical noise source and pseudo-random number generator produces extremely long sequence of random bit sequences based on a deterministic algorithm (Tsoi, Leung, & Leong, 2003).

There are three techniques based on hardware implementations are used for getting true random number generator. These are 1. oscillator sampling, 2. direct amplification and 3. discrete-time chaos. In the technique i.e. oscillator sampling, time period variation in a low-frequency clock of low-quality factor is utilized by using it to a small high-frequency clock. Discrete-time chaos can be used to produce true random number generator. Direct amplification technique digitizes thermal noise using amplifier and comparator. True random number generators based on the chaotic system can lead to very compact CMOS implementation.

Westlake suggested that if there are two different congruential generators authors perform XOR on their outputs to get a new series. For the next number authors, after rotating the next number through a random number of positions given by a set of bits extracted from the previous, again perform XOR on their output (Brody, 1984).

The author in (Brody, 1984) suggested that if the word length of the machine for which the generator is planned for p bits its cycle length must be of 2^p. This length is not too short but it is the best statistics to improve the cycle length. Such problem arises when the world length is below 32 bits; this is common in all the present models of microprocessors and mini-processors. To improving the possibility authors use multiple-precision mathmetic to achieve a sufficiently large and effective word length. McLaren and Marsaglic suggest combining two congruential generators by using one to provide a random index from the table, the value noted to the result, which is then replaced by the number calculated by the other generator. This method results an extremely long cycle length if those of the generators are mutually prime and can reduce the higher-order correlation among the generated number.

The author in (Brody, 1984) proposed some modification in this method. Authors may produce a new random number from the table by combining two random numbers with an exclusive OR operation. This idea was developed by systematic exploration of random number generators. The exclusive OR was chosen because on the average it does not change the proportion of 0's and 1's. It works on logical equivalence.

The author in (Stefanov, Gisin, Guinnard, Guinnard, & Zbinden, 2000) says that random numbers employed today are for numerical simulation as well as for cryptography. Unfortunately, computers are not able to generate a truly random number, as they are the deterministic system. The only way to get a truly random number, hence true security for cryptosystems, is to build a generator based on a random physical phenomenon. As quantum theory process is an ideal base for a physical random number generator. The randomness of a sequence of number, understand the behaviour of a random process, so as to gain confidence in its proper random operation.

Randomness Testing

Different testing agencies are using different criteria for the measurement of the usefulness of the proposed random number generator. The ENT test includes: Entropy, Compression rate, χ^2 statistics, Arithmetic mean, Monte Carlo π estimation, and Serial correlation coefficient. The Diehard Suite (p-value) contains: Birthday spacing, GCD and Gorilla, Overlapping permutations, Ranks of 31x31 and 32x32 matrices, Ranks of 6x8 matrices, Monkey test on 20 bit words, Monkey test OPSO, Monkey test OQSO, Monkey test DNA, Count the 1's in a stream of bytes, Count the 1's in a specific byte, Parking lot test, Minimum distance test, Random spheres test, The squeeze test, Overlapping surus test, Runs up and down test, The craps test, and Overall ks p-value. David Sexton's battery (p-value) is a set of 12 tests, namely: Bit run test, Frequency test, Bit test, Sum test, Matrix test, Prediction test, And test, Up/down test, Rect. distance test, Collision test, Offset XOR test, and Mod test. NIST suite (proportion) is equipped with Frequency, Block-frequency, Cumulative-sums, Runs, Longest run, Rank, Dft, Overlapping templates, Universal, Apen serial, Linear Complexity, Randomness excursions, and Random excursions variant. Bit-byte prediction test in David-Sexton's battery (p-value) consists of Bit prediction test (A, B, C, D, and E), Byte prediction test (A, B, C, and D), and Byte repetition. A serial correlation test also exists

(Martín, Millán, Entrena, Céstro, & López, 2011). Authors can see from results that Warbler design of random numbers passed for NIST test suite while AKARI-1 and AKARI-2 passed ENT test also Wu et. al passed for Diehard test suite and NIST test suite both. While designing a PRNG, the focus should be on:

1. An outsider who eavesdrop the communication will not be able to compute the algorithms internal state, there will be no effect of the observations of outputs.
2. The rival will not be able to compute the next sequence, there will be no effect of the numbers of previous sequence observations.
3. If the opponent, in any case, successfully get to find or change the input values those are fed by the algorithm, but algorithms internal state is unknown, the opponent must not be able to find the next sequence of bits or the next internal state of the algorithm.
4. If the rival has somehow gained the internal state of the algorithm, but the input values that are given-in cannot be observed, then the rival should not figure out the internal state of the algorithm after the re-keying operation.

In figure 8, TRNG, Polynomial selector, and LFSR used in PRNG of J3GEN, the architecture of a well known PRNG J3GEN is shown (Melià-Seguí, Garcia-Alfaro, & Herrera-Joancomartí, 2013). It uses a true random number generator, a polynomial selector, and a linear feedback shift register to produce a pseudo-random number.

Figure 8.

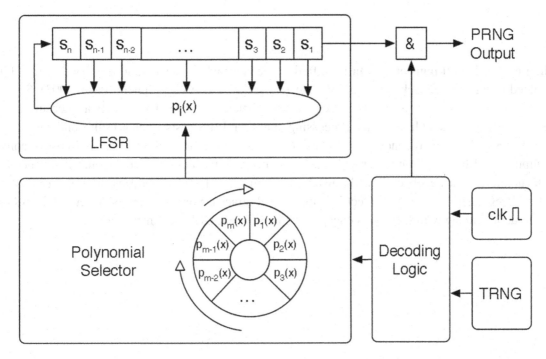

Dynamic Linear Feedback Shift Registers

Non-linearity may be achieved by using a non-linear Boolean function, filter generator, and irregular clocking. Linear feedback shift registers can generate a pseudo-random sequence. Some attacks like fast algebraic attack and correlation attack can observe its sequence. Filter generator using a non-linear function or combination generator using a non-linear Boolean function can process the output sequence of an LFSR. Dynamic Linear Feedback Shift Register is another method in which the feedback polynomial changes dynamically at runtime. The general construction of a DLFSR is depicted in figure 9, the general construction of a DLFSR.

Figure 9.

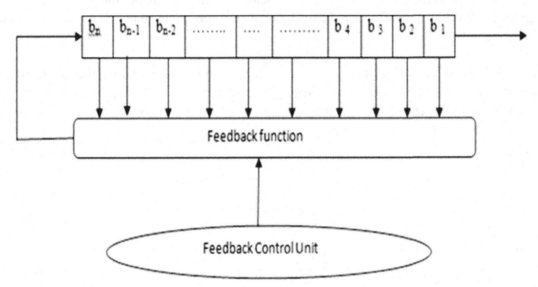

In a feedback shift register one bit is shifted to the right when needed and the new leftmost bit is calculated using the feedback function shift registers generates keys for ciphers (Page, 2003). Some of the criteria include period, linear complexity, and statistical measure. The statistical measure can be taken by using the Federal Information Processing Standard (FIPS) tests, Diehard suite, and the National Institute of Standard and Technology (NIST) statistical test suite. Several methods are in use to convert the output of an LFSR in a non-linear form, such as combination generators, clock-controlled generators, and Dynamic Linear Feedback Shift Registers. A control mechanism modifies the input to feedback function irregularly in order to protect it from several attacks. Some of the constructed DLFSRs are given in table 7 along with the basic concept used in different DLFSR construction.

Table 7. The basic concept used in different DLFSR construction

Sl. No.	Author	Year	Basic concept used
1	Mita et. al.	2002	primitive polynomial
2	Mita et. al.	2006	decoder circuits and counter
3	Horant and Guinee	2006	clocking and polynomial switching time
4	Kiyomoto et. al.	2007	secondary LFSR as well
5	Molina – Rueda et. al.	2008	irreducible polynomial
6	Cid et. al.	2009	non-LFSR state
7	Snow 2.0	2010	dynamic number generator function
8	Colbert et. al.	2011	irreducible polynomial and hash function
9	Melia – Segui et. al.	2013	round robin scheme
10	Peninado et. al.	2014	two LFSR and a counter

Edge Computing (Local Computing)

In terms of transmission delay; an algorithm should be generated to differentiate between the severities of events. It may happen that for the same work sometimes authors need information more frequently and many times less frequently. The processing unit should have all three options: (1) Periodic circulation, (2) Triggered circulation, and (3) Event-driven circulation.

In terms of storage requirement; the answer of the question *"what should be done with the large volume of gathered data if they are of no use after some times and who should be authorized to check the usefulness of these data?"* should be answered carefully because if authors are thinking that they can save space by deleting some data, they may be losing some important information. So, until they are not sure enough that they never need these data in future, they cannot delete any data. On the other hand, storing a large volume of data is already a problem. Keeping both facts in mind, authors should develop some lightweight algorithm that must be capable of performing knowledge discovery (Bonomi, Milito, Zhu, & Addepalli, 2012).

In terms of security threat; a mechanism is required for mutual authentication between the cloud service provider and the intended receiver. Also, the measures for authentication should be taken at the time of receiving the data from the sensors. As both the sensors and the end devices are working on the lightweight OS, the algorithm for mutual authentication should also be lightweight with advanced security features.

The Sensor as a Service

The sensor as a service SEaaS (A new cloud service for constrained devices) mechanism is collecting the sensed data and after processing they are delivering this information to the machines as and when required. A large number of sensing devices are deployed everywhere in order to collect local information. This information is needed by the processing unit while computing. Suppose a large number of sensors are deployed in every classroom/library/canteen/offices of our university. These sensors capture the temperature of their surrounding every second. Now suppose if these findings are sent to the central server every second then what will happen? Per second there will be lacks of readings and successively for minutes, then for hours, then for days, and in this manner, these readings will become even larger.

Some filter should be applied to sensors so that they can transfer as minimum information as possible. One variant of the sensor is known as an actuator. The actuator is a special type of sensor that can sense and can perform manipulation as and when required. Authors can take the above example where authors can insert an algorithm so that the information can be sent only when it is required or only when it is asked. A large number of unnecessary data can be avoided in this way. Authors can also apply some rule or threshold limit to the devices so that when the reading will be out of this threshold the information will be sent to the central server (Tso, Chen, Zheng, & Wu, 2014).

The main purpose of an Internet of Things environment is that it should be scalable. Data is generating very fast and also in large volume. As authors all know that before using any data, the processing is required. To process this data, authors need to send them to the processing unit. In the case of the Internet of Things, the processing units are sensors "either local or global" where they store the large volume of heterogeneous data and process it by using different rules. The sensor sends these data to the "end-nodes" and waits for the response before heading forward. Suppose doctors are looking for data that is going to be used in the medical emergency. In this case, doctors cannot wait for long. So to get the processing done at a much faster pace, researchers use the concept of edge computing. Programmers should set the priority of individual cases so that they can differentiate that which case should send to "end-nodes" and which case should be processed at edge level. For the same, researchers develop EDGE computing.

The well-known cloud platform is now offering another service known as Sensor as a service or SEaaS. Some of the elite activity and GPS data providers are **Fitbit** or **Waze**. A weather data provider in this way is known as **DarkSky**.

POSSIBLE ATTACKS ON SECURE THINGS AND THEIR COUNTERMEASURE

An intruder may trigger a transmission attack to steal some sensitive information from secure things and may send some wrong information through trusted devices. A type of electromagnetic signal leak or side-channel attack is also possible on the communicating devices. Externally or internally activated Trojan can also harm the devices. Tempering with tags or readers physically is also a matter to worry because authors are going to use these small devices remotely and in that case, their protection is not possible. In a remote location, one can inject some false data into the edge nodes, so programmers should use hash functions in order to justify the incoming packets from the devices. A tamper proofing mechanism is required to deal with physical tempering. Some methods are integrating physically non-clone-able function into the circuit modification. In the cases when programmers fail to implement any security mechanism, it is common practice to trigger a kill or sleep command and then they may isolate tag/device or block it. A type of distance estimation is used to perform the signal to noise ratio that informs researchers about any undesired physical movement of devices. Some cryptographic schemes including encryption, locked and unlocked state of hash-based schemes, lightweight cryptographic protocols are mathematically designed to improve the hardware as well as software efficiency of the particular device (Lazarescu, 2013).

One may also sniff the communication channel. The process is known as eavesdropping. While a signal travels from one node to another, an ill-suited node may encounter it in between and may read all the data associated with it or produce the modified one. There are some well-known routing attacks exists such as the black hole, grey hole, wormhole, hello flood, Sybil, etc. that needs serious attention. Reliable routing is one of the possible solutions in the case of routing attack. A scheme of role-based authorization is presented that uses de-patterning or decentralization technique to deal with the afore-said problems. Two cryptographic schemes named CLEFIA and PRESENT is presented (Neisse, Steri, Fovino, & Baldini, 2015).

Next concern is about automation. In modern devices, coders program in such a way that machines can learn by their previous output. One may playfully or wishfully insert some false logic in the method by using a non-standard framework that can change the thought process of the machines. In that case, pre-testing and outlier detection system is required. An intrusion detection system named DIGLOSSIA is presented on this behalf. The main focus is to make a lightweight secure authentication system that fulfils all the security requirements of a device that can handle the increasing data uses and can control the exponential growth of weak links ("Summary of an Open Discussion on IoT and," 2017).

APPLICATION AREAS OF INTERNET OF THINGS

The rising popularity and acceptance of the Internet of Things can be realized as now the IoT environment is moving towards (a) Transportation and Logistic Domain (with the applications in (i) Logistics, (ii) Assisted Driving, (iii) Mobile Ticketing, (iv) Environmental parameters Monitoring, and (v) Augmented Maps), (b) Healthcare Domain (with the application in (i) Tracking, (ii) Identification and Authentication, (iii) Data Collection, and (iv) Sensing), (c) Smarts Environments Domain (with the application in (i) Comfortable homes and offices, (ii) Industrial plants, and (iii) Smart Museum and gym), (d) Personal and Social Domain (with the applications in (i) Social Networking, (ii) Historical Queries, (iii) Losses, and (iv) Thefts), (e) Futuristic Applications Domain (with the applications in (i) Robot Taxi, (ii) City Information Model, (iii) Enhanced Game Room), (f) Application in Agriculture, (g) Water Scarcity Monitoring, (h) Energy Management, (i) Construction Management, and many more (Li, Xu, & Zhao, 2018).

Internet of Things is becoming an universal dependable technology. It is given greater responsibilities and to be a responsible technology it should work on odds coming in its way. In terms of the Internet of Things authors still need to work on (a) Standards, (b) Mobility Support, (c) Naming and Identity Management (Assigning an IPv6 address to each element), (d) Object safety, (e) Transport Protocol, (f) Traffic Characterization and QoS Support, (g) Authentication, (h) Data Integrity, (i) Information Privacy, and (j) greening of Internet of Things.

A smart city application is shown in figure 10, possible application areas of the Internet of Things in a Smart City (Source: Internet). Different possible applications of the Internet of Things can be seen here. Such as public safety, smart health, intelligent shopping, gas and water leak detection, smart energy, water quality, smart parking, electric vehicle charging, waste management, smart street light, smart home, and smart environment.

Figure 10.

Working Agencies

Some agencies which are working as the key development force for Internet of Things are Microsoft's Eye-on-Earth platform, Cluster of European Research Project on the Internet of Things, The Internet of Things Architecture (IoTA), Internet of Things@work, Internet of Things-initiative (Internet of Things-i), European Research Cluster on the Internet of Things, and many more. These agencies are working continuously to convert the cryptographic algorithms into their lightweight version (Bröring, Schmid, Schindhelm, & Kramer, 2017). Figure 11, Different agencies working in the field of Internet of Things. (Source: Internet), shows some of the working agencies of the Internet of Things.

Figure 11.

CONCLUSIVE REMARK

In this chapter, authors see different aspects of lightweight cryptography. For secure lightweight communication, three things should be taken care of. First is to develop a sense of trust between devices. A table containing different works on mutual authentication is shown in this regard. From large complex calculations on polynomial algebra to simple bitwise arithmetic manipulations many concepts emerge in between that changes the generation of mutual authentication such as the concept of algebraic eraser, physically unclonable functions, scalar multiplication, cyclic redundancy check, permutation mechanism, hash computation, and point addition.

FUTURE RESEARCH DIRECTIONS

Many works have been already done to protect the communicating devices from different possible attacks but as researchers are aiming towards including every object to the internet they should also work to make the new algorithms capable of a strong but comparatively small computation. Second is to protect the communication in transit (Gupta & Kumar, 2019). There are many algorithms exists for secure communication. Many of them are relying on sponge-based hash construction or on pseudo-random numbers. Authors enlist almost all the works on these two concepts and also authors have shown a comparison among many algorithms. The designer of lightweight cryptographic algorithms may choose these algorithms as per their requirement or also they can write a new one for their work. In future, researchers may work to provide a better tradeoff in terms of cost and performance or cost and security or performance and security. The third is about storage. Large storage requirement is already a big problem. Authors see that in many cases authors even do not require the stored data. Intermediate results should be treated at the local level or edge in order to make the final result only available for global storage or cloud. Researchers should work on the reliability of edge computing.

REFERENCES

Ali Eljadi, F. M., & Taha Al Shaikhli, I. F. (2014). Dynamic linear feedback shift registers: A review. In *Proceedings 2014 the 5th International Conference on Information and Communication Technology for the Muslim World, ICT4M 2014*, (January 2015). 10.1109/ICT4M.2014.7020598

Atzori, L., Iera, A., & Morabito, G. (2010). The Internet of Things: A survey. *Computer Networks*, *54*(15), 2787–2805. doi:10.1016/j.comnet.2010.05.010

Avoine, G., & Oechslin, P. (2005). A scalable and provably secure hash-based RFID protocol. In *Proceedings Third IEEE International Conference on Pervasive Computing and Communications Workshops, PerCom 2005 Workshops*, 110–114. 10.1109/PERCOMW.2005.12

Berger, T. P., D'Hayer, J., Marquet, K., Minier, M., & Thomas, G. (2012). The GLUON family: A lightweight hash function family based on FCSRs. Lecture Notes in Computer Science (Including Subseries Lecture Notes in Artificial Intelligence and Lecture Notes in Bioinformatics), 7374 LNCS, 306–323. doi:10.1007/978-3-642-31410-0_19

Bonomi, F., Milito, R., Zhu, J., & Addepalli, S. (2012). Fog computing and its role in the internet of things. *Proceedings of the First Edition of the MCC Workshop on Mobile Cloud Computing - MCC '12*, 13. 10.1145/2342509.2342513

Brody, T. A. (1984). A random-number generator, *34*, 39–46.

Bröring, A., Schmid, S., Schindhelm, C.-K., & Kramer, D. (2017). Enabling IoT Ecosystems through Platform Interoperability The Problem of Missing IoT Interoperability. *IEEE Software, 34*(1), 54–61. doi:10.1109/MS.2017.2

Bussi, K., Dey, D., Biswas, M. K., & Dass, B. K. (2016). Neeva: A Lightweight Hash Function. *IACR Cryptology EPrint Archive, 2016*, 42. Retrieved from http://dblp.uni-trier.de/db/journals/iacr/iacr2016.html#BussiDBD16

Canetti, R., Goldreich, O., & Halevi, S. (2000). The Random Oracle Methodology, Revisited, *51*(4), 557–594. Retrieved from https://arxiv.org/abs/cs/0010019

Chakraborti, A., Chattopadhyay, A., Hassan, M., & Nandi, M. (2018). TriviA and uTriviA: Two fast and secure authenticated encryption schemes. *Journal of Cryptographic Engineering, 8*(1), 29–48. doi:10.100713389-016-0137-2

Chien, H. Y. (2007). SASI: A new ultralightweight RFID authentication protocol providing strong authentication and strong integrity. *IEEE Transactions on Dependable and Secure Computing, 4*(4), 337–340. doi:10.1109/TDSC.2007.70226

GS1. (2013). EPC ™ Radio-Frequency Identity Protocols Generation-2 UHF RFID. *Specification for RFID Air Interface Protocol for Communications At*, 1–152. doi:10.100740261-017-0531-2

Gubbi, J., Buyya, R., Marusic, S., & Palaniswami, M. (2013). Internet of Things (IoT): A vision, architectural elements, and future directions. *Future Generation Computer Systems, 29*(7), 1645–1660. doi:10.1016/j.future.2013.01.010

Guo, J., Peyrin, T., & Poschmann, A. (2000). The PHOTON Lightweight Hash Functions Family. *Crypto*, 222–239. Retrieved from http://dblp.uni-trier.de/db/conf/crypto/crypto2011.html#GuoPP11

Guo, J., Peyrin, T., & Poschmann, A. (2011). The PHOTON family of lightweight hash functions. Lecture Notes in Computer Science (Including Subseries Lecture Notes in Artificial Intelligence and Lecture Notes in Bioinformatics), 6841 LNCS, 222–239. doi:10.1007/978-3-642-22792-9_13

Gupta, D. N., & Kumar, R. (2019). Lightweight Cryptography: an IoT Perspective, (8), 700–706.

Junod, P. (1999). Cryptographic secure pseudo-random bits generation: The Blum-Blum-Shub generator. *Unpublished*, (August). Retrieved from http://tlapixqui.izt.uam.mx/sem_cripto/sucesiones/CryptoSecureRandomBits.pdf

Khan, R., Khan, S. U., Zaheer, R., & Khan, S. (2012). Future internet: The internet of things architecture, possible applications and key challenges. *Proceedings - 10th International Conference on Frontiers of Information Technology, FIT 2012*, 257–260. 10.1109/FIT.2012.53

Lazarescu, M. T. (2013). Design of a WSN platform for long-term environmental monitoring for IoT applications. *IEEE Journal on Emerging and Selected Topics in Circuits and Systems*, *3*(1), 45–54. doi:10.1109/JETCAS.2013.2243032

Li, S., Da Xu, L., & Zhao, S. (2018). 5G Internet of Things: A survey. *Journal of Industrial Information Integration*, *10*, 1–9. doi:10.1016/j.jii.2018.01.005

Maimut, D., & Ouafi, K. (2012). Lightweight cryptography for RFID tags. *IEEE Security and Privacy*, *10*(2), 76–79. doi:10.1109/MSP.2012.43

Manayankath, S., Srinivasan, C., Sethumadhavan, M., & Megha Mukundan, P. (2016). Hash-One: A lightweight cryptographic hash function. *IET Information Security*, *10*(5), 225–231. doi:10.1049/iet-ifs.2015.0385

Mandal, K., Fan, X., & Gong, G. (2016). Warbler: A Lightweight Pseudorandom Number Generator for EPC C1 Gen2 Passive RFID Tags. *International Journal of RFID Security and Cryptography*, *2*(2), 82–91. doi:10.20533/ijrfidsc.2046.3715.2013.0011

Martín, H., Millán, E. S., Entrena, L., Céstro, J. C. H., & López, P. P. (2011). AKARI-X: A pseudorandom number generator for secure lightweight systems. *Proceedings of the 2011 IEEE 17th International On-Line Testing Symposium, IOLTS 2011*, 228–233. 10.1109/IOLTS.2011.5994534

Maurer, U., Renner, R., & Holenstein, C. (2004). Indifferentiability, Impossibility Results on Reductions, and Applications to the Random Oracle Methodology, (20), 21–39. doi:10.1007/978-3-540-24638-1_2

Melia-Segui, J., Garcia-Alfaro, J., & Herrera-Joancomarti, J. (2010). Analysis and improvement of a pseudorandom number generator for EPC Gen2 tags. Lecture Notes in Computer Science (Including Subseries Lecture Notes in Artificial Intelligence and Lecture Notes in Bioinformatics), 6054 LNCS, 34–46. doi:10.1007/978-3-642-14992-4_4

Melià-Seguí, J., Garcia-Alfaro, J., & Herrera-Joancomartí, J. (2013). J3Gen: A PRNG for low-cost passive RFID. *Sensors (Switzerland)*, *13*(3), 3816–3830. doi:10.3390130303816 PMID:23519344

Neisse, R., Steri, G., Fovino, I. N., & Baldini, G. (2015). SecKit: A Model-based Security Toolkit for the Internet of Things. *Computers & Security*, *54*, 60–76. doi:10.1016/j.cose.2015.06.002

Page, E. C. C. (2003). Linear Feedback Shift Registers (LFSRs) 4-bit LFSR Applications of LFSRs Galois Fields - the theory behind LFSRs Galois Fields - The theory behind LFSRs Galois Fields - The theory behind LFSRs Galois Fields - The theory behind LFSRs Building an LFSR fro.

Paper, C., & Nielsen, J. B. (2002). Advances in Cryptology — CRYPTO 2002, *2442*(September 2002). doi:10.1007/3-540-45708-9

Papers, C. F. O. R. (2019). IEEE Internet of Things Journal. *IEEE Internet of Things Journal*, *5*(6), C2–C2. doi:10.1109/jiot.2018.2887292

Peris-Lopez, P., Hernandez-Castro, J. C., Estevez-Tapiador, J. M., & Ribagorda, A. (2009). LAMED - A PRNG for EPC Class-1 Generation-2 RFID specification. *Computer Standards & Interfaces*, *31*(1), 88–97. doi:10.1016/j.csi.2007.11.013

Pointcheval, D., & Stern, J. (1996). *Security Proofs for Signature Schemes*, *96*, 387–398. doi:10.1007/3-540-68339-9_33

Robshaw, M. J. B., & Williamson, T. (2015). RAIN RFID and the Internet of Things: Industry Snapshot and Security Needs, 1–4.

Rukhin, A., Soto, J., & Nechvatal, J. (2010). SP800-22rev1a, (April), 131.

Singh, D., Tripathi, G., & Jara, A. J. (2014). A survey of Internet-of-Things: Future vision, architecture, challenges, and services. In *Proceedings 2014 IEEE World Forum on Internet of Things, WF-IoT 2014*, 287–292. 10.1109/WF-IoT.2014.6803174

Stefanov, A., Gisin, N., Guinnard, O., Guinnard, L., & Zbinden, H. (2000). Optical quantum random number generator. *Journal of Modern Optics*, *47*(4), 595–598. doi:10.1080/09500340008233380

IHS Technology. (2016). IoT platforms: enabling the Internet of Things. *IHS Technology, Whitepaper*(March), 1–19.

Tehranipoor, M., & Wang, C. (2012). Introduction to hardware security and trust. *Introduction to Hardware Security and Trust*, *9781441980*, 1–427. doi:10.1007/978-1-4419-8080-9

Tso, R., Chen, C. M., Zheng, X., & Wu, M. E. (2014). A New Ultra-Lightweight RFID Authentication Protocol Based on Physical Unclonable Functions. *Cryptology and Information Security Series*, *12*, 17–28. doi:10.3233/978-1-61499-462-6-17

Tsoi, K. H., Leung, K. H., & Leong, P. H. W. (2003). Compact FPGA-based true and pseudo random number generators. *IEEE Symposium on FPGAs for Custom Computing Machines, Proceedings, 2003-Janua*, 51–61. 10.1109/FPGA.2003.1227241

Wang, C., Daneshmand, M., Dohler, M., Mao, X., Hu, R. Q., & Wang, H. (2013). Guest Editorial Special Issue on Internet of Things (IoT): Architecture, Protocols and Services. *IEEE Sensors Journal*, *13*(10), 3505–3510. doi:10.1109/JSEN.2013.2274906

Chapter 12
Energy–Efficient Rotation Technique of Cluster–Head Method for Wireless Sensor Networks

Aruna Pathak

Government Engineering College, Bharartpur, India

Ram Shringar Raw

Ambedkar Institute of Advanced Communication Technologies and Research, India

Pratibha Kamal

Guru Gobind Singh Indraprastha University, Delhi, India

ABSTRACT

Sensor nodes are supposed to function independently for a long timespan through a restricted source of energy in Wireless sensor networks (WSNs). For prolonging the network lifespan, sensor nodes need to be energy-efficient. To split the sensing region of WSNs into clusters is a noble methodology is to lengthen network lifespan. Clustering methods rotate the extra burden of head of cluster nodes among other nodes of the network through head rotation and re-clustering techniques. Overhead cost is greater in case of Re-clustering as compared to rotation method due to its global approach. Head rotation takes place when residual energy of cluster head falls below a fixed energy threshold. However, this fixed threshold does not consider the existing load of cluster head which become foremost cause for enhancing their early death. This chapter proposes an Energy-Efficient Rotation Technique of Cluster Head (EERTCH) for WSNs, which takes existing load of cluster head in consideration for their rotation.

DOI: 10.4018/978-1-7998-2570-8.ch012

INTRODUCTION

Wireless sensor networks (WSNs) comprise a huge number of small nodes. These nodes have sensing, computation, and wireless communications capabilities (Akyildiz et al, 2002). They are deployed in sensing area. These nodes can be deployed randomly or manually installed. Main function of these nodes is to collect the facts from the sensing area, process the collected facts, and then transmit to other nodes or to a Base Station (BS) wirelessly. BS is linked to an available communications structure or to the Internet to facilitate a customer can have access to the presented data.

WSNs have found applications in industry, house, health, security, disaster relief administration and many more. They are furthermore utilized in monitoring of inaccessible location applications (Zaheeruddin et al, 2017; Ari et al, 2015). In inaccessible situation, substituting or filling up the attached battery source of the sensor is very tough work. Main limitation of WSNs is their restricted energy resource (Aruna et al, 2012; Titouna et la, 2016). Extending lifespan of the network is sparking research issue. Consequently, researchers have recommended various methods such as duty cycling, reduction of data, and management of topology etc for increasing the lifespan of the network. Duty cycling approach allows nodes to go in sleep while they are not in usage to save their energy. The data reduction technique decreases the energy consumption through diminishing the magnitude of data produced, processed, and communicated (Willett et al, 2004). The topology management constructs and preserves a reduced set of nodes for saving their energy (Yunhuai et al, 2010; Zhang et al, 2007; Ingelrest et al, 2006). Hierarchical or cluster-based communication techniques are utmost suitable for increasing the lifespan of WSNs ((Liu et al, 2012; Aruna et al, 2018).

A cluster-based communication method splits whole network into several clusters where a node has to take responsibility of head for a particular cluster and other nodes of that cluster are become member of the cluster (Afsar et al, 2014; Heinzelman et al, 2000). Gathered information from sensor nodes sends to BS into number of rounds. Every round is comprised of two sub-stages: forming the cluster structure and transmitting the gathered data. Cluster head selection and cluster membership are main tasks involved while forming the cluster structure. Second sub-stage is associated to the communicating of gathered information to the BS. All members direct their sensed data to an associated head. After that head combined the gathered information with its own and conveys it to the BS.

Head has extra burden than other nodes in the cluster. Therefore, it consumes additional energy than its member nodes and hastily drains the energy (Afsar et al, 2014; Heinzelman et al, 2000).. The cluster-dependent communication methods utilize re-clustering and rotation techniques for rotating their extra load amongst other sensors of the system. Re-clustering is global way where each sensor node of the network must be involved. With predefined criteria new cluster structure is formed that permits the network to reexamine the cluster borders. Head rotation is a local phenomenon where only cluster members can participate for selecting next head for the upcoming round. Typically, head rotation arises once the residual energy of head drops below a threshold with predefined criteria. After selecting the new cluster head, previous cluster head turn out to be a regular member of the cluster. The boundaries of the cluster are fixed in rotation.

Re-clustering and head rotation have a most important influence on the whole lifespan of the entire network. The inappropriate decision can enhance to early death of heads. The valuable lifespan of all members of that clusters finishes when head of that cluster dies prematurely. When head of cluster depletes its energy in between the data transmission, valuable energy of it and its members get unused.

Also in clustered networks, only head of cluster can communicate with the BS, hence early death of cluster head directly affects the quantity of packet received at BS.

We proposed an Energy-Efficient Rotation Technique of Cluster Head (EERTCH) for wireless sensor networks, which takes existing load of cluster head in consideration for their rotation to minimize the early death of heads of cluster and prolong network lifespan. The paper is organized as follows: related work is briefed in section II. Next section defines radio propagation model. Proposed EERTCH is presented in Section IV. Section V briefs the experimental setup of the Proposed EERTCH and Section VII shows the performance assessment of Proposed EERTCH, and an assessment is done with other methods. Conclusion and future scope of the paper is specified in the end of the paper.

RELATED WORK

Revolving the role of cluster heads is necessary to balance the energy consumption of extra burden head among the remaining nodes of the network. However most of clustering methods focus on controlling the selection of heads of clusters. A handful research work is carried towards the direction of the procedure of re-clustering or head rotation.

Low-Adaptive Clustering Hierarchy (LEACH) (Heinzelman et al, 2000)protocol is the first cluster based protocol proposed for WSNs. It selects the head of cluster on probability basis and randomly rotates the role of head in each round of communication. LEACH-C (Heinzelman et al, 2000) is centralized clustering protocol that rotates the role of head randomly amongst other sensors of the network in every round of data transmission. In (Neamtollahi et al, 2018), re-clustering is done in a controlled way by defining re-clustering time for reforming the new clusters. In (Taheri et al, 2011), authors proposes "On Demand Clustering" concept which forms new clusters on demand basis instead of each round. In (Taheri et al, 2011), a parameter termed as average cluster member energy is defined. If the above said parameter has value less than preset threshold, re-clustering occurs.

Authors proposed first clustering protocol which utilizes cluster head rotation method in (Heinzelman et al, 2002). BS defines a preset order for all nodes to become the head of cluster. In (Neamtollahi et al, 2014), when residual energy of head drops below the predefined energy threshold, protocol initiates the process of head rotation. In (Gamwarige et al, 2007), a logical method is introduced to find the optimum assessment of threshold for head rotation. In (Gamwarige et al, 2005), BS synchronized head rotation scheme is presented. When residual energy of head drops lower than the threshold, protocol prompts a new head candidacy event by notifying BS that present head is not competent to execute its functionalities as head of cluster. Then BS commences the head rotation phase. In (Yongcai et al, 2004), a termination procedure for head rotation is introduced. If residual energy falls below rotation threshold, it sends termination appeal to three linked members of cluster with highest residual energy. Subsequently, highest residual energy node becomes the next head for that cluster. In (Zhao et al, 2012) approach, in the beginning of each round the current head of cluster selects vice-head for that cluster. Vice head get duty of head if residual energy of current head falls below a preset threshold. In (Mahajan et al, 2014), rotation of head occurs if energy level goes below 75%. In (Gouxi et al, 2013), authors give emphasis to transferring responsibility of head to the next adjoining node on received signal strength indicator reading. T-LEACH (Sibahee et la, 2016) also revolves heads as per the predefined threshold. The energy overhead for the revolving of heads was diminished by employing the dual-cluster-head method in presented in (Lin et al, 2019). There is a third responsibility backup head was presented in (Lin et al,

2019) besides to the functions of cluster head and cluster member. With the support of backup head, the rotation of head occurs between the head and the backup head.

RADIO PROPAGATION MODEL

We are utilizing Radio Propagation Model (RPM) specified in (Heinzelman eta l, 2000). RPMs are free space and two-ray ground propagation model. In the former, the loss of propagation for transferring power is inversely proportionate to square of the distance between Transmitter (*Tx*) and Receiver (*Rx*). For second model, the loss of propagation for transferring power is inversely proportionate to fourth power of the distance between *Tx* and *Rx*. For distance *d* in between *Tx* and *Rx*, consumption of energy for sending *k*-bit packet from *Tx* to *Rx* distance *d* is as follows

$$E_T = \begin{cases} kE_e + kE_{fs}d^2 & if \ d < d_o \\ kE_e + kE_{tg}d^4 & if \ d \geq d_o \end{cases} \tag{1}$$

where E_e is energy per bit consumed in the transreceiver system and $kE_{fs}d^2$ or $kE_{fs}d^4$ is energy per bit consumed in the power amplifier and d_o is cross over distance given as

$$d_o = \sqrt{E_{fs} \Big/ E_{tg}} \tag{2}$$

If d_o is greater than the distance *d* between the *Tx* to *Rx*, Free space model is utilized else two-ray ground model is utilized. Consumption of energy to receive a *k*-bits message (Heinzelman et al, 2000) is:

$$E_R = kE_e \tag{3}$$

ENERGY-EFFICIENT ROTATION TECHNIQUE OF CLUSTER HEAD (EERTCH)

The Energy-Efficient Rotation Technique of Cluster Head (EERTCH) is a head rotation approach that takes existing load of cluster head in consideration for their rotation. As head of cluster execute additional task than other member nodes in the cluster, therefore it needed more energy to perform these additional duties. Foremost, energy needed by head node and member nodes of cluster in each round is computed. Afterwards, analyze successful rounds to be done by head node of cluster prior to exhaust by its battery. Before last round of head node, head rotation has to initiate to reduce early death of head node. The presented clustering protocol has given stages: Initialization of Network, forming the cluster structure, head rotation, and transmitting the gathered data. Pseudocode of the EERTCH is given in Figure 1.

1. **Initialization of Network:** Initially entire nodes are deployed randomly in the sensing area. BS sends beacon signals to every node in the sensing area. These signals comprise the location information of the BS. Each node calculates their respective Euclidian distance from the BS. Then the

distance among nearby nodes is calculated on the basis of acknowledged strength of signals and their comparative coordinates.

2. **Formation of Cluster Structure:** BS exploits k-mean clustering to segregate sensor nodes into the optimal number of clusters. Preliminary heads of clusters are decided on the basis of position information only as initial energy of all nodes are same at the instant of network initialization. Cluster centroid node is chosen as initial head of cluster. Then heads of clusters spread a message to the other nodes. It carries the information about their selection as heads. Afterwards, other nodes report to their heads to be a member of their cluster. Also, the head builds a schedule depends on Time Division Multiple Access (TDMA) and assigns it to the members of its cluster.

3. **Rotation of Cluster Head:** Responsibility of head node is supposed to be rotated among member node of cluster for energy balance in the cluster. Let's assume, there are n nodes in a cluster with one node takes responsibility of head and other nodes (n-1) become member of that cluster. Foremost, energy needed by head node and member nodes of cluster in each round is computed using the equations.

Energy needed by head node of cluster in each round is:

$$E_{HR} = \sum_{i=1}^{i=(n-1)} (i \times E_{MR}) + (n \times E_{ag}) + E_{TBS} \tag{4}$$

where E_{MR} is energy consumption to receive l-bit data from member node. E_{ag} represents energy consumption in aggregating data (head aggregate all member data with its own data) and E_{TBS} denotes consumption of energy for transmitting aggregated data to BS.

Energy needed by member node of cluster in every round (E_M) is equivalent to energy consumption to trasmit k-bit data to head node (E_{TH}) is given as:

$$E_M = E_{TH} \tag{5}$$

We utilizes energy consumption model described in section IV to estimate the values of E_{MR}, E_{ag}, E_{TBS}, and E_M.

$$E_{MR} = kE_e \tag{6}$$

$$E_{ag} = kE_a \tag{7}$$

where E_a represents the energy needed to aggregate per bit.

$$E_{TBS} = \begin{cases} kE_e + kE_{fs}d_{HB}^{2} & if \ d_{HB} < d_o \\ kE_e + kE_{tg}d_{HB}^{4} & if \ d_{HB} \geq d_o \end{cases} \tag{8}$$

where d_{HB} represents the distance form head of cluster to BS.

$$E_M = \begin{cases} kE_e + kE_{fs}d_{MH}^{\ 2} & if \ d_{MH} < d_o \\ kE_e + kE_{tg}d_{MH}^{\ 4} & if \ d_{MH} \ge d_o \end{cases} \qquad (9)$$

where d_{MH} represents the distance form member node to head node of cluster.

Number of successful rounds to be done by head node of cluster prior to exhaust by its battery is given as follows:

$$R_H = E_{HE} \Big/ E_{HR} \qquad (10)$$

where E_{HE} is existing energy of head node.

Before last round of head node, head rotation has to initiate to reduce early death of head node. There-fore, proceeding to final round head node sets a recommended bit in a data packet and transmits it to the BS. The BS receive this bit from the data packet rotates the role of head on the basis of current energy, and position in cluster. Cluster centroid or near to the cluster centroid node that has maximum energy is chosen as new head of cluster. After selecting the new head node for cluster, it transmits information to the rest of the sensor nodes in the cluster as an announcement message to become new head. Further-more, new head also creates a schedule based on TDMA and allocate it to the members of its cluster.

1. **Transmitting Data:** For every cluster, all members direct its data to their analogous heads by TDMA based scheme. After getting the data from each member, the heads aggregate all received data with its individual data to reduce redundancy. Then aggregated data will be to the BS.

Figure 1. Pseudocode of the EERTCH

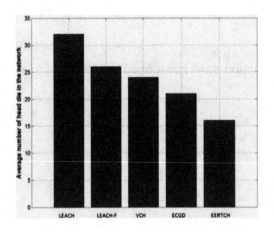

Table 1.

Pseudocode of the EERTCH
Begin
//Initialization of Network//
1. BS broadcasts beacon
2. Each nodecomputes Euclidian distance
// Formation of Cluster Structure//
3. Calculate optimal number of clusters
4. For each cluster
5. Set cluster cycle to 1
6. Repeat
7. Select head nodes
8. cluster cycle = cluster cycle+1
9. Till highestcluster cycle number
10. End For
11. For each head
12. Set head cycle to 1
13. Repeat
14. For allmember
15. Set member cycle to 1
16. Repeat
17. head broadcast messagedeclaration as head
18. Non-head node sends ACCEPTED message to head
19. member cycle = member cycle +1
20. Till highestmember cycle number
21. End For
22. head cycle = head cycle +1
23. Till highesthead cycle number
24. End For
// head rotation phase//
25.For each head; calculate number of successful rounds to be done by head
26. Set rounds to 1
27. Repeat
28. Aggergate and trasmit data
29. successful rounds = successful rounds +1
30.Till successful rounds-1
31. End For
32. Initiate head rotation
End

EXPERIMENTAL SETUP

This section describes the Experimental setup used for analyzing proposed approach. We utilized MAT-LAB2009a as simulation tool. The network model is depends on the given postulations:

1. All nodes have equivalent primary energy and the abilities of each node to process data and communicate data are similar.
2. Nodes are not fitted out with GPS.
3. All nodes and BS are static.
4. BS is not restricted in terms of energy, memory, and computational power.
5. They are utilized in monitoring of inaccessible environment applications.

The required simulation parameters for various algorithms are presented in Table 2.

Table 2. Parameters of EETCH

Parameter Value
Sensing area (W*L) (m) (100*100)
Position of BS (x, y) (50,50)
Quantity of nodes (n) 100
Energy per bit consumed in the transreceiver systemE$_e$(nJ/bit) 70
Energy per bit consumed in the power ampliðer (E$_{fs}$&E$_{tg}$)(pJ/bit/m²) 120 &0.0013
Primary energy of a node (E$_i$) (J) 1.0
Length of Data packet (L) (bits) 6400
Energy consumed in aggregation (E$_a$) (nJ) 5

PERFORMANCE ASSESSMENT

We estimate the performance of our presented approach on the basis of metrics, namely average number of head dies, average network lifespan, and throughput of the network for various numbers of rounds. Also we compare simulation results with LEACH (Heinzelman eta l, 2000) LEACH-F (Heinzelman et al, 2002), VCH (Zhao et al, 2012) and ECGD (Lin et al, 2019).

Figure 2 shows the comparative analysis of average number of head dies in the network. In LEACH, the average numbers of head die in the network are32 due to the reason being random selection of cluster-heads. The average number of head die in the network in LEACH-F occurs close to 26 whereas in VCH and ECGD (Lin et la, 2019) are 24 and 21 respectively. It is now apparent from the simulation results that EERTCH outperforms with the average number of head die in the network here around only 16.

Figure 3 demonstrates an assessment of the lifespan of network. In the literature, many descriptions are recommended for network lifespan as time till the first, half or last node dies. In LEACH, the first node death occurs near to 206 rounds, in LEACH-F, VCH and ECGD give better performance than LEACH. The first dead node in LEACH-F occurs close to 324 rounds whereas in VCH and ECGD are around 383 and 627rounds. It is now apparent from the simulation results that EERTCH outperforms as the first node is dead here around 627 rounds. In LEACH, the half node death and last node death occurs near to 427 and 510rounds respectively. However, the node death rate increases as the number of rounds increases. In EERTCH, the half node death and last node death occurs after almost 780 and 912 rounds respectively because of taken care of existing load of cluster head in consideration for their rotation method.

The throughput of the wireless sensor network for all five algorithms is shown in Figure 4.It is decipted from figure 4. that highest throughput of 0.64 Mbps is achieved with the all approaches. Nevertheless, its value decreases when the rounds enhances. Throughput reduces at very early in LEACH. InLEACH-F, it is retained to its highest value by 300 rounds, and in VCH and ECGD, it is retained to its highest value till 350 rounds and 400 rounds respectively. On the other hand, the EERTCH algorithm retains its highest value for more than 600 rounds.

We consider 10 dissimilar networks which are randomly created varying from 100 to 500 nodes with different BS positions as shown in Table 3. We run 20 independent simulations and the outcomes are occupied by taking average these simulations. A comparative analysis is specified in Table 3, Table 4, and Table 7. In all cases, the mean value of network lifespan i.e. time till the first, half or last node dies is computed and highlighted Table 4, Table 5, and Table 6 respectively. It can evidently be comprehended that EERTCH achieves highest mean value in all cases.

Figure 2. Comparative analysis of average number of head dies in the network

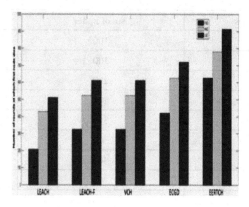

Figure 3. Comparative analysis of the network lifespan

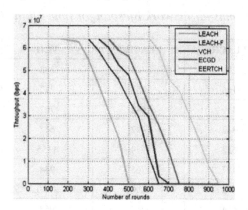

Figure 4. Comparative analysis of throughput of network

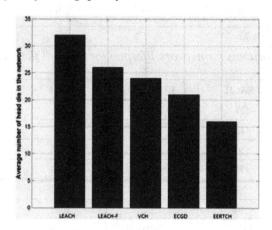

Table 3. Experimental networks cases

Experimental networks Cases	No. of nodes	Location of BS
Experimental networks Case-1	100	50-50
Experimental networks Case-2	100	100-100
Experimental networks Case-3	200	50-50
Experimental networks Case-4	200	100-100
Experimental networks Case-5	300	50-50
Experimental networks Case-6	300	100-100
Experimental networks Case-7	400	50-50
Experimental networks Case-8	400	100-100
Experimental networks Case-9	500	50-50
Experimental networks Case-10	500	100-100

Table 4. Performance of algorithms for network lifespan for time till the first node dies

Network	LEACH	LEACH-F	VCH	ECGD	EERTCH
Experimental networks Case-1	206	324	383	421	627
Experimental networks Case-2	166	258	312	398	595
Experimental networks Case-3	409	642	762	852	1257
Experimental networks Case-4	312	492	612	783	1189
Experimental networks Case-5	622	934	1155	1266	1867
Experimental networks Case-6	497	765	944	1188	1782
Experimental networks Case-7	832	1287	1530	1681	2503
Experimental networks Case-8	654	764	963	1145	1756
Experimental networks Case-9	1036	1627	1918	2112	3138
Experimental networks Case-10	830	1295	1567	1998	2976

Table 5. Performance of algorithms for network lifespan for time till the half node dies

Network	LEACH	LEACH-F	VCH	ECGD	EERTCH
Experimental networks Case-1	427	523	578	624	780
Experimental networks Case-2	412	508	563	609	765
Experimental networks Case-3	856	1056	1176	1248	1568
Experimental networks Case-4	877	1078	1189	1267	1545
Experimental networks Case-5	1256	1557	1757	1812	2344
Experimental networks Case-6	1234	1522	1683	1822	2297
Experimental networks Case-7	1771	2091	2315	2488	3120
Experimental networks Case-8	1642	2034	2250	2438	3069
Experimental networks Case-9	2136	2616	2893	3125	3908
Experimental networks Case-10	2066	2546	2813	3042	3827

Table 6. Performance algorithms for network lifespan for time till the last node dies

Network	LEACH	LEACH-F	VCH	ECGD	EERTCH
Experimental networks Case-1	510	612	645	718	912
Experimental networks Case-2	475	577	610	683	877
Experimental networks Case-3	1032	1242	1297	1438	1825
Experimental networks Case-4	945	1145	1234	1366	1754
Experimental networks Case-5	1532	1834	1931	2154	2736
Experimental networks Case-6	1426	1731	1832	2049	2631
Experimental networks Case-7	2040	2448	2585	2872	3648
Experimental networks Case-8	1906	2308	2440	2732	3508
Experimental networks Case-9	2559	3060	3227	3590	4530
Experimental networks Case-10	2375	2888	3050	3425	4388

CONCLUSION AND FUTURE WORKS

We have presented an Energy-Efficient Rotation Technique of Cluster Head (EERTCH) for WSNs is proposed, which takes existing load of cluster head in consideration for their rotation. The EERTCH confirms a node is selected as a head once its existing energy is more than the energy burden for one round. This approach diminishes the early death of head nodes. The result illustrations EERTCH outperforms LEACH, LEACH-F, VCH & ECGD by attaining higher energy efficiency, better throughput and prolonging network lifespan. We have tested the EERTCH in static wireless networks. We are planning to examine clustering in mobile sensor networks in the future work.

REFERENCES

Afsar, M. M., & Mohammad-H., T. (2014). Clustering in sensor networks: A literature survey, Elsevier. *Journal of Network and Computer Applications, 46,* 198–226. doi:10.1016/j.jnca.2014.09.005

Akyildiz, I. F., Su, W., Sankarasubramaniam, Y., & Cayirci, E. (2002). Wireless Sensor Networks: A Survey. *Elsevier Journal on Computer Networks, 38*(4), 393–422. doi:10.1016/S1389-1286(01)00302-4

Alam, M. M., Hamida, E. B., Berder, O., Menard, D., & Sentieys, O. (2016). A Heuristic Self-Adaptive Medium Access Control for Resource-Constrained WBAN Systems, *IEEE Access on Special section on body area networks for interdisciplinary research, 4,* 1287–1300.

Ari, A. A. A., Gueroui, A., Labraoui, N., & Yenke, B. O. (2015). Concepts and evolution of research in the field of wireless sensor networks. *International Journal on Computational Networks and Communication, 7*(1), 81–98. doi:10.5121/ijcnc.2015.7106

Gamwarige, S., & Kulasekere, C. (2005). An algorithm for energy driven cluster head rotation in a distributed wireless sensor network. *Proceedings of the International Conference on Information and Automation (ICIA 2005),* 354-359. Hong Kong, December 15-18.

Gamwarige, S., & Kulasekere, C. (2007). Optimization Of Cluster Head Rotation in Energy Constrained Wireless Sensor Networks. *Proceedings of IEEE Conference on Wireless and Optical Communications Networks*, 1-5. Singapore. July 2-4. 10.1109/WOCN.2007.4284155

Heinzelman, W. B. (2000). Application-specific protocol architectures for wireless networks [Ph.D. dissertation]. Massachusetts Institute of Technology, Cambridge, MA.

Heinzelman, W. B., Chandrakasan, A. P., & Balakrishnan, H. (2002). An application-specific protocol architecture for wireless microsensor networks. *IEEE Transactions on Wireless Communications*, *1*(4), 660–670. doi:10.1109/TWC.2002.804190

Heinzelman, W. R., Chandrakasan, A., & Balakrishnan, H. (2000). Energy-efficient communication protocol for wireless microsensor networks. *Proceedings of IEEE International Conference on System Sciences*. 10-20. Hawaii, January 4-7. 10.1109/HICSS.2000.926982

Ingelrest, F., Simplot-Ryl, D., & Stojmenovic, I. (2006). Optimal Transmission Radius for Energy Efficient Broadcasting Protocols in Ad Hoc Networks. *IEEE Transactions on Parallel and Distributed Systems*, *17*(6), 536–547. doi:10.1109/TPDS.2006.74

Khasawneh, A., Latiff, M., Kaiwartya, O., & Chizari, H. (2018). A reliable energy-efficient pressure-based routing protocol for underwater wireless sensor network. *Wireless Networks*, *24*(6), 2061–2075. doi:10.100711276-017-1461-x

Kimura, N., & Latifi, S. (2005). A survey on data compression in wireless sensor networks. *Proceedings of IEEE International Conference on Information Technology: Coding and computing*, 8-13. Nevada, April 4-6. 10.1109/ITCC.2005.43

Lin, D., & Wang, Q. (2019). An Energy-Efficient Clustering Algorithm Combined Game Theory and Dual-Cluster-Head Mechanism for WSNs. *IEEE Access: Practical Innovations, Open Solutions*, *7*, 49894–49905. doi:10.1109/ACCESS.2019.2911190

Liu, H., Yao, G., Wu, J., & Shi, L. (2010). An adaptive energy-efficient and low-latency MAC protocol for wireless sensor networks. *IEEE Journal of Communications and Networks*, *12*(5), 510–517. doi:10.1109/JCN.2010.6388497

Liu, H., Yao, G., Wu, J., & Shi, L. (2010). An adaptive energy-efficient and low-latency MAC protocol for wireless sensor networks. *IEEE Journal of Communications and Networks*, *12*(5), 510–517. doi:10.1109/JCN.2010.6388497

Liu, X. (2012). A survey on clustering routing protocols in wireless sensor networks. *Sensors Journal*, *12*(8), 11113–11153. doi:10.3390120811113 PMID:23112649

Liu, Y., Zhang, Q., & Lionel, N. (2010). Opportunity-based topology control in wireless sensor networks. *IEEE Transactions on Parallel and Distributed Systems*, *21*(3), 405–416. doi:10.1109/TPDS.2009.57

Lu, G., Krishnamachari, B., & Raghavendra, C. S. (2004). An adaptive energy efficient and low-latency Mac for data gathering in wireless sensor networks. *Proceedings of IEEE Parallel and Distributed Processing Symposium*, 224-30. New Mexico, Apr. 26-30.

Ma, G., & Tao, Z. (2013). A Hybrid Energy- and Time-Driven Cluster Head Rotation Strategy for Distributed Wireless Sensor Networks. *International Journal of Distributed Sensor Networks*, 6(1), 21–32. doi:10.1155/2013/109307

Mahajan, S., Malhotra, J., & Sharma, S. (2014). An energy balanced QoS based cluster head selection strategy for WSN. *Egyptian Informatics Journal*, 15(3), 189–199. doi:10.1016/j.eij.2014.09.001

Neamatollahi, P., Naghibzadeh, M., Abrishami, S., & Yaghmaee, M. (2018). Distributed Clustering-Task Scheduling for WSNs Using Dynamic Hyper Round Policy. *IEEE Transactions on Mobile Computing*, 17(2), 334–347. doi:10.1109/TMC.2017.2710050

Neamatollahi, P., Taheri, H., Naghibzadeh, M., & Abrishami, S. (2014). A distributed clustering scheme for wireless sensor networks. *Proceedings of IEEE Conference on Information and Knowledge Technology (IKT)*, 20-24. Shahrood, Iran, May 27-29. 10.1109/IKT.2014.7030326

Pathak, A., & Lobiyal, D. K. (2012, March). Maximization the lifetime of wireless sensor network by minimizing energy hole problem with exponential node distribution and hybrid routing. *Proceedings 2012 Students Conference on Engineering and Systems* (pp. 1-5). IEEE.

Pathak, A., & Tiwari, M. K. (2018, October). Clustering in WSNs based on Soft Computing: A Literature Survey. *Proceedings of IEEE Conference on Automation and Computational Engineering (ICACE)*, 29-33. Greater Noida, India, October 3-4.

Sibahee, M. A., & Lu, S. (2016). T-LEACH: the method of threshold-based cluster head replacement for wireless sensor networks. *Proceedings IEEE conference on network and information systems for computers* (ICNISC), 36–40. Wuhan, China, April 15-17.

Taheri, H., Neamatollahi, P., Yaghmaee, M. H., & Naghibzadeh, M. (2011). A local cluster head election algorithm in wireless sensor networks. *Proceedings of IEEE Symposium on Computer Science and Software Engineering (CSSE)*, 38-43. Tehran, June 15-16. 10.1109/CSICSSE.2011.5963987

Tan, L., & Wu, M. (2016). Data reduction in wireless sensor networks: A Hierarchical LMS prediction approach. *IEEE Sensors Journal*, 16(6), 1708–1715. doi:10.1109/JSEN.2015.2504106

Titouna, C., Aliouat, M., & Gueroui, M. (2016.) FDS: fault detection scheme for wireless sensor networks. *Springer Journal on Wireless Personal Communication,* 86(2), 549–562.

Wang, Y., Zhao, Q., & Dazhong, Z. (2004).Energy-driven adaptive clustering data collection protocol in wireless sensor networks. *Proceedings of International Conference on Intelligent Mechatronics and Automation*, 599-604. Chengdu: China, August 26-31.

Willett, R., Martin, A., & Nowak, R. (2004). Back casting: adaptive sampling for sensor networks, *Proceedings of IEEE International symposium on Information processing in sensor networks*, 124-133. California, April 26-27.

Zaheeruddin, D. K., Lobiyal, D. K., & Pathak, A. (2017). Energy-aware bee colony approach to extend lifespan of wireless sensor network. *Australian Journal of Multi-Disciplinary Engineering*, 13(1), 29–46. doi:10.1080/14488388.2017.1358896

Zhang, R., & Labrador, M. A. (2007). Energy-aware topology control in heterogeneous wireless multi-hop networks. *Proceedings of IEEE International Symposium on Wireless Pervasive Computing*, 1-5. Puerto Rico, February 5-7. 10.1109/ISWPC.2007.342568

Zhao, F., Xu, Y., & Li, R. (2012). Improved LEACH Routing Communication Protocol for a Wireless Sensor Network. *International Journal of Distributed Sensor Networks*, 8(12), 1–6. doi:10.1155/2012/649609

Chapter 13
Performance Investigation of Topology–Based Routing Protocols in Flying Ad–Hoc Networks Using NS–2

Sudesh Kumar

ⓘD https://orcid.org/0000-0002-9405-1890

Indira Gandhi National Tribal University, Amarkantak, India

Abhishek Bansal

Indira Gandhi National Tribal University, Amarkantak, India

ABSTRACT

Recently, with the rapid technological advancement in communication technologies, it has been possible to establish wireless communication between small, portable, and flexible devices like Unmanned Aerial Vehicles (UAVs). These vehicles can fly autonomously or be operated without carrying any human being. The workings with UAVs environment often refer to flying ad-hoc network (FANETs), currently a very important and challenging area of research. The usage of FANETs promises new applications in military and civilian areas. The data routing between UAVs also plays an important role for these real-time applications and services. However, the routing in FANETs scenario faces serious issues due to fast mobility and rapid network topology change of UAVs. Therefore, this chapter proposes a comparative study on topology-based routing protocols like AODV, DSDV, and DSR. Furthermore, investigate the performance of these different protocols for a FANETs environment based on different parameters by using the NS-2 simulator.

DOI: 10.4018/978-1-7998-2570-8.ch013

1. INTRODUCTION

A Flying Ad-hoc Network (FANETs) is a special type of network that consists of a grouping of small or mini-UAVs, which are connected in an ad-hoc manner (Bekmezci, I., et al., 2013). In FANETs, each UAV is called smart vehicle or smart node because this is configured with high resolution camera, wireless and computing devices, sensors, digital map, GPS etc. The usage of FANET environment is increasing day by day. This network first time used during Hurricane Katrina deadly cyclone in 2005 for search & rescue operation, it was the worst hurricane in Louisiana and then after in the 11th March, 2011 Fukushima Daiichi nuclear disaster and also in 25th April, 2015 used in Nepal earthquake. Many of the human lives were rescued due to this highly advanced concept and technology, which demonstrated the validity FANETs. In recent years, UAVs are being used in as civil as well as military applications (Kumar S., 2018, March). In FANETs, All UAVs design two types of communication, which is UAV-to-UAV (U2U) communication and either one or a group of UAVs, which is communicating with ground station called UAVs-to-Infrastructure (U2I) communication. In this communication if one of the UAV links fail; there is no communication breakage with the ground node because of the ad-hoc network between UAVs. FANETs use multi-UAVs scenario of tasks can be parallelized which in turn reduce the completion time of mission. This is very useful for critical applications like search, monitoring and rescue operation. Following figure 1 describe communication links with multiple UAVs.

Figure 1. Communication link in FANETs

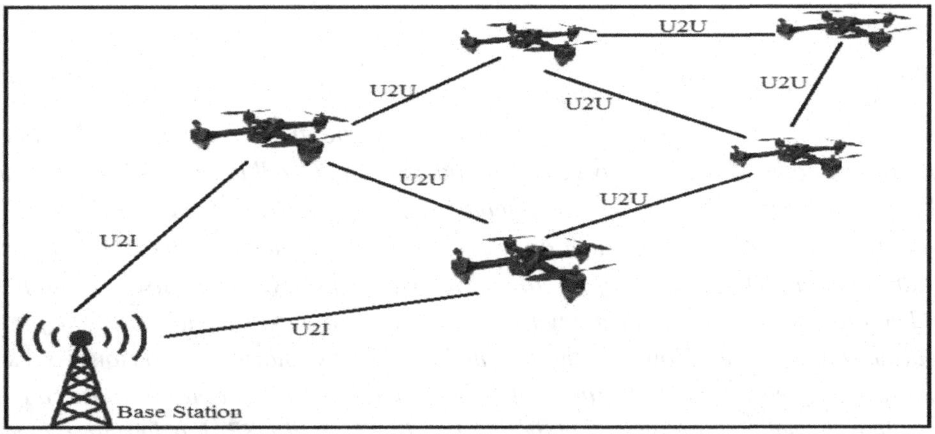

CHARECTERISTICS

Furthermore, wireless ad-hoc network categorized according to their objective and utilization. By the definition of FANETs, it is created by small multi-UAVs communication system. On the other hand, it is also the specialized form of previously existing Mobile Ad-hoc Network (MANET) as well as Vehicular Ad-hoc Network (VANET). Due to the unique characteristics of FANETs it is attracting so much attention of both academia and industry. In this section we discuss some common characteristics of FANETs, VANET and MANET in detail manner.

- **Node Mobility:** Here the node mobility mentions the movement of the nodes. Mobility degree in FANETs (UAV nodes, which are flying in 3D space) is much higher than the VANET as well as MANET nodes. Most of the time the speed of all UAVs is from 50 to 450 km/h, therefore this high mobility of UAVs, several issues occur for framing communication protocol (Bekmezci, I., et al., 2013).

- **Mobility Model:** Most of the cases in the FANETs, mobility model has been always regular. In VANET regular mobility model is required and in MANET, it is random. But the other side, in any case like autonomous multi-UAV systems, sometime the flight plan is not predetermined because of some mission updates. Therefore, the flight plan is required recalculation (Yassein, B. M., et al., 2016).

- **Node Density:** The actual meaning of node density is the total number of average nodes present in a unit area. In FANETs the distance between all UAVs (scattered in the 3D space) can be several kilometers. Therefore, FANET node density is very low other than MANET and VANET.

- **Network Topology Change:** The topology changes very frequently in FANETs due to the higher node's mobility. In such case, communication link between UAVs is also broken. Therefore, it is required to design & develop some new advanced routing methodologies for effective communication between UAVs without any link breakage.

- **Radio Propagation Model:** In the MANET as well as VANET environment, nodes are moving very near to the ground or may be on the ground, but in FANETs all UAVs nodes most of the time very far away from the ground. Therefore, need for developing some new efficient radio propagation model FANET (Peng J., 2015).

- **Power Utilization and Network Duration:** In FANETs, UAV communication hardware consists of battery-powered computing devices, but it is very typical for some large time taking applications. Therefore, new research is going on to how to charge the UAV node wirelessly so that the network duration can be maximized.

- **Computational Power:** In FANET, all UAV nodes are treated as smart vehicles and they are behaving like routers therefore; all smart UAVs have enough energy and space to support all high levels of computational power. VANET also include the high computational power. However, in MANET, the nodes have limited computational energy because of the small size of nodes as well battery constraint.

- **Localization:** Most of the FANETs application required highly efficient and accurate localization data with smaller time intervals. Therefore, in FANETs every UAV must be equipped with a special device like GPS as well IMU, which is providing exact location of UAV to the other UAVs at any time. Although, GPS is sufficient for MANET and AGPS & DGPS used by VANET (Bekmezci, I., et al., 2013).

APPLICATIONS

Due to these unique characteristics the usages of FANETs are growing day by day. In recent years, it is used in many civilian and commercial applications (A. Bujari, et al., 2017). Several flying devices (UAVs) have been deployed in 3D space for to communicate with each other, for specific applications. Some most popular applications illustrate below:

- **Research Trends and Technologies:** Now days FANETs is a hot topic for academicians as well as researchers. Recently Artificial Intelligence has become a key concept for UAVs to drive automatically without any human being. Applying advanced feature extraction algorithms of machine learning can also help to obtain new findings from real-time data through on-board UAVs. Furthermore, Cloud Computing has offered many types of services with the increase of real-time FANETs storage and Big Data and Internet of Thing is also used for capturing, storing and analyzing the FANETs data. Another hand, Image processing techniques also plays an important role for smart UAVs (configure with a camera, GPS, Sensors, etc.) for inspection and monitoring purpose (Sankarasrinivasan, S. et al., 2015).

- **Construction and Infrastructure Investigation:** FANETs can be used for real-time investigation or monitoring in inaccessible areas, which are not easily accessible by human like inspections of tanks, flues, roofs, power transmission line and critical construction sites. Therefore, the investigator human can monitor the all sites with the help of UAVs with better visibility and progress without any need of a physical presence (P. Liu et al., 2014). Also it is used for monitoring of linear network infrastructures like railway tracks, power lines, gas pipelines, etc.

- **Media and Entertainments:** News media organizations are increasingly making use of the drone's network to share the latest information within a very short time period in front of the users and also enhance their coverage area. . Also, Drones have been used in the film as well as entertainment industries for the making several types of feature films, including Wolf of Wall The Expendables, Skyfall, Chappie, Street, and many more.

- **Product Delivery:** UAVs can transport vaccines, foods, blood and retrieve medical samples, into and out of remote or inaccessible regions. Last few years some popular companies like Amazon, Walmart, Google etc. also investing huge amount of money in drone delivery related projects. Presently Amazon has Prime Air service that ships the orders safely from Amazon.com to customers. Not only Amazone, even Uber also looks for its own drone-based food delivery service by 2021.

- **Boarder Surveillances:** UAVs are equipped with a variety of sensors, high-resolution and daylight camera, GPS and can support live streaming. This UAVs network used by the military personnel for surveillance and monitoring purposes with minimized human intervention and capable of doing surveillance tasks like collecting images of objects, position of the soldier, monitoring unwanted international border activities, etc. and collected data can be immediately transmitted to a base station in a very short period.

- **Search and Rescue operation:** Many times multi-UAV framework proposed for search and rescue operation. In this context, UAVs is sensed for a target, typically on the ground. This network is used mostly used where ground networks are damaged due to natural disaster or inaccessible areas. In emergency scenarios, this framework provides all real-time information (Image, Audio, and Video) about the operation to station.

- **Relaying Network:** In FANETs relay network basically design for managing airborne communication links between a source node and destination node for efficiently and securely transmit the data, because sometimes they cannot communicate directly due to some physical obstacles like mountains, walls, large buildings etc. or may be destination node is very far away from the other source node. This is also used for increasing the communication range of networks.

- **Disaster Monitoring:** FANETs can evaluate the scenario completely in some very typical and remote areas through UAVs, which are not accessible by ground nodes like wildfires, flooding, earthquake, etc. Also, FANETs help to transmitting the correct information in real-time by using Wireless Sensor Network to the remote location of disaster areas and also help in post-fire and life-saving tasks.

- **Agriculture Management and Monitoring:** There are several possibilities for the use of Autonomous multi-UAV system for agricultural production management, because this system can perform all types of field operations like to apply fertilizer in the field and provide the information like growth and quality of crop within a very short time interval. Also use for monitoring plant health and complete crop evaluation (Kumar, S. et al., 2018).

- **Traffic Monitoring:** FANETs can involve in the ground traffic monitoring system without the travel over ground, therefore, reduce the number of labour and complicated observation infra-structure. In which each UAV configures with high quality cameras, typically involve capturing real-time images and videos data from flying nodes. Due to high UAVs movement, urgent event-specific data like any unwanted traffic and incident related information can be transferred to the nearest traffic control room or any management system (Zafar, B. et al., 2016).

- **Remote Health Monitoring:** Now days, research on FANETs application has focused on the various health monitoring planning. The combine effort of Wireless Body Area Sensor Network (WBAN) and FANETs, improving communication between medical professionals and patients. This planning can be improved to monitor patients using WBAN by sending the Personal Health Information (PHI) to the healthcare center with the help of FANETs in remote areas that is vulner-able to communication difficulties (Kumar, S. et al., 2018). These concepts provide high-quality healthcare at an early stage and provides immediate response to patients in emergency situations.

- **Wildlife Monitoring:** Now days the FANETs scenario is most popular for wildlife monitoring, which is more efficient in covering larger area. Recently the huge number of research project is going to examine individual animal's health, more accurate population counts, and observe life of all types of animals with the help of monitoring system through FANETs. Also, the wildfires are one of the very dangerous and deadliest natural disasters across the world. The immediate rescue can save the lives as well as forest resources (Thomas, D. S. et al., 2017).

- **Reconnaissance and Patrolling:** In this application, all UAVs monitor a precise determined area that usually patrols periodically for the inspection due to security purpose. For example, in the border surveillance area, a swarm of UAVs can detect and collecting images of objects like the involvement of the unplanned human disturbances, drugs and unauthorized materials, including weapons, illegal border crossings (Orfanus D., 2014).

- **Remote Sensing:** The Sensor networks are mainly used in high-flying aircraft (UAVs) equipped with GPS to access any location without great difficulties, in order to obtain important information for various typical situations (IF A. et al., 2002). Basically, FANETs improves the performance of network when evaluating the different scenarios in which they are applied at remote location (Miguel Itallo et al., 2019).

- **Environmental Sensing:** In this application, all UAVs act as smart sensor nodes that detect en-vironmental information on a specified area (Tareque, H. Md., et al., 2015). Basically, Sensor networks are mainly collecting and analysis the data according to environmental conditions in various situations, like temperature, humidity, pollution level, pressure, wind direction is typical physical quantities can analyze with the help of FANETs.

- **Business and Commerce:** We know, internet is one of the most important technologies for hu-man beings in 21st century. Recently a large number of drones related projects going on by world top most popular companies for business point of view, which aims to provide internet coverage in remote areas on mobiles directly from the sky like Facebook Aquila, Google Loon, Nokia F-Cell, Huawei Digital Sky etc. Also, UAVs are used in the commercial sector to take images and videos on any new construction sites and ground areas. Property dealers use such types of materials to be advertising purpose.

- **Security and Privacy Related:** Recently, FBI and police departments in all over the world, are buying drones that they can use for safety or protection related activities. Many authorities and industrial operations face some threats related to safety and security. Therefore, FANETs framework used for the real-time response to prevent all types of threats and provide rapid and reliable situational awareness and also, preserve evidence alike.

- **3D Mapping:** Using high quality multi-spectral cameras and laser scanners, small UAVs or drones are able to create 3D mapping. Therefore, they found applications in various areas, including photography, remote sensing, surveying & mapping, Investigation, Surveillance, precision agriculture, etc.

- **Smart Cities:** Now days UAVs is playing a major important role in developing smart cities. According to development of IoT (Internet of Things), multiple drones are applied in a verity of applications and functions in the smart cities. Some of these applications are like pollution monitoring, traffic management, Crowd management, smart transportation, environmental hazards monitoring and many more on a regular basis. Therefore, UAVs can provide several opportunities and advanced services that can beneficial to the development of any smart city.

CHALLENGES

Although, many of analyst and researchers have been done lot of works for increasing the efficiency of this ad-hoc network with UAVs, but there are still so many challenges (Bekmezci, I., et al., 2013), which is also describe below:

- **High Mobility of UAVs:** In FANETs, due to the very high mobility of UAVs nodes the efficiency of a routing protocol as well as the performance of the wireless link is degraded. Therefore, maintaining all connections between the UAVs is a very challenging issue.

- **Mobility Models:** Choosing correct mobility models in FANET are also very challenging task. As we know in MANET, node movements are always in specific regions and VANET nodes moving on the road, but in FANET nodes fly in the sky which are away from the ground. In some FANET applications, UAVs moves on a predetermined path, therefore the mobility model is regular. But some time mission may be updated, than the flight plan is recalculated, which is again affected to the mobility model of FANET.

- **Network Topology Change:** FANETs frequently change in the network because of the high mobility of UAVs. Whenever, if any UAV fails due to any reason in the network, then the links (formed by UAV) are also failing and it results the topology changed. Another cause of topology changes is a redefinition of the routes because of operation updating (addition/deletion UAVs) and environmental obstacles like weather uncertainties, very high mountains, and geographical conditions. Therefore, due to these constraints, this network increased overhead routing and decreased the packet delivery success rates. Therefore, these important aspects must be considered when designing FANETs.

- **High Reliability:** FANETs applied in sensitive military information as well search and rescue operation that required secure and guaranteed data delivery with low latency and high reliability. The reliability concept can be achieved by designing an ad-hoc network between the UAV nodes, but due to its unique characteristic (high mobility UAVs, frequent topology changes, etc.), sometime communication links fail between UAVs are challenging task for reliability.

- **Routing:** We know that topology changes very frequently in FANETs. Therefore, data routing between UAVs is a serious issue for researchers to provide effective and efficient routing protocols for FANETs, which is able to update or recalculate routing tables dynamically. Most of the previous routing protocols used by traditional ad-hoc networks partially fail in FANETs system. Therefore, there is a need of developing new routing protocols which are updated routing table dynamically.

- **Path Scheduling:** During some important mission operation, in FANETs each UAV may be to change its previous path due to some dynamic changes like weather conditions, add and deletion of UAVs, fixed obstacles (mountain, large buildings), dynamic threats etc. In such cases, new path should be re- calculated dynamically. Therefore FANETs need some new algorithms and network methods for dynamic path planning to communicate and coordinate between UAVs for efficient data transmission.

- **Size of UAVs:** Micro and mini UAVs are smaller in size, therefore; they can configure with limited capability, but in some typical operation if there is a need to use some different sensors and devices they may be restricted due to the size and weight of UAVs. Thus, there is need of some new research on UAVs size with less energy consumption.

- **Quality of Services:** There are huge numbers of application areas where FANET used to transmit verity of data like GPS location, images, streaming videos & audio, text files, etc. Therefore, researchers need to require quality services to overcome some issues like packet loss, end to end delay, low data transition rate, bandwidth, packet delivery ratio, residue energy, etc.

- **Security and Privacy:** Physically very small or mini UA Vs are always preferred in different type of applications of FANETs. Therefore, they can be very easily stolen. Moreover, unauthorized persons (hackers) may take control of the specific part of UAVs or may be complete network. This has also hampered military applications like surveillance and monitoring purposes. Another issue is complex secure hardware systems cannot be mounted on UAVs due to size constraint. Therefore, a lot of research required in security and privacy protocol for FANETs.

- **Development and Maintenance:** Another challenging issue in FANETs is the deployment and maintenance of network formation. The researchers should be designed a network which is easy to deploy and configure according to different type of operations.

- **National Regulations:** Various numbers of applications of FANETs are increasing now days. Every country has their own rules and regulation of aviation of UAVs, but such UAVs are not allowed for aviation in the public domain (Sahingoz, O. et al., 2013). Therefore, the biggest challenges to define some rules and regulations to controlled the UAV in the public domain. In other hand, some new technologies and operational regulations needed to guide the safe and secure performance of UAVs in FANETs.

- **Standardize FANETs:** Since FANETs is used in different application scenario with different UAVs for communication through satellite or GSM or CDMA networks. So they have to communicate with different frequency bands like C-band, L-band, Ku-band, etc. Hence it is standardized the frequency band for communication among FANETs network to reduce the congestion problem (Sahingoz, O. et al., 2013).

- **Scalability:** In FANETs, scalability becomes more difficult due to exponential growth of mobile nodes (vehicles, IoTs, Sensors) to this increase of data traffics, lack of service connectivity etc.
- **Weather:** Weather conditions are also an important challenge to UAVs, because weather hazards (fog, lighting, clouds, wind speed, icing) direct impact on UAVs operations. In cases of natural disasters, like Tsunamis, or wildfire, weather becomes a tough challenge. In such type of scenarios, UAVs may fail in their predefined mission (Shakhatreh, H. Et al., 2018).

All above mentions issues some additional issues also under the consideration for UAVs like insurance, criminal use, safety purpose, damage inspection etc. In other hand, Routing play a most dominating role in enhancing the performance of ad-hoc networks. At the same time, routing in FANETs is more difficult due to its nature like high mobility, 3D topology, different density, power consumption, different radio propagation model. Therefore, enhancing existing or may be evolution new routing is one of the exciting research.

The chapter is organized as follows: In Section I, authors, summaries background survey, Section II gives the detailed overview of DSDV, DSR and AODV routing protocol with the advantages and disadvantages of each of one, further differentiate all routing protocols in tabular form. Section IV analyze and visualize the performance of these Routing Protocols for FANETs scenario through NS-2 simulator along with results in various parameters like end to end delay, average throughput, and packet delivery ratio. At the end chapter is concluded with future scope.

LITERATURE REVIEW

In (Juan, Li. et al., 2014), authors proposed new routing protocol called UEDSR(UAV Energy Dynamic Source Routing Protocol) which is more suitable for small reconnaissance UAV ad hoc network. UEDSR basically used energy balancing mechanism based on DSR, which is improve network lifetime. The NS2 illustrates the comparison between UEDSR and DSR w.r.t. PDR and average throughput.

In (Singh, K. et al., 2015), three routing protocols AODV, DSDV and OLSR performance analyzed under the different parameters with respect to speed of mobile nodes. Through the NS-2 simulation explained that, OLSR routing protocol gives better result and enhancing the performs of FANETs other than two routing protocols AODV as well as DSDV in terms of different parameters like E2ED, PDR and Average Throughput. Therefore the network performance of FANETs can be optimized with the help of an OLSR protocol.

In this (Tareque, H. Md., 2015) paper, all different types of ad hoc networks among the UAVs is surveyed with emphasis on its most important challenges and compared with other networks like MANET, VANET (traditional ad hoc networks). They described that, communication between the UAVs are the most challenging tasks. They compared different routing categories based on various performance criteria. Finally, they presented several open research issues related to FANETs environment.

In this (Shilpa, K. G. et al., 2016) research paper, three routing protocols like AODV, DSDV and AOMDV are simulate with the help of an NS2 simulator under the different parameters like overhead, throughput, and PDR with respect to different speeds (5, 15, 25m/Sec.) of node. Furthermore, authors analyzed that, AODV performs better in FANET scenario other than AOMDV and DSDV in terms of E2ED, Average Throughput, PDR and overhead.

This (Rabia, B. et al., 2017) research paper is presenting the comprehensive analysis of mobility models like the RPGM, GM, RWP and MGM for various applications of FANET and simulation result show that DSR perform well as compare AODV and OLSR in highly dynamic FANETs environments which is generated by different mobility models.

In (Khan, M. A. et al., 2018) this research paper author, discussed various topology-based routing protocols with their working process and also explain their different types of advantages and limitations in the context of FANETs. They explained OPNET simulation based on key parameters like mobility, routing overhead and traffic density etc.

At (Aftab, Y. M. et al., 2019) this paper, some open issues discussed related to design and implementation of UAVs Network. Researchers surveyed the existing routing protocols for UAV networks, based on different categories like topology, position, hierarchical, deterministic, stochastic, and social network, etc. Furthermore, these are compared qualitatively on the basis their characteristics and performance.

In (Jianze, Wu et al., 2019) this paper, authors proposed new EV-AODV protocol, which is based on residual energy and relative movement of UAVs. Furthermore, the simulation results show that the EV-AODV is more suitable for UAV Ad-hoc network environment on the basis of PDR as well as network lifetime as compared to AODV.

ROUTING FOR FLYING AD HOC NETWORKS

In FANETs, routing is simply a process to find out an efficient path to deliver data between sources to destination with the help of mini-UAVs. Efficient path can be calculated in term of less packet delivery time, high packet delivery ratio, fewer relay hops, fewer control messages, etc. Although, previously different types of routing protocols exist in wireless ad-hoc network like MANET, VANET, but due to the unique characteristics of FANETs like high mobility of nodes as well as rapid topology changes, these protocols need to be update according to the requirement of UAVs network. To formulate the communication between UAVs in FANETs, routing protocols are basically classified into either topology-based or position-based routing protocols, and each one is characterized according to a number of network design issues. Topology-based routing protocol depends on the information about existing links, and this link information is used to transmit the packets between the UAV nodes. It requires the IP addresses of the source UAV as well as the destination UAV. These routing protocols are divided into four different categories like Static, Proactive, Reactive and Hybrid which will be discussed in the next paragraph (Khan, M. A., et al). Furthermore, the position based routing protocols this is also called geographical routing protocols, requires the actual position or location about the moving nodes (UAVs or drones) through the GPS system, which is based on location services (latitude and longitude of the moving UAVs). The GPS information is used to recognize the route for forwarding the packets from the source UAV to destination UAV node.

Recently, important research techniques have been proposed for topology-based routing protocols in FANETs scenario. These routing protocols are furthermore divided into four different Categories as shown in Figure 2 with a detailed description of DSDV, DSR and AODV routing protocol.

Figure 2. Types of topology-based routing protocols in FANETs

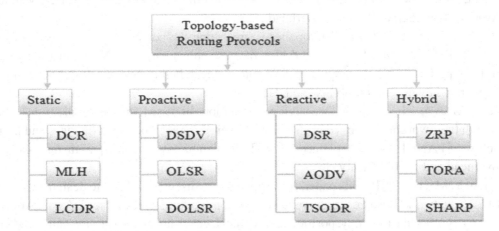

- **Static Routing Protocol:** In this routing, a routing table is calculated and uploaded with all UAV nodes before an assign any tasks and the more important is these routing tables cannot be updated (no need of refresh) during the operation or any assigned mission. So that UAVs has constant topology. There are a number of proposed algorithms under this category like Data Centric Routing (DCR), Multilevel Hierarchical Routing (MLH) and Load Carry and Deliver Routing (LCDR) (Sahingoz, O. 2013).
- **Proactive Routing Protocol:** This is based on table-driven routing; these are periodically refreshed routing tables. In this network every node shares information from its routing table at regular time interval. The key feature of this routing is, it is stored latest information about the routes. There are many algorithms in this category like DSDV, OLSR, Directional-OLSR (DOLSR) and FSR (Singh, K. et al., 2014).
- **Reactive Routing Protocol:** Also stand for on-demand routing protocols because, they discover paths for messages on demand. This protocol mainly uses two concepts, one is RREQ and another one is RREP for establishing the connection between the UAVs node. AODV, DSR and ABR are routing algorithms under this category (Bekmezci, I. et al., 2013)
- **Hybrid Routing Protocol:** These types of protocol overcome the limitation of previously existing routing protocols. It takes advantage from the grouping of proactive and reactive routing protocols. But, these protocols are only suitable for less number of UAVs (small networks), because more numbers of UAVs imply large overlapping of routing zones. TORA and ZRP are the examples under this routing protocol category (Bekmezci, I., et al. 2013).

3.1 Destination-Sequenced Distance-Vector (DSDV)

DSDV (Parkins C. E. et al., 1994) is enhanced version of the Bellman-Ford routing mechanism. This is table-driven and the part of proactive routing. In DSDV, each routing table maintains the global topology information at every UAV nodes. These routing tables are updated frequently for maintain the latest information about network and then each UAV node exchange its updated information with each other UAV. The routing table contain the information about destination ID, next node, distance and sequence number. Route broadcast massage also contain destination node, next hope, distance and recent sequence number.

In Figure 3, let UAV node U_1 want to send some data to UAV node U_2 and then also send to destination UAV node U_3. Than the routing table 1 for UAV node U_1 shown following entries:

Figure 3. FANET scenario

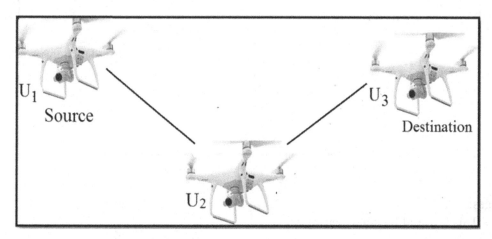

Table 1. Routing table for UAV node U_1

Destination Node	Next Hop	Distance	Sequence Number
U_2	U_2	1	14
U_3	U_2	2	18

The same routing table also generated by node U_1 as well as node U_2. Each UAV node exchanges its updated routing table with each other by using either full dump method (entire routing table is sent to the neighbours UAV) or incremental update method (only the entries that requires changes are send). For example, if new UAV node U_4 is connected to U_2 than following new entries (row 4) in table 2 either exchange the information or full table 3 is sent to other UAVs.

Table 2. Updated routing table

Destination Node	Next Hop	Distance	Sequence Number
U_2	U_2	1	14
U_3	U_2	2	18
U_4	U_2	2	22

Figure 4. FANET scenario

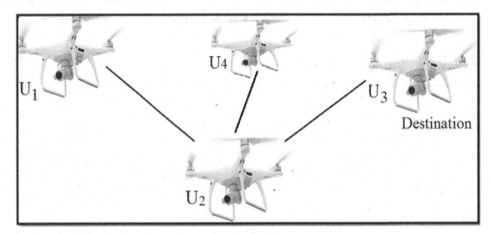

Advantages:
- ◦ This is useful for small networks.
- ◦ Always loop –free transmission.

Disadvantages:
- ◦ Not efficient for large no. of node with highly dynamic in nature.
- ◦ It supports only single path routing
- ◦ Slower protocol processing time

Dynamic Source Routing (DSR)

DSR (Johnson, D. B. at al. 2001) is a very simple with self-organizing and self-configuring routing for MANET, VANET and FANET. This is the part of reactive routing, sometime it is also called on-demand routing protocol because; it is routing is capable of determining the route to be used in transmitting its packets from source node to destination node only when required and needed. This routing was developed at CMU in 1996. Routing in DSR is done in two phases, one is route discovery and another one is route maintenance. Route discovery find the optimum rout for transmit the packet from source node to destination node by using intermediate nodes. Route Maintenance is performed only while the route is in use, if any, error is detected then it will send the error packet to the original sender which performs a new route discovery. DSR does broadcast the route to its neighbours UAVs, but does not flood the information. It only traces the route by calculating the total distance or may be calculating the number of UAVs present in between the source UAV and destination UAVs.

Consider a FANETs environment containing 5 UAVs where U_1 is the source and U_2 is the destination. Below mentioned steps will explain how DSR protocol works and how Re-Request packet is transmitted through the network.

Step 1: Start from source UAV node U_1 and broadcast the information about it to its neighbours, i.e. in this case the route information is $<U_1>$, because of its one-to-one link between UAV nodes U_1 and U_2.
Step 2: Broadcast previous route information to neighbours of node U_2 i.e. to node U_3, U_4, U_5. The new route will remain same $<U_1, U_2>$ in all the cases.

Step 3: Take node U3 and broadcast previous route <U_1, U_2> to next neighbouring nodes i.e. node U_5. New route till node U_5 will be <U_1, U_2, U_3> and the same process can be done form node U_4 to U_5 with <U_1, U_2, U_4> and direct node U2 to U5 with <U_1, U_2> .The updated routes will be as shown in figure 5.

Figure 5. Route discovery by RREQ

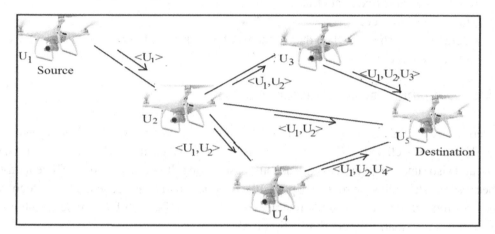

After this, "Re-Request" packet will be sent in the backward direction from destination UAV node U_5 to source UAV node U_1. It will trace the shortest route by counting the number of UAVs from route discovered in previous steps. The three possible routes are <U_1, U_2, U_3>, <U_1, U_2> and <U_1, U_2, U_4> in rout <U_1, U_2> clearly seen that, it contains the least number of UAVs and hence it will definitely be the shortest path and then data can be transferred accordingly. The Re-Request Packet route can be shown in figure 6.

Figure 6. DSR with RREP

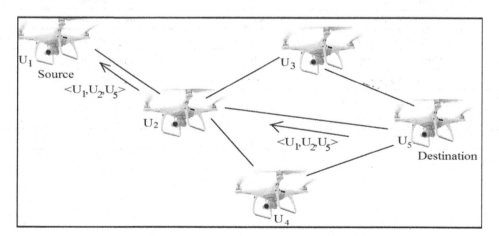

Advantages:
- A perfect route is discovered always
- Highly efficient
- Low bandwidth Consumption
- More suitable when data contents of a packet are large

Disadvantages:
- If the route gets broke, data transmission cannot happen.
- Time taking protocol.
- Degrades performance when data contents of a packet are large.
- Not efficient for large network.

Ad Hoc on Demand Distance Vector (AODV)

AODV (Perkins, C.E. et al., 1999 & Royer, E. et al., 2000) is a reactive MANET routing which is also utilized by VANET as well as FANET environments. The AODV used to reduce the limitation of DSR and DSDV and also supports unicast as well as multicast routing. It is considered as efficient on-demand routing because, it establishes the route to a particular destination only as needed. This protocol operates on two phase's route discovery and route maintenance. In FANETs, each UAV node maintains a route table that contains information about destination UAV node.

AODV consider four different types of control message: First one is Route Request (RREQ) message, which is used to initiate the route-finding process. This message broadcast by the source node that wants to connect to a destination node, the second is Route Reply (RREP), this is used to finalize the routes and the third one is a Route Error (RERR) messages, this is mainly used to notify the other nodes that the route becomes invalid and the last one is HELLO message, this is indicating the presence of neighbour UAVs. The RREQ and RREP contain the following fields.

Table 3. RREQ and RREP format

RREQ Format	RREP Format
Target IP Address	Target IP Address
Target Sequence Number	Target Sequence Number
Originator IP Address	Originator IP Address
Request ID	Other State and Routing Flags
Originator Sequence Number	Hop Count
Other State and Routing Flags	Life-Time
Hop Count	

If any source UAV node (figure 7) needs to send packets to a destination UAV node, it first must determine path for communication through route discovery. The source UAV first broadcasting a RREQ message with destination UAV IP address. After that, each neighbouring UAV checks the source ID as well as request ID on receiving a RREQ message. If one of any UAV has already received a RREQ message with the same previous ID, the new RREQ message will be discarded. When the destination UAV receives the RREQ, a RREP generated. The RREP is unicast back to the source on the reverse path along which the RREQ came. Above Figure 7 shows the working process of RREQ and RREP.

Figure 7. RREQ and RREP for AODV

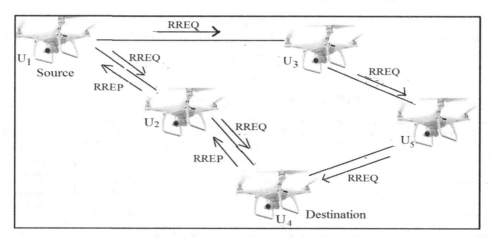

According to the above figure 7, If the source UAV U_1 wants to send a packet to the destination UAV U_4 than it follows the given steps: -

- Firstly, source UAV node U_1 will send RREQ to its neighbour U_2 and U_3.
- UAV node U_2 setup reverses path and forwards the RREQ packet to its next neighbour U_4.
- UAV node U_3 also setup reverses path and forwards the RREQ to U_5.
- UAV node U_5 (same above) forward RREQ packet to U_4.
- When the UAV U_4 receives the RREQ from other UAV U_5, it will abandon this message because it was previously received by U_2.
- UAV node U_4 creates a RREP message and updates the entries of its routing tables.
- After that it unicast the RREP to UAV node $_{U2}$ and with the same process RREP forward massage from UAV node U_2 to Source node U_1.

On the other hand, neighbouring UAVs periodically exchange hello message. Network connectivity determine by the hello message. When any UAV node detects the loss of neighbour node (not received HELLO message) that is part of an active route, a route error (RERR) packet is sent in order to inform the other UAV nodes of the loss of connectivity.

Advantages:
- ◦ Smaller Storage Space required
- ◦ Adaptability to dynamic networks
- ◦ Route Cache preserves Bandwidth
- ◦ Reduce delay and maintain Active Routes Using a timer

Disadvantages:
- ◦ High mobility of UAVs leads to more link failure and packet drop
- ◦ It do not repair broken link only inform them
- ◦ Need Periodic updates
- ◦ Do not utilize any congestion control

On the basis of above in-depth discussion of DSDV, DSR and AODV protocols, the bellow table 3 illustrates the comparison of these protocols with all properties.

Table 4. Comparison between DSDV, DSR and AODV protocols

Properties/Protocols	DSDV	DSR	AODV
Category	Proactive	Reactive	Reactive
Route Update	Periodically	On-demand	On-demand
Concept	Based on Bellman-Ford algorithm	Source-based routing	Combination of DSR and DSDV
Path Discovery	Routing table	Routing table	Routing table
Multicast Capability	No	No	Yes
Loop Free	Yes	Yes	Yes
Distributed	Yes	Yes	Yes
Topology Size	Small	Large	Large
Highly Dynamic Topology	Not suitable	Suitable	More suitable

In next section authors investigate the performance of above discussed routing protocols like DSDV, DSR and AODV. This investigation aims to help academicians and researchers to choose more efficient and reliable protocol, which is more suited to their interest areas.

SIMULATION

In this section, authors demonstrate the comparative performance of three routing protocols DSDV, DSR and AODV with the help of NS2 simulator and evaluate the performance on the basis of Packet Delivery Ratio (PDR), End-to-End Delay (E2ED), and Average throughput for FANETs scenario.

Simulation Platform

We used simulation tool NS2 (Issariyakul, T., et el, 2011), this is very simple and open- source event-driven simulation tool for studying the networks like MANET, VANET, FANET, etc. It provides simulation for routing protocols for wired and wireless. The NS2 was developed in 1989 by collaborative efforts of the University of California and Cornell University. This simulator combines two important languages: C++ (i.e., a backend) and Object-oriented Tool Command Language (OTcl) (i.e., a front-end). Whereas, the performance evaluation metrics were programmed in AWK (Aho, Weinberger and Kernighan) scripting language. AWK scripts are used for manipulating the data and generating reports from the trace files which we get from NS2.35. Further, NAM tool use for interpreting these results as a graphically and interactively.

Figure 8. Basic architecture of NS2.35

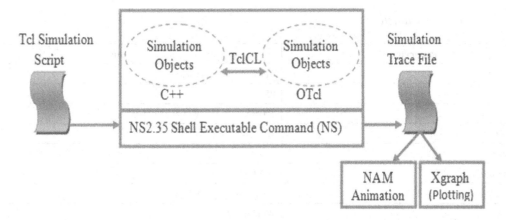

Network Animator (NAM)

NAM is a completely separate program that is distributed with the NS simulator. Basically NAM is an animator tool for real world packet tracer and graphically supported topology layout of network. It reads an input file and draws the network events graphically (Estrin D. et al., 1999). The simulator was originally developed as part of the VNIT project. Beloved figure 9 shows the typical NAM visualization.

RESULTS AND ANALYSIS

The simulation is designed for DSDV, DSR and AODV routing protocol with different parameters like PDR, E2ED, and Avg. throughput. At the beginning, all the five UAV nodes are placed uniformly and forming an ad-hoc network between all in an 800m x 800m area. After 2 Sec. UAV nodes start to move with different speed like 15, 30, 45, 60, 80m/Sec. CBR traffic type is used with the packet size 1000 bytes. We set the data rate to be 11mbps for all the UAVs, according to the IEEE 802.11g standard. The transmission range is taken to be 250 meters. Each simulation is executed in 150 seconds by NS 2.35 simulator. The other simulation parameters are given below in table 5.

Figure 9. NAM tool descriptions for 05 different UAVs

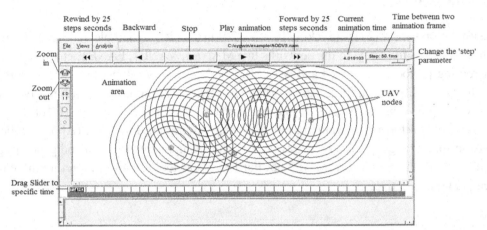

Table 5. Simulation parameters

Parameters	Value
Channel type	Channel/Wireless Channel
Number of UAV nodes	05
Simulation time	150sec
Simulation area	800×800
Packet size	1000
Mac layer protocol	802.11g
Routing protocol	DSDV, DSR and AODV
Operating system	Window 07
NS2 Version	NS2.35
Antenna model	Omni
Interface queue type	Drop tail/Priority queue, CMU priQueue
Traffic type	CBR
Transmission range	250m
Interface queue length	50
UAV Nodes speed	15, 30, 45, 60, 80

- **PDR:** The PDR is defined as the ratio of the total number of data packets successfully delivered and the total data packets transmitted by all the UAV nodes in a network. It is formulated as

$$PDR = \frac{\sum_{i=1}^{n} R_p}{\sum_{i=1}^{n} S_p} \times 100 \quad \begin{array}{l} R_p \text{ is total packetes received by each destination} \\ S_p \text{ is total packets generated by each source} \end{array}$$

- *UAV Nodes Speed vs PDR:* Table 6 shows the variation of the PDR with the change in speed of UAV nodes

Table 6. UAV nodes speed vs PDR.

Routing Protocol	Speed (m/sec)				
	15	**30**	**45**	**60**	**80**
DSDV	.075	.075	.075	.075	.075
DSR	.16	.20	.20	.19	.20
AODV	.20	.20	.20	.20	.20

The following graph shows the PDR of DSDV, DSR and AODV. X-axis represents different speed of UAV nodes and Y- axis represents the packet delivery ratio. According to the figure 10 shows that the PDR of AODV is consistent and perform well even though the speed of UAV nodes are increasing, whereas the PDR of DSDV is very low and the result of DSR decreases when the UAV nodes speed increase.

Figure 10. UAV nodes speed vs PDR

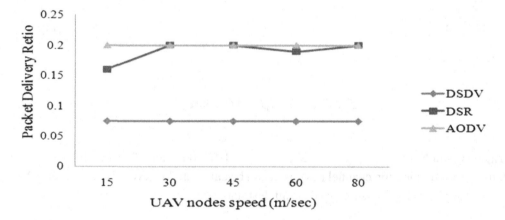

- **E2ED:** The E2ED is calculates all possible delays occurred in the networks. In other words E2ED is the time taken by a packet to travel from source to a destination UAV node. It can be formulated as
  E2ED = TR-TS
  TR is packet received time
  TS is packet sent time
- **UAV Nodes Speed vs E2ED:** Table 7 shows the variation in E2ED of different protocols with the change in speed of the UAV nodes.

Table 7. UAV nodes speed vs E2ED

Routing Protocol	Speed (m/sec)				
	15	**30**	**45**	**60**	**80**
DSDV	3.41	3.41	3.41	3.41	3.41
DSR	4.19	3.69	3.70	3.70	3.70
AODV	3.46	3.51	3.42	3.56	3.51

The below graph (figure 11), clearly shows that, the E2ED of DSR protocol is higher than as compared to AODV and DSDV, So in case of E2ED AODV as well as DSDV perform well as compare to DSR.

Figure 11. UAV nodes speed vs E2ED

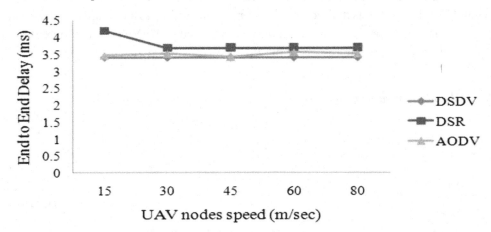

Average Throughput: The Avg. throughput can be defined as rate of successful message transmission through a communication channel in kbps. It can be calculated as, Avg. Throughtput = Np * Packet Size *8/Seconds (Np is total bits received by all destinations.

- **UAV Nodes Speed vs Avg.Throughput:** The given table 8 shows the change of average throughput with the different speed (15 to 80m/Sec.) of the UAV nodes.

Table 8. UAV nodes speed vs avg. throughput

Routing Protocol	Speed (m/Sec.)				
	15	**30**	**45**	**60**	**80**
DSDV	73.14	73.14	73.14	73.14	73.14
DSR	154.69	191.03	189.50	189.39	191.21
AODV	196.77	195.94	195.64	194.57	195.13

Figure 12. UAV nodes speed vs average throughput

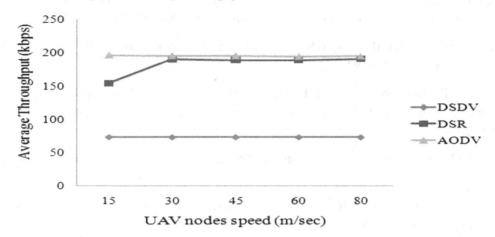

Above graph shows, the avg. throughput of AODV is consistent even when the speed of UAV nodes is increased, but the other side in DSR and DSDV, it is degraded with the high speed of UAV nodes. So above simulation result verified that AODV gives better avg. throughput as compare to DSR and DSDV in FANETs scenario.

CONCLUSION

In this research, authors firstly discuss main characteristics of FANETs and also focus on popular applications with its key challenges. Secondly, the authors briefly described DSDV, DSR and AODV routing protocol and evaluate these popular protocols with different parameters in FANETs. Through the simulation results by using NS2.35 simulator, it can be clearly seen that, AODV is performs better than the other two routing protocol DSR and DSDV in terms of E2ED, PDR, and avg. throughput. The resulting graph also describes the DSDV routing protocol is not as good as compared DSR and AODV, the meaning is that, the DSDV routing protocol is not a better choice for FANETs scenario due to high mobility as well as frequent topology changes of UAV nodes. Therefore, AODV has better performance than DSR in higher-mobility scenarios, in this, FANETs can be optimized by choosing AODV as a routing protocol.

In the near future, this research work can be extended and compare with the different type of position-based routing protocols for enhancing the performances of FANETs.

REFERENCES

Lilien, L. T., ben Othmane, L., Angin, P., DeCarlo, A., Salih, R. M., & Bhargava, B. (2013, May). A simulation study of ad hoc networking of UAVs with opportunistic resource utilization networks. *Journal of Network and Computer Applications, 38*, 3–15.

Akyildiz, I. F., Su, W., Sankarasubramaniam, Y., & Cayirci, E. (2002). A survey on sensor networks. *IEEE Communications Magazine, 40*(8), 102–114. doi:10.1109/MCOM.2002.1024422

Arafat, Y. M., & Moh, S. (2019, July), Routing Protocols for Unmanned Aerial Vehicle Networks: A Survey, *IEEE Access, 7,* 99694-99720.

Azevedo, M. I. B., Coutinho, C., Toda, E. M., Carvalho, T. C., & Jailton, J. (2019, June). Wireless Communications Challenges to Flying Ad Hoc Networks (FANET). *IntechOpen.* doi: . doi:10.5772/intechopen.86544

Bamburry, D. (2015). Drones: Designed for product delivery. *Design Management Review, 26*(1), 40–48. doi:10.1111/drev.10313

Bekmezci, I., Sahingoz, O. K., & Temel, S. (2013). *Flying Ad-Hoc Networks (FANETs): A Survey* (pp. 1254–1270). ELSEVIER Ad Hoc Networks.

Bilal, R., & Khan, B. M. (2017). Analysis of Mobility Models and Routing Schemes for Flying Ad–Hoc Networks (FANETS). *International Journal of Applied Engineering Research, 12*(12), 3263–3269.

Bujari, A., Calafate, C. T., Cano, J. C., Manzoni, P., Palazzi, C. E., & Ronzani, D. (2017). Flying ad–hoc network application scenarios and mobility models. *International Journal of Distributed Sensor Networks, 13*(10), 1–17. doi:10.1177/1550147717738192

Bujari, A., Palazzi, C. E., & Ronzani, D. (2017). FANET application scenarios and mobility models. *Proceedings of the 3rd Workshop on Micro Aerial Vehicle Networks, Systems, and Applications* (pp. 43–46). ACM

Chezhiyan, U. (2013, April) Measurement Based Analysis of Reactive Protocols in MANET, *International Journal of Wired and Wireless Communications, 1*(2).

Estrin, D., Handley, M., Heidemann, J., McCanne, S., Xu, Y., & Yu, H. (1999, November). Network Visualization with the VINT Network Animator Nam. Retrieved from https://pdfs.semanticscholar.org/08e3/c15700c229ab3b91218dd36e1aa902c1922d.pdf

Garcia-Santiago, A., Castaneda-Camacho, J., Guerrero-Castellanos, J. F., & Mino-Aguilar, G. (2018, February). Evaluation of AODV and DSDV routing protocols for a FANET: Further results towards robotic vehicle networks. *Proceedings 2018 IEEE 9th Latin American Symposium on Circuits & Systems* (pp. 1-4). IEEE.

Gupta, L., Jain, R., & Vaszkun, G. (2015, November). Survey of Important Issues in UAV Communication Networks. *IEEE Communications Surveys & Tutorials, 18*(2), 1123-1152. doi: . doi:10.1109/COMST.2015.2495297

Ham, Y., Han, K. K., Lin, J. J., & Golparvar-Fard, M. (2016). Visual monitoring of civil infrastructure systems via camera-equipped unmanned aerial vehicles (UAVs): A review of related works. *Visualization in Engineering, 4*(1), 1. doi:10.118640327-015-0029-z

Hayat, S., Yanmaz, E., & Muzaffar, R. (2016). Survey on Unmanned Aerial Vehicle Networks for Civil Applications: A Communications Viewpoint. *IEEE Communications Surveys and Tutorials, 18*(4), 2624–2661. doi:10.1109/COMST.2016.2560343

Issariyakul, T., & Hossain, E. (2011). *Introduction to network simulator NS2*. Springer Science & Business Media.

Johnson, D. B., Maltz, D. A., & Broch, J. (2001). DSR: The dynamic source routing protocol for multihop wireless ad hoc networks. *Ad Hoc Networks, 5*, 139–172.

Khan, M. A., Khan, I. U., Safi, A., & Quershi, I. M. (2018). Dynamic routing in flying ad-hoc networks using topology-based routing protocols. *Drones, 2*(3), 27. doi:10.3390/drones2030027

Khan, M. A., Safi, A., Qureshi, I. M., & Khan, I. U. (2017, November). Flying ad-hoc networks (FANETs): A review of communication architectures, and routing protocols. *Proc. 1st Int. Conf. Latest Trends Elect. Eng. Comput. Technol. (INTELLECT)*, pp. 1-9. Karachi, Pakistan. IEEE. 10.1109/INTELLECT.2017.8277614

Kumar, S., Bansal, A., & Raw, S. R. (2018, December 22-24). Health Monitoring Planning for On-board Ships through Flying Ad-hoc Network. In *3rd International Conference on Advanced Computing and Intelligent Engineering*, Siksha 'O' Anusandhan Deemed to be University, Bhubaneswar, India.

Kumar, S., & Raw, S. R. (2018, March 14-16). Flying Ad-Hoc Networks (FANETs): Current State, Challenges, and Potentials. In 12th INDIACom-2018; 5th International Conference on Computing for Sustainable Global Development, BVICAM, New Delhi, India.

Leonov, A. V. (2016). Application of bee colony algorithm for FANET routing. *17th International Conference of Young Specialists on Micro/Nanotechnologies and Electron Devices (EDM)*, Erlagol, Russia, pp. 124–132. Retrieved from 10.1109/EDM.2016.7538709

Leonov, A. V., & Litvinov, G. A. (2018). Simulation-Based Packet Delivery Performance Evaluation with Different Parameters in Flying Ad-Hoc Network (FANET) using AODV and OLSR. *International Conference Information Technologies in Business and Industry*. 10.1088/1742-6596/1015/3/032178

Li, J., Liu, X., Pang, Y., & Zhu, W. (2014, June). A Novel DSR-based Protocol for Small Reconnaissance UAV Ad Hoc Network. *Applied Mechanics and Materials, 568-570*, 1272–1277. doi:10.4028/www.scientific.net/AMM.568-570.1272

Liu, P., Chen, A. Y., Huang, Y.-N., Han, J.-Y., Lai, J.-S., Kang, S.-C., ... Tsai, M. (2014). A review of rotorcraft unmanned aerial vehicle (UAV) developments and applications in civil engineering. *Smart Structures and Systems, 13*(6), 1065–1094. doi:10.12989ss.2014.13.6.1065

Nayyar, A. (2018, August). Flying Adhoc Network (FANETs): Simulation Based Performance Comparison of Routing Protocols: AODV, DSDV, DSR, OLSR, AOMDV, and HWMP. *Proceedings International Conference on Advances in Big Data, Computing, and Data Communication Systems (icABCD). IEEE.* 10.1109/ICABCD.2018.8465130

Orfanus, D., & De Freitas, E. (2014, October). Comparison of UAV-based reconnaissance systems performance using realistic mobility models. *Proceedings 6th international congress on ultra-modern telecommunications and control systems and workshops (ICUMT),* pp. 248–253. New York: IEEE.

Oubbati, O. S., Lakas, A., Zhou, F., Güneş, M., & Yagoubi, M. B. (2017, October). A survey on position-based routing protocols for Flying Ad hoc Networks (FANETs). *Vehicular Communications, 10*(October), 29–56. doi:10.1016/j.vehcom.2017.10.003

Oubbati, O. S., Atiquzzaman, M., Lorenz, P., Tareque, M. H., & Hossain, M. S. (2019). Routing in flying Ad Hoc networks: Survey, constraints, and future challenge perspectives. *IEEE Access, 7,* 81057-81105. doi:10.1109/ACCESS.2019.2923840

Peng, J. (2015, May). Radio propagation models in wireless networks of unmanned aerial vehicles. *International Journal of Computer Networks & Communications, 7*(3).

Perkins, C. E., & Watson, T. J. (1994). Highly Dynamic Destination Sequenced Distance Vector Routing (DSDV) for Mobile Computers. ACM SIGCOMM computer communication review, 24(4), 234-244.

Perkins, C. E., & Royer, E. M. (1999, February). Ad-hoc on-demand distance vector routing. Proceedings WMCSA'99. Second IEEE Workshop on Mobile Computing Systems and Applications (pp. 90-100). IEEE.

Rabia, B., & Bilal, M. K. (2017, November). Analysis of Mobility Models and Routing Schemes for Flying Ad-Hoc Networks (FANETS). *International Journal of Applied Engineering Research, 12,* 3263–3269.

Rosati, S., Kruelecki, K., Heitz, G., Floreano, D., & Rimoldi, B. (2016). Dynamic routing for flying ad hoc networks. *IEEE Transactions on Vehicular Technology, 65*(3), 1690–1700. doi:10.1109/TVT.2015.2414819

Royer, E., & Perkins, C. (2000). An Implementation Study of the AODV Routing Protocol. *Proceedings of Wireless Communication and Networking Conference.* Retrieved from http://erdos.csie.ncnu.edu.tw/~ccyang/WirelessNetwork/Papers/MANET/AdHocUnicast-17.pdf

Sahingoz, O. (2013, September). Networking Models in Flying Ad-Hoc Networks (FANETs): Concepts and Challenges. *Journal of Intelligent & Robotic Systems, 74.*

Sankarasrinivasan, S., Balasubramanian, E., Karthik, K., Chandrasekar, U., & Gupta, R. (2015). Health monitoring of civil structures with integrated UAV and image processing system. *Procedia Computer Science, 54,* 508–515. doi:10.1016/j.procs.2015.06.058

Santhiya, K. G., & Arumugam, N. (2012, March). Energy Aware Reliable Routing Protocol (EARRP) for Mobile Ad Hoc Networks Using Bee Foraging Behavior and Ant Colony Optimization. *International Journal of Computer Science Issues, 9*(2), 171.

Scherer, J., Yahyanejad, S., Hayat, S., Yanmaz, E., Vukadinovic, V., Andre, T., ... Hellwagner, H. (2015). *An autonomous multi-UAV system for search and rescue* (pp. 33–38). DroNet. doi:10.1145/2750675.2750683

Shilpa, K. G., et al. (2016, August). Efficient Data Routing Analysis In FANETS To Achieve QOS. *International Journal of Innovative Science, Engineering & Technology, 3*(8).

Singh, A., Singh, G., & Singh, M. (2018). Comparative study of OLSR, DSDV, AODV, DSR, and ZRP routing protocols under black hole attack in mobile ad hoc network. In *Intelligent Communication, Control, and Devices* (pp. 443–453). Singapore: Springer. doi:10.1007/978-981-10-5903-2_45

Singh, K., & Verma, A. K. (2014, May). Applying OLSR routing in FANETs. *Proceedings International Conference on Advanced Communication Control and Computing Technologies (ICACCCT)*, pp. 1212-1215. IEEE.

Singh, K., & Verma, A. K. (2015, March). Experimental Analysis of AODV, DSDV and OLSR Routing Protocol for Flying Ad-hoc Networks (FANETs). *Proceedings IEEE International Conference on Electrical, Computer, and Communication Technologies (ICECCT)*, IEEE. Coimbatore, India, doi: 10.1109/ICECCT.2015.7226085

Sumra, I. A., Sellappan, P., Abdullah, A., & Ali, A. (2018, April). Security issues and Challenges in MANET-VANET-FANET: A Survey. *EAI Endorsed Transactions on Energy Web and Information Technologies.* . doi:10.4108/eai.10-4-2018.155884

Tareque, H. Md., Hossain, S. Md., & Atiquzzaman, Mh. (2015). On the Routing in Flying Ad hoc Networks. *Proceedings of the Federated Conference on Computer Science and Information Systems*, ACSIS, 5, pp. 1–9. doi: 10.15439/2015F002

Shakhatreh, H., Sawalmeh, A. H., Al-Fuqaha, A., Dou, Z., Almaita, E., Khalil, I., ... & Guizani, M. (2018, April). Unmanned Aerial Vehicles: A Survey on Civil Applications and Key Research Challenges. *Robotics*, *10*. doi:10.1109/ACCESS.2019

Vijaya, I., & Rath, A. K. (2011). Simulation and Performance Evaluation of AODV, DSDV, and DSR in TCP and UDP Environment. *Proceedings 3rd International Conference on Electronics Computer Technology*, 6. 10.1109/ICECTECH.2011.5942047

Wu, J., Shuo, S., Liu, Z., & Gu, X. (2019). Optimization of AODV Routing Protocol in UAV Ad Hoc Network. *Proceedings International Conference on Artificial Intelligence for Communications and Networks (AICON), LNICST*, 286, pp. 472-478. 10.1007/978-3-030-22968-9_43

Yassein, M. B., & Damer, N. A. (2016). Flying ad–hoc networks: Routing protocols, mobility models, issues. *International Journal of Advanced Computer Science and Applications*, 7(6), 162–168.

Zafar, W., & Muhammad, K. B. (2016, June). Technological and social Implications Flying Ad-Hoc Network. *IEEE Technology and Society Magazine*.

Zhan, P., Yu, K., & Swindlehurst, A. L. (2011, July). Wireless relay communications with unmanned aerial vehicles: Performance and optimization. *IEEE Transactions on Aerospace and Electronic Systems*, *47*(3), 2068–2085. doi:10.1109/TAES.2011.5937283

Chapter 14
Vehicular Cloud and Fog Computing Architecture, Applications, Services, and Challenges

Priyanka Gaba
Ambedkar Institute of Advanced Communication Technologies and Research, India

Ram Shringar Raw
Ambedkar Institute of Advanced Communication Technologies and Research, India

ABSTRACT

VANET, a type of MANET, connects vehicles to provide safety and non-safety features to the drivers and passengers by exchanging valuable data. As vehicles on road are increasing to handle such data cloud computing, functionality is merged with vehicles known as Vehicular Cloud Computing(VCC) to serve VANET with computation, storage, and networking functionalities. But Cloud, a centralized server, does not fit well for vehicles needing high-speed processing, low latency, and more security. To overcome these limitations of Cloud, Fog computing was evolved, extending the functionality of cloud computing model to the edge of the network. This works well for real time applications that need fast response, saves network bandwidth, and is a reliable, secure solution. An application of Fog is with vehicles known as Vehicular Fog Computing (VFC). This chapter discusses cloud computing technique and its benefits and drawbacks, detailed comparison between VCC and VFC, applications of Fog Computing, its security, and forensic challenges.

1. INTRODUCTION

The basic building block in making vehicle communication possible is through VANET which enables various features to support various applications. To facilitate VANET in computing and storage, Cloud computing plays an important role. Detail description of VANET and cloud is mentioned below.

DOI: 10.4018/978-1-7998-2570-8.ch014

Vehicular Ad-Hoc Network

Vehicular Ad-hoc Network (VANET) is a kind of Mobile Ad-hoc Network (MANET) which consists of vehicles like the mobile nodes and Road Side Units (RSU). The key features of Vehicular Ad-hoc Network that differentiate it from MANET are highly mobile nodes, boundless network size, Time Critical, recurrent exchange of information, Wireless Communication and frequent topology changes. VANET is a self-governing as well as a self-organizing wireless communication network, wherein the nodes of VANET entail themselves as clients or servers for exchanging & sharing information. A smart vehicle for computation and communication,(Nguyen et al. 2018) can be equipped with some of the following types of equipment internally and externally like: On-board device, GPS device, wireless transceiver, camera, sensors, RADAR, LIDAR, I/O interfaces. (Raza et al. 2019)

For achieving VANET Communication information can be exchanged using Vehicle-to-Vehicle (V2V) and Vehicle-to-Infrastructure (V2I) communications. This communication is achieved through OBU and using DSRC (Dedicated Short Range Communication) signals within an area of around 1 km forming an Ad-hoc communication which provides the feature that connected vehicles can move freely, they don't need any wires. (Shrestha et al., 2018)

Safety applications are concerned with the safety of the drivers and passengers while traveling to make it safe and include sending timely warning messages just to assist the driver to take proper actions to avoid accidental situations. Safety messages also include details about traffic jams, road construction, and diversions, accident reports, etc. The need for safety applications is low latency and high reliability. (Zekri & Jia, 2018)

Non-safety applications offer a comfortable and efficient driving experience. It is further categorized into two sets: traffic management and infotainment. Traffic management is related to improving the flow of traffic on the road and to avoid obstruction so as to save the time of all the passengers. Infotainment is for entertainment purpose i.e to provide internet access to the passengers so as to facilitate video calling, video streaming, data storage, etc. These kinds of applications are not latency-sensitive.

Although researchers have already deployed some route planning and surveillance still many issues exist in VANET systems. The reason behind that is technical hitches in both exploitation and supervision. Few issues still look to be impenetrable in the present design like a great increase in the number of interconnected devices, competent resources exploitation, uneven traffic flow, geographical addressing, delay restriction because of high mobility and unpredictable connectivity between devices; and Quality of Service (QoS)(Truong et al., 2015)

Simulation tools like NS-2, SUMO, and GlomoSIM, etc. can be used for VANET implementation and to simulate the performance of the proposed system.

Cloud Computing

Cloud computing is the on-demand deliverance of computing resources like servers, storage, databases, software, networking, analytics, intelligence and much more onto the Internet ("the cloud") to propose quicker innovation, flexible resources, and the option of scaling. The name cloud computing was stimulated by the cloud symbol which is often used to represent the internet in diagrams. Cloud computing works on the rule of "Pay as you go" Model to lower down the operating cost and to run infrastructure more effectively (Vaquero et al., 2009). Using cloud computing, users are capable to use storage, software, and applications from anywhere; their programs are being hosted by an external party and exist in the cloud. This means that users do not have to be concerned about things such as storage and power, they can simply get it from the cloud by economical spending. The demand for cloud computing is because of the huge data produced by the billions of IoT devices, it's a challenging task to handle such persistent and tremendous amount of data in real-time so, from last few years, cloud computing technology has become an appropriate solution for the needs of high computation and storage capabilities. The amazing fact about cloud computing is that currently, we are probably using it but we don't realize it like when we are using an online service to send emails, watch movies, edit documents, playing games and storing any file, it is expected that cloud is making this possible. Three vendors that propose services ranging from big data in the cloud to serverless computing and more are Google, Azure, and AWS.

A single type of cloud is not appropriate for all so several different categories are there to offer a perfect solution as per your needs. To deploy your cloud services, three different types are: on a public or private or hybrid cloud. Cloud computing provides four broad categories of services: Infrastructure as a Service (IaaS), Software as a Service (SaaS), Platform as a Service (PaaS), Serverless computing(Whaiduzzaman et al., 2014). Cloud computing provides these benefits: adaptable, multitenant, reliable, scalable, cost-effective, speedy, global scale, productivity, performance, and safety(Microsoft Azure).

VEHICULAR CLOUD COMPUTING (VCC)

Although VANET itself is well-developed technology offering real-time service for providing services to safety and non-safety applications because of the current dynamic vehicular environment, it's a big challenge to propagate time-critical messages reliably to the target area. The present VANET architecture has been facing this difficulty because of poor connectivity, flexibility, scalability, intelligence, computation, and storage. Thus there is a need for technological shifting to deal with the above-stated issues being faced by VANET. To handle such issues various solutions have been proposed by different researchers. Vehicular cloud computing is one of the prominent resolutions which takes the advantages of the cloud to assist VANET with a variety of computational facilities. VCC can work well with a highly dynamic environment to provide on-demand solutions in case of unpredictable traffic conditions, road safety by using resources like computing networking and storage (Talib et al., 2017).

Benefits of VCC

Cloud computing offers a lot of benefits when merged with Vehicular Ad-hoc networks which are as follows(Sharma & Kaur, 2015):

1. Virtualization: The huge amount of demands are being handled by one single server machine although but still appears to be as handled by separate machines to users or vehicles.
2. Pay as you go: It is like the business model for the user to pay only for those services which he desires and only when he desires which gives a benefit of cost-saving to the users.
3. Network as a Service: Every car on-road may probably not be having internet connection so they can borrow the internet connection from the nearby moving cars on the road whenever required and can pay for it. This is known as Network as a Service (NaaS).
4. Storage as a Service: Every vehicle's onboard device may not having the same capacity so chances are there that a vehicle may have less storage capacity on its onboard device then it may require so

can borrow the same from other nearby devices to run their application or services. This is known as Storage as a Service (STaaS).

5. Disaster Management: VCC has great benefits in disaster management to offer instantaneous communication of vehicle with nearby resources like to other vehicles or nearby base station or authorized authorities regarding any happening so as further action could be taken.

Drawbacks of VCC

Vehicular Cloud computing when merged with VANET apart from various benefits also suffers from various drawbacks as shown in figure 1.

Figure 1. Drawback of VCC

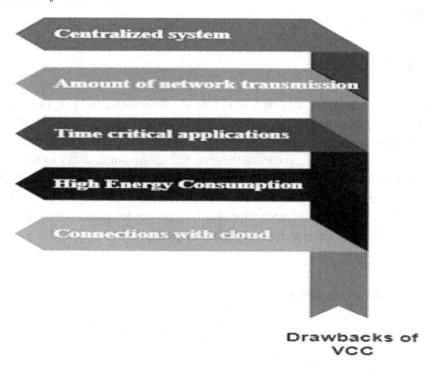

1. Centralized System: As the IoT emerges and flourishes into almost all business spheres, so there is an intense need for high-speed data processing, big-data analytics, and fewer response times. Achieving these needs via the existing centralized cloud-based model is proving to be difficult. (Siddiqui & Mahmood 2018)
2. Amount of Network Transmission: In 2016, as an estimation the average person generates around 650MB of data every day and so by 2020, some of them will project to more than double. However because of combinations of light detection and ranging (LIDAR), global positioning systems (GPS), cameras, etc., smart autonomous cars will produce multiple terabytes of data every day. As the network bandwidth is now going to be the bottleneck of cloud computing, it is approximately

impractical to transmit all the produced data from IoT devices to the cloud for handling and storing (Aliyu et al. 2017)

3. Time-Critical Applications: IoT applications, like traffic light systems in smart transportation, smart grids, healthcare, emergency response system, and other latency-sensitive applications, may necessitate a very less response time and sustain mobility but there is an unacceptable delay caused due to transferring of data. (Aliyu et al. 2017)
4. High Energy Consumption: Cloud computing for its functioning is based on the sustain of immense infrastructures that primarily include a huge number of data centers covering numerous server units and other opinionated tools, like, cooling system. The energy utilization of such components will be massive. (Kumar & Goyal, 2019)
5. Connections with the Cloud: Connecting additional and diverse Kind of Things Directly to the cloud is impractical.

FOG COMPUTING

Fog computing an idiom being produced by Cisco, refers to a decentralized geographically distributed computing architectural pattern that brings traditional cloud computing facility to the edge of network as shown in Figure 2, which provides a more proficient resolution to the shortcomings of cloud computing, and offers the cloud an escort which can handle the remarkable amount of data produced daily from the Internet of Things (Pereira et al. 2019). The devices, that perform this task are called fog nodes, which can be situated anywhere within the network. The important fact which needs to accentuate here is that fog computing technology is not an alternative for cloud computing technique instead it works as a helping hand for the expansion and development of cloud computing.

Figure 2. Architecture of fog computing

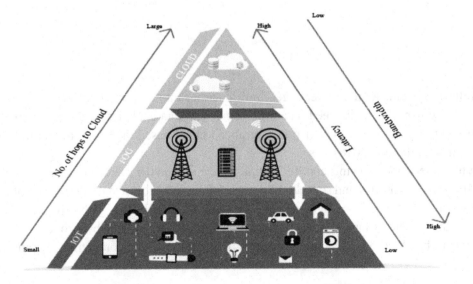

How Fog works

The fog nodes which lie very near to the network boundary transmits the information from IoT devices connected primarily by various modes of wireless connection like 4G, Bluetooth, or could be by WiFi. Fog nodes are moreover associated with the cloud through the internet so as to acquire complete benefit of the gigantic computing and storage resources of the cloud. The fog IoT application needs to take a crucial decision of directing a different variety of information to the best place for analysis. (Kai et al., 2016). The various task performed by fog are:

1. Handle the crucial time-crucial information at the network boundary, which means near proximity to where actually it is produced rather than transferring an immense quantity of IoT data onto the cloud.
2. Based on policy, it takes actions on IoT data within milliseconds.
3. After that, it sends only the particular information to the cloud for historical analysis purposes in the future or for long-term storage.

What Happens in the Fog and the Cloud

Fog and cloud nodes work in co-ordination with each other to speed up the task as shown in figure 3.

Figure 3. Working of fog and cloud nodes

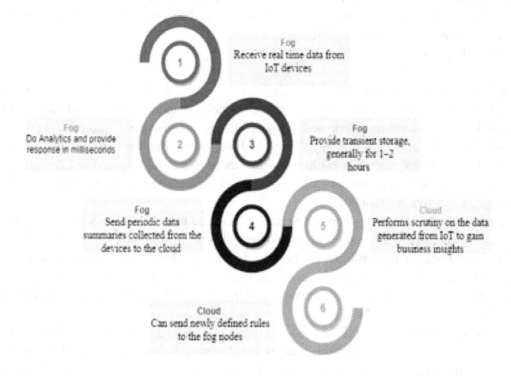

1. Fog nodes
   a. It receives real-time information from actual working IoT devices through the help of any protocol.
   b. Run IoT-enabled application data for real-time control and analytics, and provides a reply in milliseconds
   c. Offer short-lived storage, generally for 1–2 hours till the time the essential data is being transmitted to the cloud.
   d. Send periodic data summaries collected from the devices to the cloud for storage.

2. The Cloud platform
   a. Cloud accepts the data from the fog and creates cumulative data summaries of data from many fog nodes distributed all over the service area.
   b. Performs scrutiny on the data generated from IoT and other resources to get business insights.
   c. Can forward newly defined rules & regulations to the fog device which are based on these observations for future implementation.

Who Can Be a Fog Node

The core of the fog computing model is fog node. Any device having features of cloud-like computing, storage, and networking can be a fog node. Fog nodes are geologically scattered resource-rich devices that could be placed anywhere in a network like on a factory floor, on top of a power pole, alongside a railway track, within a vehicle, or on the oil industry, etc. Examples of fog node include switches, industrial controllers, routers, embedded servers, and video surveillance cameras or could be any privately owned device. (Nath et. al. 2018)

Benefits of Fog Computing

1. Conserve Network Bandwidth: It is excessively costly and almost infeasible to upload every bit of data to the cloud and moreover very time-taking to seek out and download required data from the cloud through the internet so Fog nodes process and accumulate some information produced by sensors and edge devices. Then only the residual worthy information is transmitted to the cloud server for permanent storage or could be for further processing if required and thus the time required to transmit the information and the amount of network transmission required in the cloud is reduced. (Dahiya & Dalal 2018)
2. Minimize Latency: As in fog computing data is analyzed at local centers so the round trip time needed to send data to the cloud is saved and hence latency is minimized. (Zhu et al. 2019)
3. **Real-Time Data Analytics:** In fact, milliseconds matters when you are putting efforts to fulfill the load of real-time applications and on the contrary, if analysis of data is done near to the device which collected the information can create a great impact in avoiding disaster and cascading system failure. (Bonomi et al. 2012)
4. Address Security Concerns: IoT data needs to be secluded both during transfer and at rest. so there is a need to monitor during the whole journey of IoT data i.e before, during and after sending. The benefit of using the fog node is that it can be protected very efficiently. it also offers better privacy of user's data as not transferring the complete information to the cloud. (Menon 2017)

5.   Mobile Fog Nodes: As fog nodes are mobile in nature so it's for them to join or leave the network anytime.

6.   **Widespread Geographical Distribution**: fog computing is a decentralized form of cloud computing and so it offers a wider range of geographical distribution than conventional cloud computing and hence offers an improved quality of service to the end-user. (Nath et. al. 2018)

7.   Heterogeneity: fog nodes appear in diverse forms and are also installed in a mixture of environments either as physical or as a virtual node. They could come in the form of high-performance servers, gateways, access points, edge routers or base stations, etc. and all these could have a different level of capabilities in the form of computation or storage. As the fog nodes could be heterogeneous and so network infrastructure is as well heterogeneous which comprises high-speed connections to connect to the data center and moreover wireless access technology to connect to edge devices. (Hu et al., 2017)

8.   Interoperability: As the end devices and in fact, fog nodes draw closer from different providers and also being installed in a diversity of environments. Hence fog computing must be capable of interoperating with different providers to provide seamless support and to deal with a range of services. (Hu et al., 2017)

Applications of Fog Computing

Fog Computing technique operates in a cloud-based atmosphere to tender control and better insight across a variety of nodes. Below given Figure 4 shows a few of the examples of real-life where and how fog computing can be useful.

1.   Vehicular Fog Computing: One significant application of fog computing is with vehicles on road, which is the amalgamation of fog computing with traditional VANET which forms the Internet of Vehicles (IoV) or also known as Vehicular Fog Computing(VFC). In this structural design, any intelligent device which has the features of cloud i.e computation, storage, and networking can act as fog node and these nodes are positioned at the edge of the network. This works on the principle that vehicle should interact with themselves and don't transmit all the data to the cloud because of which it gives benefits like low latency, less network bandwidth, security, privacy, reliability. VFC offers a variety of services for safety and non-safety purpose. (Bonomi et al. 2012)

2.   Healthcare: In the world of IoT, the healthcare field has also developed from 1.0 to 4.0 generation. Healthcare 3.0 was just hospital-centric, in which patients with prolonged illnesses have to suffer a lot due to visits in several hospitals for their checkups. Hence, the long-lasting treatment of these patients comes with an overall hike in the cost of treatment of patients. However, with fog computing, these inconveniences could be diminished with the least amount of funding in computing and storage provision associated with the information of the patients. This provides continual context-responsive functionalities to the end-users whenever needed. This concept works well in case of emergency as little delay in treatment could be the reason for the patient's death. (Nath et. al. 2018)

3.   Smart Cities: A city can face issues because of traffic jamming, public protection, high energy need and in delivering municipal functionalities. To deal with such issues IoT networks with various fog nodes can be installed. As because most of the bandwidth is being used by cellular networks very limited bandwidth is left for advanced municipal services of a smart city. This less bandwidth does

Figure 4. Applications of fog computing

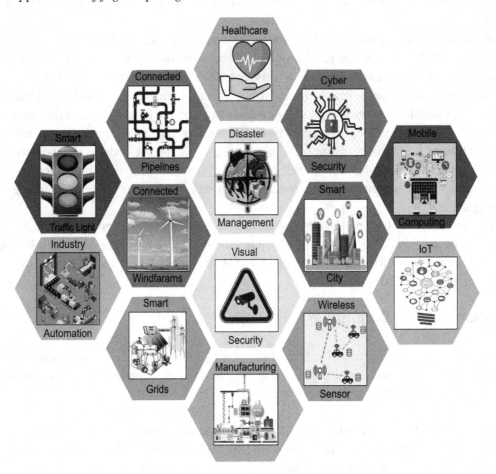

not allow transferring whole information of smart city to the cloud so deployment of fog nodes near the event provides lot of benefits like optimizes network usage, security for susceptible jam and resident related information, as well as in life-sensitive systems like emergency response even in case of network failure suppose in case of a disaster, an emergency response application running in a smart city which offers wireless connectivity to the common public to offer a response plans, evacuation routes, or emergency instructions. In a natural disaster, the consequence could be that the municipal emergency website may be unreachable which is being run based on cloud servers but still if the internet is down pubic can get significant directives if suppose wireless access points have battery backup, and connected local fog nodes have pre-stored this data. (Perera et al. 2017)

4. Smart Grids: Another key application of fog computing is the smart grid. A smart grid is the potential production network for the circulation of electricity which comprises automation at all significant levels of the power grid which includes smart devices, smart houses, smart meter, smart vehicles, and transmission lines. A smart grid renders clearness between the customer and distributor and also has a characteristic of self-healing, self-adaptive and self-monitoring. The traditional power grids are made smart by the incorporation of technology like IoT, Cloud, Fog and turned the current power grid into a smart grid (Yi et al. 2015). Fog computing extends its characteristics to the

edge users on the smart grid in a way like an edge process the information gathered by fog nodes and produces a control directive to the actuator. The cleaned data is consumed in the near vicinity by fog and the important data is being sent to the cloud for revelation, real-time intelligence, and transactional analytics.

5. **Smart Traffic Lights:** With the increase in the number of vehicles on the road day by day, traffic efficiency is becoming a worldwide problem. Conventional mechanized traffic lights systems plan the vehicles waiting time at an intersection on the basis of a fixed pre-decided time slot manner(Grover et al. 2018). This pre-timed controller approach doesn't consider emergency conditions like traffic congestion, bypassing huge roadside sensors, opposing wicked vehicles and avoiding single-point breakdown, and so fails to diminishes the waiting time of vehicles at the traffic intersection. This system works on the principle of, once vehicles enter into the zone of the traffic signal, the vehicles send their positional information to the nearby fog node on the traffic signal and accordingly traffic signal is monitored. Smart lights in some emergency cases transmit a warning indication to the approaching vehicles This significantly reduces the waiting time of ambulance, Fire Brigades, and Police Vans(Giang et al. 2016).

6. **Self Maintaining Train:** Another significant application of fog computing is with self-maintaining trains. Sensors are placed on self-maintaining trains to monitor train components. It senses the modifying temperature intensity and any chaos, then it will involuntarily aware of the train operator immediately using fog nodes so that he can take the correct actions and make maintenance accordingly. Thus can avoid major disasters(Peter 2016).

7. Connected Pipelines: Oil and gas mining are a high-venture technology-determined task that is based on real-time onsite intellect to offer practical monitoring and security against device breakdown and ecological harm. Huge manufacturing setting up could produce a tremendous amount of unprocessed sensor data per day. The network bandwidth to transfer this information to the cloud will be very costly and also the cloud can't work well for emergency situations. The solution is the installation of local fog nodes in nearby area so that local analysis and storage potential can endlessly monitor the information flow, carry out local analytics to sense probable troubles and generates early caution messages, and converts the interpretation into quite minor necessary messages that can be powerfully and inexpensively transferred over to the cloud-based systems. (Peter 2016)

8. Visual Security and Fog Computing: Video cameras are very beneficial nowadays to enhance security as being installed at various places like parking areas, buildings, offices, and other public and private spaces. It's really impractical to transfer the whole data being collected from cameras to the cloud to get real-time insights and take any action in case needed. These cameras are being installed at such places that need real-time monitoring and finding in case of any anomalies and hence create harsh low-latency needs on supervision systems. Timeliness is essential for both recognition and reaction. A fog computing architecture can help out in processing the video intelligently by fog nodes located near to the cameras. (Khan et al. 2017)

9. Smart Buildings and Fog Computing: A building may include a massive quantity of sensors to evaluate various building functional factors like temperature, key card readers and parking space possession smoke level, etc. Information collected from these sensors must be analyzed immediately to see if there is a need for any action, like prompting a fire alarm when smoke is notified. Fog computing works well for these real-time functions in taking spontaneous decisions. Fog nodes could be installed on each floor or tower or in rooms for carrying out urgent situation monitor-

ing and reaction functions and also provides storage service and to further send the aggregated data, actions are taken for future use to the cloud. The stored operational history data of cloud can then be used to train machine learning models, and then to additionally optimize building functions by employing these learning representations of the cloud-trained machine in the home fog infrastructure(Stojmenovic & Wen 2014).

10. Wireless Sensor and Actuator Networks: To extend battery life Wireless sensor nodes (WSN) are designed so as to operate at very low power. These WSN also involve low bandwidth, energy, processing power, etc. These are able to work in several directions like multiple and mobile sensing and sinking but they shortfall in applications that works beyond this. Actuators help sensors in controlling a system or the measurement process. The features of the fog like proximity, geo-distribution and location awareness make it an apt policy to sustain together energy-constrained WSNs as well as WSANs.(Bonomi et al. 2012)

VEHICULAR FOG COMPUTING (VFC)

Fog is a novel concept of computing, which expands the functionality offered by the cloud to the edge of the network. In fog computing, the task of data processing and analytics happens nearby the end devices where the actual data is generated which give the advantage of eliminating unnecessary hops and so reduce the time. To make it possible a collection of smart vehicles within a short-range can attach together to create a vehicular fog that could be via dedicated short-range communication with a range of 75 MHz of spectrum in 5.9 GHz band (Kui et al. 2018). Vehicle to vehicle and vehicle to infrastructure both can be used for VFC. Fog service providers if using vehicles power for this communication then it is beneficial for both vehicle owners and for service providers as fog service providers don't need to spend more to enhance the infrastructure to support this computing. The advantage for vehicle owners is that they can rent out their additional computing power and can get incentives which could be used to pay parking amount, pay toll charges, avail free Wi-Fi, etc.(Sookhak et al. 2017)

Architecture of VFC

Fog computing is the latest computational concept, that expands the conventional cloud computing facilities like computation, communication, storage to the boundary of the network. The design of Vehicular Fog Computing is a three-layer configuration and explained below in detail. Fog computing expands functionalities of cloud to the network boundary by bringing in a fog layer among end devices which are vehicles and the cloud. (et al., 2017)

1. Terminal Layer: A layer that exists very near to the end-user and it comprises an assortment of IoT devices like sensors, mobile phones, smart vehicles, smart cards, readers, etc. Among these mobile phones and elegant vehicles are smart sensing devices and are geographically scattered. These devices sense the information of events or objects and spread that information to a higher level for handing out and storage.

2. Fog Layer: Fog Layer is located on the edge of the network and is made of a large number of fog nodes, that can be routers, switches, gateways, access points, or base stations, etc. These nodes could be a static device or could be mobile and these are scattered between end devices and the cloud.

Fog nodes have the competence to figure out, spread and stock up the information temporarily. This processes the real time-sensitive applications and is also connected to the cloud so fog forward the only that data which demands more powerful computing or storage to the cloud. (Wang et al. 2017)

3. Cloud Layer: The topmost layer of VFC is the cloud layer that is composed of devices for storage, high-performance servers to support high computing and storage needs in various applications like smart home, factory, transportation, etc. But unlike traditional cloud architecture, all the data does not pass through the cloud but just the filtered data from the fog which fog thinks is necessary to store for future analysis is transmitted to cloud for added computing or storage hence the cloud is not overloaded so resource utilization of the cloud is improved.

As shown in figure 5, VFC architecture, the end devices are associated with the fog node by wireless technology like WiFi, WLAN, 3G, 4G, Bluetooth, etc. or could be through a wired connection. For the interconnection of fog nodes together wired or wireless could be used. For the connection of Fog with cloud IP network is used.

Figure 5. Architecture of VFC

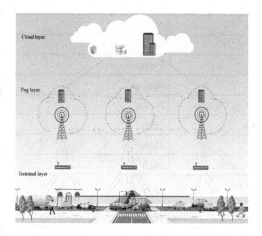

VCC VS VFC

Vehicular cloud computing and vehicular fog computing on the basis of various parameters are discussed and their significant differences are shown below in Table 1. (Shrestha et al., 2018 and Hou e al. 2016).

SERVICES PROVIDED THROUGH VANET USING FOG

Below given is the review of the work done by various authors in terms of services provided to benefit VANET by using fog computing and make VFC a better approach.

Table 1. VCC Vs VFC

S. No.	Criteria	VCC	VFC
1	Technology Proposed By	Amazon	Cisco in Aug 2012
2	Technology Promoted By	Microsoft, Google, Amazon	Cisco, Princeton, Microsoft, Intel, Dell
3	Technology Industry Organizations	Open Cloud Consortium	Open Fog Consortium
4	Geographical Distribution	Centralized	Decentralized
5	Location of Service	Globally Distributed server	Local Area Network/Edge of network
6	Latency	High	Low
7	Bandwidth	High	Low
8	Delay/Jitter	High	Low
9	No of servers	Thousands	Millions
10	Real-Time Interaction	Supported	Supported
11	Mobility	Limited	Highly
12	Communication Mode	IP Network	Wireless(WLAN, Wifi, Zigbee, 3G, 4G) or Wired
13	Communication Type	Bandwidth Constraint	Real-Time
14	Location Awareness	No	Yes
15	Security	Prone to attack	Safe from attack
16	Security Decision	Complex	Simple
17	Decision Making	Remote	Local
18	Computation & Storage Capacity	Strong	Weak
19	Energy Consumption	High	Low
20	Scalability	High	Average
21	Reliability	High	Low
22	No of Hops required for Communication	Multiple	Single or could be very Few
23	Congestion	High	Limited
24	Cost Saving	Low deployment cost	Low storage & Networking i.e Bandwidth
25	How long IoT data is stored	Short duration: perhaps hours, days, or weeks	Months or years
26	Dynamic Broadcasting range depending on the message type	Yes	N/A
27	Applications	That is not time-sensitive & do not necessitate real-time reaction	Critical time-sensitive Applications that do not require real-time response

Using Vehicles as Infrastructure

As in VFC just to reduce the cost of implementation we don't deploy any special infrastructure. In this regard, we can make use of the unutilized power of vehicles on roads. Two categories of vehicles are on the road "Moving" and "Parked". Both can be used for communication and computation. so we end up with four different scenarios:(Hou et al. 2016).

1. Moving vehicles as communication
2. Moving vehicles as computation
3. Parked vehicles as communication
4. Parked vehicles as computation

Using Moving Vehicles

In Urban areas due to huge traffic especially during peak hours, the vehicles are moving at a very slow speed so these can be used to communicate with each other and as they are connected together they can form a powerful cloudlet that is competent to offer high computation power.

Using Parked Vehicles

Except for hustle timings, during an extended time of day and night, the majority of the vehicles are either parked along the roadside or in parking areas near offices and houses. These parked vehicles along the roadside can participate in a crucial task in transmitting packets, whereas those in a parking bundle can construct a huge computation cloud. With this way out, both the communication and computational competence of that particular region could be improved to a great extent.

1. Moving Vehicles as Communication: In vehicular communication, two variety of nodes work Vehicles and RSU which enables V2V and V2I communication. In V2I, to have a strong network the whole dependency is on RSU. In V2V, the distance between the two vehicles should be small for better communication.

    Now in the case of VFC, that uses Moving Vehicles as communication brings better connectivity and hence solves communication problems? VFC take the benefit of multihop feature and moving quality of vehicles to move the data from one point to another. Moving vehicles turn out to be good data transporter and can constantly convey data by constructed up new associations. Because of the geo-distribution and local assessment making features of VFC moving vehicles in close vicinity can communicate with each other and hence play the role of the communication hub, now all because of these hubs, fog is formed. Rather than transmitting information to cloud servers, it can now be dealt with in fog using local resources and hence bring less delay, low cost, and high efficiency.

2. Moving Vehicles as Computation: Slow-moving cars on a jammed road can create a cloud utilizing embedded computers of the vehicles and RSU could be positioned so as to attach to these distant clouds. In such a VFC system, the computation could be attained via V2V communications. Vehicles that are congested can also communicate data through V2I exchanges with RSUs, whereas RSUs

exchange with distant cloud computing centers via the Internet. Hence, the entire scheme forms an amalgam cloud, which combines together computation assets from both movable cloudlets and distant clouds and then allocates them to various vehicles to fulfill the computation requirements of a particular vehicle.

3. Parked Vehicles as Communication: The number of parked vehicles in an urban area is quite high especially during working hours cars are parked near offices on-road or maybe underground parking. During these long hours, cars have relatively unchanged locations. With the help of wireless devices and rechargeable (vehicle) battery, parked vehicles can simply exchange data with one another and as well with the close-by moving vehicles. These parked vehicles can give out as stationary strength and service infrastructure to enhance connectivity. These vehicles carry and forward data to other vehicles. Conveying packets can improve to a great level the opportunistic approach connectivity, which will advantage the content-exchange application considerably. Because of the characteristics of the massive number, long-period residing, extensive geo-distribution, and fixed position, parked vehicles are able to turn out to be an abundant, reliable, and well-situated communication node in urban areas.

4. Parked Vehicles as Computation: While the parked vehicles are parked in an office parking area during working hours can unite with VFC, which together can form a miniature data center and, as a result, able to deal with different difficult tasks, which necessitate huge computation potential.

Security and Privacy

Due to amplifying the number of vehicles on the road, the problem of efficient traffic handling is also booming out. To deal with such a problem intelligent traffic light plays an important role. Current traffic lights are not able to cope up with challenges like avoiding huge traffic area, single-point failure, resisting malicious vehicles, fixed time traffic lights. The authors (Liu et al., 2017) projected two intellectual traffic light system to handle the above issues. These schemes are based on fog devices and provide the feature of resisting from the malicious vehicle attacks and can also avoid a single point failure problem. The first method is based on the computational Diffie–Hellman (CDH) puzzle which is a kind of cryptographic puzzle that is originally used to protect the Denial of Service attack. In this scheme Traffic light which is the fog devices generates the number of CDH puzzles and encrypts it by means of a location-based encryption scheme and forwards it to nearby vehicles. Vehicles that solve this puzzle generate the proof and send it to the traffic light, which verifies the strength based on the proofs. On the basis of these proofs, traffic lights run a traffic schedule algorithm to regulate its plan. They also proposed an improved scheme of the above where the traffic light is just forwarding a single puzzle and so traffic light needs to execute a very lightweight function to validate the proofs.

Carpooling is an efficient way to somehow control the problems like traffic and pollution occurring because of the increasing population and hence increasing the number of cars on roads. Various cab booking services nowadays providing the feature of cab pooling which makes the journey quite convenient and reasonable for all and also works towards environment betterment. This system of cab polling needs to store lot of data regarding drivers and passengers and need to take real-time fast decisions of allocating cabs to different passengers going on almost same route for which cloud does not fit well as it is going to take more time for these decisions and so fog computing came into picture that fits well for low latency. fog computing, on the other hand, raises issues like security and privacy of user's private information which are being shared during cab pooling. Issues that can occur are like a person's private information, frequently visited locations could be disclosed and may be used somewhere else like an evil-intentioned driver could use that information later to show a false pickup of passenger and make money out of it. Another issue is to provide adequate data audit-ability for cab pooling records in case if the cloud server collapse or reports data tempering, all the cab pooling records will be lost and so can't get data if a passenger reports any issue. The next issue that arises is that with anonymization and encryption it's difficult to do one-much proximity matching i.e finding many drivers nearby passengers on his desired time. To deal with the above problems an efficient scheme is being proposed by the author (Li et al. 2019) using Block-chain assisted vehicular fog computing. They proposed a competent and privacy-conserving carpooling (FICA) scheme which is able to provide provisional privacy, one-to-many propinquity similarities, target identicalness.

Resource Allocation and Application Offloading

Authors (Chen et al. 2017) stated that in case of connected car systems the application of coordinated lane change assistance can't be addressed by implementing it on cloud so fog server could be used to lower down the latency requirements but in case of fog computing the problem of load balancing still needs to be addressed for improved timing. For load balancing problem the authors predicted the travel pattern of the cars and to avoid deadline misses and lower the processing times they formulated a load balancing optimization problem which tried to pre-assign the sources to the preeminent fit servers. They also compared their solution with other heuristics like subjective round-robin, lively monitoring, and throttled load balancer and showed that it performs better than the earlier ones.

As cloud computing technology is not enough to support VANET applications due to its high network congestion and greater than before delay problems so fog computing has opted. In this regard, the Authors (Sutagundar et al. 2019) proposed "Fog Enhanced Vehicular Services (FEVS)" which serves the purpose of cloud by providing features like compute, network, store at the edge of the network. FEVS is also compared with the Cloud model. To make the FEVS system possible there is a need to carry out better utilize resources and services to its utmost extent. For better utilization of resources presented by the fog layer, resource assessment and source allotment in this level is required which is the main focal point of the author for that authors used a game theory-based approach. Their designed model provides many benefits over cloud-based models like lowering the latency, response time and processing time but leads to a complex system somehow due to the insufficiency of resources in fog node. They also suggested that complexity can be reduced via high-performance edge devices to accomplish the improved performance constraint like latency, response time, processing time, cost and resource utilization.

To mitigate the burden of the base station and diminish the processing postponement all through the pinnacle time. VFC acts as an emerging solution by offloading the computational task of base stations to under-exploited computation resource vehicles in close proximity. Authors(Zhou et al. 2019) stated that it still faces some challenges like incentive, task assignment and resource allocation from a contract corresponding incorporation perception. To solve these problems they proposed a "Contract-based incentive system" so as to encourage vehicles to exchange resources and a pricing-based toning mechanism was devised to tackle the task assignment trouble. The designed contract is customized so as to make the best use of the accepted effectiveness of the base station by the exclusive characteristic of each sort of vehicle. They also transformed the problem into the corresponding problem between vehicles and user equipment which is resolved by a pricing based mechanism that carries the "purpose and worth increasing" iteratively so as to obtain a constant identical on the basis of the reorganized performance list. Through results, they showed that the incentive mechanism gives optimal performance and task assignment is capable to accomplish optimal network postponement as a previous extensive searching mechanism but with the benefit of lesser complication. Unlike cloud in which servers are managed by dedicated service providers, fog nodes are maintained by developers or users so there is a need of several security methods like integrity, access control, confidentiality, authenticity, etc. for the trustworthy operation of VFC so the security of VFC still needs researchers attention and further development.

Vehicular Routing

In vehicular communications, if applied fog computing, fog servers reside near to the end devices (vehicles) and servers are directly connected to vehicles. However, the number of hops needed would be more when working for a large scale network. so for this routing algorithms are required to determine how data is transmitted from the end device to its own fog node or neighboring fog node keeping little latency and little bandwidth and high security. (Nabil et al. 2019) Fog computing- enabled IoT services demands for various routing approaches so author(Okay & Ozdemir, 2018) has analyzed various services like mobility, Content delivery and caching, calculation offloading, Load balancing, task scheduling, resource allocation and sharing with reverence to their routing requirements when fog computing is applied and gave a summary report showing the work done by various other authors with respect to these services and their proposed protocol, performance metrics and evaluation method which they have used. Then various SDN based Fog- Enabled IoT services are analyzed. SDN(Software Defined Networking) a networking paradigm that has the feature of separating network traffic as for control and data plane to obtain an easy and flexible routing conclusion. It keeps a comprehensive vision of various dispersed forward essentials like fog servers and end devices for routing mechanisms. These SDN based Fog- Enabled IoT services, work better than those applied without SDN in terms of QoS, latency, bandwidth utilization. Authors had proposed a Hierarchical Software Defined Networking based Fog computing approach for routing as because when the network dimension enhances, it's difficult to deal with all forwarding rudiments by a single controller so there are multiple controllers dispersed over fog and cloud layers and works on the principle that local decisions are being taken by fog servers and global decisions are forwarded to cloud. Every controller in the network can be actually centralized or dispersed. This architecture is suitable for Fog computing to amplify the routing potential of IoT services. Mininet, an open-source SDN emulator is used for the performance evaluation of this architecture with the quantity of organizer in terms of delay, data transmission overhead, and throughput over the diverse situation.

(Lu et al. 2018) proposed an IGR(Improved Geographic Routing) scheme for inter-vehicle transfer of messages in city environments. IGR is based on vehicular Fog computing for the better exploitation of vehicular communication and computation sources. Geographic routing is position-dependent routing and it takes the routing decisions locally. Two previous routing techniques are GPSR(Global Positioning System Routing), GPCR(Greedy Perimeter Coordinator Routing). GPCR executes superior to GPSR in city situation but in both of these protocols, the lossy features of wireless channels and vehicle density are not being measured during path selection and this is the improvement of IGR. IGR is made up of three modes: i) junction selection, which is based on higher score value given by the starting vehicle and forwarding vehicles according to the Euclid distance to the destination and the vehicle density between the current junction and the next junction, ii) an enhanced covetous forwarding scheme to transfer information packets to vehicles between two junctions which will incur the minimum transmission cost and iii) repair mode when the packet is not yet delivered to the destination and about to reach local maximum, so finds a new flexible path. To evaluate the performance of IGR, the authors used the ns-2 simulator and showed that there is significant improvement being done by using IGR in terms of attained packet pace and end-to-end hindrance.

VANET can also be made to provide a feature that vehicles can communicate videos with each other regarding road mishappening or disasters that present more precise data about the same as compared to context messages and these videos could be transmitted to civic service authorities so as to diminish liberate period. (Bezerra et al. 2019) Authors proposed a Collaborative routing protocol (CRPV), transmits multimedia packets on the highway using fog storage to reduce the data to be shared and could enhance videos with less QoE by taking fast decisions of forwarding to those nodes which have better network capacities. The CRPV protocol determines the number of vehicles in the cluster and for each vehicle according to its speed, location, and recording angle creates a routing table and calculates the Gateway Quality Indicator (GQI) then calculate the best collaborative gateway(CG) to take the decision of to whom to broadcast the video within the V2I so as to diminish the needless transfer of video. The CRPV protocol is analyzed using simulations and contrasted with two previous routing protocols, PassCAR and SRB protocol. CRPV model performs better in terms of packet deliverance speed, typical packet hindrance, and throughput. Hence it proves to be a realistic solution for the problems of road accidents.

Vehicular Software-Defined Networking

In the vehicular network, the burden on V2V communication will not increase if doing fog and cloud integration rather it will give a better experience to the user. As stated by (Khan et al. 2018) Software-defined networking an innovative technology that controls the network by separating the two planes' data and control in a programmable and centralized way. The data plane is for forwarding functions and the control plane is for network control. Due to its features, it can assist in the case of a flexible network and controlling of large scale applications. Hence it can be assumed as one of the best solutions to tackle the dynamic nature and intense deployment states of VANET while minimizing the functioning cost. (Nobre et al. 2019) Authors proposed a "Fog enabled Vehicular Software Defined Networks" on the perception of system, network, services and examined it's design principles. They also presented a real example of the rescue of vehicles in fast-moving traffic using the traffic data picked up from a city of Brazil. They analyzed that combination of VSDN and fog computing would be able to reduce the time needed to arrive at the emergency vehicles where the accident actually happened and identified while integrating SDN and Fog computing together what are the possible chances of research challenges and opportunities.

1.   Offloading

Internet of Vehicle (IoV), a branch of IoT Manages Traffic Management System (TMS) and road safety. With the tremendous growth of vehicles, air pollution, traffic congestion and accidents on roads are also growing at a high pace. There is a need for a decentralized server to reduce the reaction time of the Traffic Management Server (TMS). Fog computing, when combined with IoV, provides a guaranteed low latency response. In this regard, the Authors (Wang et al. 2018) designed "FORT" which is an offloading algorithm to reduce the average reaction period of the messages of TMS. For this they establish a 3 layer model having a cloud layer, cloudlets and fog layer, and partitioned the city into regions. In each region, messages are being managed by Cloudlet and fog nodes which are nearby parked or moving vehicles on road. They modeled this TMS as a queuing system with processing server if cloudlet then M/M/n queue and if fog nodes then M/M/1 queue. This problem is NP-hard so to find the optimal solution an iterative scheme is used to divide the problem into sub-problem and so on. To reveal the feasibility of their system, they analyzed the real-time data of Shanghai for 30 days of around 100- taxies and considered its 2 districts Hongkou and Jingan. Then compared the usual reaction time based on "dissimilar content appearance rates", " overall quantity of parked vehicle-based fog node" and "diverse facility rates of fog nodes" which shows their system FORT is superior to the previous system.

To provide low latency, fog computing is an emerging application. Authors (Zeng et al. 2018) have proposed that to unburden the huge task of computing of fog, edge devices that have idle resources can share them and could participate in computation offloading. To motivate them to participate in sharing with the fog computing system, the authors proposed a contract theoretic incentive mechanism, which tells the negotiation between fog nodes and task publisher. The publisher of the task has assorted options when it wishes to offload its computing task taking into consideration the excellence of communication connections, power utilization and few other hardware restrictions of fog nodes. They proposed the "Nash equilibrium" as an optimal contract solution. Through simulations, they had shown that a most favorable deal can make the best use of the utility of task publisher in the meantime also guarantees to keep the person's rationality and inducement compatibility of various fog nodes. They also stated that in the future investigation could be done to check the generalization of a contract-based incentive approach when fog node has diverse distributions and work in other multifaceted circumstances.

Autonomous driving is in demand that could be somehow because of the smart vehicle components which have enormous computing resources and also because of seamless connectivity through wireless technologies. Vehicular Fog Network (VeFN) also supports autonomous driving which enables sharing of computational resources sharing through task offloading concept. But it's hard to guarantee the delay in communication of messages and computing those when dealing with high mobility vehicles during the task offloading process. Authors (Sun et al. 2019) had proposed an architecture of VeFN with three important modes of offloading and did a brief analysis of its advantages and challenges. They had also considered the significance of mobility for the purpose of well-timed computing in "VeFN as a foe and also as a friend" and concluded that mobility just acts as a barrier in VeFN for timely computation but instead also proofs to be a benefit for delay performance. They also introduced machine learning techniques and coded computing methods to address and take advantage of mobility in the case of VeFN. To prove the capability for timely computation in VeFN through their proposed learning and coded methods they carried out two case studies "Learning-based assignment Offloading in VeFN" and "Delay-Constrained assignment Replication Exploiting Vehicle Mobility" which also illustrated how to adapt those methods.

Connected and Automated Vehicles (CAVs) fully incorporated with the number of sensors generates huge data about the surrounding environment which needs to be communicated with nearby vehicles. To supervise CAVs, Authors (Tassi et al. 2019) proposed Cloud-based systems are used which also collects the data from CAV for the whole city using an agile strategy. For better performance, they used fog computing techniques and proposed a new framework for an Intelligent transportation system based on fog computing which utilizes "Random Linear Network Coding (RLNC)" to accomplish reliable and agile offloading of CAV data. The enormous data generated by CAVs would not be generated while in range of a single RSU but instead within a limited period CAVs would be the range of number of RSUs obliging data to bring together across diverse RSUs, if conventional schemes of data off-loading were to be utilized. To establish communication between RSUs and CAVs, ETSI's ITS-G5 communication heap is being used which they had extended by incorporating an "RLNC Facility Sub-layer" into the original

"ITS-G5 Facility layer". They proposed CAVs to offload their generated sensor records in a network implied style while utilizing a new sort of CAM and named it as the RLNCCAM. For the performance evaluation of their proposed system, they considered a network installed in the city Bristol, UK, consisting of 4 RSUs. The result showed the feasibility and effectiveness of their system using parameters like packet delivery rate, packet error probability, and recovery probability.

2.   Message Dissemination through Vehicles using Fog

Authors (Paranjothi et al. 2018) first studied various challenges being faced by the connected vehicles in heavy traffic areas like bad resource utilization, more delay, and recurrent vehicle disconnection. Earlier researchers have tried to solve the above issues by using mobility in fog computing or cloud computing, but they still endure from the problems like packet delays losses. Authors have proposed an approach based on fog computing itself known as "Dynamic Fog for Connected Vehicles (DFCV)", which on the basis of communication needs dynamically construct, increase and devastate fog nodes. DFCV tries to make sure a reduced amount of delay and definite message deliverance to the vehicles in close proximity. To evaluate DFCV authors discussed two involved options of fog splitting and fog merging depending on the different scenarios. For performance assessment, they calculated the formulas for chances of collapse and capacity of the system. Simulation is being carried out on urban and highway scenarios using simulators like ns-2, Sumo and cloudsim. Their comparison showed the best performance in end-to-end delay, the likelihood of message deliverance in urban areas and collision ratio, a split condition in highway scenarios.

Various applications of VANET like traffic monitoring, route sharing, video streaming need to exchange a huge amount of messages, which is quite challenging when there is no consistency in vehicles' speed, direction, and neighbors while moving. Another challenge is congestion avoidance to evade communication failure especially at the time of busy hours in case of emergency situations. Fog computing merged with VANET plays an essential role to improve communication among vehicles. In this context, Authors (Ullah et al. 2018) had examined in detail various efficient existing schemes for message dissemination and also for congestion avoidance and then presented a detailed comparison of various such schemes. Congestion avoidance schemes are categorized into 2 types: static and Dynamic. Dynamic are further classified according to transmission control, transmission power control, security preservation, aggregation, and segmentation. They have also discussed in detail challenges in VANET like latency, throughput, availability, congestion, security, and routing which are to be considered while designing responsible solutions via FoG based VANET. After that, they had proposed the architecture of Fog based VANET. Another aspect that they focussed is open research problems like continues connectivity support, low latency, real-time data storage support, mobility and position tracking management, secure communication, quality of service, software up-gradation in vehicles, etc.

3.   Performance

For the transmission of information in the VANET system, the need for storage and processing is increasing rapidly as the number of cars on road and interest in research on autonomous vehicles is increasing. There is a need to improve the problem of latency to transmit data between device and data-center and the problem is also related to faulty sensing nodes operating under VANET. Fault in nodes could be because of internal or external factors which may origin considerable accidents. Hence need is of proper protocol to transfer correct and consistent information to the user even after the existence of faulty nodes. The author mentioned the proposal of a researcher which is the "Byzantine Agreement (BA) problem". Furthermore, the authors (Chiang et al., 2019) have projected a method based on consensus agreement for the VANET system under Fog Computing that ensures the appropriateness and steadiness to make sure that the system would be capable to deal with the traffic situation accurately in real-time.

The problem of data sharing in VANET is so gigantic that could not be addressed using cloud computing only as it can't satisfy latency-sensitive real-time applications. Fog computing a type of cloud computing that is able to achieve optimum data exchange between vehicles. Authors (Fan et al. 2018) had proposed a novel scheme " Ciphertext Policy Attribute-Based Encryption (CP-ABE) " in vehicular fog computing system with efficient decryption techniques, but still keeping their system protected against the collusion attack. They also designed a method for the proficient user and attribute revocation for their scheme that is able to achieve forward as well as backward security. Their discussion is also based on properties contained in the security analysis of their proposed CP-ABE system and those are Collusion tolerant, Forward and backward security, Data confidentially. The properties which they used for the performance evaluation of their system are Flexibility analysis, Computation cost, Efficiency analysis which is based on Storage overhead and Communication cost. All the above properties showed that their proposed CP-ABE system is more efficient and secure.

4. Intelligent Transportation

Intelligent Transportation System (ITS) a field of VANET aims to improve road safety, the efficiency of the transportation system and to conserve the green environment. Big data analytics is applied to ITS to manage the enormous amount of information produced by this system. Transferring such huge data to centralized cloud system results in network bottlenecks and high latency which is not acceptable by the delay-sensitive ITS. Moreover, the cloud is also not able to provide location knowledge and support for mobility which an ITS system needs. The above issues can be resolved by Fog computing which is able to grant the cloud services at the edge of the network. However, fog is not able to satisfy the huge computational and storage requirement of the big data of ITS so Authors (Darwish & Bakar 2018) stated that both cloud and fog have to used together to support big data of ITS and they proposed a new architecture for this consisting of three dimensions including computing layer (could be a cloud or a fog), real-time big data analytics layer, and IoV layer. They discussed in detail about the IoV environment opportunities and challenges, then features of ITS big data, also the real-time big data analytics architecture, and also discussed various techniques for intelligent computing. They also discussed security, privacy issues, the trustworthiness of the IoV system and VFC concerns related to their proposed system.

5. Smart City Concept using IoT and Vehicular Fog

To improve the standard of living in an urban environment, the smart city makes it possible for various devices like mobile devices, walkers, and electronic appliances to exchange data with each other. Similar to these because of the smart city concept role of IoT and Vehicular network has also emerged. Because of the issues of cloud-based techniques, Fog computing had come into existence. Authors (Shah et al., 2019) had anticipated a framework for vehicular Fog computing which is a rising field from the perspective of Smart City. The concept of Vehicular Fog computing can facilitate to sustain delay-sensitive applications and can also help in diminishing the workload on the networks. Vehicles in vFog provide infrastructure- as -a- service functionality which poses a big challenge for vehicles to provide computation while they are moving. Authors had proposed a term for their framework called vFog, which was designed to offer computing amenities from fog vehicles that are nearby. The framework exploits the onboard computing capability of the vehicles with not taking the hold of roadside units (RSUs). They had designed their proposed vFog model on " OMNeTCC, using SUMO and Veins". Their framework is based on algorithms on fog vehicle, user's vehicle and relay mechanism for the proper functioning of the system. For performance evaluation of their system, they had considered the number of simulation parameters like area, time, run, fog vehicles, roadside units, data transmission rate, etc. on taking particular values of these parameters they analyzed their system. Their results showed the graphs on these parameters: packet delivery ratio, transmission delay, system resources usage, system efficiency, and multi-hop dissemination.

SECURITY AND FORENSIC PROPERTIES OF VEHICULAR FOG COMPUTING

Research related to security risks related to vehicular fog computing is still immature and needs some more attention. Its major focus is on threats, potential attacks, and vulnerability. (Huang et al., 2017)

In VFC attacks could be of two types one type is Active attacks which is an intentional attempt to interrupt the operations of VFC. The second type of attack is Passive attack which is an attempt to disclose private information and does not destroy the functionality of VFC.

Two kinds of attackers for VANET system are Internal attackers and the External attackers. An internal attacker is the one occurring from an internal system that is from vehicles or from fog or cloud nodes that hold the key material of the VFC system. An External attacker is the one occurring from the outside system which does not hold the key materials of the VFC system.

The security Threats which may occur in case of Vehicular Fog Computing are(Jhariya et al. 2014):

1. Distributed Denial of Service: This is harsher than DOS attack in this attacker uses different locations and different timeslots to attack with a target to down the whole network so as it is not available for anyone to use.
2. Node Impersonation: To exchange information in the network every vehicle has a unique id that is used for vehicle identification. In the Node Impersonation attack, the attacker uses someone else's identity to send a modified or fake message.
3. Sending False Information: An attacker can intentionally deviate other vehicles from the path by sending fake information regarding traffic so that he can get a clear path.
4. ID Disclosure: In this attack, the attacker captures the ID of the target node and its present location then generates the malicious code which is being transmitted to the target node and by this attacker collects the required information of the vehicle. The attacker makes use of the RSU for this purpose.
5. Sybil Attack: A type of attack where an invader operates as the manifold personalities of the system at the equivalent instance and sends the identical fake message so as to pretend it to others that this message is genuine as being forwarded by many and forced the vehicle owner to take a wrong decision.

6. Repudiation Attack: Repudiation means a node denies that he is responsible for this message. This could be because an attacker has used his identity to send messages and the vehicle is not aware of it so he denies.

A secure VFC should grant the following security and forensic features: (Huang et al. 2017)

1. Confidentiality: This is to ensure that data is accessed only by authorized users that are to prevent its access from the unauthorized users of the VFC system.
2. Integrity: This ensures that the information is in its original form as sent by the sender. (Yi et al. 2015)
3. Availability: This makes sure that whenever a vehicle tries to contact the fog nodes or cloud servers, they should be accessible.
4. Authentication: This makes sure that any two transmitting units are able to substantiate the information during communication. (Yi et al. 2015)
5. Access control: This is intended to limit the right to use the fog node just to authoritative entities. (Yi et al. 2015)
6. Non-repudiation: It makes sure that anytime a node in the system won't refuse its preceding acts means the information being sent.
7. Reliability: To ensure that the information collected from various smart vehicles and fog nodes haven't been altered.
8. Forensics: Forensics feature makes sure that the potential to discover, assemble, and analyze information gathered from smart vehicles, fog nodes, and the fundamental infrastructure for outlining and discovering the nasty resource.

CHALLENGES AND OPEN PROBLEMS

As for the practical vehicular services we need better capacity and resources, VFC employs vehicles as infrastructure and utilizes its power. Still there exists a lot of challenges and open problems which are discussed below:

1. Mobility Model for Vehicles: Learning the mobility representation for the vehicles is of primary significance in proposing a VFC system. We need an improved mobility representation to offer us important data about the precise vehicular behaviors, like its speed and distribution in time as well as space domains. In particular, we have to learn mobility further cautiously to originate a better precise and perfect mobility representation for assorted surroundings which are additionally supportive for realistic purpose. Getting the fundamental mobility prototype and the vehicular behavior will assist us to perform improved communication and computational resource exploitation and task to recognize an efficient VFC system, which will lead to the utmost effectiveness in both equipment and energy. (Lin et al. 2008)
2. Capacity Analysis and Resource Management: To enhance the capacity needs of VFC we can still enhance the more usage of moving and vehicles that are parked as infrastructures. Although they are still used but need new proposals and mechanisms to take full advantage of the capacity of the vehicle. Persons will be more engrossed to offer their vehicles to unite VFC once they realize the

benefits offered by it and so they will be ready to pay off some amount. To attract vehicles to rent out the capacity of their vehicle some approaches like incentive-based method and punishment-based method are still in the system and need some improvement. (Xiao & Zu 2017)

3. System Implementation: To work with VFC scheme a vehicle wishes to have definite devices like incorporated embedded computers, GPS, sensors, communication devices, and intelligent algorithms. Although the current modern vehicles are equipped with many of these devices but surely upcoming vehicles will even have advanced hardware and software to hold VFC. (Xiao & Zu 2017)

4. Incentives: VANET deals with various safety and non-safety applications. VFC provides support for massive communication and computational needs. All the applications of VANET need to exchange an enormous amount of information and so needs a powerful communication and computational capacity. To solve this purpose power of VFC and vehicles can be used. Vehicles equipped with high power can rent out their unutilized capacity only if they get some benefit. For this giving incentive to VFC and vehicles is a good way to attract vehicle possessors to lease out their assets. There should be a proper protocol defined for renting out resources and giving incentives.

5. Security: Exchanging content and getting data results in a few major defensive troubles like frail validation, lack of adequate security and maltreatment of protocols, etc. which could arise problems like information hack, virus infection and hostile attacks. Thus it is essential to design a security mechanism for VFC. (Zekri & Jia, 2018)

CONCLUSION

This chapter presents a review on Vehicular Ad-hoc Network technology, its features, and applications supported by it to make a safer and convenient drive for both passengers and drivers. To facilitate VANET in computing & storage, cloud computing plays a crucial role & helps VANET to accomplish communication between devices and take suitable actions by taking a crucial decision in situations occurring in VANET. Vehicles need to pay for the services needed from the cloud. Cloud due to its drawbacks like centralized server, consumes high energy, needs large network bandwidth, faces challenges in dealing with VANET so as to support cloud, fog computing was proposed which works together with the cloud to offload its burden and to support real-time applications. Fog apart from VANET also plays a vital role in a range of applications like smart city, IoT, smart grids, Healthcare, cyber and visual security, etc. This chapter also covered significant differences between Vehicular Fog Computing and Vehicular Cloud Computing. A detailed review of various author's contributions with respect to various services of VANET using Fog computing like routing, offloading, security, privacy, message dissemination, etc are also presented in this chapter. Fog apart from its advantages also suffers from various security issues and open problems which could be considered by authors as a future scope.

REFERENCES

Aliyu, A., Abdullah, A. H., Kaiwartya, O., Cao, Y., Usman, M. J., Kumar, S., ... Raw, R. S. (2017). Cloud Computing in VANETs: Architecture, Taxonomy, and Challenges. *IETE Technical Review*. doi: 10.1080/02564602.2017.1342572

Bezerra, P., Melo, A., Douglas, A., Santos, H., Rio, D. R., & Cerqueira, E. (2019). A collaborative routing protocol for video streaming with fog computing in vehicular ad hoc networks, doi:10.1177/15501 47719832839(online)

Bonomi, F., Milito, R., Zhu, J., & Addepalli, S. (2012). Fog Computing and its Role in the Internet of Things. *MCC '12 Proceedings of the first edition of the MCC Workshop on Mobile Cloud Computing*, 13-16.

Chen, Y. A., Walters, J. P., & Crago, S. P. (2017). Load Balancing for Minimizing Deadline Misses and Total Runtime for Connected Car Systems in Fog Computing. *Proceedings 2017 IEEE International Symposium on Parallel and Distributed Processing with Applications and 2017 IEEE International Conference on Ubiquitous Computing and Communications (ISPA/IUCC)*. 10.1109/ISPA/IUCC.2017.00107

Chiang, M. L., Lin, Y., Hsieh, H. C., & Tsai, W. C. (2019). Improving Latency and Reliability for Vehicle System Under Fog Computing Networks. In J. S. Pan, A. Ito, P. W. Tsai, & L. Jain (Eds.), *Recent Advances in Intelligent Information Hiding and Multimedia Signal Processing. IIH-MSP 2018. Smart Innovation, Systems, and Technologies* (Vol. 109). Cham, Switzerland: Springer. doi:10.1007/978-3-030-03745-1_28

Dahiya, V., & Dalal, S. (2018) Fog Computing: A Review on Integration of Cloud Computing and Internet of Things. *Proceedings 2018 IEEE International Students' Conference on Electrical, Electronics, and Computer Science (SCEECS) (pp. 1-6). IEEE.*

Darwish, T. S. J., & Bakar, K. A. (2018). *Fog Based Intelligent Transportation Big Data Analytics in The Internet of Vehicles Environment: Motivations, Architecture, Challenges, and Critical Issues. IEEE Access, 6,* 15679–15701.

Fan, K., Wang, J., Wang, X., Li, H., & Yang, Y. (2018). Secure, efficient, and revocable data sharing scheme for vehicular fogs. *Peer-to-Peer Networking and Applications, 11*(4), 766–777. doi:10.100712083-017-0562-8

Giang, N. K., Leung, V. C. M., & Lea, R. (2016). On Developing Smart Transportation Applications in Fog Computing Paradigms. *DIVANet '16 Proceedings of the 6th ACM Symposium on Development and Analysis of Intelligent Vehicular Networks and Applications*, 91-98.

Grover, J., Jain, A., Singhal, S., & Yadav, A. (2018). Real-Time VANET Applications Using Fog Computing. *Proceedings of First International Conference on Smart System, Innovations, and Computing. Smart Innovation, Systems and Technologies, 79.* Springer, Singapore. 10.1007/978-981-10-5828-8_65

Hou, X., Li, Y., Chen, M., Wu, D., Jin, D., & Chen, S. (2016). Vehicular Fog Computing: A Viewpoint of Vehicles as the Infrastructures. *IEEE Transactions on Vehicular Technology, 65*(6), 3860–3873. doi:10.1109/TVT.2016.2532863

Hu, P., Dhelim, S., Ning, H., & Qui, T. (2017). Survey on fog computing: Architecture, key technologies, applications and open issues. *Journal of Network and Computer Applications, 98,* 27–42. doi:10.1016/j.jnca.2017.09.002

Huang, C., Lu, R., & Choo, K. K. R. (2017). Vehicular Fog Computing. *Architecture, Use Case, and Security and Forensic Challenges. IEEE Communications Magazine, 55*(11), 105–111.

Jhariya, M. K., Shukla, P. K., & Barskhar, R. (2014) Assessment of Different Attacks and Security Schemes in Vehicular Ad-hoc Network, *International Journal of Computer Applications 98*(22), 24-28.

Kai, K., Cong, W., & Tao, L. (2016). Fog computing for vehicular Ad-hoc networks: Paradigms, scenarios, and issues. *Journal of China Universities of Posts and Telecommunications, 23*(2), 56–65, 96. doi:10.1016/S1005-8885(16)60021-3

Khan, A. A., Abolhasan, M., & Ni, W. (2018). 5G Next generation VANETs using SDN and Fog Computing Framework. Proceedings 2018 15th IEEE Annual Consumer Communications & Networking Conference (CCNC) (pp. 1-6). IEEE.

Khan, S., Parkinson, S., & Qin, Y. (2017) Fog computing security: a review of current applications and security solutions, *Journal of Cloud Computing, 6*(19).

Kui, X., Sun, Y., Zhang, S., & Li, Y. (2018). Characterizing the Capability of Vehicular Fog Computing in Large-scale Urban Environment. *Mobile Networks and Applications, 23*(4), 1050–1067. doi:10.100711036-017-0969-8

Kumar, R., & Goyal, R. (2019). On Cloud security requirements, threats, vulnerabilities, and countermeasures: A survey. *Computer Science Review. Elsevier Journal, 33*, 1–48.

Kwon, B. W., Kang, J., & Park, J. H. (2019). A Fog Computing-Based Automotive Data Overload Protection System with Real-Time Analysis. In J. Park, V. Loia, K. K. Choo, & G. Yi (Eds.), *Advanced Multimedia and Ubiquitous Engineering. MUE 2018, FutureTech 2018. Lecture Notes in Electrical Engineering* (Vol. 518). Singapore: Springer. doi:10.1007/978-981-13-1328-8_89

Li, M., Zhu, L., & Lin, X. (2019). *Efficient and Privacy-Preserving Carpooling Using Blockchain-Assisted Vehicular Fog Computing. IEEE Internet of Things Journal, 6*(3), 4573–4584.

Liao, S., Li, J., Wu, J., Yang, W., & Guan, Z. (2018). *Fog-Enabled Vehicle as a Service for Computing Geographical Migration in Smart Cities. IEEE Access, 7*, 8726–8736.

Lin, X., Lu, R., Zhang, C., Zhu, H., Ho, P. H., & Shen, X. (2008). *Security in Vehicular Ad Hoc Networks. IEEE Communications Magazine, 46*(4), 88–95.

Liu, J., Li, J., Zhang, L., Dai, F., Zhang, Y., Meng, X., & Shen, J. (2017). Secure intelligent traffic light control using fog computing. *Future Generation Computer Systems, 78*(Part 2), 817–824.

Lu, T., Chang, S., & Li, W. (2018). Fog computing enabling geographic routing for urban area vehicular network. *Peer-to-Peer Networking and Applications, 11*(4), 749–775. doi:10.100712083-017-0560-x

Menon, V. G. (2017). Moving From Vehicular Cloud Computing to Vehicular Fog Computing: Issues and Challenges. *International Journal on Computer Science and Engineering, 9*(2).

Nabil, M., Hajami, A., & Haqiq, A. (2019). Predicting the Route of the Longest Lifetime and the Data Packet Delivery Time between Two Vehicles in VANET. *Mobile Information Systems Volume 2019, Article ID 2741323.* . doi:10.1155/2019/2741323

Nath, S. B., Gupta, H., Chakraborty, S., & Ghosh, S. K. (2018). A Survey of Fog Computing and Communication: Current Researches and Future Directions, Networking and Internet Architecture. *arXiv:1804.04365*.

Nguyen, T. D. T., Nguyen, T. D., Nguyen, V. D., Pham, X. Q., & Huh, E. N. (2018). Cost-Effective Resource Sharing in an Internet of Vehicles-Employed Mobile Edge Computing Environment. *Symmetry*, *10*(11), 594. doi:10.3390ym10110594

Nobre, J. C., Souza, A. M. D., Rosário, D., Both, C., Villas, L. A., Cerqueira, E., ... Gerla, M. (2019). Vehicular Software-Defined Networking and Fog Computing: Integration and Design Principles. *Ad Hoc Networks*, *82*, 172–181. doi:10.1016/j.adhoc.2018.07.016

Okay, F. Y., & Ozdemir, S. (2018). Routing in Fog-Enabled IoT Platforms: A Survey and an SDN-based Solution. *IEEE Internet of Things Journal, 5*(6), 4871–4889. doi:10.1109/JIOT.2018.2882781

Paranjothi, A., Khan, M. S., & Atiquzzaman, M. (2018). DFCV: A Novel Approach for Message Dissemination in Connected Vehicles using Dynamic Fog, In K. Chowdhury, M. Di Felice, I. Matta, & B. Sheng (Eds.), Wired/Wireless Internet Communications. Lecture Notes in Computer Science, 10866. Cham, Switzerland: Springer. doi:10.1007/978-3-030-02931-9_25

Pereira, J., Ricardo, L., Luís, M., Senna, C., & Sargento, S. (2019). Assessing the reliability of fog computing for smart mobility applications in VANETs. *Future Generation Computer Systems*, *94*, 317–332. doi:10.1016/j.future.2018.11.043

Perera, C., Qin, Y., Estrella, J. C., Reiff- Marganiec, S., & Vasilakos, A. V. (2017). Fog Computing for Sustainable Smart Cities: A Survey. *Journal ACM Computing Surveys, 50*(3), 32.

Peter, N. (2015). FOG Computing and Its Real Time Applications. *International Journal of Emerging Technology and Advanced Engineering*, *5*(6).

Raza, S., Wang, S., Ahmed, M., & Anwar, M. R. (2019). A Survey on Vehicular Edge Computing: Architecture, Applications, Technical Issues, and Future Directions. *Wireless Communications and Mobile Computing*, 1–19. doi:10.1155/2019/3159762

Shah, S. S., Ali, M., Malik, A. W., Khan, M. A., & Ravana, S. D. (2019). vFog: A Vehicle-Assisted Computing Framework for Delay-Sensitive Applications in Smart Cities. *IEEE Access, 7*, 34900–34909. doi:10.1109/ACCESS.2019.2903302

Sharma, M. K., & Kaur, A. (2015). A Survey on Vehicular Cloud Computing and its Security. *Proceedings 1st International Conference on Next Generation Computing Technologies*. 10.1109/NGCT.2015.7375084

Shrestha, R., Bajracharya, R., & Nam, S. Y. (2018). Challenges of Future VANET and Cloud-Based Approaches. *Wireless Communications and Mobile Computing*, 1–15. doi:10.1155/2018/5603518

Siddiqui, S. A., & Mahmood, A. (2018). Towards Fog-based Next Generation Internet of Vehicles Architecture. *Proceedings of the 1st International Workshop on Communication and Computing in Connected Vehicles and Platooning*, 15-21.

Sookhak, M., Yu, F. R., He, Y., Talebian, H., Safa, N. S., Zhao, N., ... Kumar, N. (2017). Fog Vehicular Computing. *Augmentation of Fog Computing Using Vehicular Cloud Computing. IEEE Vehicular Technology Magazine, 12*(3), 55–64.

Stojmenovic, I., & Wen, S. (2014). The Fog Computing Paradigm: Scenarios and Security Issues. *Proceedings 2014 Federated Conference on Computer Science and Information Systems* 10.15439/2014F503

Sun, Y., Guo, Y., Song, J., Zhou, S., Jiang, Z., Liu, X., & Niu, Z. (2019). *Adaptive Learning-Based Task Offloading for Vehicular Edge Computing Systems. IEEE Transactions on Vehicular Technology, 68*(4), 3061–3074.

Sutagundar, A. V., Attar, A. H., & Hatti, D. I. (2019). Resource Allocation for Fog Enhanced Vehicular Services. *Wireless Personal Communications, 104*(4), 1473–1491. doi:10.100711277-018-6094-6

Talib, M. S., Hussin, B., & Hassan, A. (2017). Converging VANET with Vehicular Cloud Networks to reduce the Traffic Congestions: A review. *International Journal of Applied Engineering Research, 12*(21), 10646-10654.

Tassi, A., Mavromatis, I., Piechocki, R., Nix, A., Compton, C., Poole, T., & Schuster, W. (2019). Agile Data Offloading over Novel Fog Computing Infrastructure for CAVs. *Proceedings IEEE 89th Vehicular Technology Conference.*

Truong, N. B., Lee, G. M., & Doudane, Y. G. (2015). Software defined networking-based vehicular Ad-hoc Network with Fog Computing. *Proceedings IEEE International Symposium on Integrated Network Management.* 10.1109/INM.2015.7140467

Ullah, A., Yaqoob, S., Imran, M., & Ning, H. (2018). *Emergency Message Dissemination Schemes Based on Congestion Avoidance in VANET and Vehicular Fog Computing. IEEE Access, 7*, 2169–3536.

Vaquero, L. M., Rodero-Merino, L., Caceres, J., & Lindner, M. (2009). A Break in the Clouds: Towards a Cloud Definition. *Computer Communication Review, 39*(1), 50–55. doi:10.1145/1496091.1496100

Wang, L., Liu, G., & Sun, L. (2017). A Secure and Privacy-Preserving/ Navigation Scheme Using Spatial Crowdsourcing in Fog-Based VANETs. *Sensors (Basel), 2017*(17), 668. doi:10.339017040668 PMID:28338620

Wang, X., Ning, Z., & Wang, L. (2018). Offloading in Internet of Vehicles: A Fog-Enabled Real-Time Traffic Management System. *IEEE Transactions on Industrial Informatics, 14*(10), 4568–4578. doi:10.1109/TII.2018.2816590

Whaiduzzaman, M., Sookhak, M., Gani, A., & Buyya, R. (2014). A survey on vehicular cloud computing. *Journal of Network and Computer Applications, 40*, 325–344. doi:10.1016/j.jnca.2013.08.004

What is cloud computing? A beginner's guide. Retrieved from https://azure.microsoft.com/en-in/overview/what-is-cloud-computing/

Xiao, Y., & Zu, C. (2017) Vehicular Fog Computing: Vision and Challenges. *Proceedings 2017 IEEE International Conference on Pervasive Computing and Communications Workshops.* 10.1109/PER-COMW.2017.7917508

Yi, S., Hao, Z., Qui, Z., & Li, Q. (2015). Fog Computing: Platform and Applications. *Proceedings 2015 Third IEEE Workshop on Hot Topics in Web Systems and Technologies*. 10.1109/HotWeb.2015.22

Yi, S., Li, C., & Li, Q. (2015). A survey of Fog Computing: Concepts, Applications and Issues. *Proceedings of the 2015 workshop on Mobile Big Data*, 37-42. 10.1145/2757384.2757397

Yi, S., Qin, Z., & Li, Q. (2015). Security and Privacy Issues of Fog Computing: A Survey. In K. Xu & H. Zhu (Eds.), Lecture Notes in Computer Science: Vol. 9204. *Wireless Algorithms, Systems, and, Applications*. Cham, Switzerland: Springer. doi:10.1007/978-3-319-21837-3_67

Zekri, A., & Jia, W. (2018). Heterogeneous Vehicular Communications: A Comprehensive Study. *Ad Hoc Networks, 75–76*, 52–79. doi:10.1016/j.adhoc.2018.03.010

Zeng, M., Li, Y., Zhang, K., Waqas, M., & Jin, D. (2018). Incentive Mechanism Design for computation Offloading in Heterogeneous Fog Computing: a Contract-based Approach. *Proceedings IEEE International Conference on Communications*. 10.1109/ICC.2018.8422684

Zhou, S., Sun, Y., Jiang, Z., & Niu, Z. (2019). *Exploiting Moving Intelligence: Delay-Optimized Computation Offloading in Vehicular Fog Networks. IEEE Communications Magazine, 57*(5), 49–55.

Zhou, Z., Liu, P., Feng, J., Zhang, Y., Mumtaz, S., & Rodriguez, J. (2019). Computation Resource Allocation and Task Assignment Optimization in Vehicular Fog Computing: A Contract-Matching Approach. *IEEE Transactions on Vehicular Technology, 68*(4), 3113–3125. doi:10.1109/TVT.2019.2894851

Zhu, C., Tao, J., Pastor, G., Xiao, Y., Ji, Y., Zhou, Q., ... Yia-Jaaski, A. (2019). Folo: Latency and quality optimized task allocation in vehicular fog computing. *IEEE Internet of Things Journal, 6*(3), 4150–4161. doi:10.1109/JIOT.2018.2875520

Compilation of References

(2010). Evaluation of the public health impacts of traffic congestion: A health risk assessment, Harvard Center for Risk Analysis. *Environmental Health*, 9(65). Retrieved from http://www.ehjournal.net/content/9/1/65

Abdel Wahab, A., Khattab, A., & Fahmy, Y. A. (2013). Two-Way TOA with Limited Dead Reckoning for GPS-Free Vehicle Localization Using Single RSU. In *Proceedings 13th International Conference on ITS Telecommunications (ITST)*, 244 -249. IEEE.

Abdelhamid, S., Hassanein, H. S., & Takahara, G. (2015). Vehicle as a resource (VaaR). *IEEE Network*, 29(1), 12–17. doi:10.1109/MNET.2015.7018198

Abdelmagid Elsadig, M., & Fadlalla, Y. A. (2016). VANETs Security Issues and Challenges: A Survey. *Indian Journal of Science and Technology*, 9(28), 1–8. doi:10.17485/ijst/2016/v9i28/97782

Abusalah, L., Khokhar, A., & Guizani, M. (2008). A survey of secure mobile ad hoc routing protocols (pp. 78–93). IEEE Communication: Surveys & Tutorials, IEEE.

Ackaah, W., Bogenberger, K., & Bertini, R. L. (2019). Empirical evaluation of real-time traffic information for in-vehicle navigation and the variable speed limit system. *Journal of Intelligent Transport Systems*, 23(5), 499–512. doi:10.1080/15472450.2018.1563864

Afsar, M. M., & Mohammad-H., T. (2014). Clustering in sensor networks: A literature survey, Elsevier. *Journal of Network and Computer Applications*, 46, 198–226. doi:10.1016/j.jnca.2014.09.005

Agarwal, P., & Alam, A. (2018). Use of ICT for Sustainable Transportation, in *Proceedings of International Conference on Future Environment and Energy*, 150(1), pp. 1-7.

Aggarwal, A., Gandhi, S., Chaubey, N., & Jani, K. A. (2014, February). Trust based secure on demand routing protocol (TSDRP) for MANETs. In *Proceedings 2014 Fourth International Conference on Advanced Computing & Communication Technologies* (pp. 432-438). IEEE. Retrieved from https://ieeexplore.ieee.org/xpl/articleDetails.jsp?arnumber=6783493

Ahammed, F., Taheri, J., Zomaya, A. Y., & Ott, M. (2012). VLOCI: Using Distance Measurements to Improve the Accuracy of Location Coordinates in GPS-Equipped VANETs. Institute for Computer Sciences, Social Informatics, and Telecommunications Engineering, 149–161.

Ahmad, A., Doughan, M., Mougharbel, I., & Marot, M. (2012, June). A new adapted back-off scheme for broadcasting on IEEE 1609.4 control channel in VANET. In 2012 The 11th Annual Mediterranean Ad Hoc Networking Workshop (Med-Hoc-Net) (pp. 9-15). IEEE.

Ahmad, F., Adnane, A., Franqueira, V. N. L., Kurugollu, F., & Liu, L. (2018). Man-in-the-middle attacks in vehicular ad-Hoc networks: Evaluating the impact of attackers' strategies. *Sensors (Switzerland)*, 18(11), 4040. doi:10.339018114040 PMID:30463282

Ahmed, W., Saeed, N., & Dost, M. S. B. (2018). *Localization of vehicular ad hoc networks with RSS based distance estimation. In Proceedings international conference on computing, mathematics, and engineering technologies.* IEEE.

Akyildiz, I. F., Su, W., Sankarasubramaniam, Y., & Cayirci, E. (2002). A survey on sensor networks. *IEEE Communications Magazine, 40*(8), 102–114. doi:10.1109/MCOM.2002.1024422

Akyildiz, I. F., Su, W., Sankarasubramaniam, Y., & Cayirci, E. (2002). Wireless Sensor Networks: A Survey. *Elsevier Journal on Computer Networks, 38*(4), 393–422. doi:10.1016/S1389-1286(01)00302-4

Alam, F. (2011). Node Feed-Back Based Tcp Scheme For Mobile Ad-Hoc Network. *Computer Science & Telecommunications, 31*(2).

Alam, K. M., Saini, M., Ahmed, D. T., & El Saddik, A. (2014). VeDi: A vehicular crowd-sourced video social network for VANETs. In *Proceedings - Conference on Local Computer Networks, LCN, 2014-November,* 738–745. 10.1109/LCNW.2014.6927729

Alam, M. M., Hamida, E. B., Berder, O., Menard, D., & Sentieys, O. (2016). A Heuristic Self-Adaptive Medium Access Control for Resource-Constrained WBAN Systems, *IEEE Access on Special section on body area networks for interdisciplinary research, 4,* 1287–1300.

Alba, E., Luna, S., & Toutouh, J. (2008). Accuracy and Efficiency in Simulating VANETs. *Communications in Computer and Information Science, 14,* 568–578. doi:10.1007/978-3-540-87477-5_60

Ali Eljadi, F. M., & Taha Al Shaikhli, I. F. (2014). Dynamic linear feedback shift registers: A review. In *Proceedings 2014 the 5th International Conference on Information and Communication Technology for the Muslim World, ICT4M 2014,* (January 2015). 10.1109/ICT4M.2014.7020598

Ali, M. E.-C., Artail, H., & Nasser, Y. (2017). An Intelligent Transportation Systems cooperative and roadside unit-aided schema for vehicular ad hoc networks. In Proceedings international conference on electrical and computing technologies and applications, 1-5. IEEE.

Aliyu, A., Abdullah, A. H., Kaiwartya, O., Cao, Y., Lloret, J., Aslam, N., & Joda, U. M. (2018). Towards video streaming in IoT Environments: Vehicular communication perspective. *Computer Communications, 118,* 93–119. doi:10.1016/j.comcom.2017.10.003

Aliyu, A., Abdullah, A. H., Kaiwartya, O., Cao, Y., Usman, M. J., Kumar, S., ... Raw, R. S. (2017). Cloud Computing in VANETs: Architecture, Taxonomy, and Challenges. *IETE Technical Review.* doi:10.1080/02564602.2017.1342572

Alotaibi, M. M., Boukerche, A., & Mouftah, H. (2014). Distributed Relative Cooperative Positioning in Vehicular Ad-hoc Networks. In *Proceedings Global Information Infrastructure and Networking Symposium (GIIS),* IEEE. 10.1109/GIIS.2014.6934255

Al-Rabayah, M., & Malaney, R. (2012). A new scalable hybrid routing protocol for VANETs. *IEEE Transactions on Vehicular Technology, 61*(6), 2625–2635. doi:10.1109/TVT.2012.2198837

Al-Sultan, S., Al-Doori, M. M., Al-Bayatti, A. H., & Zedan, H. (2014). A comprehensive survey on vehicular ad hoc network. *Journal of Network and Computer Applications, 37,* 380–392. doi:10.1016/j.jnca.2013.02.036

Altoaimy, L., Mahgoub, I., & Rathod, M. (2014). Weighted localization in vehicular ad hoc networks using vehicle-to-vehicle communication. In *Proceedings Global Information Infrastructure and Networking Symposium (GIIS),* 1-5, IEEE. 10.1109/GIIS.2014.6934270

Anand, A. (2013). Performance evaluation of vehicular ad hoc network (VANET). *Using, 3*(2), 25–33.

Anda, C., Erath, A., & Fourie, P. J. (2017). Transport modelling in the age of big data. *International Journal of Urban Sciences*, *21*(1), 19–42. doi:10.1080/12265934.2017.1281150

Anwer, M. S., & Guy, C. (2014). A survey of VANET technologies. *Journal of Emerging Trends in Computing and Information Sciences*, *5*(9), 661–671.

Arafat, Y. M., & Moh, S. (2019, July), Routing Protocols for Unmanned Aerial Vehicle Networks: A Survey, *IEEE Access, 7*, 99694-99720.

Ari, A. A. A., Gueroui, A., Labraoui, N., & Yenke, B. O. (2015). Concepts and evolution of research in the field of wireless sensor networks. *International Journal on Computational Networks and Communication*, *7*(1), 81–98. doi:10.5121/ijcnc.2015.7106

Aslam, N. S., Cheng, T., & Cheshire, J. (2019). A high-precision heuristic model to detect home and work locations from smart card data. *Geo-Spatial Information Science*, *22*(1), 1–11. doi:10.1080/10095020.2018.1545884

Atzori, L., Iera, A., & Morabito, G. (2010). The Internet of Things: A survey. *Computer Networks*, *54*(15), 2787–2805. doi:10.1016/j.comnet.2010.05.010

Avoine, G., & Oechslin, P. (2005). A scalable and provably secure hash-based RFID protocol. In *Proceedings Third IEEE International Conference on Pervasive Computing and Communications Workshops, PerCom 2005 Workshops*, 110–114. 10.1109/PERCOMW.2005.12

Ayaida, M., Messai, N., Najeh, S., & Boris Ndjore, K. (2019). A Macroscopic Traffic Model-based Approach for Sybil Attack Detection in VANETs. *Ad Hoc Networks, 90*(February), 0–12. doi:10.1016/j.adhoc.2019.01.010

Ayaida, M., Messai, N., Wilhelm, G., & Najeh, S. (2019). A Novel Sybil Attack Detection Mechanism for C-ITS. In *Proceedings 2019 15th International Wireless Communications & Mobile Computing Conference (IWCMC)*, 913–918. doi:10.1109/iwcmc.2019.8766572

Azevedo, M. I. B., Coutinho, C., Toda, E. M., Carvalho, T. C., & Jailton, J. (2019, June). Wireless Communications Challenges to Flying Ad Hoc Networks (FANET). *IntechOpen*. doi: . doi:10.5772/intechopen.86544

Azura, C. S., & Lai, G. R. (2010). MATLAB simulation of fuzzy traffic controller for multilane isolated intersection. *International Journal on Computer Science and Engineering*, *2*(4), 924–933.

Bachir, B., Ali, O., Ahmed, H., Mohamed, E., (2014). Proactive schema-based link lifetime estimation and connectivity ratio. Hindawi Publishing Corporation the Scientific World Journal, 2014(4), 1-6.

Bai, F., Stancil, D. D., & Krishnan, H. (2010, September). Toward understanding characteristics of dedicated short range communications (DSRC) from a perspective of vehicular network engineers. In *Proceedings of the 16th Annual International Conference on Mobile Computing and Networking* (pp. 329-340). ACM. 10.1145/1859995.1860033

Baldessari, R., Bödekker, B., Deegener, M., Festag, A., Franz, W., Kellum, C. C., ... & Peichl, T. (2007). Car-2-car communication consortium-manifesto.

Bamburry, D. (2015). Drones: Designed for product delivery. *Design Management Review*, *26*(1), 40–48. doi:10.1111/drev.10313

Barbeau, S. J., Winters, P. L., Georggi, N. L., Labrador, M. A., & Perez, R. (2010). Travel assistance device: Utilizing global positioning system-enabled mobile phones to aid transit riders with special needs. *Intelligent Transport Systems*, *4*(1), 12–23. doi:10.1049/iet-its.2009.0028

Baza, M., Nabil, M., Bewermeier, N., Fidan, K., Mahmoud, M., & Abdallah, M. (2019). *Detecting Sybil Attacks using Proofs of Work and Location in VANETs.* 1–15. Retrieved from https://arxiv.org/abs/1904.05845

Bazzi, A., Zanella, A., & Masini, B. M. (2015). An OFDMA-based MAC protocol for next-generation VANETs. *IEEE Transactions on Vehicular Technology*, *64*(9), 4088–4100. doi:10.1109/TVT.2014.2361392

Bedi, P., & Jindal, V. (2014). Use of Big Data Technology in Vehicular Ad-Hoc Networks. In *Proceedings of. IEEE ICACCI*, 1677–83.

Bedi, R., Singh, B., & Devi, M. (2019). Position Depended Sybil Attack Detection using Efficient KNN technique with Clustering. *International Journal on Computer Science and Engineering*, *7*(2), 266–272. doi:10.26438/ijcse/v7i2.266272

Beijar, N. (2002). Zone routing protocol (ZRP). Networking Laboratory, Helsinki University of Technology, Finland, 9, 1-12.

Bekmezci, I., Sahingoz, O. K., & Temel, S. (2013). *Flying Ad-Hoc Networks (FANETs): A Survey* (pp. 1254–1270). ELSEVIER Ad Hoc Networks.

Bekmezci, S. O., Sahingoz, O. K., & Temel, Ş. (2013). Flying ad-hoc networks: A survey. *Ad Hoc Networks*, *11*(3), 1254–1270. doi:10.1016/j.adhoc.2012.12.004

Belding-Royer, E., & Toh, C. (1999). *A review of current routing protocols for ad-hoc mobile wireless networks*(pp. 46-55). IEEE Personal Communication magazine.

Belkadi, M., Lalam, M., M'zoughi, A., Tamani, N., Daoui, M., & Aoudjit, R. (2010). Intelligent routing and flow control in manets. *CIT. Journal of Computing and Information Technology*, *18*(3), 233–243. doi:10.2498/cit.1001470

Benenson, I., Elia, E. B., Rofé, E., & Geyzersky, D. (2017). The benefits of a high-resolution analysis of transit accessibility. *International Journal of Geographical Information Science*, *31*(2), 213–236. doi:10.1080/13658816.2016.1191637

Benslimane, A. (2005, August). Localization in vehicular ad hoc networks. In Proceedings 2005 Systems Communications (ICW'05, ICHSN'05, ICMCS'05, SENET'05) (pp. 19-25). IEEE. doi:10.1109/ICW.2005.54

Benslimane. (2005). Localization in Vehicular Ad Hoc Networks, In *Proceedings Systems Communications,* 19–25.

Berger, T. P., D'Hayer, J., Marquet, K., Minier, M., & Thomas, G. (2012). The GLUON family: A lightweight hash function family based on FCSRs. Lecture Notes in Computer Science (Including Subseries Lecture Notes in Artificial Intelligence and Lecture Notes in Bioinformatics), 7374 LNCS, 306–323. doi:10.1007/978-3-642-31410-0_19

Bezerra, P., Melo, A., Douglas, A., Santos, H., Rio, D. R., & Cerqueira, E. (2019). A collaborative routing protocol for video streaming with fog computing in vehicular ad hoc networks, doi:10.1177/1550147719832839(online)

Bilal, R., & Khan, B. M. (2017). Analysis of Mobility Models and Routing Schemes for Flying Ad–Hoc Networks (FANETS). *International Journal of Applied Engineering Research*, *12*(12), 3263–3269.

Blessy, A., & Devi, H., R., & LaxmiPriya, C. (2013). An automatic traffic light management using vehicle sensor and GSM model. *International Journal of Scientific and Engineering Research*, *4*(6), 2354–2358.

Böhm, A., Lidström, K., Jonsson, M., & Larsson, T. (2010, October). Evaluating CALM M5-based vehicle-to-vehicle communication in various road settings through field trials. In *IEEE Local Computer Network Conference* (pp. 613-620). IEEE. 10.1109/LCN.2010.5735781

Bonomi, F., Milito, R., Zhu, J., & Addepalli, S. (2012). Fog Computing and its Role in the Internet of Things. *MCC '12 Proceedings of the first edition of the MCC Workshop on Mobile Cloud Computing*, 13-16.

Bonomi, F., Milito, R., Zhu, J., & Addepalli, S. (2012). Fog computing and its role in the internet of things. *Proceedings of the First Edition of the MCC Workshop on Mobile Cloud Computing - MCC '12*, 13. 10.1145/2342509.2342513

Boukerche, A., Oliveira, H. A., Nakamura, E. F., & Loureiro, A. A. (2008). Vehicular ad hoc networks: A new challenge for localization-based systems. *Computer Communications*, *31*(12), 2838–2849. doi:10.1016/j.comcom.2007.12.004

Brody, T. A. (1984). A random-number generator, *34*, 39–46.

Bröring, A., Schmid, S., Schindhelm, C.-K., & Kramer, D. (2017). Enabling IoT Ecosystems through Platform Interoperability The Problem of Missing IoT Interoperability. *IEEE Software*, *34*(1), 54–61. doi:10.1109/MS.2017.2

Bujari, A., Calafate, C. T., Cano, J. C., Manzoni, P., Palazzi, C. E., & Ronzani, D. (2017). Flying ad–hoc network application scenarios and mobility models. *International Journal of Distributed Sensor Networks*, *13*(10), 1–17. doi:10.1177/1550147717738192

Bujari, A., Palazzi, C. E., & Ronzani, D. (2017). FANET application scenarios and mobility models. *Proceedings of the 3rd Workshop on Micro Aerial Vehicle Networks, Systems, and Applications* (pp. 43–46). ACM

Bussi, K., Dey, D., Biswas, M. K., & Dass, B. K. (2016). Neeva: A Lightweight Hash Function. *IACR Cryptology EPrint Archive, 2016*, 42. Retrieved from http://dblp.uni-trier.de/db/journals/iacr/iacr2016.html#BussiDBD16

Canetti, R., Goldreich, O., & Halevi, S. (2000). The Random Oracle Methodology, Revisited, *51*(4), 557–594. Retrieved from https://arxiv.org/abs/cs/0010019

Cao, Z., Shi, K., Song, Q., & Wang, J. (2017). Analysis of correlation between vehicle density and network congestion in VANETs. In *Proceedings 2017 7th IEEE International Conference on Electronics Information and Emergency Communication (ICEIEC)*, pp. 409-412. IEEE. 10.1109/ICEIEC.2017.8076593

Castillo, E., Menendez, J. M., & Cambronero, S. S. (2008). Predicting traffic flow using Bayesian networks. *Transportation Research Part B: Methodological*, *42*(5), 482–509. doi:10.1016/j.trb.2007.10.003

Chai, H., Ma, R., & Michael, H. (2019). Search for parking: A dynamic parking and route guidance system for efficient parking and traffic management. *Journal of Intelligent Transport Systems*, *23*(6), 541–556. doi:10.1080/15472450.2018.1488218

Chakraborti, A., Chattopadhyay, A., Hassan, M., & Nandi, M. (2018). TriviA and uTriviA: Two fast and secure authenticated encryption schemes. *Journal of Cryptographic Engineering*, *8*(1), 29–48. doi:10.100713389-016-0137-2

Chakraborty, S., Pal, A. K., Dey, N., Das, D., & Acharjee, S. (2014). Foliage Area Computation using Monarch Butterfly Algorithm. In *2014 International Conference on Non-Conventional Energy*, Kalyani, India: IEEE. 10.1109/ICONCE.2014.6808740

Chandre, P. R., Mahalle, P. N., & Shinde, G. R. (2019). Machine Learning Based Novel Approach for Intrusion Detection and Prevention System: A Tool Based Verification. *Proceedings - 2018 IEEE Global Conference on Wireless Computing and Networking, GCWCN 2018*. 10.1109/GCWCN.2018.8668618

Chaubey, N. K. (2016). Security Analysis of Vehicular Ad Hoc Networks (VANETs): A Comprehensive Study. *International Journal of Security and Its Applications*, *10*(5), 261–274. doi:10.14257/ijsia.2016.10.5.25

Chen, K., Nahrstedt, K., & Vaidya, N. (2004, March). The utility of explicit rate-based flow control in mobile ad hoc networks. In *Proceedings 2004 IEEE Wireless Communications and Networking Conference (IEEE Cat. No. 04TH8733)*, 3, pp. 1921-1926. IEEE. 10.1109/WCNC.2004.1311847

Cheng, H. T., Shan, H., & Zhuang, W. (2011). Infotainment and road safety service support in vehicular networking: From a communication perspective. *Mechanical Systems and Signal Processing, 25*(6), 2020–2038. doi:10.1016/j.ymssp.2010.11.009

Cheng, N., Lyu, F., Chen, J., Xu, W., Zhou, H., Zhang, S., & Shen, X. S. (2018). Big Data Driven Vehicular Networks. *IEEE Network, 32*(6), 160–167. doi:10.1109/MNET.2018.1700460

Cheng, X., Fang, L., Hong, X., & Yang, L. (2017). Exploiting mobile big data: Sources, features, and applications. *IEEE Network, 31*(1), 72–79. doi:10.1109/MNET.2017.1500295NM

Cheng, X., Yang, L., & Shen, X. (2015). D2D for intelligent transportation systems, A feasibility study. *IEEE Transactions on Intelligent Transportation Systems, 16*(4), 1784–1793. doi:10.1109/TITS.2014.2377074

Chen, S., Chen, F., Liu, J., Wu, J., & Bienkiewicz, B. (2010). Mobile mapping technology of wind velocity data along highway for traffic safety evaluation. *Transportation Research Part C, Emerging Technologies, 18*(4), 507–518. doi:10.1016/j.trc.2009.10.003

Chen, Y. A., Walters, J. P., & Crago, S. P. (2017). Load Balancing for Minimizing Deadline Misses and Total Runtime for Connected Car Systems in Fog Computing. *Proceedings 2017 IEEE International Symposium on Parallel and Distributed Processing with Applications and 2017 IEEE International Conference on Ubiquitous Computing and Communications (ISPA/IUCC)*. 10.1109/ISPA/IUCC.2017.00107

Chezhiyan, U. (2013, April) Measurement Based Analysis of Reactive Protocols in MANET, *International Journal of Wired and Wireless Communications, 1*(2).

Chi, T. N., & Oh, H. (2014). A link quality prediction metric for location-based Routing protocols under shadowing and fading effects in vehicular ad-hoc networks. In *Proceedings International Symposium on Emerging Inter-Networks, Communication, and Mobility, 34*, 565-570.

Chia-Ho Ou (2012). A roadside unit-based localization scheme for vehicular ad hoc networks, *International Journal of Communication Systems, 27*, 135–150.

Chiang, M. L., Lin, Y., Hsieh, H. C., & Tsai, W. C. (2019). Improving Latency and Reliability for Vehicle System Under Fog Computing Networks. In J. S. Pan, A. Ito, P. W. Tsai, & L. Jain (Eds.), *Recent Advances in Intelligent Information Hiding and Multimedia Signal Processing. IIH-MSP 2018. Smart Innovation, Systems, and Technologies* (Vol. 109). Cham, Switzerland: Springer. doi:10.1007/978-3-030-03745-1_28

Chien, H. Y. (2007). SASI: A new ultralightweight RFID authentication protocol providing strong authentication and strong integrity. *IEEE Transactions on Dependable and Secure Computing, 4*(4), 337–340. doi:10.1109/TDSC.2007.70226

Chong, L., Abbas, M. M., Flintsch, A. M., & Higgs, B. (2013). A rule-based neural network approach to model driver naturalistic behavior in traffic. *Transportation Research Part C, Emerging Technologies, 32*, 207–223. doi:10.1016/j.trc.2012.09.011

Choudhary, P. (2015, March). A literature review on vehicular Adhoc Network for intelligent transport. In *2015 2nd International Conference on Computing for Sustainable Global Development (INDIACom)* (pp. 2209-2213). IEEE.

Choudhary, P. (2018). Analyzing virtual traffic light using state machine in vehicular ad hoc network. *Advances in Intelligent Systems and Computing, 638*, 239–245. doi:10.1007/978-981-10-6005-2_25

Chowdhury, S. I., Lee, W. I., Choi, Y. S., Kee, G. Y., & Pyun, J. Y. (2011, October). Performance evaluation of reactive routing protocols in VANET. In *The 17th Asia Pacific Conference on Communications* (pp. 559-564). IEEE. 10.1109/APCC.2011.6152871

Courcoubetis, C. A., Dimakis, A., & Kanakakis, M. (2017). Congestion Control for Background Data Transfers with Minimal Delay Impact. *IEEE/ACM Transactions on Networking, 25*(5), 2743–2758. doi:10.1109/TNET.2017.2710879

Cruz, S. B., Abrudan, T. E., Xiao, Z., Trigoni, N., & Barrosn, J. (2017). Neighbor-Aided Localization in Vehicular Networks. *Transactions on Intelligent Transportation Systems, IEEE, 18*(10), 2693–2702. doi:10.1109/TITS.2017.2655146

Cunha, F., Villas, L., Boukerche, A., Maia, G., Viana, A., Mini, R. A., & Loureiro, A. A. (2016). Data communication in VANETs: Protocols, applications and challenges. *Ad Hoc Networks, 44*, 90–103. doi:10.1016/j.adhoc.2016.02.017

Dahiya, V., & Dalal, S. (2018) Fog Computing: A Review on Integration of Cloud Computing and Internet of Things. *Proceedings 2018 IEEE International Students' Conference on Electrical, Electronics, and Computer Science (SCEECS) (pp. 1-6). IEEE.*

Dahmane, S., & Lorenz, P. (2016). Weighted probabilistic next-hop forwarder decision-making in VANET environments. In *Proceedings IEEE International Conference on Global Communication Conference,* 1-6.

Dakhole, A. Y., & Moon, M. P. (2014). Design of intelligent traffic control system based on ARM. *The Journal of VLSI Signal Processing, 4*(4), 37–40.

Daniker, V. M. (2009). Visualizing real time and archived traffic incident data. In *Proceedings of the 10th IEEE International Conference on Information Reuse and Integration,* 206–211, IEEE Press: Piscataway

Darwish, T. S. J., & Bakar, K. A. (2018). *Fog Based Intelligent Transportation Big Data Analytics in The Internet of Vehicles Environment: Motivations, Architecture, Challenges, and Critical Issues. IEEE Access, 6*, 15679–15701.

Darwish, T., & Bakar, K. A. (2015). Traffic density estimation in vehicular ad hoc networks: A review. *Ad Hoc Networks, 24*, 337–351. doi:10.1016/j.adhoc.2014.09.007

Dey, K. C., Rayamajhi, A., Chowdhury, M., Bhavsar, P., & Martin, J. (2016). Vehicle-to-vehicle (V2V) and vehicle-to-infrastructure (V2I) communication in a heterogeneous wireless network–Performance evaluation. *Transportation Research Part C, Emerging Technologies, 68*, 168–184. doi:10.1016/j.trc.2016.03.008

Dey, N., Samanta, S., Yang, X. S., Chaudhri, S. S., & Das, A. (2013). Optimisation of scaling factors in electrocardiogram signal watermarking using cuckoo search. *International Journal of Bio-inspired Computation, 5*(5), 315–326. doi:10.1504/IJBIC.2013.057193

Dia, H., & Thomas, K. (2011). Development and evaluation of arterial incident detection models using fusion of simulated probe vehicle and loop detector data. *Information Fusion, 12*(1), 20–27. doi:10.1016/j.inffus.2010.01.001

Diakaki, C., Papageorgiou, M., Papamichail, I., & Nikolos, I. (2015). Overview and analysis of vehicle automation and communication systems from a motorway traffic management perspective. *Transportation Resource part A, 75*, 147–165. doi:10.1016/j.tra.2015.03.015

Drawil, N. M., & Basir, O. (2010). Intervehicle-communication-assisted localization. Intelligent Transportation Systems. *IEEE Transactions on Intelligent Transportation Systems, 11*(3), 678–691. doi:10.1109/TITS.2010.2048562

Drawil, N., & Basir, O. (2010). Toward Increasing the Localization Accuracy of Vehicles in VANET. In *Proceedings International Conference on Vehicular Electronics and Safety,* 13-18. IEEE.

Dukkipati, N., Kobayashi, M., Zhang-Shen, R., & McKeown, N. (2005, June). Processor sharing flows in the internet. In *Proceedings International Workshop on Quality of Service* (pp. 271-285). Berlin, Germany: Springer.

Dutta, N., & Chellappan, S. (2013). A Time-series Clustering Approach for Sybil Attack Detection in Vehicular Ad hoc Networks. In *Proceedings VEHICULAR 2013: The Second International Conference on Advances in Vehicular Systems, Technologies, and Applications,* (February), 35–40.

Eichler, S. (2007, September). Performance evaluation of the IEEE 802.11 p WAVE communication standard. In *Proceedings 2007 IEEE 66th Vehicular Technology Conference* (pp. 2199-2203). IEEE.

Elazab, M., Noureldine, A., & Hassanein, H. S. (2015). Integrated cooperative localization for connected vehicles in urban canyons. In *Proceedings IEEE Global Communications Conference (GLOBECOM),* 1-6. 10.1109/GLOCOM.2015.7417819

Elumalai, P., Murukanantham, P., & Technology, I. (n.d.). *Reliable Data Dissemination for Car Safety Application in VANET.* 1–62.

Emad, I., Kareem, A., & Jantan, A. (2011). An intelligent traffic light monitor system using an adaptive associative memory. *International Journal of Information Processing and Management,* 2(2), 23–39. doi:10.4156/ijipm.vol2.issue2.4

Engineering, C. (2015). *Review on Intelligent Traffic Management System Based on VANET.* 2001–2004.

Engoulou, R. G., Bellaïche, M., Pierre, S., & Quintero, A. (2014). VANET security surveys. *Computer Communications,* 44, 1–13. doi:10.1016/j.comcom.2014.02.020

Estrin, D., Handley, M., Heidemann, J., McCanne, S., Xu, Y., & Yu, H. (1999, November). Network Visualization with the VINT Network Animator Nam. Retrieved from https://pdfs.semanticscholar.org/08e3/c15700c229ab3b91218dd36e1aa902c1922d.pdf

Faghri, A., & Hamad, K. (2002). Application of GPS in Traffic Management Systems. *GPS Solutions,* 5(3), 52–60. doi:10.1007/PL00012899

Fan, K., Wang, J., Wang, X., Li, H., & Yang, Y. (2018). Secure, efficient, and revocable data sharing scheme for vehicular fogs. *Peer-to-Peer Networking and Applications,* 11(4), 766–777. doi:10.100712083-017-0562-8

Fascista, A., & Ciccarese, G. (2016). A localization algorithm based on V2I communications and AOA estimation. *IEEE Signal Processing Letters,* 1–5.

Fazio, P., De Rango, F., Sottile, C., Manzoni, P., & Calafate, C. (2011, March). *A distance vector routing protocol for VANET environment with Dynamic Frequency assignment. In Proceedings 2011 IEEE Wireless Communications and Networking Conference* (pp. 1016–1020). IEEE. doi:10.1109/WCNC.2011.5779274

Feizhou, Z., Xuejun, C., & Dongkai, Y. (2008). Intelligent Scheduling of Public Traffic Vehicles Based on a Hybrid Genetic Algorithm. *Tsinghua Science and Technology,* 13(5), 625–631. doi:10.1016/S1007-0214(08)70103-2

Figueiredo, L., Jesus, I., Machado, J. T., Ferreira, J. R., & De Carvalho, J. M. (2001, August). Towards the development of intelligent transportation systems. In Proceedings 2001 IEEE Intelligent Transportation Systems (Cat. No. 01TH8585) ITSC 2001. (pp. 1206-1211). IEEE. doi:10.1109/ITSC.2001.948835

Fille, E., Legara, T., & Monterola, C. P. (2018). Inferring passenger types from commuter eigentravel matrices. *Transportmetrica B. Transport Dynamics,* 6(3), 230–250. doi:10.1080/21680566.2017.1291377

Fiore, M., Harri, J., Filali, F., & Bonnet, C. (2007, March). Vehicular mobility simulation for VANETs. In *Proceedings 40th Annual Simulation Symposium (ANSS'07)* (pp. 301-309). IEEE. 10.1109/ANSS.2007.44

Fischer, H. J. (2015). Standardization and harmonization activities towards a global C-ITS. In *Vehicular ad hoc Networks* (pp. 23–36). Cham, Switzerland: Springer. doi:10.1007/978-3-319-15497-8_2

Fu, L. P., & Rilett, L. P. (2000). Estimation of time-dependent, stochastic route travel times using artificial neural networks. *Transportation Planning and Technology, 24*(1), 25–48. doi:10.1080/03081060008717659

Fussler, H., Schnaufer, S., Transier, M., & Effelsberg, W. (2007). Vehicular ad-hoc networks: from vision to reality and back. In *Proceedings 2007 Fourth Annual Conference on Wireless on Demand Network Systems and Services*, 80–83. 10.1109/WONS.2007.340477

Gambardella, L. M. (2003). Ant colony optimization for ad-hoc networks. In *The first MICS workshop on routing for Mobile Ad-Hoc Networks*. Zurich, Switzerland.

Gamwarige, S., & Kulasekere, C. (2005). An algorithm for energy driven cluster head rotation in a distributed wireless sensor network. *Proceedings of the International Conference on Information and Automation (ICIA 2005)*, 354-359. Hong Kong, December 15-18.

Gamwarige, S., & Kulasekere, C. (2007). Optimization Of Cluster Head Rotation in Energy Constrained Wireless Sensor Networks. *Proceedings of IEEE Conference on Wireless and Optical Communications Networks*, 1-5. Singapore. July 2-4. 10.1109/WOCN.2007.4284155

Garcia-Santiago, A., Castaneda-Camacho, J., Guerrero-Castellanos, J. F., & Mino-Aguilar, G. (2018, February). Evaluation of AODV and DSDV routing protocols for a FANET: Further results towards robotic vehicle networks. *Proceedings 2018 IEEE 9th Latin American Symposium on Circuits & Systems* (pp. 1-4). IEEE.

Garip, M. T., Kim, P. H., Reiher, P., & Gerla, M. (2017). *INTERLOC: An interference-aware RSSI-based localization and sybil attack detection mechanism for vehicular ad hoc networks*. 1–6. doi:10.1109/ccnc.2017.8013424

Gerla, M., Lee, S., & Su, W. (2000). *On-Demand Multicast Routing Protocol (ODMRP) for Ad Hoc Networks*. Retrieved from draft-ietfmanet-odmrp-02.txt.

Geroliminis, N., Karlaftis, M. G., & Skabardonis, A. (2009). A spatial queuing model for the emergency vehicle districting and location problem. *Transportation Research Part B: Methodological, 43*(7), 798–811. doi:10.1016/j.trb.2009.01.006

Ghaemi, M. S., Agard, B., Trépanier, M., & Nia, V. P. (2017). A visual segmentation method for temporal smart card data. *Transportmetrica A: Transport Science, 13*(5), 381–404. doi:10.1080/23249935.2016.1273273

Ghanim, M. N., & Lebdeh, G. A. (2015). Real-time dynamic transit signal priority optimization for coordinated traffic networks using genetic algorithms and artificial neural networks. *Journal of Intelligent Transport Systems, 19*(4), 327–338. doi:10.1080/15472450.2014.936292

Giang, N. K., Leung, V. C. M., & Lea, R. (2016). On Developing Smart Transportation Applications in Fog Computing Paradigms. *DIVANet '16 Proceedings of the 6th ACM Symposium on Development and Analysis of Intelligent Vehicular Networks and Applications*, 91-98.

Golestan, K., Sattar, F., Karray, F., Kamel, M., & Seifzadeh, S. (2015). Localization in vehicular ad hoc networks using data fusion and V2V communication. Computer Communications. Retrieved from www.elsevier.com/locate/comcom, 1-12

Gómez, A. A., & Mecklenbräuker, C. F. (2016). Dependability of decentralized congestion control for varying VANET density. *IEEE Transactions on Vehicular Technology, 65*(11), 9153–9167. doi:10.1109/TVT.2016.2519598

Gonzalez Gonzalez, H., & Ferré, R. V. (n.d.). *Títol: Study of the protocol for home automation Thread*.

Govindaswamy, V., Blackstone, W., & Balasekaran, G. (2011). Survey of Recent Position Based Routing Mobile Ad-hoc Network Protocols (pp. 467-471). *Proceedings of 2011, UKSim, 13th International Conference on Modelling and Simulation*. 10.1109/UKSIM.2011.95

Gregoriades, A., & Mouskos, K. (2013). Black spots identification through a Bayesian networks quantification of accident risk index. *Transportation Research Part C, Emerging Technologies, 28*, 28–43. doi:10.1016/j.trc.2012.12.008

Grover, J., Jain, A., Singhal, S., & Yadav, A. (2018). Real-Time VANET Applications Using Fog Computing. *Proceedings of First International Conference on Smart System, Innovations, and Computing. Smart Innovation, Systems and Technologies, 79.* Springer, Singapore. 10.1007/978-981-10-5828-8_65

GS1. (2013). EPC ™ Radio-Frequency Identity Protocols Generation-2 UHF RFID. *Specification for RFID Air Interface Protocol for Communications At*, 1–152. doi:10.100740261-017-0531-2

Gubbi, J., Buyya, R., Marusic, S., & Palaniswami, M. (2013). Internet of Things (IoT): A vision, architectural elements, and future directions. *Future Generation Computer Systems, 29*(7), 1645–1660. doi:10.1016/j.future.2013.01.010

Gunther, H. J., Trauer, O., & Wolf, L. (2015, December). The potential of collective perception in vehicular ad-hoc networks. In *Proceedings 2015 14th International Conference on ITS Telecommunications (ITST)* (pp. 1-5). IEEE. 10.1109/ITST.2015.7377190

Guo, J., Peyrin, T., & Poschmann, A. (2000). The PHOTON Lightweight Hash Functions Family. *Crypto*, 222–239. Retrieved from http://dblp.uni-trier.de/db/conf/crypto/crypto2011.html#GuoPP11

Guo, J., Peyrin, T., & Poschmann, A. (2011). The PHOTON family of lightweight hash functions. Lecture Notes in Computer Science (Including Subseries Lecture Notes in Artificial Intelligence and Lecture Notes in Bioinformatics), 6841 LNCS, 222–239. doi:10.1007/978-3-642-22792-9_13

Guo, J., Baugh, J. P., & Wang, S. (2007, May). *A group signature based secure and privacy-preserving vehicular communication framework. In Proceedings 2007 Mobile Networking for Vehicular Environments* (pp. 103–108). IEEE. doi:10.1109/MOVE.2007.4300813

Gu, P., Khatoun, R., Begriche, Y., & Serhrouchni, A. (2017). K-Nearest Neighbours classification based Sybil attack detection in Vehicular networks. In *Proceedings of the 2017 3rd Conference on Mobile and Secure Services, MOBISEC-SERV 2017.* 10.1109/MOBISECSERV.2017.7886565

Gupta, D. N., & Kumar, R. (2019). Lightweight Cryptography: an IoT Perspective, (8), 700–706.

Gupta, L., Jain, R., & Vaszkun, G. (2015, November). Survey of Important Issues in UAV Communication Networks. *IEEE Communications Surveys & Tutorials, 18*(2), 1123-1152. doi: . doi:10.1109/COMST.2015.2495297

Hamdan, S., Hudaib, A., & Awajan, A. (2019). Detecting Sybil attacks in vehicular ad hoc networks. *International Journal of Parallel Emergent and Distributed Systems, 34*, 1–11. doi:10.1080/17445760.2019.1617865

Hamid, B., & El Mokhtar, E. N. (2015, December). Performance analysis of the Vehicular Ad hoc Networks (VANET) routing protocols AODV, DSDV, and OLSR. In *Proceedings 2015 5th International Conference on Information & Communication Technology and Accessibility (ICTA)* (pp. 1-6). IEEE.

Ham, Y., Han, K. K., Lin, J. J., & Golparvar-Fard, M. (2016). Visual monitoring of civil infrastructure systems via camera-equipped unmanned aerial vehicles (UAVs): A review of related works. *Visualization in Engineering, 4*(1), 1. doi:10.118640327-015-0029-z

Hartenstein, H., & Laberteaux, K. (2010). *VANET: vehicular applications and inter-networking technologies* (Vol. 1). Chichester, UK: Wiley. doi:10.1002/9780470740637

Hartenstein, H., & Laberteaux, L. P. (2008). A tutorial survey on vehicular ad hoc networks. *IEEE Communications Magazine, 46*(6), 164–171. doi:10.1109/MCOM.2008.4539481

Hasnat, M. A., Haque, M. M., & Khan, M. (2006). GIS Based Real Time Traveler Information System: An Efficient Approach to Minimize Travel Time Using Available Media. Retrieved from www.bracu.ac.bd

Hatem, B. A., & Habib, H. (2009). Bus Management System Using RFID In WSN, in the *proceedings of European and Mediterranean Conference on Information Systems*, Abu Dhabi, UAE. Academic Press.

Hayat, S., Yanmaz, E., & Muzaffar, R. (2016). Survey on Unmanned Aerial Vehicle Networks for Civil Applications: A Communications Viewpoint. *IEEE Communications Surveys and Tutorials*, *18*(4), 2624–2661. doi:10.1109/COMST.2016.2560343

He, Z., & Zhang, Q. (2009). Public Transport Dispatch and Decision Support System Based on Multi-Agent. *In the proceedings of Second International Conference on Intelligent Computation Technology and Automation*, Zhangjiajie, China.

Heinzelman, W. B. (2000). Application-specific protocol architectures for wireless networks [Ph.D. dissertation]. Massachusetts Institute of Technology, Cambridge, MA.

Heinzelman, W. B., Chandrakasan, A. P., & Balakrishnan, H. (2002). An application-specific protocol architecture for wireless microsensor networks. *IEEE Transactions on Wireless Communications*, *1*(4), 660–670. doi:10.1109/TWC.2002.804190

Heinzelman, W. R., Chandrakasan, A., & Balakrishnan, H. (2000). Energy-efficient communication protocol for wireless microsensor networks. *Proceedings of IEEE International Conference on System Sciences*. 10-20. Hawaii, January 4-7. 10.1109/HICSS.2000.926982

He, L., Agard, B., & Trépanier, M. (2018). A classification of public transit users with smart card data based on time series distance metrics and a hierarchical clustering method. *Transportmetrica A: Transport Science*, 1–20.

Hernandez, J. Z., Ossowski, S., & Serrano, G. A. (2002). Multiagent Architectures for Intelligent Traffic Management Systems. *Transportation Research Part C, Emerging Technologies*, *10*(5-6), 473–506. doi:10.1016/S0968-090X(02)00032-3

Hezam Al Junaid, M. A., Syed, A. A., Mohd Warip, M. N., Fazira Ku Azir, K. N., & Romli, N. H. (2018). Classification of Security Attacks in VANET: A Review of Requirements and Perspectives. *MATEC Web of Conferences, 150*, 1–7. 10.1051/matecconf/201815006038

Hickman, J., & Hanowski, R. J. (2011). Use of a video monitoring approach to reduce at-risk driving behaviors in commercial vehicle operations. *Transportation Research Part F: Traffic Psychology and Behaviour*, *14*(3), 189–198. doi:10.1016/j.trf.2010.11.010

Hoang, G.-M., Denis, B., H"arri, J., & Slock, D. T. M. (2017). Robust Data Fusion for Cooperative Vehicular Localization in Tunnels. In *Proceedings IEEE Intelligent Vehicles Symposium (IV)*, 1372-1377. 10.1109/IVS.2017.7995902

Hoebeke, J., Moerman, I., Dhoedt, B., & Demeester, P. (2004). An overview of mobile ad hoc networks: Applications and challenges. *Journal-Communications Network*, *3*(3), 60–66.

Hofmann-Wellenhof, B., Lichtenegger, H., & Collins, J. (2012). *Global positioning system: theory and practice*. Springer Science & Business Media.

Ho, I. W. H., Leung, K. K., Polak, J. W., & Mangharam, R. (2007). Node Connectivity in Vehicular Ad Hoc Networks with Structured Mobility. In *Proceedings 32nd IEEE Conference on Local Computer Networks (LCN 2007)*, 635–642. 10.1109/LCN.2007.22

Hossain, M., & Muromachi, Y. (2012). A Bayesian network based framework for real-time crash prediction on the basic freeway segments of urban expressways, *Accident Analysis and Prevention*, *45*, 373–381. PMID:22269521

Hou, X., Li, Y., Chen, M., Wu, D., Jin, D., & Chen, S. (2016). Vehicular Fog Computing: A Viewpoint of Vehicles as the Infrastructures. *IEEE Transactions on Vehicular Technology, 65*(6), 3860–3873. doi:10.1109/TVT.2016.2532863

Huang, C., Lu, R., & Choo, K. K. R. (2017). Vehicular Fog Computing. *Architecture, Use Case, and Security and Forensic Challenges. IEEE Communications Magazine, 55*(11), 105–111.

Hu, P., Dhelim, S., Ning, H., & Qui, T. (2017). Survey on fog computing: Architecture, key technologies, applications and open issues. *Journal of Network and Computer Applications, 98*, 27–42. doi:10.1016/j.jnca.2017.09.002

Hussain, R., Sharma, S., Sharma, V., & Sharma, S. (2013). WSN applications: Automated intelligent traffic control system using sensors. *International Journal of Soft Computing and Engineering, 3*(3), 77–81.

IHS Technology. (2016). IoT platforms: enabling the Internet of Things. *IHS Technology, Whitepaper*(March), 1–19.

Indra, A., & Murali, R. (2014). Routing Protocols for Vehicular Adhoc Networks (VANETs). *RE:view, 5*(1).

Ingelrest, F., Simplot-Ryl, D., & Stojmenovic, I. (2006). Optimal Transmission Radius for Energy Efficient Broadcasting Protocols in Ad Hoc Networks. *IEEE Transactions on Parallel and Distributed Systems, 17*(6), 536–547. doi:10.1109/TPDS.2006.74

Issariyakul, T., & Hossain, E. (2011). *Introduction to network simulator NS2*. Springer Science & Business Media.

Jagadeesh, G. R., Srikanthan, T., & Zhang, X. D. (2004). A Map Matching Method for GPS Based Real-Time Vehicle Location. *The Journal of Navigation, 57*, 429–440.

Jánošíková, L., Slavík, J., & Koháni, M. (2014). Estimation of a route choice model for urban public transport using smart card data. *Transportation Planning and Technology, 37*(7), 638–648. doi:10.1080/03081060.2014.935570

Jarašūnienė, A. (2007). Research into Intelligent Transport systems: Technologies and efficiency. *Transport, 22*(2), 61–67. doi:10.3846/16484142.2007.9638100

Jayapal, C., & Roy, S. S. (2016, March). Road traffic congestion management using VANET. In *Proceedings 2016 International Conference on Advances in Human Machine Interaction (HMI)* (pp. 1-7). IEEE.

Jhariya, M. K., Shukla, P. K., & Barskhar, R. (2014) Assessment of Different Attacks and Security Schemes in Vehicular Ad-hoc Network, *International Journal of Computer Applications 98*(22), 24-28.

Jiang, D., & Delgrossi, L. (2008). IEEE 802.11p: Towards an International Standard for Wireless Access in Vehicular Environments, *IEEE Vehicular Technology Conference*, 2036–2040.

Johnson, D. B., Maltz, D. A., & Broch, J. (2001). DSR: The dynamic source routing protocol for multi-hop wireless ad hoc networks. *Ad Hoc Networks, 5*, 139–172.

Junod, P. (1999). Cryptographic secure pseudo-random bits generation: The Blum-Blum-Shub generator. *Unpublished*, (August). Retrieved from http://tlapixqui.izt.uam.mx/sem_cripto/sucesiones/CryptoSecureRandomBits.pdf

Kafi, A. M., Challal, Y., Djenouri, D., Bouabdallah, A., Khelladi, L., & Badache, N. (2012). A study of wireless sensor network architectures and projects for traffic light monitoring. In *Proceedings International Conference on Ambient Systems, Networks and Technologies*, 543–552. 10.1016/j.procs.2012.06.069

Kai, K., Cong, W., & Tao, L. (2016). Fog computing for vehicular Ad-hoc networks: Paradigms, scenarios, and issues. *Journal of China Universities of Posts and Telecommunications, 23*(2), 56–65, 96. doi:10.1016/S1005-8885(16)60021-3

Kaleem, M., Hussain, S. A., Raza, I., Chaudhry, S. R., & Raza, M. H. (2014). A direction and relative speed (DARS) based routing protocol for VANETs in a highway scenario. *Taylor Francis Journal of the Chinese Institute of Engineers, 38*(3), 399-405.

Karagiannis, G., Altintas, O., Ekici, E., Heijenk, G., Jarupan, B., Lin, K., & Weil, T. (2011). Vehicular networking: A survey and tutorial on requirements, architectures, challenges, standards and solutions. *IEEE Communications Surveys and Tutorials, 13*(4), 584–616. doi:10.1109/SURV.2011.061411.00019

Karnadi, F. K., Mo, Z. H., & Lan, K. C. (2007). Rapid generation of realistic mobility models for VANET. In *Proceedings IEEE Wireless Communications and Networking Conference, WCNC*, 2508–2513. 10.1109/WCNC.2007.467

Karp, B., & Kung, H. T. (2000). GPSR: greedy perimeter stateless routing for wireless networks. *MobiCom 00 proceedings of the 6th annual international conference on mobile computing and networking*, 243-254. 10.1145/345910.345953

Keith, J. (2001). Video Demystified: a handbook for the digital engineering, 3rd edition. Eagle Rock, VA: LLH Technology Publishing.

Kejun, L., Yong, L., & Xiangwu, L. (2008). Emergency Accident Rescue System in Freeway Based on GIS, in the *proceedings of International Conference on Intelligent Computation Technology and Automation. Academic Press.*

Khalid, A. S., Khateeb, A., Jaiz, A. Y., Johari Wajdi, F., & Khateeb, A. (2008). Dynamic Traffic Light Sequence, Science Publications. *Journal of Computational Science, 4*(7), 517–524. doi:10.3844/jcssp.2008.517.524

Khan, A. A., Abolhasan, M., & Ni, W. (2018). 5G Next generation VANETs using SDN and Fog Computing Framework. Proceedings 2018 15th IEEE Annual Consumer Communications & Networking Conference (CCNC) (pp. 1-6). IEEE.

Khan, M. A., Khan, I. U., Safi, A., & Quershi, I. M. (2018). Dynamic routing in flying ad-hoc networks using topology-based routing protocols. *Drones, 2*(3), 27. doi:10.3390/drones2030027

Khan, M. A., Safi, A., Qureshi, I. M., & Khan, I. U. (2017, November). Flying ad-hoc networks (FANETs): A review of communication architectures, and routing protocols. *Proc. 1st Int. Conf. Latest Trends Elect. Eng. Comput. Technol. (INTELLECT)*, pp. 1-9. Karachi, Pakistan. IEEE. 10.1109/INTELLECT.2017.8277614

Khan, R., Khan, S. U., Zaheer, R., & Khan, S. (2012). Future internet: The internet of things architecture, possible applications and key challenges. *Proceedings - 10th International Conference on Frontiers of Information Technology, FIT 2012*, 257–260. 10.1109/FIT.2012.53

Khan, S., Parkinson, S., & Qin, Y. (2017) Fog computing security: a review of current applications and security solutions, *Journal of Cloud Computing, 6*(19).

Khan, M. (2016, December). Cross layer design approach for congestion control in MANETs. In *Proceedings 2016 IEEE International Conference on Advances in Electronics, Communication and Computer Technology (ICAECCT)* (pp. 464-468). IEEE. 10.1109/ICAECCT.2016.7942633

Khasawneh, A., Latiff, M., Kaiwartya, O., & Chizari, H. (2018). A reliable energy-efficient pressure-based routing protocol for underwater wireless sensor network. *Wireless Networks, 24*(6), 2061–2075. doi:10.100711276-017-1461-x

Khattab, A., Fahmy, Y. A., & Abdel Wahab, A. (2016). High Accuracy GPS-Free Vehicle Localization Framework via an INS-Assisted Single RSU. *International Journal of Distributed Sensor Networks,* Hindawi Publishing Corporation, 1-16.

Khelifi, H., Luo, S., Nour, B., & Shah, S. C. (2018). Security and privacy issues in vehicular named data networks: An overview. *Mobile Information Systems, 2018*, 1–11. doi:10.1155/2018/5672154

Kikuchi, S. (2009). Artificial intelligence in transportation analysis: Approaches, methods, and applications. *Transportation Research Part C, Emerging Technologies, 17*(5), 455. doi:10.1016/j.trc.2009.04.002

Kimura, N., & Latifi, S. (2005). A survey on data compression in wireless sensor networks. *Proceedings of IEEE International Conference on Information Technology: Coding and computing*, 8-13. Nevada, April 4-6. 10.1109/ITCC.2005.43

Ko, Y. B., & Vaidya, N. H. (1998). Location-aided routing (LAR) in mobile ad-hoc networks. In *Proceedings of ACM/ IEEE MOBICOM'98*, 66 –75. IEEE.

Ko, Y. B., & Vaidya, N. H. (2000). Location-aided routing (LAR) in mobile ad-hoc networks. *International Journal of Wireless Networks, 6*(4), 307–321.

Kolte, S. R., & Madankar, M. S. (2014). Adaptive congestion control for transmission of safety messages in VANET. In *Proceedings 2014 International Conference for Convergence of Technology (I2CT)*, pp. 1-5. IEEE. 10.1109/ I2CT.2014.7092177

Kshirsagar, N., & Sutar, U. S. (2015). *An Intelligent Traffic Management and Accident Prevention System based on VANET, 4*(7), 2013–2015.

Kui, X., Sun, Y., Zhang, S., & Li, Y. (2018). Characterizing the Capability of Vehicular Fog Computing in Large-scale Urban Environment. *Mobile Networks and Applications, 23*(4), 1050–1067. doi:10.100711036-017-0969-8

Kuklinski, S., Matei, A., & Wolny, G. (2010, June). NGVN: A framework for Next Generation Vehicular Networks. In *Proceedings 2010 8th International Conference on Communications* (pp. 297-300). IEEE. 10.1109/ICCOMM.2010.5509082

Kumar Karn, C., & Prakash Gupta, C. (2016). A Survey on VANETs Security Attacks and Sybil Attack Detection. *International Journal of Sensors, Wireless Communications and Control, 6*(1), 45–62. doi:10.2174/22103279059991 51103170103

Kumar, P., Kataria, H. S., & Ghosh, T. (2015). Congestion control approach by reducing the number of messages in VANET. In 2015 4th International Conference on Reliability, Infocom Technologies, and Optimization (ICRITO) (Trends and Future Directions), pp. 1-5. IEEE. 10.1109/ICRITO.2015.7359297

Kumar, S., & Raw, S. R. (2018, March 14-16). Flying Ad-Hoc Networks (FANETs): Current State, Challenges, and Potentials. In 12th INDIACom-2018; 5th International Conference on Computing for Sustainable Global Development, BVICAM, New Delhi, India.

Kumar, S., Bansal, A., & Raw, S. R. (2018, December 22-24). Health Monitoring Planning for On-board Ships through Flying Ad-hoc Network. In *3rd International Conference on Advanced Computing and Intelligent Engineering*, Siksha 'O' Anusandhan Deemed to be University, Bhubaneswar, India.

Kumar, V., & Kumar, S. (2015). Position based beaconless routing in wireless sensor networks. *International Journal Wireless Personal Communication, 86*(2), 1061-1085.

Kumar, H., & Singh, P. (2014, February). TCP congestion control with delay minimization in MANET. In *Proceedings International Conference on Information Communication and Embedded Systems (ICICES2014)* (pp. 1-6). IEEE. 10.1109/ICICES.2014.7033929

Kumar, P., Singh, V., & Reddy, D. (1999). Advanced Traveler Information System for Hyderabad City. *IEEE Transactions on Intelligent Transportation Systems, 6*(1), 26–37. doi:10.1109/TITS.2004.838179

Kumar, R., & Goyal, R. (2019). On Cloud security requirements, threats, vulnerabilities, and countermeasures: A survey. *Computer Science Review. Elsevier Journal, 33*, 1–48.

Kumar, S., Basavaraju, T., & Puttamadappa, C. (2008). *Ad-hoc Mobile Wireless Networks Principles, Protocols, and Applications*. New York: Auerbach Publications.

Kumar, V., Mishra, S., & Chand, N. (2013). Applications of VANETs: Present & future. *Communications and Network*, 5(1), 12–15. doi:10.4236/cn.2013.51B004

Kuutti, S., Fallah, S., Katsaros, K., Dianati, M., Mccullough, F., & Mouzakitis, A. (2018). A survey of the state-of-the-art localization techniques and their potentials for autonomous vehicle applications. *IEEE Internet of Things Journal*, 5(2), 829–846. doi:10.1109/JIOT.2018.2812300

Kwon, B. W., Kang, J., & Park, J. H. (2019). A Fog Computing-Based Automotive Data Overload Protection System with Real-Time Analysis. In J. Park, V. Loia, K. K. Choo, & G. Yi (Eds.), *Advanced Multimedia and Ubiquitous Engineering. MUE 2018, FutureTech 2018. Lecture Notes in Electrical Engineering* (Vol. 518). Singapore: Springer. doi:10.1007/978-981-13-1328-8_89

Lagraa, N., Yagoubi, M. B., & Benkouider, S. (2010). Localization technique in VANets using Clustering (LVC). *IJCSI International Journal of Computer Science*, 7, 4-9.

Lazarescu, M. T. (2013). Design of a WSN platform for long-term environmental monitoring for IoT applications. *IEEE Journal on Emerging and Selected Topics in Circuits and Systems*, 3(1), 45–54. doi:10.1109/JETCAS.2013.2243032

Lèbre, M.-A., Le Mouël, F., Ménard, E., Dillschneider, J., & Denis, R. (2014). *VANET Applications: Hot Use Cases*. Retrieved from https://arxiv.org/abs/1407.4088

Lee, J., & Gerla, M. (2000). AODV-BR: Backup routing in Ad Hoc networks. *Proceedings of IEEE, WCNC*. 10.1109/WCNC.2000.904822

Lee, K. C., Lee, U., & Gerla, M. (2010). Survey of routing protocols in vehicular ad hoc networks. In Proceedings *Advances in vehicular ad-hoc networks: Developments and challenges* (pp. 149–170). IGI Global. doi:10.4018/978-1-61520-913-2.ch008

Lee, S., Gahng-Seop,, A., Zhang,, X.,, & Campbell,, A. (2000). INSIGNIA: An IP-based Quality of Service Framework for Mobile Ad-hoc Networks (pp. 374-406). Journal of Parallel and Distributed Computing8. Scalability study of the ad hoc on-demand distance vector routing protocol (pp. 97-114). *International Journal of Network Management*, 13.

Leonov, A. V. (2016). Application of bee colony algorithm for FANET routing. *17th International Conference of Young Specialists on Micro/Nanotechnologies and Electron Devices (EDM)*, Erlagol, Russia, pp. 124–132. Retrieved from 10.1109/EDM.2016.7538709

Leonov, A. V., & Litvinov, G. A. (2018). Simulation-Based Packet Delivery Performance Evaluation with Different Parameters in Flying Ad-Hoc Network (FANET) using AODV and OLSR. *International Conference Information Technologies in Business and Industry*. 10.1088/1742-6596/1015/3/032178

Levin, M., & Boyles, S. (2016). A cell transmission model for dynamic lane reversal with autonomous vehicles. *Transportation Research Part C, Emerging Technologies*, 68, 126–143. doi:10.1016/j.trc.2016.03.007

Levin, M., & Boyles, S. (2016). A multiclass cell transmission model for shared human and autonomous vehicle roads. *Transportation Research*, 62(part C), 103–106.

Liang, W., Li, Z., Zhang, H., Sun, Y., & Bie, R. (2015). Vehicular ad hoc networks: Architectures, Research issues, Challenges, and trends. *International Journal of Distributed Sensor Networks*, 2015(1)(1), 1–11. doi:10.1155/2015/745303

Liang, L., Peng, H., Li, G. Y., & Shen, X. (2017). Vehicular communications: A physical layer perspective. *IEEE Transactions on Vehicular Technology*, 66(12), 647–659. doi:10.1109/TVT.2017.2750903

Liao, S., Li, J., Wu, J., Yang, W., & Guan, Z. (2018). *Fog-Enabled Vehicle as a Service for Computing Geographical Migration in Smart Cities. IEEE Access, 7,* 8726–8736.

Li, D., Miwa, T., & Morikawa, T. (2016). Modeling time-of-day car use behavior: A Bayesian network approach. *Transportation Research Part D, Transport and Environment, 47,* 54–66. doi:10.1016/j.trd.2016.04.011

Li, F., & Wang, Y. (2007). Routing in vehicular ad hoc networks: A survey. *IEEE Vehicular Technology Magazine, 2*(2), 12–22. doi:10.1109/MVT.2007.912927

Li, J., Liu, X., Pang, Y., & Zhu, W. (2014, June). A Novel DSR-based Protocol for Small Reconnaissance UAV Ad Hoc Network. *Applied Mechanics and Materials, 568-570,* 1272–1277. doi:10.4028/www.scientific.net/AMM.568-570.1272

Lilien, L. T., ben Othmane, L., Angin, P., DeCarlo, A., Salih, R. M., & Bhargava, B. (2013, May). A simulation study of ad hoc networking of UAVs with opportunistic resource utilization networks. *Journal of Network and Computer Applications, 38,* 3–15.

Li, M., Zhu, L., & Lin, X. (2019). *Efficient and Privacy-Preserving Carpooling Using Blockchain-Assisted Vehicular Fog Computing. IEEE Internet of Things Journal, 6*(3), 4573–4584.

Lin, D., & Wang, Q. (2019). An Energy-Efficient Clustering Algorithm Combined Game Theory and Dual-Cluster-Head Mechanism for WSNs. *IEEE Access: Practical Innovations, Open Solutions, 7,* 49894–49905. doi:10.1109/AC-CESS.2019.2911190

Lin, X., Lu, R., Zhang, C., Zhu, H., Ho, P. H., & Shen, X. (2008). *Security in Vehicular Ad Hoc Networks. IEEE Communications Magazine, 46*(4), 88–95.

Li, S., Da Xu, L., & Zhao, S. (2018). 5G Internet of Things: A survey. *Journal of Industrial Information Integration, 10,* 1–9. doi:10.1016/j.jii.2018.01.005

Liu, H., Yao, G., Wu, J., & Shi, L. (2010). An adaptive energy-efficient and low-latency MAC protocol for wireless sensor networks. *IEEE Journal of Communications and Networks, 12*(5), 510–517. doi:10.1109/JCN.2010.6388497

Liu, J., Li, J., Zhang, L., Dai, F., Zhang, Y., Meng, X., & Shen, J. (2017). Secure intelligent traffic light control using fog computing. *Future Generation Computer Systems, 78*(Part 2), 817–824.

Liu, J., Wan, J., Wang, Q., Deng, P., Zhou, K., & Qiao, Y. (2016). A survey on position-based routing for vehicular ad hoc networks. *Telecommunication Systems, 62*(1), 15–30. doi:10.100711235-015-9979-7

Liu, K., Lim, H. B., Frazzoli, E., Ji, H., & Lee, V. C. S. (2014). Improving Positioning Accuracy Using GPS Pseudo range Measurements for Cooperative Vehicular Localization. *IEEE Transactions on Vehicular Technology, 63*(6), 2544–2556. doi:10.1109/TVT.2013.2296071

Liu, P., Chen, A. Y., Huang, Y.-N., Han, J.-Y., Lai, J.-S., Kang, S.-C., ... Tsai, M. (2014). A review of rotorcraft unmanned aerial vehicle (UAV) developments and applications in civil engineering. *Smart Structures and Systems, 13*(6), 1065–1094. doi:10.12989ss.2014.13.6.1065

Liu, X. (2012). A survey on clustering routing protocols in wireless sensor networks. *Sensors Journal, 12*(8), 11113–11153. doi:10.3390120811113 PMID:23112649

Liu, Y., & Cheng, T. (2018). Understanding public transit patterns with open geodemographics to facilitate public transport planning. *Transportmetrica A: Transport Science,* 1–28.

Liu, Y., Zhang, Q., & Lionel, N. (2010). Opportunity-based topology control in wireless sensor networks. *IEEE Transactions on Parallel and Distributed Systems, 21*(3), 405–416. doi:10.1109/TPDS.2009.57

Lobo, F., Grael, D., Oliveira, H., Villas, L., Almehmadi, A., & El-Khatib, K. (2019). Cooperative Localization Improvement Using Distance Information in Vehicular Ad Hoc Networks. *International Journal of Sensors,* 1-27. Retrieved from www.mdpi.com/journal/sensors

Local Authority Guide to Emerging Transport Technology, the Institution of Engineering and Technology and ITS (UK), 2014. Retrieved from http://www.its-uk.org

Lochert, C., Scheuermann, B., & Mauve, M. (2007). A Survey on Congestion Control for Mobile Ad-Hoc Networks Wiley. *Wireless Communications and Mobile Computing, 7*(5), 655–676. doi:10.1002/wcm.524

Lochin, E., Jourjon, G., Ardon, S., & Sénac, P. (2010). Promoting the use of reliable rate-based transport protocols: the Chameleon protocol.

Logi, F., & Ritchie, S. G. (2001). Development and Evaluation of a Knowledge-Based System for Traffic Congestion Management and Control. *Transportation Research Part C, Emerging Technologies, 9*(6), 433–459. doi:10.1016/S0968-090X(01)00002-X

Lu, R., Lin, X., Zhu, H., & Shen, X. (2009, April). SPARK: A new VANET-based smart parking scheme for large parking lots. In Proceedings IEEE INFOCOM 2009 (pp. 1413-1421). IEEE. doi:10.1109/INFCOM.2009.5062057

Lu, G., Krishnamachari, B., & Raghavendra, C. S. (2004). An adaptive energy efficient and low-latency Mac for data gathering in wireless sensor networks. *Proceedings of IEEE Parallel and Distributed Processing Symposium,* 224-30. New Mexico, Apr. 26-30.

Luo, H., Lu, S., Bharghavan, V., Cheng, I., & Zhong, G. (2004). *A Packet Scheduling Approach to QoS Support in Multi-hop Wireless Networks* (pp. 193-206). International Journal of Mobile Networks and Applications.

Luo, Y., Zhang, W., & Hu, Y. (2010, April). A new cluster-based routing protocol for VANET. In *Proceedings 2010 Second International Conference on Networks Security, Wireless Communications, and Trusted Computing* (Vol. 1, pp. 176-180). IEEE. 10.1109/NSWCTC.2010.48

Lu, T., Chang, S., & Li, W. (2018). Fog computing enabling geographic routing for urban area vehicular network. *Peer-to-Peer Networking and Applications, 11*(4), 749–775. doi:10.100712083-017-0560-x

Ma, G., & Tao, Z. (2013). A Hybrid Energy- and Time-Driven Cluster Head Rotation Strategy for Distributed Wireless Sensor Networks. *International Journal of Distributed Sensor Networks, 6*(1), 21–32. doi:10.1155/2013/109307

Mahajan, S., Malhotra, J., & Sharma, S. (2014). An energy balanced QoS based cluster head selection strategy for WSN. *Egyptian Informatics Journal, 15*(3), 189–199. doi:10.1016/j.eij.2014.09.001

Mahmoud, A., Noureldin, A., & Hassanein, H. S. (2015). VANETs Positioning in Urban Environments: A Novel Cooperative Approach. In *Proceedings Vehicular Technology Conference (VTC),* 1-7. IEEE. 10.1109/VTCFall.2015.7391188

Mai, Y., Rodriguez, F. M., & Wang, N. (2018, January). CC-ADOV: An effective multiple paths congestion control AODV. In *Proceedings 2018 IEEE 8th Annual Computing and Communication Workshop and Conference (CCWC)* (pp. 1000-1004). IEEE.

Maimut, D., & Ouafi, K. (2012). Lightweight cryptography for RFID tags. *IEEE Security and Privacy, 10*(2), 76–79. doi:10.1109/MSP.2012.43

Malik, T., Yi, S., & Hongchi, S. (2007). Adaptive traffic light control with wireless sensor networks. In *Proceedings of IEEE Consumer Communications and Networking Conference,* pp. 187–191, Las Vegas, NV: IEEE.

Manayankath, S., Srinivasan, C., Sethumadhavan, M., & Megha Mukundan, P. (2016). Hash-One: A lightweight cryptographic hash function. *IET Information Security, 10*(5), 225–231. doi:10.1049/iet-ifs.2015.0385

Mandal, K., Fan, X., & Gong, G. (2016). Warbler: A Lightweight Pseudorandom Number Generator for EPC C1 Gen2 Passive RFID Tags. *International Journal of RFID Security and Cryptography, 2*(2), 82–91. doi:10.20533/ijrfidsc.2046.3715.2013.0011

Mariagrazia, D., Pia, F. M., & Carlo, M. (2003). Real time traffic signal control: application to coordinated intersections. In IEEE International Conference on Systems, Man and Cybernetics, vol. 4, 3288-3295. Washington, DC: IEEE.

Martinez, F. J., Cano, J.-C., Calafate, C. T., & Manzoni, P. (2009). A performance evaluation of warning message dissemination in 802.11 p based VANETs. In *Proceedings 2009 IEEE 34th Conference on Local Computer Networks,* pp. 221-224. IEEE.

Martín, H., Millán, E. S., Entrena, L., Céstro, J. C. H., & López, P. P. (2011). AKARI-X: A pseudorandom number generator for secure lightweight systems. *Proceedings of the 2011 IEEE 17th International On-Line Testing Symposium, IOLTS 2011,* 228–233. 10.1109/IOLTS.2011.5994534

Maurer, U., Renner, R., & Holenstein, C. (2004). Indifferentiability, Impossibility Results on Reductions, and Applications to the Random Oracle Methodology, (20), 21–39. doi:10.1007/978-3-540-24638-1_2

Mautz, R. (2012). Indoor Positioning Technologies. Institute of Geodesy and Photogrammetry, Department of Civil, Environmental, and Geomatic Engineering, ETH Zurich.

Mecklenbrauker, C. F., Molisch, A. F., Karedal, J., Tufvesson, F., Paier, A., Bernadó, L., ... & Czink, N. (2011). Vehicular Channel Characterization and Its Implications for Wireless System Design and Performance. *Proceedings of the IEEE, 99*(7), 1189–1212.

Melia-Segui, J., Garcia-Alfaro, J., & Herrera-Joancomarti, J. (2010). Analysis and improvement of a pseudorandom number generator for EPC Gen2 tags. Lecture Notes in Computer Science (Including Subseries Lecture Notes in Artificial Intelligence and Lecture Notes in Bioinformatics), 6054 LNCS, 34–46. doi:10.1007/978-3-642-14992-4_4

Melià-Seguí, J., Garcia-Alfaro, J., & Herrera-Joancomartí, J. (2013). J3Gen: A PRNG for low-cost passive RFID. *Sensors (Switzerland), 13*(3), 3816–3830. doi:10.3390130303816 PMID:23519344

Menon, V. G. (2017). Moving From Vehicular Cloud Computing to Vehicular Fog Computing: Issues and Challenges. *International Journal on Computer Science and Engineering, 9*(2).

Menouar, H., Lenardi, M., & Filali, F. (2007).Movement Prediction-Based Routing (MOPR) Concept for Position-Based Routing in Vehicular Networks. In *Proceedings IEEE International conference on vehicular technology conference,* 556-561. IEEE.

Menouar, H., Filali, F., & Lenardi, M. (2006). A survey and qualitative analysis of MAC protocols for vehicular ad hoc networks. *IEEE Wireless Communications, 13*(5), 30–35. doi:10.1109/WC-M.2006.250355

Messelodi, S., Modena, C. M., Zanin, M., De Natale, F. G. B., Granelli, F., Betterle, E., & Guarise, A. (2009). Intelligent extended floating car data collection. *Expert Systems with Applications, 36*(3, Part 1), 4213–4227. doi:10.1016/j.eswa.2008.04.008

Ming-Fong Tsai, Po-Ching Wang, Ce-Kuen Shieh ·Wen-Shyang Hwang, Naveen Chilamkurti, Seungmin Rho& Yang Sun Lee(2015).Improving positioning accuracy for VANET in real city environments. Springer Science+Business Media,1975–1995.

Mittal, P., & Ahlawat, D. (2016). Sybil Node Detection Using Neighbourhood Information Passing. *International Journal of Computer Science and Mobile Computing, 5*(8), 230–240.

Mohamed, S. A. E. (2013). Smart Street Lighting Control and Monitoring System for Electrical Power Saving by Using VANET. *International Journal of Communications, Network, and System Sciences, 6*(8), 351–360. doi:10.4236/ijcns.2013.68038

Molina, M. (2005). An Intelligent Assistant for Public Transport Management. In *Proceedings of International Conference on Intelligent Computing*, LNCS 3645, 199-208, Hefei, China: Springer.

Mondal, A., & Mitra, S. (2014). Dynamic and distributed channel congestion control strategy in VANET. In *Proceedings 2014 International Conference on Advances in Computing, Communications, and Informatics (ICACCI)*, pp. 1697-1703. IEEE. 10.1109/ICACCI.2014.6968382

Mouhcine, E., Khalifa, M., & Mohamed, Y. (2018). Solving Traffic Routing System using VANet Strategy Combined with a Distributed Swarm Intelligence Optimization.

Moustafa, H., & Zhang, Y. (2009). *Vehicular Networks: Techniques, Standards, and Applications*. Boca Raton, FL: CRC Press.

Mughal, B. M., Wagan, A. A., & Hasbullah, H. (2010). Efficient congestion control in VANET for safety messaging. In *Proceedings 2010 International Symposium in Information Technology (ITSim)*, vol. 2, pp. 654-659. IEEE. 10.1109/ITSIM.2010.5561609

Mulay, S. A., Dhekne, C. S., Bapat, R. M., Budukh, T. U., & Gadgil, S. D. (2013). Intelligent City Traffic Management and Public Transportation System. *International Journal of Computer Science Issues, 10*(3), 46–50.

Muller, M. (2012). Flying Adhoc Network. In *Proceedings of the 4th Seminar on Research Trends in Media Informatics*. Institute of Media Informatics, Ulm University.

Murthy, C., & Manoj, B. (2004). *Ad-hoc Wireless Networks Architectures and Protocols* (p. 07458). Upper Saddle River, NJ: Prentice Hall.

Nabil, M., Hajami, A., & Haqiq, A. (2019). Predicting the Route of the Longest Lifetime and the Data Packet Delivery Time between Two Vehicles in VANET. *Mobile Information Systems Volume 2019, Article ID 2741323.* . doi:10.1155/2019/2741323

Naguib, A., Pakzad, P., Palanki, R., Poduri, S., & Chen, Y. (2013). Scalable and Accurate Indoor Positioning on Mobile Devices. In *Proceedings International Conference on Indoor Positioning and Indoor Navigation*, 1-10. IEEE. 10.1109/IPIN.2013.6817856

Namarpreet, K., & Aman, A. (2015). A review on security issues in VANET. *International Journal of Advanced Research in Computer Science, 6*(2), 161–165.

Nath, S. B., Gupta, H., Chakraborty, S., & Ghosh, S. K. (2018). A Survey of Fog Computing and Communication: Current Researches and Future Directions, Networking and Internet Architecture. *arXiv:1804.04365.*

Nayyar, A. (2018, August). Flying Adhoc Network (FANETs): Simulation Based Performance Comparison of Routing Protocols: AODV, DSDV, DSR, OLSR, AOMDV, and HWMP. *Proceedings International Conference on Advances in Big Data, Computing, and Data Communication Systems (icABCD). IEEE.* 10.1109/ICABCD.2018.8465130

Neamatollahi, P., Taheri, H., Naghibzadeh, M., & Abrishami, S. (2014). A distributed clustering scheme for wireless sensor networks. *Proceedings of IEEE Conference on Information and Knowledge Technology (IKT)*, 20-24. Shahrood, Iran, May 27-29. 10.1109/IKT.2014.7030326

Neamatollahi, P., Naghibzadeh, M., Abrishami, S., & Yaghmaee, M. (2018). Distributed Clustering-Task Scheduling for WSNs Using Dynamic Hyper Round Policy. *IEEE Transactions on Mobile Computing*, *17*(2), 334–347. doi:10.1109/TMC.2017.2710050

Neisse, R., Steri, G., Fovino, I. N., & Baldini, G. (2015). SecKit: A Model-based Security Toolkit for the Internet of Things. *Computers & Security*, *54*, 60–76. doi:10.1016/j.cose.2015.06.002

Nellore, K., & Hancke, G. P. (2016). *Traffic Management for Emergency Vehicle Priority Based on Visual Sensing.* doi:10.339016111892

Nguyen, T. D. T., Nguyen, T. D., Nguyen, V. D., Pham, X. Q., & Huh, E. N. (2018). Cost-Effective Resource Sharing in an Internet of Vehicles-Employed Mobile Edge Computing Environment. *Symmetry*, *10*(11), 594. doi:10.3390ym10110594

Ni, D., Huang, H., & Zheng, L. (2015). Support vector machine in crash prediction at the level of traffic analysis zones: Assessing the spatial proximity effects. *Accident; Analysis, and Prevention*, *82*, 192–198. doi:10.1016/j.aap.2015.05.018 PMID:26091769

Nidhi, & Lobiyal, D. K. (2012). *Performance Evaluation of Realistic Vanet Using Traffic Light Scenario.* Retrieved from https://arxiv.org/abs/1203.2195

Nobre, J. C., Souza, A. M. D., Rosário, D., Both, C., Villas, L. A., Cerqueira, E., ... Gerla, M. (2019). Vehicular Software-Defined Networking and Fog Computing: Integration and Design Principles. *Ad Hoc Networks*, *82*, 172–181. doi:10.1016/j.adhoc.2018.07.016

Oakland, S., & Follower, R. (2003). *Statistical process control* (5th ed.). Cornwall, UK: MPG Books Limited.

Oguz-Ekim, P., Ali, K., Madadi, Z., Quitin, F., & Tay, W. P. (2016, November). Proof of Concept Study Using DSRC, IMU and Map Fusion for Vehicle Localization in GNSS-Denied Environments. In *Proceedings IEEE 19th International Conference on Intelligent Transportation Systems (ITSC),* 841-846. IEEE.

Okay, F. Y., & Ozdemir, S. (2018). Routing in Fog-Enabled IoT Platforms: A Survey and an SDN-based Solution. *IEEE Internet of Things Journal*, *5*(6), 4871–4889. doi:10.1109/JIOT.2018.2882781

Orfanus, D., & De Freitas, E. (2014, October). Comparison of UAV-based reconnaissance systems performance using realistic mobility models. *Proceedings 6th international congress on ultra-modern telecommunications and control systems and workshops (ICUMT),* pp. 248–253. New York: IEEE.

Ossowski, S., Hernandez, J. Z., Belmonte, M. V., Fernandez, A., Garcia-Serrano, A., Perez-de-la-Cruz, J., ... Triguero, F. (2005). Decision Support for Traffic Management Based on Organizational and Communicative Multiagent Abstractions. *Transportation Research Part C, Emerging Technologies*, *13*(4), 272–298. doi:10.1016/j.trc.2005.07.005

Oubbati, O. S., Atiquzzaman, M., Lorenz, P., Tareque, M. H., & Hossain, M. S. (2019). Routing in flying Ad Hoc networks: Survey, constraints, and future challenge perspectives. *IEEE Access*, *7*, 81057-81105. doi:10.1109/ACCESS.2019.2923840

Oubbati, O. S., Lakas, A., Zhou, F., Güneş, M., & Yagoubi, M. B. (2017, October). A survey on position-based routing protocols for Flying Ad hoc Networks (FANETs). *Vehicular Communications*, *10*(October), 29–56. doi:10.1016/j.vehcom.2017.10.003

oussama Cherif, M., Senouci, S. M., & Ducourthial, B. (2009, June). A new framework of self-organization of vehicular networks. In *Proceedings 2009 Global Information Infrastructure Symposium* (pp. 1-6). IEEE.

Ozkurt, C., & Camci, F. (2009). Automatic traffic density estimation and vehicle classification for traffic surveillance systems using neural network. *Mathematical and Computational Applications*, *14*(3), 187–196. doi:10.3390/mca14030187

Page, E. C. C. (2003). Linear Feedback Shift Registers (LFSRs) 4-bit LFSR Applications of LFSRs Galois Fields - the theory behind LFSRs Galois Fields - The theory behind LFSRs Galois Fields - The theory behind LFSRs Galois Fields - The theory behind LFSRs Building an LFSR fro.

Pal, S., & Singh, V. (2011). GIS Based Transit Information System for Metropolitan Cities in India. In *Proceedings of Geospatial World Forum*, (pp. 18-21), Hyderabad, India.

Panchal, A., & Singh, D. D. (2017). Segregation of Sybil Attack using Neighbouring Information in VANET. *Iarjset*, *4*(6), 172–180. doi:10.17148/IARJSET.2017.4631

Paper, C., & Nielsen, J. B. (2002). Advances in Cryptology — CRYPTO 2002, *2442*(September 2002). doi:10.1007/3-540-45708-9

Papers, C. F. O. R. (2019). IEEE Internet of Things Journal. *IEEE Internet of Things Journal*, *5*(6), C2–C2. doi:10.1109/jiot.2018.2887292

Paranjothi, A., Khan, M. S., & Atiquzzaman, M. (2018). DFCV: A Novel Approach for Message Dissemination in Connected Vehicles using Dynamic Fog, In K. Chowdhury, M. Di Felice, I. Matta, & B. Sheng (Eds.), Wired/Wireless Internet Communications. Lecture Notes in Computer Science, 10866. Cham, Switzerland: Springer. doi:10.1007/978-3-030-02931-9_25

Park, E. S., Rilett, L. R., & Spiegelman, C. H. (2008). A Markov Chain Monte Carlo-Based Origin Destination Matrix Estimator that is Robust to Imperfect Intelligent Transportation Systems Data. *Journal of Intelligent Transport Systems*, *12*(3), 139–144. doi:10.1080/15472450802262364

Parmar, U., & Singh, S. (2015). Overview of Various Attacks in VANET. *International Journal of Engineering Research and General Science*, *3*(3), 120–125.

Pathak, A., & Lobiyal, D. K. (2012, March). Maximization the lifetime of wireless sensor network by minimizing energy hole problem with exponential node distribution and hybrid routing. *Proceedings 2012 Students Conference on Engineering and Systems* (pp. 1-5). IEEE.

Pathak, A., & Tiwari, M. K. (2018, October). Clustering in WSNs based on Soft Computing: A Literature Survey. *Proceedings of IEEE Conference on Automation and Computational Engineering (ICACE)*, 29-33. Greater Noida, India, October 3-4.

Paul, B., Ibrahim, M., Bikas, M., & Naser, A. (2012). Experimental analysis of aodv & dsr over tcp & cbr connections with varying speed and node density in vanet. *arXiv preprint arXiv:1204.1206*.

Peng, J. (2015, May). Radio propagation models in wireless networks of unmanned aerial vehicles. *International Journal of Computer Networks & Communications, 7*(3).

Peng, Z. R. (1997). A Methodology for Design of a GIS-Based Automatic Transit Traveler Information System. *Computers, Environment, and Urban Systems*, *21*(5), 359–372. doi:10.1016/S0198-9715(98)00006-4

Perallos, A., Hernandez-Jayo, U., Zuazola, I. J. G., & Onieva, E. (Eds.). (2015). *Intelligent Transport Systems: Technologies and Applications*. John Wiley & Sons. doi:10.1002/9781118894774

Pereira, J., Ricardo, L., Luís, M., Senna, C., & Sargento, S. (2019). Assessing the reliability of fog computing for smart mobility applications in VANETs. *Future Generation Computer Systems*, *94*, 317–332. doi:10.1016/j.future.2018.11.043

Perera, C., Qin, Y., Estrella, J. C., Reiff- Marganiec, S., & Vasilakos, A. V. (2017). Fog Computing for Sustainable Smart Cities: A Survey. *Journal ACM Computing Surveys, 50*(3), 32.

Peris-Lopez, P., Hernandez-Castro, J. C., Estevez-Tapiador, J. M., & Ribagorda, A. (2009). LAMED - A PRNG for EPC Class-1 Generation-2 RFID specification. *Computer Standards & Interfaces, 31*(1), 88–97. doi:10.1016/j.csi.2007.11.013

Perkins, C. E., & Royer, E. M. (1999, February). Ad-hoc on-demand distance vector routing. Proceedings WMCSA'99. Second IEEE Workshop on Mobile Computing Systems and Applications (pp. 90-100). IEEE.

Perkins, C. E., & Watson, T. J. (1994). Highly Dynamic Destination Sequenced Distance Vector Routing (DSDV) for Mobile Computers. ACM SIGCOMM computer communication review, 24(4), 234-244.

Peter, N. (2015). FOG Computing and Its Real Time Applications. *International Journal of Emerging Technology and Advanced Engineering, 5*(6).

Pinart, C., Sanz, P., Lequerica, I., García, D., Barona, I., & Sánchez-Aparisi, D. (2008, March). DRIVE: a reconfigurable testbed for advanced vehicular services and communications. In *Proceedings of the 4th International Conference on Testbeds and research infrastructures for the development of networks & communities* (p. 16). ICST (Institute for Computer Sciences, Social-Informatics and Telecommunications Engineering). 10.4108/weedev.2008.3141

Pinto, E. M. D. L., Lachowski, R., Pellenz, M. E., Penna, M. C., & Souza, R. D. (2018). A machine learning approach for detecting spoofing attacks in wireless sensor networks. In *Proceedings - International Conference on Advanced Information Networking and Applications, AINA*. 10.1109/AINA.2018.00113

Placzek, B. (2011). Performance evaluation of road traffic control using a fuzzy cellular model. In *6th International Conference on Hybrid Artificial Intelligence Systems*, (59-66), Wroclaw, Poland. 10.1007/978-3-642-21222-2_8

Pointcheval, D., & Stern, J. (1996). *Security Proofs for Signature Schemes, 96*, 387–398. doi:10.1007/3-540-68339-9_33

Prakash, R., & Kamal, S. (2014). Improved session key-based certificate to detect sybil attack. *IJERT, 3*(5), 116–119.

Priyanka, S., & Dhonde, S. (2017). VANET System for Traffic Management. *International Journal of Innovative Research in Computer and Communication Engineering, 5*(5), 9689–9693. .0505167 doi:10.15680/IJIRCCE.2017

Qi, L. (2008). Research on intelligent transportation system technologies and applications. In Proceedings *Power Electronics and Intelligent Transportation System*. IEEE. doi:10.1109/PEITS.2008.124

Queen, C., M., & Albers, C. J. (2008). Forecasting traffic flows in road networks: a graphical dynamic model approach. 1-24.

Qureshi, K. N., & Abdullah, A. H. (2013). A Survey on Intelligent Transportation Systems. *Journal of Scientific Research, 15*(5), 629–642.

Rabia, B., & Bilal, M. K. (2017, November). Analysis of Mobility Models and Routing Schemes for Flying Ad-Hoc Networks (FANETS). *International Journal of Applied Engineering Research, 12*, 3263–3269.

Rahbari, M., & Jabreil Jamali, M. A. (2011). Efficient Detection of Sybil attack Based on Cryptography in Vanet. *International Journal of Network Security & Its Applications*. doi:10.5121/ijnsa.2011.3614

Rahman, K. C., & Hasan, S. F. (2010). Explicit rate-based congestion control for multimedia streaming over mobile ad hoc networks. *International Journal of Electrical & Computer Sciences IJECS-IJENS, 10*(4), 28–40.

Ramachandran, N., & Devi, G. (2011). Accident Emergency Response and Routing Software (AERARS) Using Genetic Algorithm. *International Journal on Computer Science and Engineering, 3*(7), 2835–2845.

Rana, K. K., Tripathi, S., & Raw, R. S. (2017).Analytical analysis of improved directional-location aided routing protocol for VANETs. *International Journal of Wireless Personal Communication, 98*(2), 2403-2426.

Rana, K., K., Triparhi, S, Rao, R., S., (2016). Analysis of expected hop counts and distance in VANETs. *International Journal of Electronics, Electrical, and Computational System, 5*(4), 66-71.

Rana, K., K., Triparhi, S., & Rao, R. S. (2016). VANET: Expected delay analysis for location aided routing protocol. *International Journal of Information Technology, 8*(2), 1029-1037.

Rana, K., K., Triparhi, S., Rao, R., S., (2017). Analysis of expected progress distance in vehicular ad-hoc network using greedy forwarding. In *Proceedings IEEE International Conference on Computing for Sustainable Global Development,* 5171-5175.

Rana, K. K., Triparhi, S., & Rao, R. S. (2019). Opportunistic Directional Location Aided Routing Protocol for Vehicular Ad-hoc Network. *International Journal of Wireless Personal Communication, 108*(392), 119–137.

Rana, K. K., Tripathi, S., & Raw, R. S. (2016). Feasibility Analysis of Directional-Location Aided Routing Protocol for Vehicular Ad-hoc Networks. [IJCSIS]. *International Journal of Computer Science and Information Security, 16*(4), 214–225.

Rana, K. K., Tripathi, S., & Raw, R. S. (2016). VANET: Expected Delay Analysis for Location Aided Routing (LAR) Protocol. *International Journal of Information Technology, 8*(2), 1029–1037.

Rathore, S., & Khan, M. R. (2016, November). Enhance congestion control multipath routing with ANT optimization in Mobile ad hoc Network. In *Proceedings 2016 International Conference on ICT in Business Industry & Government (ICTBIG)* (pp. 1-7). IEEE. 10.1109/ICTBIG.2016.7892721

Raw, R. S., Kumar, M., & Singh, N. (2013). Security challenges, issues and their solutions for VANET. *International journal of network security & its applications, 5*(5), 95.

Raw, R. S., Lobiyal, D. K., Das, S., & Kumar, S. (2015).Analytical evaluation of improved directional-location aided routing protocol for VANETs. *International Journal of Wireless Personal Communication, 82*(3), 1877 - 1891.

Rawat, ASantosh, S., & Rama, S. (2014). Vanet: Security Attacks and Its Possible Solutions. *Journal of Information and Operations Management, 3*(1), 301–304. doi:10.100713398-014-0173-7.2

Rawat, D. B., Bista, B. B., Yan, G., & Olariu, S. (2014, July). Vehicle-to-vehicle connectivity and communication framework for vehicular ad-hoc networks. In *2014 Eighth International Conference on Complex, Intelligent, and Software Intensive Systems* (pp. 44-49). IEEE. 10.1109/CISIS.2014.7

Raw, R. S., Das, S., Singh, N., & Kumar, S. (2012). Feasibility evaluation of VANET using directional-location aided routing ((D-LAR) protocol. *International Journal of Computational Science, 9*(5), 404–410.

Raw, R. S., Kumar, M., & Singh, N. (2013). Security Challenges, Issues and their Solutions for VANET. [IJNSA]. *International Journal of Network Security & Its Applications, 5*(5). doi:10.5121/ijnsa.2013.5508

Raya, M., & Hubaux, J. P. (2005, November). The security of vehicular ad hoc networks. In *Proceedings of the 3rd ACM workshop on Security of ad hoc and sensor networks* (pp. 11-21). ACM. 10.1145/1102219.1102223

Raza, S., Wang, S., Ahmed, M., & Anwar, M. R. (2019). A Survey on Vehicular Edge Computing: Architecture, Applications, Technical Issues, and Future Directions. *Wireless Communications and Mobile Computing*, 1–19. doi:10.1155/2019/3159762

Rizwan, P., Suresh, K., & Rajasekhara Babu, M. (2017). Real-time smart traffic management system for smart cities by using Internet of Things and big data. *Proceedings of IEEE International Conference on Emerging Technological Trends in Computing, Communications and Electrical Engineering, ICETT 2016.* 10.1109/ICETT.2016.7873660

Robshaw, M. J. B., & Williamson, T. (2015). RAIN RFID and the Internet of Things: Industry Snapshot and Security Needs, 1–4.

Rohani, M., Gingras, D., & Gruyer, D. (2014). Vehicular Cooperative Map Matching. In *Proceedings International Conference on Connected Vehicles and Expo*, 779-803. IEEE.

Rohani, M., Gingras, D., & Gruyer, D. (2015). A Novel Approach for Improved Vehicular Positioning Using Cooperative Map Matching and Dynamic Base Station DGPS Concept. *IEEE Transactions on Intelligent Transportation Systems*, 1–10.

Roncoli, C., Papageorgiou, M., & Papamichail, I. (2015). Traffic flow optimization in presence of vehicle automation and communication systems — part I: A first-order multi-lane model for motorway traffic. *Transportation Research Part C, Emerging Technologies, 57*, 241–259. doi:10.1016/j.trc.2015.06.014

Roncoli, C., Papageorgiou, M., & Papamichail, I. (2015). Traffic flow optimization in presence of vehicle automation and communication systems – part II: Optimal control for multi-lane motorways. *Transportation Research Part C, Emerging Technologies, 57*, 260–275. doi:10.1016/j.trc.2015.05.011

Roncoli, C., Papamichail, I., & Papageorgiou, M. (2016). Hierarchical model predictive control for multilane motorways in presence of vehicle automation and communication systems. *Transportation Research Part C, Emerging Technologies, 62*, 117–132. doi:10.1016/j.trc.2015.11.008

Rosati, S., Kruelecki, K., Heitz, G., Floreano, D., & Rimoldi, B. (2016). Dynamic routing for flying ad hoc networks. *IEEE Transactions on Vehicular Technology, 65*(3), 1690–1700. doi:10.1109/TVT.2015.2414819

Ros, F. J., Martinez, J. A., & Ruiz, P. M. (2014). A survey on modeling and simulation of vehicular networks: Communications, mobility, and tools. *Computer Communications, 43*, 1–15. doi:10.1016/j.comcom.2014.01.010

Rossi, G. V., Leung, K. K., & Gkelias, A. (2015). Density-based optimal transmission for throughput enhancement in vehicular ad-hoc networks communications. In *Proceedings IEEE International Conference on Communications,* 6571-6576. IEEE.

Rouse, M. (2013). Sharing economy. Retrieved from https://searchcio.techtarget.com/definition/sharing-economy

Roweis, S., & Saul, L. (2000). Nonlinear dimensionality reduction by locally linear embedding. *Science, 290*(5500), 2323–2326. doi:10.1126cience.290.5500.2323 PMID:11125150

Roy, A., & Chakraborty, J. (2015). Communication based accident avoidance and congestion control mechanism in VANETs. In *Proceedings 2015 International Symposium on Advanced Computing and Communication (ISACC)*, pp. 320-327. IEEE. 10.1109/ISACC.2015.7377363

Royer, E., & Perkins, C. (1999). Multicast Operation of the Ad Hoc On Demand Distance Vector Routing Protocol (pp. 207-218). *Proc. ACM/IEEE MobiCom.*

Royer, E., & Perkins, C. (2000). An Implementation Study of the AODV Routing Protocol. *Proceedings of Wireless Communication and Networking Conference.* Retrieved from http://erdos.csie.ncnu.edu.tw/~ccyang/WirelessNetwork/Papers/MANET/AdHocUnicast-17.pdf

Rukhin, A., Soto, J., & Nechvatal, J. (2010). SP800-22rev1a, (April), 131.

Russell, S., & Norvig, P. (2009). *Artificial Intelligence: A Modern Approach* (3rd ed.). New Jersey: Prentice Hall.

Rzepecki, W., Iwanecki, L., & Ryba, P. (2018). IEEE 802.15.4 thread mesh network - Data transmission in harsh environment. *Proceedings - 2018 IEEE 6th International Conference on Future Internet of Things and Cloud Workshops, W-FiCloud 2018*, 42–47. 10.1109/W-FiCloud.2018.00013

Sahasrabudhe, M. S., & Chawla, M. (2014). Survey of Applications based on Vehicular Ad-Hoc Network (VANET) Framework. [IJCSIT]. *International Journal of Computer Science and Information Technologies, 5*, 3.

Sahingoz, O. (2014*)*. Networking models in flying Ad-hoc networks (FANETs): Concepts and challenges (pp. 513-527). *Journal of Intelligent & Robotic Systems*.

Sahingoz, O. (2013, September). Networking Models in Flying Ad-Hoc Networks (FANETs): Concepts and Challenges. *Journal of Intelligent & Robotic Systems, 74*.

Sailhan, F., Fallon, L., Quinn, K., Farrell, P., Collins, S., & Parker, D., … Huang, Y. (2007). Wireless mesh network monitoring: Design, implementation and experiments. *GLOBECOM - IEEE Global Telecommunications Conference*. 10.1109/GLOCOMW.2007.4437816

Saini, M., Alelaiwi, A., & El Saddik, A. (2015). How close are we to realizing a pragmatic VANET solution? A meta-survey. *ACM Computing Surveys, 48*(2), 1–40. doi:10.1145/2817552

Samanta, S., Acharjee, S., Mukherjee, A., Das, D., & Dey, D. (2013). Ant Weight Lifting Algorithm for Image Segmentation. In *Proceedings IEEE International Conference on Computational Intelligence and Computing Research*, Enathi, India: IEEE. 10.1109/ICCIC.2013.6724160

Samanta, S., Chakraborty, S., Acharjee, S., Mukherjee, A., & Dey, N. (2013). Solving 0/1 Knapsack Problem using Ant Weight Lifting Algorithm. In *Proceedings IEEE International Conference on Computational Intelligence and Computing Research*, Enathi, India: IEEE. 10.1109/ICCIC.2013.6724162

Sanchez, J. F., & Cobo, L. A. (2014). Theoretical model of congestion control in VANET networks. In *Proceedings 2014 IEEE Colombian Conference on Communications and Computing (COLCOM)*, pp. 1-6. IEEE. 10.1109/ColComCon.2014.6860400

Sankarasrinivasan, S., Balasubramanian, E., Karthik, K., Chandrasekar, U., & Gupta, R. (2015). Health monitoring of civil structures with integrated UAV and image processing system. *Procedia Computer Science, 54*, 508–515. doi:10.1016/j.procs.2015.06.058

Santhiya, K. G., & Arumugam, N. (2012, March). Energy Aware Reliable Routing Protocol (EARRP) for Mobile Ad Hoc Networks Using Bee Foraging Behavior and Ant Colony Optimization. *International Journal of Computer Science Issues, 9*(2), 171.

Sarakis, L., Orphanoudakis, T., Leligou, H. C., Voliotis, S., & Voulkidis, A. (2016). Providing entertainment applications in VANET environments. *IEEE Wireless Communications, 23*(1), 30–37. doi:10.1109/MWC.2016.7422403

Saul, L., & Roweis, S. (2003). *Think globally, fit locally: Unsupervised learning of nonlinear manifolds*. JMLR.

Scherer, J., Yahyanejad, S., Hayat, S., Yanmaz, E., Vukadinovic, V., Andre, T., … Hellwagner, H. (2015). *An autonomous multi-UAV system for search and rescue* (pp. 33–38). DroNet. doi:10.1145/2750675.2750683

Shah, S. S., Ali, M., Malik, A. W., Khan, M. A., & Ravana, S. D. (2019). vFog: A Vehicle-Assisted Computing Framework for Delay-Sensitive Applications in Smart Cities. *IEEE Access, 7*, 34900–34909. doi:10.1109/ACCESS.2019.2903302

Shakhatreh, H., Sawalmeh, A. H., Al-Fuqaha, A., Dou, Z., Almaita, E., Khalil, I., … & Guizani, M. (2018, April). Unmanned Aerial Vehicles: A Survey on Civil Applications and Key Research Challenges. *Robotics, 10*. doi:10.1109/ACCESS.2019

Shakya, R. K., Rana, K. K., Gaurav, A., Mamoria, P., & Srivastava, P. K. (2019). Stability Analysis of Epidemic Modeling Based on Spatial Correlation for Wireless Sensor Networks. *International Journal of Wireless Personal Communication*. doi:10.100711277-019-06473-0

Sharma, A. K., Saroj, S. K., Chauhan, S. K., & Saini, S. K. (2017). Sybil attack prevention and detection in vehicular ad hoc network. In *Proceeding - IEEE International Conference on Computing, Communication, and Automation, ICCCA 2016*, (April), 594–599. 10.1109/CCAA.2016.7813790

Sharma, A., Chaki, R., & Bhattacharya, U. (2011). Applications of wireless sensor network in Intelligent Traffic System: A review. In *Proceedings 3rd International Conference on Electronics, Computer Technology*, Kanyakumari, India: IEEE. 10.1109/ICECTECH.2011.5941955

Sharma, M. K., & Kaur, A. (2015). A Survey on Vehicular Cloud Computing and its Security. *Proceedings 1st International Conference on Next Generation Computing Technologies*. 10.1109/NGCT.2015.7375084

Shelly, S., & Babu, A. V. (2015). Link reliability based greedy perimeter stateless routing for vehicular ad-hoc networks. International Journal of Vehicular Technology. *Hindawi Publishing Corporation, 2015*(1), 1–16.

Shelly, S., & Babu, A. V. (2017). Link residual lifetime-based next hop selection scheme for vehicular ad-hoc networks. *EURASIP Journal on Wireless Communications and Networking, 2*(6), 1–13. doi:10.118613638-017-0810-x

Shendurkar, A., M., & Chopde, N., R. (2014). A review of position-based routing protocol in mobile ad-hoc networks. *International Journal of Advanced Research in Computer Engineering and Technology, 3*(6), 2047-2053.

Sherry, L. (2001). *Report on non-traditional traffic country methods* (p. 85748). Tucson, AZ: Tanque Verde Loop Rd.

Shilpa, K. G., et al. (2016, August). Efficient Data Routing Analysis In FANETS To Achieve QOS. *International Journal of Innovative Science, Engineering & Technology, 3*(8).

Shipra, D., & Kashyap, R. (2017). *DETECTING SYBIL ATTACK USING HYBRID FUZZY K-MEANS ALGORITHM IN WSN., 5*(2), 1560–1565.

Shrestha, R., Bajracharya, R., & Nam, S. Y. (2018). Challenges of Future VANET and Cloud-Based Approaches. *Wireless Communications and Mobile Computing*, 1–15. doi:10.1155/2018/5603518

Sibahee, M. A., & Lu, S. (2016). T-LEACH: the method of threshold-based cluster head replacement for wireless sensor networks. *Proceedings IEEE conference on network and information systems for computers* (ICNISC), 36–40. Wuhan, China, April 15-17.

Siddiqui, S. A., & Mahmood, A. (2018). Towards Fog-based Next Generation Internet of Vehicles Architecture. *Proceedings of the 1st International Workshop on Communication and Computing in Connected Vehicles and Platooning*, 15-21.

Singh, D., Tripathi, G., & Jara, A. J. (2014). A survey of Internet-of-Things: Future vision, architecture, challenges, and services. In *Proceedings 2014 IEEE World Forum on Internet of Things, WF-IoT 2014*, 287–292. 10.1109/WF-IoT.2014.6803174

Singh, H., Bala, M., & Kumar, M. Performance Analysis of Zrp Star and Dsr Using Blackhole Attack Under Vanet's.

Singh, H., Bala, M., & Kumar, M. Performance Evaluation of Zrp Star and Dsr under Vanet's. IOSR Journal of Computer Engineering (IOSR-JCE) e-ISSN: 2278-0661.

Singh, K., & Verma, A. (2014). Applying OLSR routing in FANETs. In *Proceedings International Conference on Advanced Communication Control and Computing Technologies* (pp. 1212-1215). IEEE. 10.1109/ICACCCT.2014.7019290

Singh, S., & Agrawal, S. (2014, March). VANET routing protocols: Issues and challenges. In Proceedings 2014 Recent Advances in Engineering and Computational Sciences (RAECS) (pp. 1-5). IEEE.

Singh, Y., & Sharma, A. (2012). A new tree-based double covered broadcast protocol for VANET. In *Proceedings 2012 Ninth International Conference on Wireless and Optical Communications Networks (WOCN)*, pp. 1-3. IEEE. 10.1109/WOCN.2012.6331905

Singh, A., Singh, G., & Singh, M. (2018). Comparative study of OLSR, DSDV, AODV, DSR, and ZRP routing protocols under black hole attack in mobile ad hoc network. In *Intelligent Communication, Control, and Devices* (pp. 443–453). Singapore: Springer. doi:10.1007/978-981-10-5903-2_45

Singh, B., & Gupta, A. (2015). Recent trends in intelligent transportation systems: A review. *Journal of Transport Literature, 9*(2), 30–34. doi:10.1590/2238-1031.jtl.v9n2a6

Singh, K., & Kaur, H. (2018). Evaluation of proposed technique for detection of Sybil attack in VANET. *International Journal of Scientific Research in Computer Science and Engineering, 6*(5), 10–15. doi:10.26438/ijsrcse/v6i5.1015

Singh, K., & Verma, A. K. (2014, May). Applying OLSR routing in FANETs. *Proceedings International Conference on Advanced Communication Control and Computing Technologies (ICACCCT)*, pp. 1212-1215. IEEE.

Singh, K., & Verma, A. K. (2015, March). Experimental Analysis of AODV, DSDV and OLSR Routing Protocol for Flying Ad-hoc Networks (FANETs). *Proceedings IEEE International Conference on Electrical, Computer, and Communication Technologies (ICECCT)*, IEEE. Coimbatore, India, doi: 10.1109/ICECCT.2015.7226085

Sinhmar, P. A. (2012). Intelligent traffic light and density control using IR sensors and microcontroller. *International Journal of Advanced Technology & Engineering Research, 2*(2), 30–35.

Sivakumar, T., & Manoharan, R. (2015). OPRM: An efficient hybrid routing protocol for sparse VANETs. *International Journal of Computer Applications in Technology, 51*(2), 97–104. doi:10.1504/IJCAT.2015.068920

Skog, I., & Handel, P. (2009). In-Car Positioning and Navigation Technologies—A Survey. Intelligent Transportation Systems. *IEEE Transactions on Intelligent Transportation Systems, 10*(1), 4–2. doi:10.1109/TITS.2008.2011712

Soelistijanto, B., & Howarth, M. P. (2013). Transfer reliability and congestion control strategies in opportunistic networks: A survey. *IEEE Communications Surveys and Tutorials, 16*(1), 538–555. doi:10.1109/SURV.2013.052213.00088

Song, J. H., Wong, V. W., & Leung, V. C. (2014). Secure Location Verification for Vehicular Ad-Hoc Networks, in *Journal of Theoretical and Applied Information Technology, 63*(3), 636-644.

Sookhak, M., Yu, F. R., He, Y., Talebian, H., Safa, N. S., Zhao, N., ... Kumar, N. (2017). Fog Vehicular Computing. *Augmentation of Fog Computing Using Vehicular Cloud Computing. IEEE Vehicular Technology Magazine, 12*(3), 55–64.

Soundararajan, S., & Bhuvaneswaran, R. S. (2012, May). Multipath load balancing & rate-based congestion control for mobile ad hoc networks (MANET). In *Proceedings 2012 Second International Conference on Digital Information and Communication Technology and its Applications (DICTAP)* (pp. 30-35). IEEE. 10.1109/DICTAP.2012.6215393

Srinivasan, D., Sanyal, S., & Sharma, V. (2007). Freeway incident detection using hybrid fuzzy neural network. *IET Intelligent Transport Systems, 1*(4), 249–259. doi:10.1049/iet-its:20070003

Srivastava, M. D., Prerna Sachin, S., Sharma, S., & Tyagi, U. (2012). Smart traffic control system using PLC and SCADA. *International Journal of Innovative Research in Science Engineering and Technology, 1*(2), 169–172.

Stefanov, A., Gisin, N., Guinnard, O., Guinnard, L., & Zbinden, H. (2000). Optical quantum random number generator. *Journal of Modern Optics, 47*(4), 595–598. doi:10.1080/09500340008233380

Stern, R. E., Cui, S., Monache, S. L., Bhadani, R., Bunting, M., Churchill, M., . . . Work, J. B. (2017). Dissipation of stop-and-go waves via control of autonomous vehicles: field experiments, [On-line]. Retrieved from https://arxiv.org/abs/1705.01693

Stojmenovic, I., Ruhil, A. P., & Lobiyal, D. K. (2006). Voronoi diagram and convex hull based geocasting and routing in wireless networks. *Wireless Communications and Mobile Computing, 6*(2), 247-258.

Stojmenovic, I., & Wen, S. (2014). The Fog Computing Paradigm: Scenarios and Security Issues. *Proceedings 2014 Federated Conference on Computer Science and Information Systems* 10.15439/2014F503

Sujatha, V., & Anita, E. A. M. (2019). FEM-hybrid machine learning approach for the detection of sybil attacks in the wireless sensor networks. *International Journal of Innovative Technology and Exploring Engineering.*

Sumra, I. A., Sellappan, P., Abdullah, A., & Ali, A. (2018, April). Security issues and Challenges in MANET-VANET-FANET: A Survey. *EAI Endorsed Transactions on Energy Web and Information Technologies.* . doi:10.4108/eai.10-4-2018.155884

Sumra, I., Sellappan, P., Abdullah, A., & Ahmad, A. (2018). Security issues and Challenges in MANET-VANET-FANET: A Survey. *EAI Endorsed Transactions on Energy Web, 5*(17), 1–6. doi:10.4108/EAI.10-4-2018.155884

Sun, J., & Sun, J. (2016). Real-time crash prediction on urban expressways: Identification of key variables and a hybrid support vector machine model. *IET Intelligent Transport Systems, 10*(5), 331–337. doi:10.1049/iet-its.2014.0288

Sun, Y., Guo, Y., Song, J., Zhou, S., Jiang, Z., Liu, X., & Niu, Z. (2019). *Adaptive Learning-Based Task Offloading for Vehicular Edge Computing Systems. IEEE Transactions on Vehicular Technology, 68*(4), 3061–3074.

Sutagundar, A. V., Attar, A. H., & Hatti, D. I. (2019). Resource Allocation for Fog Enhanced Vehicular Services. *Wireless Personal Communications, 104*(4), 1473–1491. doi:10.100711277-018-6094-6

Swarnapriyaa, U., Vinodhini, A. S., & Anand, R. (2011). Auto Configuration in Mobile Ad Hoc Networks (pp. 61-66). In *Proceedings of the National Conference on Innovations in Emerging Technology.*

Taheri, H., Neamatollahi, P., Yaghmaee, M. H., & Naghibzadeh, M. (2011). A local cluster head election algorithm in wireless sensor networks. *Proceedings of IEEE Symposium on Computer Science and Software Engineering (CSSE), 38-43.* Tehran, June 15-16. 10.1109/CSICSSE.2011.5963987

Taleb, T., Sakhaee, E., Jamalipour, A., Hashimoto, K., Kato, N., & Nemoto, Y. (2007). A stable routing protocol to support ITS services in VANET networks. *IEEE Transactions on Vehicular Technology, 56*(6 I), 3337–3347. doi:10.1109/TVT.2007.906873

Talebpour, A., & Mahmassani, H. S. (2016). Influence of connected and autonomous vehicles on traffic flow stability and throughput. *Transportation Research Part C, Emerging Technologies, 71*, 143–163. doi:10.1016/j.trc.2016.07.007

Talib, M. S., Hussin, B., & Hassan, A. (2017). Converging VANET with Vehicular Cloud Networks to reduce the Traffic Congestions: A review. *International Journal of Applied Engineering Research, 12*(21), 10646-10654.

Tang, K., Obraczka, K., Lee, S. J., & Gerla, M. (2002, July). Congestion controlled adaptive lightweight multicast in wireless mobile ad hoc networks. In *Proceedings ISCC 2002 Seventh International Symposium on Computers and Communications* (pp. 967-972). IEEE. 10.1109/ISCC.2002.1021789

Tan, L., & Wu, M. (2016). Data reduction in wireless sensor networks: A Hierarchical LMS prediction approach. *IEEE Sensors Journal, 16*(6), 1708–1715. doi:10.1109/JSEN.2015.2504106

Tareque, H. Md., Hossain, S. Md., & Atiquzzaman, Mh. (2015). On the Routing in Flying Ad hoc Networks. *Proceedings of the Federated Conference on Computer Science and Information Systems*, ACSIS, 5, pp. 1–9. doi: 10.15439/2015F002

Tassi, A., Mavromatis, I., Piechocki, R., Nix, A., Compton, C., Poole, T., & Schuster, W. (2019). Agile Data Offloading over Novel Fog Computing Infrastructure for CAVs. *Proceedings IEEE 89th Vehicular Technology Conference.*

Tay, J. H., Chandrasekhar, V. R., & Seah, W. K. G. (2006). Selective Iterative Multilateration for Hop Count-Based Localization in Wireless Sensor Networks. In *Proceedings 7th International Conference on mobile data management*, 152-152. IEEE. 10.1109/MDM.2006.139

Tehranipoor, M., & Wang, C. (2012). Introduction to hardware security and trust. *Introduction to Hardware Security and Trust, 9781441980*, 1–427. doi:10.1007/978-1-4419-8080-9

Tenenbaum, J., de Silva, V., & Langford, J. (2000). A global geometric framework for nonlinear dimensionality reduction. *Science, 290*(5500), 2319–2323. doi:10.1126cience.290.5500.2319 PMID:11125149

Thomas, D. (2001). Expanding Infrastructure: the ITS option, *20th South African Transport Conference*, Pretoria, South Africa.

Titouna, C., Aliouat, M., & Gueroui, M. (2016.) FDS: fault detection scheme for wireless sensor networks. *Springer Journal on Wireless Personal Communication, 86*(2), 549–562.

Tonguz, O., Wisitpongphan, N., Bai, F., Mudalige, P., & Sadekar, V. (2007). Broadcasting in VANET. *2007 Mobile Networking for Vehicular Environments, MOVE*, 7–12. doi:10.1109/MOVE.2007.4300825

Truong, N. B., Lee, G. M., & Doudane, Y. G. (2015). Software defined networking-based vehicular Adhoc Network with Fog Computing. *Proceedings IEEE International Symposium on Integrated Network Management.* 10.1109/INM.2015.7140467

Tsoi, K. H., Leung, K. H., & Leong, P. H. W. (2003). Compact FPGA-based true and pseudo random number generators. *IEEE Symposium on FPGAs for Custom Computing Machines, Proceedings, 2003-Janua*, 51–61. 10.1109/FPGA.2003.1227241

Tso, R., Chen, C. M., Zheng, X., & Wu, M. E. (2014). A New Ultra-Lightweight RFID Authentication Protocol Based on Physical Unclonable Functions. *Cryptology and Information Security Series, 12*, 17–28. doi:10.3233/978-1-61499-462-6-17

Ullah, A., Yaqoob, S., Imran, M., & Ning, H. (2018). *Emergency Message Dissemination Schemes Based on Congestion Avoidance in VANET and Vehicular Fog Computing. IEEE Access, 7*, 2169–3536.

Unwala, I., Taqvi, Z., & Lu, J. (2018). Thread: An IoT protocol. In *Proceedings IEEE Green Technologies Conference, 2018-April*, 161–167. 10.1109/GreenTech.2018.00037

Vanderschuren, M., van Katwijk, R., & Schuurman, H. (2000). Increase of the Highway Capacity without additional infrastructure. In *Proceedings of the Conference on Technology Transfer in Developing Countries, Automation in Infrastructure Creation.* Pretoria, South Africa.

Vanderschuren, M., van Katwijk, R., & Schuurman, H. (2000). Increasing the Highway Capacity without Additional Infrastructure. TNO Netherlands Organization for Applied Scientific Research and Transport Research Centre. Delft, The Netherlands.

Vaquero, L. M., Rodero-Merino, L., Caceres, J., & Lindner, M. (2009). A Break in the Clouds: Towards a Cloud Definition. *Computer Communication Review, 39*(1), 50–55. doi:10.1145/1496091.1496100

Venkatasubramanian, S., & Gopalan, N. P. (2010). A Quality of service architecture for resource provisioning and rate control in mobile ad hoc networks. International Journal of Ad hoc [IJASUC]. *Sensor & Ubiquitous Computing, 1*(3), 106–120. doi:10.5121/ijasuc.2010.1309

Vèque, V., Kaisser, F., Johnen, C., & Busson, A. (2013). CONVOY: A New Cluster-Based Routing Protocol for Vehicular Networks. *Vehicular Networks: Models and Algorithms*, 91-129.

Vijaya, I., & Rath, A. K. (2011). Simulation and Performance Evaluation of AODV, DSDV, and DSR in TCP and UDP Environment. *Proceedings 3rd International Conference on Electronics Computer Technology*, 6. 10.1109/ICECTECH.2011.5942047

Vodopivec, S., Bešter, J., & Kos, A. (2012, July). A survey on clustering algorithms for vehicular ad-hoc networks. In *Proceedings 2012 35th International Conference on Telecommunications and Signal Processing (TSP)* (pp. 52-56). IEEE. 10.1109/TSP.2012.6256251

Voorhees, A. M. (2013). A general theory of traffic movement. *Transportation, 40*(6), 1105–1116. doi:10.100711116-013-9487-0

Wang, Y., Zhao, Q., & Dazhong, Z. (2004).Energy-driven adaptive clustering data collection protocol in wireless sensor networks. *Proceedings of International Conference on Intelligent Mechatronics and Automation*, 599-604. Chengdu: China, August 26-31.

Wang, C., Daneshmand, M., Dohler, M., Mao, X., Hu, R. Q., & Wang, H. (2013). Guest Editorial Special Issue on Internet of Things (IoT): Architecture, Protocols and Services. *IEEE Sensors Journal, 13*(10), 3505–3510. doi:10.1109/JSEN.2013.2274906

Wang, L., Liu, G., & Sun, L. (2017). A Secure and Privacy-Preserving/ Navigation Scheme Using Spatial Crowdsourcing in Fog-Based VANETs. *Sensors (Basel), 2017*(17), 668. doi:10.339017040668 PMID:28338620

Wang, X., Ning, Z., & Wang, L. (2018). Offloading in Internet of Vehicles: A Fog-Enabled Real-Time Traffic Management System. *IEEE Transactions on Industrial Informatics, 14*(10), 4568–4578. doi:10.1109/TII.2018.2816590

Wang, Y., Chuang, C., & Hsu, C., & Hung, C. (2003). Ad hoc on-demand routing protocol setup with backup routes (pp. 137-141). In *Proceedings of ITRE, International Conference on Information Technology, Research, and Education.*

Wenjie, C., Lifeng, C., Zhanglong, C., & Shiliang, T. (2005). A realtime dynamic traffic control system based on wireless sensor network, parallel processing. *In Proceedings International Conference on ICPP Workshops*, pp. 258–264.

Werf, J. V., Shladover, S. E., Miller, M. A., & Kourjanskaia, N. (2002). Evaluation of the Effects of Adaptive Cruise Control on Highway Traffic Flow Capacity. *Transportation Research Record: Journal of the Transportation Research Board, 1800*(1), 78–84. doi:10.3141/1800-10

Whaiduzzaman, M., Sookhak, M., Gani, A., & Buyya, R. (2014). A survey on vehicular cloud computing. *Journal of Network and Computer Applications, 40*, 325–344. doi:10.1016/j.jnca.2013.08.004

What is cloud computing? A beginner's guide. Retrieved from https://azure.microsoft.com/en-in/overview/what-is-cloud-computing/

Willett, R., Martin, A., & Nowak, R. (2004). Back casting: adaptive sampling for sensor networks, *Proceedings of IEEE International symposium on Information processing in sensor networks*, 124-133. California, April 26-27.

Wu, J., Shuo, S., Liu, Z., & Gu, X. (2019). Optimization of AODV Routing Protocol in UAV Ad Hoc Network. *Proceedings International Conference on Artificial Intelligence for Communications and Networks (AICON), LNICST*, 286, pp. 472-478. 10.1007/978-3-030-22968-9_43

Xi, L., Liu, Q., Li, M., & Liu, Z. (2007, October). Map matching algorithm and its application. *International Journal of Computational Intelligence Systems,* 1-7.

Xiang, X., Wang, X., & Yang, Y. (2011). Supporting Efficient and Scalable Multicasting over Mobile [IEEE Transactions on mobile computing.]. *Ad Hoc Networks*, 544–550.

Xiao, J., & Liu, Y. (2012). Traffic incident detection using multiple-kernel support vector machine. *Transportation Research Record: Journal of the Transportation Research Board, 2324*(1), 44–52. doi:10.3141/2324-06

Xiao, Y., & Zu, C. (2017) Vehicular Fog Computing: Vision and Challenges. *Proceedings 2017 IEEE International Conference on Pervasive Computing and Communications Workshops.* 10.1109/PERCOMW.2017.7917508

Xie, S., Hu, Y., & Wang, Y. (2014). Weighted centroid localization for wireless sensor networks. International Conference on Consumer Electronics - China, 1-4. IEEE.

Xie, G., & Hoeft, B. (2012). Freeway and Arterial System of Transportation Dashboard. *Transportation Research Record: Journal of the Transportation Research Board, 2271*(1), 45–56. doi:10.3141/2271-06

Xiong, G., Zhu, F., Liu, X., Dong, X., Huang, W., Chen, S., & Zhao, K. (2015). Cyber-physical social system in intelligent transportation, IEEE/CAA. *Journal of Automatica Sinica, 2*(3), 320–333.

Xu, B., Shen, L., Yan, F., & Zheng, J. (2011). Doppler-shifted frequency measurement-based positioning for roadside-vehicle communication systems. Wireless communications and mobile computing, Wiley Online Library, 866-875.

Xu, W., Zhou, H., Cheng, N., Lyu, F., Shi, W., Chen, J., & Shen, X. (2018). Internet of vehicles in big data era, *IEEE/CAA Journal of Automatica. Sinica, 5*(1), 19–35.

Yadav, S., & Singh, D. (2016, March). A survey on congestion control mechanism in multi-hop wireless network. In *Proceedings 2016 3rd International Conference on Computing for Sustainable Global Development (INDIACom)* (pp. 683-688). IEEE.

Yan, F., Yang, C., & Ukkusuri, S. (2019). Alighting stop determination using two-step algorithms in bus transit systems. *Transportmetrica A: Transport Science, 15*(2), 1522–1542. doi:10.1080/23249935.2019.1615578

Yang, S., Rongxi, H., Lin, S., Lin, B., & Wang, Y. (2014). An improved geographical routing protocol and its OPNET-based simulation in VANETs. In *Proceedings IEEE International Conference on Bio Medical Engineering and Informatics,* 913-917.

Yao, Y., Xiao, B., Wu, G., Liu, X., Yu, Z., Zhang, K., & Zhou, X. (2019). Multi-Channel Based Sybil Attack Detection in Vehicular Ad Hoc Networks Using RSSI. *IEEE Transactions on Mobile Computing, 18*(2), 362–375. doi:10.1109/TMC.2018.2833849

Yap, W., Liu, J., Tan, S., & Goi, B. (2015). On the security of a lightweight authentication and encryption scheme for mobile ad hoc network. *International Journal of Security and Communication Networks.*

Yap, M., Cats, O., & Arem, B. V. (2018). Crowding valuation in urban tram and bus transportation based on smart card data. *Transportmetrica A: Transport Science,* 1–20.

Yassein, M. B., & Damer, N. A. (2016). Flying ad–hoc networks: Routing protocols, mobility models, issues. *International Journal of Advanced Computer Science and Applications, 7*(6), 162–168.

Ye, H., Liang, L., Li, G. Y., Kim, J., Lu, L., & Wu, M. (2018). Machine Learning for Vehicular Networks: Recent Advances and Application Examples. *IEEE Vehicular Technology Magazine, 13*(2), 94–101. doi:10.1109/MVT.2018.2811185

Ye, Q., Szeto, W., & Wong, S. C. (2012). Short-term traffic speed forecasting based on data recorded at irregular intervals. *IEEE Transactions on Intelligent Transportation Systems, 13*(4), 1727–1737. doi:10.1109/TITS.2012.2203122

Yi, S., Hao, Z., Qui, Z., & Li, Q. (2015). Fog Computing: Platform and Applications. *Proceedings 2015 Third IEEE Workshop on Hot Topics in Web Systems and Technologies.* 10.1109/HotWeb.2015.22

Yi, S., Li, C., & Li, Q. (2015). A survey of Fog Computing: Concepts, Applications and Issues. *Proceedings of the 2015 workshop on Mobile Big Data*, 37-42. 10.1145/2757384.2757397

Yi, S., Qin, Z., & Li, Q. (2015). Security and Privacy Issues of Fog Computing: A Survey. In K. Xu & H. Zhu (Eds.), Lecture Notes in Computer Science: Vol. 9204. *Wireless Algorithms, Systems, and, Applications.* Cham, Switzerland: Springer. doi:10.1007/978-3-319-21837-3_67

Yousef Al-Raba'nah, G. S. (2015). Security Issues in Vehicular Ad Hoc Networks (VANET): A survey. *International Journal of Sciences & Applied Research, 2*(4), 50–55.

Yousefi, S., Mousavi, M. S., & Fathy, M. (2006, June). Vehicular ad hoc networks (VANETs): challenges and perspectives. In *Proceedings 2006 6th International Conference on ITS Telecommunications* (pp. 761-766). IEEE.

Yu, X., Sun, F., & Cheng, X. (2012). Intelligent urban traffic management system based on cloud computing and internet of things. *Proceedings - 2012 International Conference on Computer Science and Service System, CSSS 2012*, 2169–2172. 10.1109/CSSS.2012.539

Yuan, F., & Cheu, R. L. (2003). Incident detection using support vector machines. *Transportation Research Part C, Emerging Technologies, 11*(3–4), 309–328. doi:10.1016/S0968-090X(03)00020-2

Zafar, W., & Muhammad, K. B. (2016, June). Technological and social Implications Flying Ad-Hoc Network. *IEEE Technology and Society Magazine.*

Zaheeruddin, D. K., Lobiyal, D. K., & Pathak, A. (2017). Energy-aware bee colony approach to extend lifespan of wireless sensor network. *Australian Journal of Multi-Disciplinary Engineering, 13*(1), 29–46. doi:10.1080/14488388.2017.1358896

Zarza, H., Yousefi, S., & Benslimane, A. (2016). RIALS: RSU/INS-aided localization system for GPS-challenged road segments. *Wireless Communications and Mobile Computing*, 1290–1305.

Zeadally, S., Hunt, R., Chen, Y. S., Irwin, A., & Hassan, A. (2012). Vehicular ad hoc networks (VANETS): Status, results, and challenges. *Telecommunication Systems, 50*(4), 217–241. doi:10.100711235-010-9400-5

Zekri, A., & Jia, W. (2018). Heterogeneous Vehicular Communications: A Comprehensive Study. *Ad Hoc Networks, 75–76*, 52–79. doi:10.1016/j.adhoc.2018.03.010

Zeng, M., Li, Y., Zhang, K., Waqas, M., & Jin, D. (2018). Incentive Mechanism Design for computation Offloading in Heterogeneous Fog Computing: a Contract-based Approach. *Proceedings IEEE International Conference on Communications.* 10.1109/ICC.2018.8422684

Zhai, H., Chen, X., & Fang, Y. (2005, March). Rate-based transport control for mobile ad hoc networks. In *Proceedings IEEE Wireless Communications and Networking Conference*, 4, (pp. 2264-2269). IEEE.

Zhang, J., Liao, F., Arentze, T., & Timmersans, H. (2011). A multimodal transport network model for advanced traveler information systems. *Procedia: Social and Behavioral Sciences, 20*, 313–322. doi:10.1016/j.sbspro.2011.08.037

Zhang, R., & Labrador, M. A. (2007). Energy-aware topology control in heterogeneous wireless multi-hop networks. *Proceedings of IEEE International Symposium on Wireless Pervasive Computing*, 1-5. Puerto Rico, February 5-7. 10.1109/ISWPC.2007.342568

Zhang, T., Li, Y., Yang, H., Cui, C., Li, J., & Qiao, Q. (2018). Identifying primary public transit corridors using multisource big transit data. *International Journal of Geographical Information Science*, 1–25. doi:10.1080/13658816.2018.1554812

Zhang, W., Aung, N., Dhelim, S., & Ai, Y. (2018). DIFTOS: A Distributed Infrastructure-Free Traffic Optimization System Based on Vehicular Ad Hoc Networks for Urban Environments. *Sensors (Basel)*, *18*(8), 2567. doi:10.339018082567 PMID:30082595

Zhang, X., & Jacob, L. (2003). *Multicast Zone Routing Protocol in Mobile Ad Hoc Wireless Networks*. Proc. Local Computer Networks.

Zhang, Y., & Liu, Y. (2009). Traffic forecasting using least squares support vector machines. *Transportmetrica*, *5*(3), 193–213. doi:10.1080/18128600902823216

Zhang, Y., & Xe, Y. (2008). Travel mode choice modeling with support vector machines. *Transportation Research Record: Journal of the Transportation Research Board*, *2076*(1), 141–150. doi:10.3141/2076-16

Zhan, P., Yu, K., & Swindlehurst, A. L. (2011, July). Wireless relay communications with unmanned aerial vehicles: Performance and optimization. *IEEE Transactions on Aerospace and Electronic Systems*, *47*(3), 2068–2085. doi:10.1109/TAES.2011.5937283

Zhao, F., Xu, Y., & Li, R. (2012). Improved LEACH Routing Communication Protocol for a Wireless Sensor Network. *International Journal of Distributed Sensor Networks*, *8*(12), 1–6. doi:10.1155/2012/649609

Zhou, B., Cao, J., Zeng, X., & Wu, H. (2010). Adaptive traffic light control in wireless sensor network-based intelligent transportation MATLAB. In *Vehicular Technology Conference Fall* (pp. 1–5). IEEE.

Zhou, M., Qu, X., & Jin, S. (2017). On the impact of cooperative autonomous vehicles in improving freeway merging: A modified intelligent driver model-based approach. *IEEE Transactions on Intelligent Transportation Systems*, *18*(6), 1422–1428.

Zhou, S., Sun, Y., Jiang, Z., & Niu, Z. (2019). *Exploiting Moving Intelligence: Delay-Optimized Computation Offloading in Vehicular Fog Networks*. IEEE Communications Magazine, *57*(5), 49–55.

Zhou, Z., Liu, P., Feng, J., Zhang, Y., Mumtaz, S., & Rodriguez, J. (2019). Computation Resource Allocation and Task Assignment Optimization in Vehicular Fog Computing: A Contract-Matching Approach. *IEEE Transactions on Vehicular Technology*, *68*(4), 3113–3125. doi:10.1109/TVT.2019.2894851

Zhu, L., Yang, A., Wu, D., & Liu, L. (2014). Survey of Indoor Positioning Technologies and Systems. *Communications in Computer and Information Science*, 400–409. Springer.

Zhu, W., Gao, D., Foh, C. H., Zhao, W., & Zhang, H. (2016). A collision avoidance mechanism for emergency message broadcast in urban VANET. In *Proceedings IEEE 83rd Vehicular Technology Conference (VTC Spring)*, pp. 1-5. IEEE. 10.1109/VTCSpring.2016.7504057

Zhu, C., Tao, J., Pastor, G., Xiao, Y., Ji, Y., Zhou, Q., ... Yia-Jaaski, A. (2019). Folo: Latency and quality optimized task allocation in vehicular fog computing. *IEEE Internet of Things Journal*, *6*(3), 4150–4161. doi:10.1109/JIOT.2018.2875520

Zhu, F., & Ukkusuri, S. (2015). A linear programming formulation for autonomous intersection control within a dynamic traffic assignment and connected vehicle environment. *Transportation Research*, *55*(Part C), 363–378.

Zhu, F., & Ukkusuri, S. (2018). Modeling the proactive driving behavior of connected vehicles: A cell-based simulation approach. *Computer-Aided Civil and Infrastructure Engineering*, *33*(4), 262–281. doi:10.1111/mice.12289

Zhu, X. Y., Yuan, Y. F., Hu, X. B., Chiu, Y., & Ma, Y. L. (2017). A Bayesian network model for contextual versus non-contextual driving behavior assessment. *Transportation Research Part C, Emerging Technologies*, *81*, 172–187. doi:10.1016/j.trc.2017.05.015

Zhu, Z., Peng, B., Xiong, C. F., & Zhang, L. (2016). Short-term traffic flow prediction with linear conditional Gaussian Bayesian network. *Journal of Advanced Transportation*, *50*(6), 1111–1123. doi:10.1002/atr.1392

About the Contributors

Ram Shringar Rao received his Ph.D. (Computer Science and Technology) from School of Computer and Systems Sciences, Jawaharlal Nehru University, New Delhi, India in 2011. He has worked as an Associate Professor in the Department of Computer Science, Indira Gandhi National Tribal University (A Central University, MP). He is currently working as an Assistant Professor in the Department of Computer Science and Engineering of Ambedkar Institute of Advanced Communication Technologies and Research, GGSIP University, Delhi, India. He has more than 18 years of teaching, administrative and research experience. Dr. Rao has worked administrative works in the capacities of Member Academic Council (IGNTU), Chief Warden, Coordinator University Cultural Cell, Coordinator University Computer Center, HoD of Computer Sc. and Eng., Proctor, Warden, etc. Dr. Rao has published around 90 research papers with good impact factors in reputed International Journals and Conferences including IEEE, Springer, Wiley & Sons, Taylor & Fransise, Inderscience, Hindawi, IERI Letters, etc. His current research interest includes Mobile Ad hoc Networks, Vehicular Ad hoc Networks and Cloud Computing.

Vishal Jain is currently working as Associate Professor with Bharati Vidyapeeth's Institute of Computer Applications and Management (BVICAM), New Delhi Affiliated to GGSIPU and Accredited by AICTE, since July, 2017 to present. He has joined BVICAM, New Delhi in year 2010 and worked as Assistant Professor from August, 2010 to July, 2017. Before joined BVICAM, New Delhi, he has worked four years in Guru Presmsukh Memorial College of Engineering, Affiliated to GGSIPU and Accredited by AICTE, from July 2004 to July, 2008. He has more than 300 research citation indices with Google scholar h-index score 9 and i-10 index 9. His research area includes Information Retrieval, Semantic Web, Ontology Engineering, Data Mining, Adhoc Networks and Sensor Networks. He has received Young Active Member award for the year 2012 – 13 from Computer Society of India.

Omprakash Kaiwartya is currently working as a Senior Lecturer at the School of Science and Technology, Nottingham Trent University (NTU), UK. Previously, He was a Research Associate at the Northumbria University, Newcastle, UK, in 2017 and a Postdoctoral Research Fellow at the Universiti Teknologi Malaysia (UTM) in 2016. He received his Ph.D. degree in Computer Science from Jawaharlal Nehru University, New Delhi, India, in 2015. His research interest focuses on IoT centric future technologies for diverse domain areas focusing on Transport, Healthcare, and Industrial Production. His recent scientific contributions are in Internet of connected Vehicles (IoV), Electronic Vehicles Charging Management (EV), Internet of Healthcare Things (IoHT), and Smart use case implementations of Sensor Networks. He is Associate Editor of reputed SCI Journals including IET Intelligent Transport Systems, EURASIP Journal on Wireless Communication and Networking, Ad-Hoc & Sensor Wireless

Networks, IEEE Access, and Transactions on Internet and Information Systems. He is also Guest Editor of many recent special issues in reputed journals including IEEE Internet of Things Journal, IEEE Access, MDPI Sensors, and MDPI Electronics.

* * *

Walaa A. Afifi received the M.Sc. in Information systems from Faculty of Graduate Studies for Statistical Research - Cairo University in 2015. She is currently a Ph.D. student. Her major interest include: wireless sensor networks (WSN), fuzzy systems, routing protocol, vehicle ad hoc network and Data mining.

Parul Agarwal is associated with Jamia Hamdard since 2002. Currently employed as Associate Professor in Department of CSE. The research areas include Big data, Cloud computing, Applications of Sustainable Development in Health Care and Smart Cities and Machine learning. Having published several papers in Scopus and SCI indexed journals, she also has few publications in Springer. Member of several committees of highly reputed conferences and editorial board member of several journals, she is the member of IEEE and life member of ISTE.

Jawed Ahmed is working as Assistant Professor, Department of Computer Science & Engineering, School of Engineering Sciences and Technology Jamia Hamdard, New Delhi, India. His area of research is Algorithm, Bioinformatics and Mathematical Modeling. He has 15 years of teaching experience.

Vikram Bali has received his B.Tech (CSE) from REC, Kurukshetra, M.E. (CSE) from NITTTR, Chandigarh and Ph.D from Banasthali Vidyapith, Rajasthan. He has more than 18 years of rich academic experience. He is a Professor & Head of Department (CSE) at JSS Academy of Technical Education, Noida. He is lifetime member of IEEE, Indian Society for Technical Education (ISTE), Computer Society of India (CSI) and Institution of Engineers (IE). He has contributed 27 Research papers in International Journal and 9 Research papers in National Conferences/ proceedings and Edited Books. He has written books on Fundamental of "Cyber Security and Laws", "Software Engineering" and "Operating System". He is reviewer to many International Journals of repute like Inderscience and IGI Global. His research interest includes Software Engineering, Cyber Security, Automata Theory, CBSS and ERP.

Abhishek Bansal has received PhD degree in Computer Science from University of Delhi, New Delhi, India. He is working as an Assistant Processor in the Department of Computer Science, Indira Gandhi National Tribal University, Amarkantak, Madhya Pradesh, India. He has almost 10 years of teaching and research experience. His research areas are Information Security, Wireless Sensor Network, Data Science. He has authored 8 research papers published in International Journals, 10 research papers published in conference proceedings.

Nirbhay Kumar Chaubey is working as a Dean of Computer Science, Ganpat University, Gujarat India. Prior to joining Ganpat University, he worked as an Associate Dean and Associate Professor of Computer Science at SSAICS College Code 554, Gujarat Technological University, Ahmedabad, Gujarat, India. Before joining as the Associate Professor, he was working as an Assistant Professor of Computer Science, at Institute of Science & Technology for Advanced Studies & Research (ISTAR), Vallabh Vidyanagar, affiliated to the Sardar Patel University, Vallabh Vidyanagar and then to the Gujarat Technological University, Ahmedabad, Gujarat, India. Before that, he has worked as a Lecturer, Computer Science Department, C.U.Shah College of Engineering and Technology, Surendranagar, Saurastra University, Gujarat, India. Professor Chaubey also worked as an Officer on Special Duty (OSD) to the Gujarat Technological University(GTU) for year 2011-2012. Professor Nirbhay Chaubey received his Ph.D in Computer Science, Faculty of Engineering, from Gujarat University, Ahmedabad, India. He has worked in the area of network communication and security for the past two decades. His research interests lie in the areas of Computer and Network Security, Cyber Security, Algorithms, Wireless Networks (Architecture, Protocol Design, QoS, Routing, Mobility and Security), Sensor Network and Cloud Computing. He has published several research papers in peered reviewed International Journals and Conferences, his published research works well cited by the research community worldwide which shows his exception research performance. Prof. Chaubey is a Senior Member of the IEEE, Senior Member of the ACM and a Life Member of Computer Society of India. He has been actively associated with the IEEE India Council and IEEE Gujarat Section and served IEEE in various volunteer positions. He has received numerous awards including IEEE Outstanding Volunteer Award- Year 2015(IEEE Region 10 Asia Pacific), Gujarat Technological University (GTU) Pedagogical Innovation Awards (PIA) -2015, IEEE Outstanding Branch Counselor Award - Year 2010 (IEEE Region 10 Asia Pacific).

Nagy Ramadan Darwish received his PhD. in Information Systems from Faculty of Computers and Information, Cairo University, Egypt. He is an Associate Professor and Acting Head of Department of Information Systems and Technology, Faculty of Graduate Studies for Statistical Research, Cairo University. He is a reviewer in many national and international conferences and Journals such as: IJCSIS, IJACSA, IJARAI, and IJST. He is an editorial board member of Circulation in Computer Science. He published about 90 papers in International Journals and conferences. He is a Consultant of Software Project Management, Software Quality, Business Information Systems, Quality of Education, and Institutional Development.

Sanjoy Das received his B.E. (Computer Science and Engineering) from G. B. Pant Engineering College, Pauri-Garhwal, UK, India and M. Tech (Computer Sc. and Eng.) from Sam Higginbottom Institute of Agriculture, Technology and Sciences, Allahabad (UP), India in 2001 and 2006, respectively. He has obtained his Ph.D. (Computer Science and Technology) from School of Computer and Systems Sciences, Jawaharlal Nehru University, New Delhi, India in 2013. He has more than 14 years of teaching experience. He has worked as an Assistant Professor in the Department of Computer Science and Engineering in G. B. Pant Engineering College, Uttarakhand Technical University, India. Currently he is working as Associate Professor in Indira Gandhi National Tribal University Regional Campus Manipur Makhan, P.O. Awang Sekmai, Kangpokpi District, Manipur, India. His current research interest includes Mobile Ad hoc Networks and Vehicular Ad hoc Networks.

Mekelleche Fatiha was born in Oran, Algeria in 1991. She received her Licence on System of Data Processing and the Communication (SDPC) in 2010 and her Master degree in Engineering of the Data and Web Technology (EDWT) in 2013 at University of Oran 1 Ahmed Benbella, Algeria. She is a Ph.D. Student in the R. I. I. R. Laboratory, Graduate school of Advanced Data Models and emerging networks. Her main research area is on Wireless Sensor Networks (WSNs).

Ananthi Govindasamy received the B. E. degree in Electronics and Communication Engineering, from R. V. S. College Engineering and Technology, Dindigul, India in 2000 and M. E. Degree in Applied Electronics P. S. N. A. College of Engineering and Technology, Dindigul, India in 2005. From 2001 to 2003 and from 2005 to 2006, she was a Lecturer with a Department of Electronics and Communication Engineering, P. S. N. A. College of Engineering and Technology, Dindigul, India. From 2006 to present, she was Assistant Professor with a Department of Electronics and Communication Engineering, Thiagarajar College of Engineering, Madurai, India. She has published six International Journal papers and 22 research papers in National and International conferences. Her Research interests include in physical layer aspects of wireless communication systems.

Deena Nath Gupta is a Research Scholar in the Department of Computer Science, Faculty of Natural Sciences, Jamia Millia Islamia (Central University), New Delhi-110025, India. He has done M.Tech in Computer Science and Engineering from Galgotia's College Of Engineering And Technology, Greater Noida, Gautam Buddha Nagar, Uttar Pradesh – 201306, India and B.Tech in Computer Science and Engineering from ABES Engineering College, Ghaziabad, Uttar Pradesh – 201009, India. He has an excellent academic background with academics and research experiences. He has published various research papers in the conferences and journals of international/national repute. His research interest includes Cryptography and cyber-security, Internet of Things.

Sachin Gupta is currently working as an Assistant Professor in the Department of Electronics & Communication Engineering Shri Mata Vaishno Devi University, Katra, Jammu, India. He received his B.Tech in Electronics and Telecommunication Engineering from National Institute of Technology, Raipur, Chhattisgarh, India in 2008 and M.Tech & Ph.D. with specialization in Systems Engineering (Wireless Communication), Department of Electrical Engineering from Indian Institute of Technology (Banaras Hindu University), Varanasi, Uttar Pradesh, India in 2011 & 2016 respectively. Previously, he was the former research fellow in Mobile Computing and Broadband Networking Lab (MBL), Department of Computer Science at National Chiao Tung University (NCTU), Hsinchu, Taiwan (Republic of China), and IIT Jodhpur, India. His research interest includes Ad-hoc Networks, SDN, and FSO etc. He has published many papers in the International/National journals and prestigious Conference Proceedings. He has served as coordinator, organizing committee members, session chair of the various workshop, seminar, and conferences.

Hafid Haffaf was born in Oran, Algeria in 1964. He obtained doctor degree in computer Science in 2000; is a senior lecturer at the University of Oran 1 Ahmed Benbella (Algeria). He actually heads the R. I. I. R. Laboratory at Computer science department–Oran University-. His researchers concern different domain as Automatic control and diagnosis, optimization reconfiguration using system of system approaches and their applications in Bond graph and monitoring. He has many collaborations projects with European laboratory: Polytech Lille where he worked in Intelligent transport systems infrastructures- and LIAU Pau (France) in the domain of Wireless sensor Networks (CMEP project).

Syed Imtiyaz Hassan works as an Associate Professor at the Department of CS & IT, Maulana Azad National Urdu University, Telangana (India). His professional experience spans over more than 18 years of teaching, research, and project supervision. He has supervised more than 90 students for interdisciplinary research and industrial projects. Over the years, he has published many research papers with national and international journals of repute. In addition to these, he is also in the Editorial Boards and Reviewers' Panels of various journals. His primary area of research is "Computational Intelligence & Sustainability". To meet the above objective, he explores the role of Data Science, Machine Learning, Fog Computing, and Internet of Things for developing sustainable systems in healthcare and Smart City domains.

Hesham A. Hefny received the B.Sc., M.Sc. and Ph.D. all in Electronics and Communication Engineering from Cairo University in 1987, 1991 and 1998 respectively. He is currently a professor of Computer Science at Faculty of Graduate Studies for Statistical Research, Cairo University. He is also the vice dean of graduate studies and researches of Faculty of Graduate Studies for Statistical Research. Prof. Hefny has authored more than 150 papers in international conferences, journals and book chapters. His major research interest includes: computational intelligence (neural networks – Fuzzy systems-genetic algorithms – swarm intelligence), data mining, deep learning, uncertain decision making. He is a member in the following professional societies: IEEE Computer, IEEE Computational Intelligence, and IEEE System, Man and Cybernetics.

Ashwani Kumar is presently working as Assistant Professor in the Department of Computer Science Engineering and Information Technology, United College of Engineering And Research, Greater Noida, Uttar Pradesh-201306, India. He has done his M.Tech in Computer Science from B.I.T Mesra, Ranchi, Jharkhand-835215, India and B.E in Electronics and Communication Engineering from G.B.Pant Engineering College, Pauri Garhwal, Uttarakhand-246194, India. He has an excellent academic background with academics and research experiences. He has published various research papers in the conferences and journals of international and national repute. His research interest includes Cryptography and Cyber Security, Internet of Things.

Rajendra Kumar is presently working as Professor in the Department of Computer Science, Faculty of Natural Sciences, Jamia Millia Islamia (Central University), New Delhi-110025, India. He has an excellent academic background with a very sound academic and research experience. He has published various research papers in the conferences and journals of international/national repute. His research interest includes cyber-security, Cloud Security and Privacy, Big Data Analytics, Data Mining, Internet of Things, Software Security, Requirements Engineering, Security Policies and Standards, Software Engineering, Access control and Identity Management, Vulnerability Assessment etc.

Sudesh Kumar is currently pursuing Ph.D. degree in Computer Science. He is working as an Assistant Professor in the Department of Computer Science, Indira Gandhi National Tribal University, Amarkantak, Madhya Pradesh, India. He has almost 10 years of teaching and research experience. His current research interest include MANET, Flying Adhoc Network and Theoretical Computer Science. He has published papers and chapters in International Journals and Conferences.

Aruna Pathak received the B.Tech. degree in Electronics and communication engineering from U.P. Technical University, Lucknow in 2004, M.Tech. degree in Electronic design & Technology from Tezpur central University, Assam in 2008 and Ph.D. degree from Jamia Millia Islamia Central University, New Delhi. She is currently an Assistant Professor with the Department of Electronics and communication engineering in Govt. Engineering College Bharatpur, Rajasthan. Her research interests include mobile networking and computing, wireless sensor networks, IoT and cloud computing.

Kamlesh Rana is engineering graduate in Computer Science & Engineering from Madan Mohan Malviya Engineering College, Gorakhpur, Uttar Pradesh, India in 2001, M. Tech. in Information Technology from Guru Gobind Singh Indraprastha University, Delhi, India in 2010, and PHD from Indian Institute of Technology (ISM) Dhanbad. He is working as Associate Professor in Computer Science & Engineering Department at Galgotias College of Engineering and Technology, Greater Noida, Uttar Pradesh, India. His current research interest includes Vehicular Ad-hoc Network and Mobile Ad-hoc Network.

Mamoon Rashid is currently working as an Assistant Professor in the School of Computer Science & Engineering, Lovely Professional University, Jalandhar, India. The main area of interest is Cloud Computing, Big Data Analytics, Machine Learning and Neuro Imaging. The author has published several research papers in Cloud Computing, Big Data Analytics and Machine Learning indexed in Scopus and Web of Science based Journals.

Vishnu Sharma has completed his B.Tech, M.Tech and Ph. D (CSE) from Madhav Institute of Technology & Science (M.I.T.S.) Gwalior (M.P.) in Computer Science & Engineering and Affiliated to Rajiv Gandhi Technical University, Bhopal. Dr Sharma is working as Professor and Head of the Department Computer Science and Engineering at Galgotia College of Engineering and Technology, Greater Noida, Uttar Pradesh, India. He is having around 21 years of teaching experience in various reputed engineering institutes and Universities. He has published more than 53 research papers in the area of Mobile Ad-hoc Networks and Mobile Computing in International/National Conferences and International/ National Journals. He has also published three books on Mobile Computing, Advanced Mobile Computing and Cyber Security. He has been involved in organizing several International /National conferences and workshops. He was the editor of IEEE Conference ICCCA proceedings. He was the Conference Technical Chair of several IEEE conferences.

Harjit Singh received his B.Tech Degree from Punjab Technical University, Jalandhar, Punjab, India in year 2009, M.Tech Degree from Punjab Technical University, Jalandhar, Punjab, India in year 2014. He Currently pursuing his Ph.D From Guru Kashi University, Talwandi Sabo, Bathinda, Punjab. Presently He is working as a Assistant Professor in Computer Science and Engineering Department in Lovely Professional University Punjab. He has 10 years of teaching experience. His research interests include Wireless Networks, Ad hoc networks, Security.

S. J. Thiruvengadam received his BE degree in electronics and communication engineering from Thiagarajar College of Engineering, Tamil Nadu, India, in 1991. He obtained his ME degree in applied electronics from the College of Engineering, Tamil Nadu, India, in 1994 and his PhD degree in the area of signal detection algorithms from Madurai Kamaraj University, Tamil Nadu, India, in 2005. At present, he is working as a professor with the Department of Electronics and Communication Engineering, Thiagarajar College of Engineering. Previously, he was a visiting associate professor with the Department of Electrical Engineering, Stanford University, CA, USA, under a postdoctoral fellowship sponsored by the Department of Science and Technology, Government of India, from January to December 2008. His current areas of research include statistical signal processing and massive multiple-input and multiple-output wireless communications and NOMA.

Gagan Tiwari received his MCA from Dr. B. R. Ambedkar University, Agra Uttar Pradesh, India in 2001, M. E. in Computer Science from Dr. B. R. Ambedkar University, Agra Uttar Pradesh, India in 2009 and Ph. D. in Computer Science & Engineering from Mewar University, Chittorgarh Rajasthan in 2018. Dr. Gagan has teaching experience of 18 years and working as Associate Professor in Department of Computer Applications at Galgotias College of Engineering and Technology, Greater Noida, Uttar Pradesh, India. His Current research interest includes Maintainability Predictions, Vehicular Ad-hoc Network and Cloud Computing. Dr Gagan has published a number of research papers in reputed SCI and Scopus indexed journals including IEEE international conference. He was the Conference Technical Chair of several IEEE conferences.

Aabid Wani has completed M.Tech in Electronics & Communication Engineering from Shri Mata Vaishno Devi University, Katra, Jammu, India. The main area of interest is Network Security, Microwaves and Internet of Things. The author has published several research papers on UAV Integrated HetNets indexed in Scopus and Web of Science based Journals.

Index

Ensure Quality Research is Introduced to the Academic Community

Become an IGI Global Reviewer for Authored Book Projects

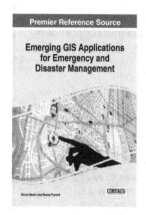
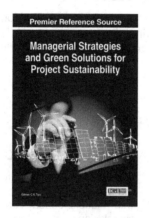

The overall success of an authored book project is dependent on quality and timely reviews.

In this competitive age of scholarly publishing, constructive and timely feedback significantly expedites the turnaround time of manuscripts from submission to acceptance, allowing the publication and discovery of forward-thinking research at a much more expeditious rate. Several IGI Global authored book projects are currently seeking highly-qualified experts in the field to fill vacancies on their respective editorial review boards:

Applications and Inquiries may be sent to:
development@igi-global.com

Applicants must have a doctorate (or an equivalent degree) as well as publishing and reviewing experience. Reviewers are asked to complete the open-ended evaluation questions with as much detail as possible in a timely, collegial, and constructive manner. All reviewers' tenures run for one-year terms on the editorial review boards and are expected to complete at least three reviews per term. Upon successful completion of this term, reviewers can be considered for an additional term.

If you have a colleague that may be interested in this opportunity, we encourage you to share this information with them.

Printed in the United States
By Bookmasters